Hyper Terminal.

Ryerson - 9797970

Business Systems Analysis and Design

Business Systems Analysis and Design

William S. Davis
Miami University

COURSE
TECHNOLOGY

ONE MAIN STREET, CAMBRIDGE, MA 02142

an International Thomson Publishing company I(T)P®

Cambridge • Albany • Bonn • Boston • Cincinnati • London • Madrid • Melbourne • Mexico City
New York • Paris • San Francisco • Singapore • Tokyo • Toronto • Washington

Publisher:	Kathy Shields
Editorial Assistant:	Tamara Huggins
Production Editor:	Jerilyn Emori
Managing Designer:	Carolyn Deacy
Print Buyer:	Karen Hunt
Art Editor:	Donna Kalal
Permissions Editor:	Peggy Meehan
Designer:	Bruce Kortebein, Design Office
Copy Editor:	Denise Cook-Clampert
Cover:	Stuart Paterson, Image House
Compositor and Technical Illustrator:	Thompson Type, Inc.
Printer:	R. R. Donnelley & Sons, Crawfordsville

© 1994 by Course Technology.
An International Thomson Publishing Company – I(T)P®

For more information contact:

Course Technology
One Main Street
Cambridge, MA 02142

International Thomson Publishing Europe
Berkshire House 168-173
High Holborn
London WCIV 7AA
England

Thomas Nelson Australia
102 Dodds Street
South Melbourne, 3205
Victoria, Australia

Nelson Canada
1120 Birchmount Road
Scarborough, Ontario
Canada M1K 5G4

International Thomson Editores
Campos Eliseos 385, Piso 7
Col. Polanco
11560 Mexico D.F. Mexico

International Thomson Publishing GmbH
Königswinterer Strasse 418
53227 Bonn
Germany

International Thomson Publishing Asia
211 Henderson Road
#05-10 Henderson Building
Singapore 0315

International Thomson Publishing Japan
Hirakawacho Kyowa Building, 3F
2-2-1 Hirakawacho
Chiyoda-ku, Tokyo 102
Japan

ISBN 0-534-18954-7

Printed in the United States of America

10 9 8 7 6 5 4

Contents

Part II

Defining the Problem 25

Part III

Requirements Analysis

Part V

Physical Design   361

Preface

This book was written to support the systems analysis and design course (or courses) required by many MBA, MIS, CIS, and BIS major and minor programs. It is also appropriate for comparable applied computer science, community college, and professional training courses. The material assumes a knowledge of basic computer concepts and an exposure to computer programming. An introduction to database concepts, data structures, or both would be useful but is not essential. No mathematics is assumed beyond high school algebra.

Systems analysis is a profession in transition. Once an art, it is evolving into an engineering-like discipline. Perhaps that is why so many analysis and design texts focus on tools and theory and ignore the more subjective aspects of the analyst's job. That, in turn, may explain why so many students see systems analysis as a rather dull profession practiced by desk-bound types who are more comfortable communicating with computers than people.

That image is unfortunate because it is simply untrue. Rather than sitting at a desk and communing with a computer, a systems analyst spends much of his or her time meeting and talking with people ranging from users, to technical experts, to managers, about topics ranging from application needs, to technical details, to resource allocations. The work is varied and challenging. It demands a unique combination of creativity, initiative, and attention to detail. Systems analysis is a fascinating profession.

One of my objectives in writing this book is to communicate to the reader a sense of my own fascination with the discipline. Rather than just introducing and explaining modern systems analysis concepts, tools, and techniques, the book presents them *in the context* of a broader sense of the analyst's job. Rather than just showing you how to use the tools, the narrative emphasizes why those tools are useful. Rather than just developing system documentation, the narrative adds coverage of the assumptions, intuition, and "street smarts" that underlie the documentation. The idea is to convey a sense of what a professional systems analyst *really* does. To help achieve these objectives, *Business Systems Analysis and Design* incorporates the following elements.

Business-oriented Case Studies

One of the best ways to learn about systems analysis and design is to follow a project from conception to completion. *Business Systems Analysis and Design* features a running case study of an inventory system. As you read through the case, you will see how a problem is defined and analyzed and how a solution is designed. The traditional system development life cycle, the analyst's tools and techniques, and important principles and theoretical concepts are introduced and explored in the context of that case study. A second running case study shows how an analyst might deal with a much larger problem.

CASE Coverage

If you plan to be a systems analyst, computer-aided software engineering (CASE) is in your future. Numerous CASE products are available today, and several analysis and design texts are built around a particular methodology. Some of these books are excellent but only if you have the appropriate software.

Business Systems Analysis and Design describes a generic system development life cycle and shows how CASE software affects each stage. The book can be used in conjunction with virtually any commercial CASE product. Additionally, Chapter 10 shows how the tools and techniques introduced in the preceding chapters might be implemented using a popular CASE package called Excelerator. You should be able to read and understand Chapter 10 even if you do not have Excelerator.

Up-to-Date Tools and Techniques

There is no universally accepted, standard way to analyze and design systems. Instead, the analyst must select, from a variety of alternatives, the tools and techniques that best fit the job. Many books emphasize one approach and provide only limited coverage of several others. This book, in contrast, covers logical modeling, data modeling, and prototyping in considerable depth and clearly explains their relative strengths and weaknesses.

In presenting the design stage, most analysis and design books do a reasonable job of presenting basic file, database, software, report, and screen design principles. This book also includes solid coverage of project management, process design, dialogue design, and testing. Additionally, chapters on object-oriented analysis and design are included.

Clear Step-to-Step Transitions

Documentation is rarely prepared for its own sake. Instead, the point of the system development process is to use the output from one stage as the input to subsequent stages, thus allowing the analyst continually to enhance his or her understanding of the system.

It is easy to become so bogged down in the details of a particular tool, technique, or step that you lose sight of the real objective. Perhaps the best way to avoid that pitfall is to develop a clear sense of how the various stages and tools are related and how they reinforce and verify each other. This book emphasizes those links. For example, the process of mapping a logical model into one or more high-level physical alternatives and then selecting the best one is a crucial task that is covered superficially (if at all) in most competitive books. This book devotes three chapters to the topic.

Coverage of Competitive Procurement

In an effort to control operating costs, many organizations prepare a set of formal requirements specifications and then subcontract information system development. The competitive procurement process is a standard model for selecting and managing subcontractors. Most systems analysis and design texts cover the competitive procurement process superficially (if at all). This book devotes a complete chapter to the topic.

Features

Although systems analysis and design is in the process of becoming an engineering-like discipline, it retains a creative, almost artistic component. Most competitive texts dismiss the analyst's art. This text doesn't. Instead, it shows how art and creativity are applied in the context of a methodology. For example, one feature, *Professional Pointer*, shows how a professional analyst sometimes relies on street smarts to recognize problems or suggest likely avenues of investigation. This feature helps humanize systems analysis and design by showing the student that human insight is still valuable.

The point of another feature, *Management's Perspective*, should be obvious. Additionally, key "sound bites" are pulled from the narrative and set in the margins, giving the reader a sense of the chapter's main points that goes beyond the usual key terms and definitions. Chapter previews and summaries, suggestions for additional readings, and end-of-chapter exercises are also included. At least three exercises in each chapter support projects that allow the instructor to assign students realistic, hands-on, out-of-class work that parallels the text's case studies.

Supplements

One of the best ways to learn how to analyze and design a system is to complete an analysis and design project. To support such projects, Wadsworth has commissioned several project manuals that provide the student with the kind of information an analyst might collect during the preliminary analysis stage. These project manuals do not present "the" solution to the problem. Instead, they are designed to help students get started and develop their own solutions.

Additionally, those who want to focus on CASE can purchase a set of easy-to-follow, self-paced tutorials that teach the basics of Excelerator. After completing this supplement, students will be able to use Excelerator as a tool to complete one or more projects.

Acknowledgments

Over a decade ago, I wrote a book entitled *System Analysis and Design: A Structured Approach* (Addison-Wesley Publishing Company, 1983). Since then I have made several starts on a new version, but other projects always seemed to take precedence. So much has changed since the early 1980s that this new book bears little resemblance to my earlier one, but I still owe a debt to the instructors, students, and reviewers who provided so much valuable feedback.

My first Wadsworth editor was Frank Ruggirello. He and Peter G. W. Keen were largely responsible for convincing me that the time had come to do a new systems analysis and design book. Since early 1993, my editor has been Kathy Shields, and I would like to acknowledge her contributions and those of her editorial assistants Rhonda Sands and Karen Mandel. Production was in the able hands of Jerilyn Emori, and Denise Cook-Clampert did an excellent job of copyediting the manuscript.

I would also like to thank the following reviewers: Robert G. Brookshire, James Madison University; Paul H. Cheney, University of South Florida; Carl Clavadetscher, California State Polytechnic University–Pomona; David M. Collopy, Ohio University, Lancaster; Jack P. Curry, University of Alaska Southeast; Albert L. Harris, Appalachian State University; John E. Melrose, University of Wisconsin, Eau Claire; Dolly Samson, Weber State University; and George P. Schell, University of North Carolina, Wilmington. Finally, I must acknowledge Donald Dawley, T. M. Rajkumar, Chi-Chung Yen, and the Miami University MIS 485 students who helped me class test the material.

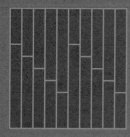

PART I

The System Development Process

You can have it fast,
you can have it cheap,
or you can have it right.
Pick any two.

1

Information Systems Analysis

When you finish reading this chapter you should be able to:

—Define the terms *system* and *information system.*

—Distinguish between electronic data processing, management information systems, decision support systems, and executive information systems.

—Explain the purpose of systems analysis.

—Distinguish between a customer, a user, and an end user.

—Discuss the advantages and disadvantages of using a methodology.

—List and briefly explain the steps in the system development life cycle.

—Briefly discuss CASE.

Systems

Quality Components Are Not Enough

Just west of San Jose, not too far from the freeways that cut through California's Silicon Valley, is a fascinating place called the Winchester Mystery House. It was built a century ago by Sarah Winchester, the widow of the man who manufactured and sold the famous repeating rifle.

FIGURE 1.1
The Winchester Mystery House.

Photos in Figures 1.1, 1.2, 1.3, and 1.4 courtesy of Winchester Mystery House.

As you approach the old mansion, it seems like an oasis among the urban sprawl (Figure 1.1). Your first impression is reinforced when you enter the main foyer (Figure 1.2). Surrounded by rich, dark woods, the sun streaming through colorful stained glass windows, you can't help but appreciate the exquisite taste and workmanship that went into Sarah's house. Everything is first class. Mrs. Winchester knew what she wanted and she had the money to pay for it.

Your impression changes as you move (or attempt to move) from room to room, however. One door opens to a blank wall. Another leads to an eight-foot drop. A stairway ends at the ceiling. Other stairways wind capriciously from level to level (Figure 1.3). Windows reveal other rooms. A chimney links fireplaces on the first three floors and then ends abruptly,

FIGURE 1.2
The main foyer.

FIGURE 1.3
Stairways wind capriciously from level to level.

less than a foot below the roof, making all three fireplaces useless. Without a guide or a good map, you might never find your way out.

Apparently, Sarah feared the ghosts of the people killed by her late husband's rifles. A seer told her that she would die when she stopped building her house, so she just kept building. She commissioned work on her living room. When that work neared completion, she moved on to some other room, or added a new one. When that room neared completion, she added yet another.

The problem was that she had no master plan. She seemed to choose each new project almost by whim. (Perhaps, to be fair, she was trying to confuse the ghosts.) The result is a rambling mansion that simply makes no sense (Figure 1.4). Each room, by itself, exudes quality, featuring the best materials money could buy installed by the very best craftspeople of Sarah Winchester's time. But the house is unlivable. The components are excellent, but the system is faulty.

The computing field abounds with comparable examples. An expensive report goes unread because no one really needs the information it contains.

FIGURE 1.4
An aerial view of the Winchester Mystery House.

A sophisticated program is ignored because no one can learn how to use it. An application fails because the necessary input data cannot be economically captured. A local area network is scrapped because it is incompatible with the organization's network. The fact that the components are of top quality means little if the system is faulty.

A **system** is a set of components that function together in a meaningful way. The solar system consists of the sun, the planets, their moons, comets, and so on. An ecological system consists of flora, fauna, water, air, land, and other components. The human body is a system of bones, flesh, muscles, brains, organs, nerves, blood, and so on. The components, by themselves, are not enough. If the system is to be effective (indeed, if it is to survive), *all* the components must work together.

If the system is to be effective, *all* the components must work together.

FIGURE 1.5
Modern information systems have evolved over time.

System Type	Characteristics
Electronic data processing	Serial-batch
	Single task
	Custom files
	Transaction processing
Management information system	Integrated applications
	Interactive
	Central database
	Data communication
Decision support system	Remote intelligence
	Network
	Query processing
	What-if analysis
Executive information system	Enterprise modeling
	Parallel processing
	Virtual reality
	Multimedia
	Electronic data interchange

Information Systems

This book is concerned with **information systems**. An information system is a set of hardware, software, data, procedural, and human components that work together to generate, collect, store, retrieve, process, analyze, and/or distribute information. The purpose of an information system is to get the right information to the right people at the right time.

The purpose of an information system is to get the right information to the right people at the right time.

Information systems are not new. They have been around ever since people began trading and bartering. The abacus, ledger books (or scrolls), and counting boards are at least as old as recorded history.

The very first **electronic data-processing systems** (Figure 1.5) were stand-alone, serial-batch applications such as payroll, accounts receivable, accounts payable, general ledger, and inventory. In addition to programs, files, forms, and reports, these systems included manual procedures for recording, verifying, and distributing information.

Serial-batch applications represented the state of the art until well into the 1960s when transaction processing systems began to emerge. Soon, database and data communication software were supporting true integrated applications. By the early 1980s, **management information systems** (Figure 1.5) with multiple users interactively sharing a central database and integrated applications over data communication lines had become the accepted standard.

By the mid-1980s the ability to network microcomputers changed the very nature of information systems. A remote *computer* implies remote *intelligence*. Given access to a networked microcomputer or a workstation, an end user can issue a query to a central database, ask the system to down-load relevant data, and then process those data or perform what-if analysis locally, without affecting the database. Add remote intelligence to a management information system and you get a **decision support system** (Figure 1.5).

Executive information systems (Figure 1.5) add such technical innovations as enterprise modeling, parallel processing, virtual reality, and multimedia to the decision support system base. Additionally, an electronic data interchange network might be used to link a corporation to its suppliers, its customers, and its business partners. The scope of an executive information system extends well beyond the boundaries of the firm.

Systems Analysis

A system begins with a **user**. The user needs information but often lacks technical expertise. Programmers and other specialists know a great deal about computers and technology but may lack a clear understanding of the user's needs. The user knows the problem but can't solve it. The technical personnel could solve the problem, if only they understood it. Complicating matters is a communication gap. At times, technical experts and users seem to speak different languages.

Successful systems require careful planning. The person who plans and designs a system is called a **systems analyst**. The systems analyst defines the user's problem, deals with management to obtain the necessary resources, translates the user's needs into technical terms, and then develops a plan for coordinating the efforts of the various technical experts assigned to the job (Figure 1.6). Remember that the analyst's focus is on the *system*, not just its component parts.

The analyst's focus is on the *system*, not just its component parts.

FIGURE 1.6
The analyst acts as an intermediary between the user, the technical professionals, and management.

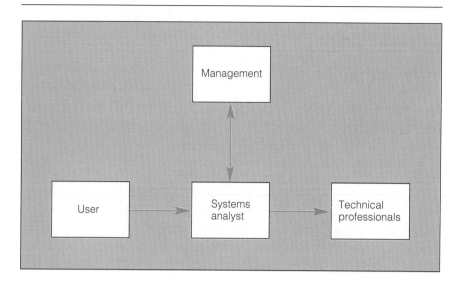

Carefully distinguish between the user and the **customer** (or the client). A user is a person who affects or is affected by the system. The customer, on the other hand, is the person who pays the bill and thus makes the final decision. Often (but not always) the customer and the user are the same.

It is sometimes useful to distinguish between a user and an **end user,** too. A user can best be defined as an application expert, while an end user is a person who utilizes all or part of the system. Sometimes the user and the end user are the same, but not always. For example, the end users of a supermarket bar code scanner system might be checkout clerks, while the users might be professionals assigned to the regional distribution or marketing manager's staff. (The customer in this example might be the distribution manager.) The end user knows what and how; the user knows what and why.

The analyst normally works with the user. End users are excellent sources of detailed information about individual system components, but the user's viewpoint tends to be somewhat broader. The customer's involvement might be limited to status reviews at key decision points.

Methodologies

Users are concerned with the details of their jobs. Technical people worry about bits, bytes, and data structures. Management deals with strategic planning, budgets, schedules, and the allocation of resources.

Because the analyst must communicate with all three groups, he or she must understand the user's task, the technical details associated with the various system components, the proposed system's budget, schedule, and resource implications, and the relationship of the proposed system to the organization's strategic business plan. Because modern systems are highly complex, the analyst must consider the relationships between numerous components. It is a demanding job, and it's easy to overlook something. That is why most professional analysts follow a methodology.

For example, consider an architect's methodology. The first step in creating a new building is to prepare sketches and submit them to the client. After the preferred sketch is selected, a scale model is built, modified as necessary, and eventually approved. Then blueprints are prepared. Only after the blueprints are approved does physical construction begin. The idea is simple: Plan first, then do.

The process starts with a logical model on paper. Gradually, step by step, the physical details are introduced. At each step, specific tools are used to create documents or models that must be completed before the next step can begin. That is the essence of a methodology: a set of tools used in the context of clearly defined steps that end with specific, measurable exit criteria.

■   **PROFESSIONAL POINTER**

Please the User

Back in the "good old days," when hardware was expensive and people were (relatively) cheap, the best programmers were technical experts who wrote efficient code. (In those days, to be called a hacker was a compliment.) Their focus was the computer, and users (literally) took what they could get and were happy to get it.

Today, hardware is cheap and skilled people are expensive, so the definition of efficiency has changed. Today, pleasing the user has become far more important than pleasing the computer, and this shift in perspective has dramatically changed the nature of the analyst's job.

The System Development Life Cycle

The basis for most systems analysis and design methodologies is the **system development life cycle,** or **SDLC** (Figure 1.7). It is sometimes called the waterfall method because the model visually suggests work cascading from step to step like a series of waterfalls, but it rarely happens that way. For example, errors in problem definition are sometimes discovered during analysis, and implementation difficulties often force a change in design. A more realistic view of the process would include numerous loops back to prior steps as a system plan is gradually refined. In other words, systems analysis and design is an iterative process.

The basis for most systems analysis and design methodologies is the system development life cycle.

It is also possible to view the system development life cycle as a loop (Figure 1.8). A system is "born" when a problem is recognized. The system is then created (analysis, design, development), tested, implemented, and maintained. Eventually, a change in the nature of the problem or increasing maintenance costs degrade the value of the system, so it "dies." That creates a new problem, and recognizing that problem starts a new cycle for the replacement system. The point is that systems do not last forever.

Problem Definition

Because it makes little sense to try to solve a problem you don't understand, the first step in the system development life cycle is **problem definition** (Figure 1.9). The intent is to identify the problem, determine its cause, and outline a strategy for solving it. A poor problem definition virtually guarantees that the system will fail to solve the real problem.

It makes little sense to try to solve a problem you don't understand.

Larger projects often call for a formal **feasibility study**. The objective of the feasibility study is to determine if the problem can be solved and if it is worth solving before significant resources are committed.

FIGURE 1.7
The system development life cycle (SDLC).

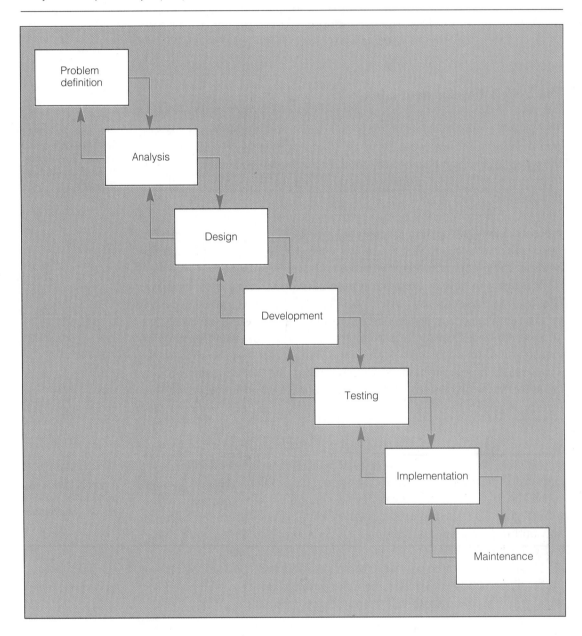

FIGURE 1.8
Another view of the system development life cycle.

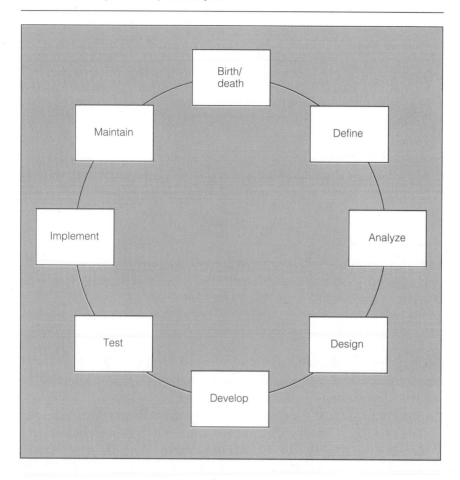

Analysis

Given a clear problem definition, **analysis** (Figure 1.9) begins. The objective of this phase is to determine exactly *what* must be done to solve the problem. During analysis the analyst works with the user to develop a *logical* model that identifies essential processes, data elements, objects,

FIGURE 1.9
The steps in the traditional system development life cycle.

Phase	Description	Exit Criteria
1. Problem definition	Identify the problem, define the cause, and outline a solution strategy.	Problem statement Feasibility study
2. Analysis	Determine *what* must be done to solve the problem.	Logical model Requirements
3. Design	Determine *how* the problem will be solved.	Physical plan
4. Development	Create the system. Write the programs, install the hardware, write procedures, and so on.	Code Procedures Manuals
5. Testing	Test the system.	System test
6. Implementation	Release the system to the user.	User sign-off Review
7. Maintenance	Keep the system functioning.	Ongoing

and other key entities without reference to how those components will be implemented. Analysis ends with a detailed set of **requirements specifications** that clearly define what the system must do.

Design

Analysis is concerned with doing the right thing. Design is concerned with doing the thing right.

Once analysis is completed, the analyst knows what must be done to solve the problem. The objective of the next phase, **design** (Figure 1.9), is to determine *how* the problem will be solved. Analysis is concerned with doing the right thing. Design is concerned with doing the thing right.

During design the analyst's focus shifts from the logical to the *physical*. Processes are converted to manual procedures or computer programs. Data elements are grouped to form physical data structures, screens, reports, files, and databases. The hardware components that support the programs and the data are defined. A system test plan is developed. The logical model often suggests several alternative physical designs, and part of the analyst's responsibility is selecting the best alternative.

The first step in design is to identify the primary physical components and the interfaces that link them. Next, the individual components are defined at a black-box level. Think of a **black box** (Figure 1.10) as a sealed box. The inputs to, the outputs from, and the function performed by the box are known. You can provide inputs and predict and observe the

FIGURE 1.10
You can provide inputs to a black box and observe the resulting outputs from it, but you cannot determine its contents.

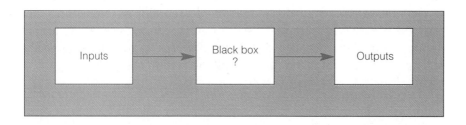

resulting outputs, but you cannot determine the contents of the black box except by deduction. In other words, the initial design objective is to specify what each component does, not how it works.

The next step is to plan the contents of the black boxes by specifying how each component works. For example, an analyst might define a system composed of a database, two programs, and appropriate input and output media and data and then define the precise database structure, the input and output data structures, and the logic of the two programs.

Development

The system is created during **development** (Figure 1.9). Programs are coded, debugged, documented, and tested. New hardware is selected and ordered. Operating, security, and auditing procedures are written and tested. End-user documentation is prepared. Databases and files are initialized, and users are trained.

Testing

Once the system is developed, it is tested to ensure that it does what it was designed to do (Figure 1.9). **Testing** usually begins with module tests, followed by component tests and a final system test. The system test parameters are derived from the requirements specification. Component and module test parameters are, in turn, based on the system test parameters. Because the requirements specification is derived (via the analysis process) from the original problem definition, a well-designed test plan ensures that the system meets the user's needs.

Implementation

After the system passes its final test and any remaining problems are corrected, the system is **released** to the user (Figure 1.9). In most cases, the system release process incorporates formal **user sign-off** procedures that mark the user's acceptance of the system. At this point the analyst's formal responsibility ends, although additional end-user training may be necessary. Often, a postinstallation review follows system release.

Maintenance

After the system is released, **maintenance** begins (Figure 1.9). The objective is to keep the system functioning at an acceptable level. Almost inevitably, some errors slip undetected through the system test, and fixing them is a maintenance function. Over time the parameters and algorithms used to develop the original programs change, so the programs must be updated. Hardware must be maintained. Even procedures change. Eventually, the cost of maintaining the system will become a problem in its own right. When that happens, the old system dies and is replaced by a new system. That marks the end of the system life cycle.

Although typically not responsible for maintenance, the analyst does influence this phase. Simply put, systems will change, and a well-designed system anticipates, allows for, and simplifies change.

■   **PROFESSIONAL POINTER**

Be Creative But Be Precise

Is systems analysis an art, or is it primarily a set of tools? Initially, as work begins, it is very much an art because the ability to recognize and describe problems demands creativity. Increasingly, however, as work progresses, emphasis shifts to the precise application of technical tools, so the correct answer is "both." We need creative architects. We do not need creative bricklayers. The best systems analysts are creative people who know how to shift gears and work within the context of a plan.

Advantages

Several advantages are derived from following a methodology such as the system development life cycle. First, the methodology acts as a memory aid. Modern information systems tend to be complex. A good methodology imposes a discipline on the analyst, and that discipline helps to minimize the risk that key details will be overlooked.

Second, communication is enhanced because most methodologies impose a consistent set of documentation standards. If everyone follows the same methodology, then the members of an analysis, design, or programming team will find it relatively easy to understand each other. If everyone follows the same methodology, then a new analyst entering a team after a project has begun will find it relatively easy to get up to speed.

Management control is a third advantage. A methodology, by definition, consists of a set of steps and well-defined exit criteria. The exit criteria represent milestones or checkpoints, and a step is not completed until its exit criteria are completed. The steps provide a framework for developing a schedule and a budget.

Fourth, a methodology generally incorporates tools, and the tools associated with a good methodology make it easier for the analyst to solve the problem. Another mark of a good methodology is that the tools are compatible, with the output from one step serving as a foundation for subsequent steps.

A fifth advantage is that a good methodology increases the likelihood that significant errors are detected early. The cost of a system accelerates as work progresses (Figure 1.11). If an error is detected early, only the work performed to that point is lost. However, if the error is not detected until just before the system is finished, the efforts of designers, programmers, and other technical professionals might be wasted. Even worse is the possibility that a bad system will be installed in spite of crucial errors simply because "We've already spent all this money."

Some Cautions

There are dangers associated with using a methodology, too. For example, some analysts fall into the trap of focusing excessively on preparing the exit criteria. Like English students who can't see past spelling, punctuation, and grammar, they become so bogged down in mechanics that they fail to analyze the system. Filling out forms *is* easier than thinking, but completing the paperwork is *not* the real job. The point of the exit criteria is to document and communicate what the analyst has done.

There is a fine line between discipline and rigidity. No matter what methodology you might choose, you will eventually encounter a problem for which that methodology is (at best) inappropriate, and it is a mistake to force the application to fit the tool. If, as you are developing a model or completing a set of documentation, you feel that you are wasting your

If you feel that you are wasting your time, you are probably right.

FIGURE 1.11
The cost of a system accelerates as work progresses.

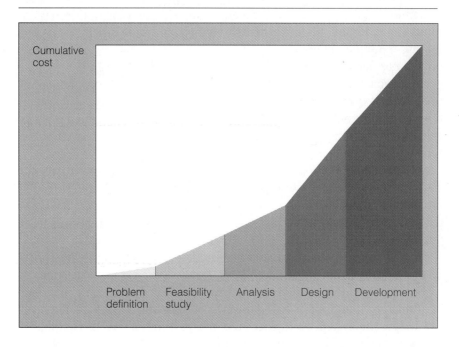

time, you are probably right. Stop and ask for help. Either the tool is inappropriate for the task or you don't understand the tool.

A good methodology makes a competent analyst more productive, but no methodology can convert an unskilled, untrained person into a competent analyst. Technical experts are expensive. Sometimes management is tempted to believe (or hope) that technology can replace the technical experts, but there is simply no substitute for skilled people.

Computer-aided Software Engineering

R. M. Graham once said, "We build systems like the Wright brothers built airplanes—build the whole thing, push it off a cliff, let it crash, and start over again." That's not quite fair to the Wright brothers (who were pretty good engineers), but it reflects a very real frustration with computer people who, over the years, have developed a well-deserved reputation for delivering less than adequate systems late and over budget.

To make matters worse, the simple jobs have already been done. We no longer plan and develop stand-alone, serial-batch applications. Instead we work with complex, integrated systems that interface with people throughout the organization. We must find a way to do better. We must find a way to impose an engineering-like discipline on the systems development process. In fact, many experts believe that systems analysis and design must evolve into software engineering and/or systems engineering before the "late and over-budget" image can be corrected.

A well-defined methodology can help to improve our performance, but we need better tools, too. CASE, an acronym for **computer-aided software engineering,** represents a significant step in the right direction. The objective of CASE is to automate all or part of the system development life cycle.

The most obvious CASE feature is a set of tools and a graphic interface that together support creating and maintaining models. However, the real key to CASE is a special database called the **repository** that holds information about and defines relationships between the system's data elements, processes, and other objects (Figure 1.12).

During analysis, logical descriptions of these entities are input to the repository. Subsequently, logical models are created to define the relationships. Because the information is stored in the repository, the CASE software can trace ripple effects that result from changes and make necessary corrections to the model. Other CASE routines can be used to check the model for completeness and consistency. During subsequent stages the analyst can build on the logical model to create physical models (design) and physical components (development). By automating much of the detail, CASE enhances the analyst's productivity.

Numerous CASE products are commercially available. Some of them automate a single life cycle phase. Others are little more than collections of loosely integrated tools. Still others cut across the entire life cycle and impose a specific methodology on the analyst. In any event, learning a CASE product is a bit like learning a new programming language.

Rather than selecting a single CASE product and teaching you how to use it, this book will explain several common analysis and design tools and show you how they might be integrated by a hypothetical CASE product. Concrete examples always help, so Chapter 10 will overview a CASE package called Excelerator, but Excelerator access will not be necessary. If you understand the tools and how they relate to each other, you should have

FIGURE 1.12
The real key to CASE is the repository.

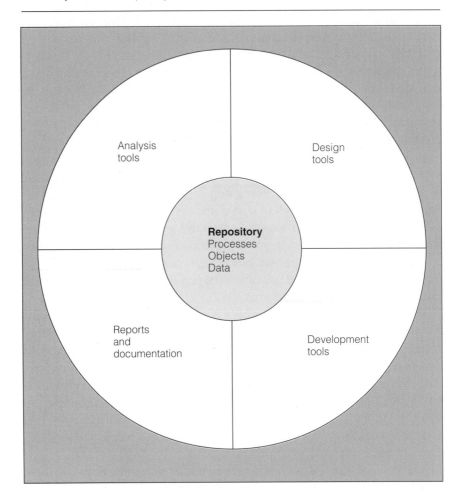

little difficulty learning whatever CASE product your school or your employer uses.

Object-oriented analysis, design, and programming is another approach that shows promise. The idea is to define a system as a set of independent objects that incorporate their own data and processes (or methods). One key objective of object-oriented software is reusability. Perhaps someday we will assemble software much as we assemble hardware: by selecting existing objects from a repository and writing a limited amount of application-specific code to link them.

The object-oriented approach is a natural for CASE, and object-oriented features are already beginning to appear in commercial CASE products. In this book, object-oriented analysis is introduced in Chapter 9 and object-oriented design is the topic of Chapter 21.

Of course, there will always be problems that are too messy for formal solution, so information systems analysis and design will remain, at least in part, an art. Also, no methodology can *guarantee* quality. An old friend named Don Stearns used to tell his managers, "You can have it fast, you can have it cheap, or you can have it right. Pick any two." The point is simple. If you allocate enough resources and take the time to do the job right, you will probably get a quality system, but there are no shortcuts.

PROFESSIONAL POINTER   ■

Concentrate on Concepts

Learning a new tool, a new methodology, or a new CASE product is a bit like learning a new programming language. Each one has its own rules, grammar, and syntax, and it is easy to become so bogged down in details that you forget the tool's purpose.

After you complete your studies and begin working, it is unlikely that your employer will use exactly the same methodology you studied in this book. If you understand *why* you used a given tool, you should find it relatively easy to learn a new one that performs the same basic function, but if all you know is how to use the tool, learning a new one means starting over.

It has been said that change is the only constant in the computer field. Methodologies change. Tools change. CASE products change. Details change. Concepts don't. Concentrate on the underlying concepts.

MANAGEMENT'S PERSPECTIVE   ■

Concentrate on the Organization's Objectives

Historically, data processing was driven by technology, but that is changing. Today, many organizations insist that computer people concentrate on those applications that contribute the most to meeting the organization's objectives.

The starting point is to develop a model of the enterprise that links information system strategy to the organization's strategic plan. Individual application projects are then selected, planned, and developed within the context of that plan. An in-depth discussion of strategic planning is beyond the scope of this book, but if you can take a course in enterprise modeling, do so.

At the project level, the system development life cycle provides a framework for allocating resources, defining a schedule and a budget, and implementing traditional management controls. Because each step ends with a set of measurable exit criteria, the checkpoints are defined by analysis, design, development, testing, and implementation. The time and effort needed to complete each step can be monitored and the plan adjusted as necessary.

Summary

A system is composed of several components that function together in a meaningful way. An information system is a set of hardware, software, data, procedural, and human components that work together to generate, collect, store, retrieve, process, analyze, and/or distribute information. Early electronic data processing systems evolved into management information systems which, in turn, provided a base for decision support systems. Today, the trend is toward executive information systems.

The person who plans and designs an information system is called a systems analyst. The analyst translates user needs into technical specifications and communicates resource requirements to management. The final decision is made by the customer. An end user is a person who utilizes all or part of the system.

A methodology imposes discipline on the system development process. The system development life cycle is the basis for most system development methodologies. Problem definition is sometimes followed by a feasibility study. During analysis, the analyst develops a logical model of the proposed system and writes detailed requirements specifications. During design, components are first defined as black boxes and then the contents of those black boxes are specified. The system is created during the development stage. Once the system is developed, it is tested to ensure that it does what it was designed to do. Once the system passes its final test, the system is released to the user. In most cases, the release process calls for formal user sign-off. Maintenance begins after the system is released.

The objective of computer-aided software engineering (CASE) is to automate key parts of the system development life cycle and thus impose an engineering-like discipline on the process. The key to CASE is a special database called the repository that holds information about and defines relationships between the system's data elements, processes, and other objects. The object-oriented approach to system development shows great promise for the future.

Suggestions for Additional Reading

Eliason, Alan L. 1990. *Systems Development. Analysis, Design, and Implementation.* 2d ed. Glenview, IL: Scott Foresman/Little Brown Higher Education.

Ince, Darrell, and Derek Andrews. 1990. *The System Life Cycle.* London: Butterworths.

Weinberg, Gerald M. 1982. *Rethinking Systems Analysis and Design.* Boston: Little, Brown and Company.

Wurman, Richard Saul. 1989. *Information Anxiety: What to Do When Information Doesn't Tell You What You Need to Know.* New York: Bantam Books.

Exercises

1. What is a system? What is an information system? Don't just copy the definitions from the book; explain what they mean.

2. Consider an information system about which you know something and identify the hardware, software, human, and procedural components that compose it. If you can't think of one, pick your school's registration system or grade distribution system.

3. Briefly distinguish between electronic data processing, management information systems, decision support systems, and executive information systems.

4. What does a systems analyst do? Why is systems analysis necessary?

5. Distinguish between a customer, a user, and an end user.

6. What is a methodology? What advantages are derived from following a methodology? What are some dangers?

7. List the steps in the system development life cycle and state the objective of each step.

8. What is systems analysis? An art? A science? A craft? A set of procedures? An engineering discipline? What *should* systems analysis be? Why?

9. Briefly, what is computer-aided software engineering? Why is CASE significant?

10. When you purchase hardware you get a warranty. When you purchase software you get a *disclaimer* of warranty. We must learn to build systems and software the way we build hardware: by selecting existing components and assembling them. Do you agree or disagree with this statement? Why?

PART II

Defining the Problem

You cannot solve a problem unless you know what caused it.

2

Recognizing and Defining the Problem

When you finish reading this chapter you should be able to:

—Explain what a problem is.

—Distinguish between problem recognition and problem definition.

—Identify a problem, define a set of objectives, and estimate the problem's scope.

—Write a problem statement.

—List and explain the objectives of a feasibility study.

—Discuss the nature of the go/no go decision that marks the end of the problem definition phase.

Problem Recognition

What Is a Problem?

In their highly readable book entitled *Are Your Lights On?*, Donald Gause and Gerald Weinberg define a **problem** as "a difference between things as *desired* and things as *perceived*." According to the authors of *The One Minute Manager*, "A problem only exists if there is a difference between what is *actually* happening and what you *desire* to be happening."

The only "problem" with those definitions is that perceptions and desires are subjective; they vary with the observer. If the star of a Broadway play breaks a leg, the producers might sense a disaster, but the star's understudy would probably see things differently. One person's problem is another person's opportunity. **Problem recognition** demands a point of view.

One person's problem is another person's opportunity.

Some problems are obvious. If the government issues new income tax withholding rules, your firm's payroll system will have to change. If a company is losing sales to its competitors, something is wrong. Most concerned observers can quickly agree on the nature of such problems.

Other problems are less clear, however. For example, imagine a breakfast cereal firm reacting to a report from the Surgeon General entitled *Oat Bran: The Silent Killer*. Some managers might argue that the report itself is the problem and that it should be discredited or ignored. Others might suggest that the firm's product line must change because the sale of oat bran cereals will almost certainly decline. Still others might see an opportunity for increasing the sale of rice pops.

Defining Desires

Before people can agree on a solution, they must first agree on the problem.

Before people can agree on a solution, they must first agree on the problem. Before you and several coworkers can agree on the nature of a problem within your organization, you must first share a sense of what the organization wants. Explicitly defining the *organization's* desires is a key objective of business planning.

Top management starts the process by identifying strategic goals. Those goals are converted to measurable objectives and critical success factors. The goals and objectives are the organization's official desires; they represent a shared sense of how things should be. The critical success factors provide a basis for prioritizing those desires.

If actual or expected performance is inconsistent with the goals and objectives, there is a problem, and the bigger the perceived difference, the bigger the problem. The most significant problems are those that have the greatest impact on the organization's critical success factors. Within an organization a problem can be defined as a difference between the way things are and the way the organization's goals and objectives say they should be (Figure 2.1).

Be careful to distinguish between real problems and special cases, however. For example, consider the control chart pictured in Figure 2.2. It

FIGURE 2.1

A problem is a difference between the way things are and the way the organization's goals and objectives say they should be.

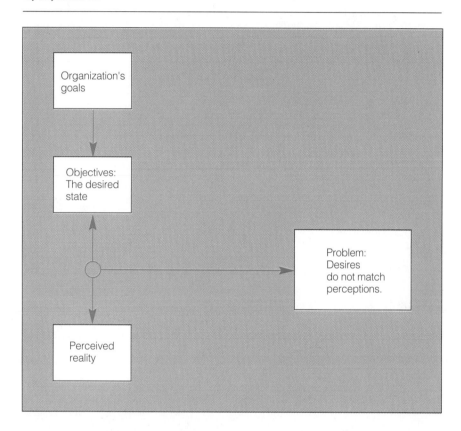

tracks actual daily production for a manufacturing concern. The average or mean production rate represents the official (or expected) target (the desire), but there will be variations in performance from day to day. As long as the actual production for any given day lies between the statistically computed upper and lower control limits, the process is in control, and the fact that Thursday's output is below the mean value is not, by itself, significant.

An occasional point that lies outside the control limits can often be explained by extreme or unusual conditions. For example, the second Wednesday's low production might be attributed to an untrained worker, a

FIGURE 2.2
A control chart for a manufacturing process.

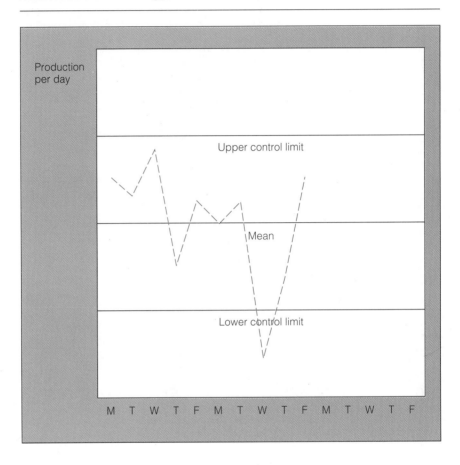

broken machine, or a planned meeting that interrupted the day's work. Dealing with such special cases is fire fighting, and solving such short-term problems, while often necessary, has little or no long-term effect because it does not change or improve the basic process. Such tasks are usually handled by user personnel and rarely call for the services of a systems analyst.

Chronically out-of-control processes are different because if performance does not consistently lie between the upper and lower control

FIGURE 2.3
Trends sometimes suggest real problems.

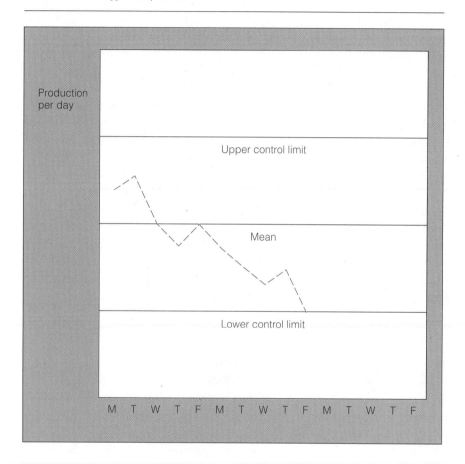

limits, something is basically wrong. Trends can also suggest real problems; for example, Figure 2.3 shows a control chart that depicts declining performance. Sometimes, due to competitive pressures or a desire to improve, an organization will decide to tighten its control limits. Bringing a process under control, reversing a trend, or tightening the control limits often means changing the process, and changing the process has long-term implications. These are the problems that require systems analysis.

Problem Definition

Once a problem has been recognized you can begin to define it. Some people stop at this point, apparently assuming that problem recognition and problem definition are the same thing. They aren't. *You cannot solve a problem unless you know what caused it.*

You cannot solve a problem unless you know what caused it.

Defining a problem is comparable to developing a scientific hypothesis or diagnosing an illness (Figure 2.4). A scientist observes a phenomenon, formulates a hypothesis, and then designs an experiment to test the hypothesis. A doctor observes symptoms, identifies possible causes, and then conducts diagnostic tests to accept or reject each possibility. A systems analyst recognizes a problem, lists possible causes, and then tests those possible causes by interviewing users and studying the present system.

Bad scientists conduct experiments, collect data, and then fashion a hypothesis. Bad doctors treat symptoms. Bad analysts develop "solutions" and hope they solve the problem. None of these approaches works very well because they focus on the symptoms (the effects), not the cause (the problem). You might get lucky, but there is no substitute for a good problem definition.

Finding the Cause

Without some idea of the problem's magnitude, management cannot judge if it is worth solving.

The first step in discovering what caused a problem is to state the symptoms in measurable form. Without some idea of the problem's magnitude, management cannot judge if it is worth solving. Without some measurable sense of what is wrong, no one can ever be sure if the problem was actually solved.

For example, imagine that your company's profits are 5 percent lower than expected. One possible explanation is that the sales department failed to meet its quota. There is an easy way to test that hypothesis. If actual sales (things as perceived) are less than expected sales (things as desired), you have a problem, and such actions as increasing advertising or hiring additional sales personnel might solve it. If, on the other hand, the problem is really excessive spending, those solutions might make matters worse.

Figure 2.5 shows a partial **cause-and-effect diagram,** sometimes called a fish bone diagram (after its shape) or an Ishikawa diagram (after

FIGURE 2.4

Defining a problem is comparable to developing a scientific hypothesis or diagnosing an illness.

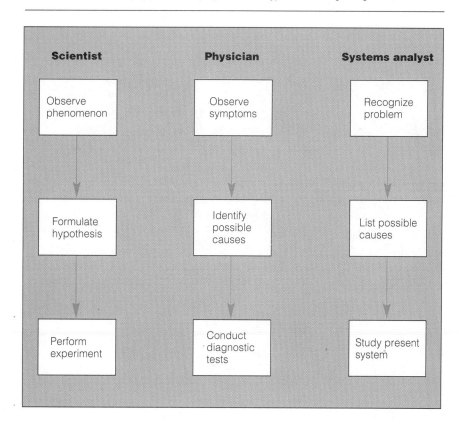

its originator), for the low-profit problem. The long horizontal line represents the primary problem: Profits are too low. The line that joins it at a 45-degree angle represents a possible cause: Sales are below quota.

The horizontal lines that join the cause line are possible explanations (or secondary causes); for example, the sales staff might have performed poorly, the sales department might be understaffed, and so on. Joining those secondary cause lines are short 45-degree angle lines that represent possible secondary symptoms. For example, if the real problem is an understaffed

FIGURE 2.5
A cause-and-effect diagram can be used to document possible causes and secondary symptoms.

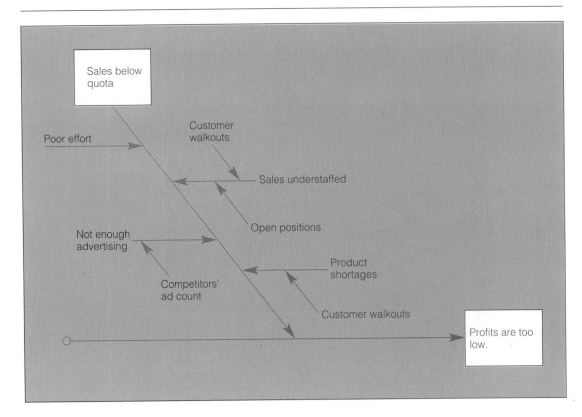

sales department, then the analyst should find evidence of unfilled sales positions and might discover customers who went to a competitor because salespeople were not available. If those secondary symptoms are not present, the hypothesis (sales department understaffed) can probably be rejected.

Next, you might turn your attention to operating costs (Figure 2.6). Are there too many people on the payroll? Are inventory costs out of control? By comparing actual expenses (things as perceived) to budgeted expenses (things as desired) you can test those possibilities.

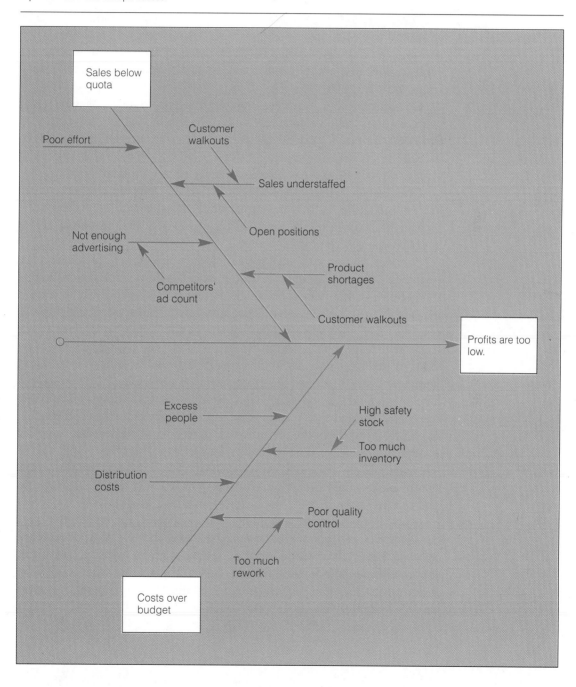

FIGURE 2.6
A problem can have multiple causes.

Note that a problem can have multiple causes. It is possible that profits are 5 percent lower than expected because the sales department missed its quota *and* marketing overspent its budget *and* there are too many people working in sales support positions. Don't stop looking for causes when you find the first discrepancy between perceptions and desires. One advantage of a cause-and-effect diagram is that it simplifies the task of visualizing multiple causes.

Consider another example. Imagine that corporate management has charged the warehouse manager with reducing the value of inventory by $100,000. If nothing is done, the actual value (the perception) is likely to exceed the goal (the organization's desire) when the next physical inventory is conducted, so the warehouse manager has a problem.

One strategy is to challenge the goal. For example, if management can be convinced that cutting inventory will hurt sales and reduce revenues, they might change the goal to match the expected level of inventory. If that happens, there is no problem.

Another option is to accept the goal and thus, implicitly, accept the hypothesis that the amount of money invested in inventory is $100,000 too high. That theory might or might not be true. The best way to test the hypothesis is to try to prove cause and effect. Start by listing possible causes. Then, for each possible cause, identify likely secondary symptoms. If the secondary symptoms are present, the hypothesis might be valid. If the secondary symptoms don't exist, the hypothesis is probably wrong.

For example, one possible explanation for excess inventory is obsolete merchandise (Figure 2.7). If the warehouse actually contains obsolete merchandise, a review of the records or a quick tour should reveal some old inventory. (Look for dust-covered boxes.) If, on the other hand, the responsible people seem to know exactly what is in inventory and can confidently explain their procedures for monitoring and controlling stock life, you can probably discount the obsolete inventory theory.

Another possible cause is poor stock turnover. If the warehouse has a turnover problem, you might expect to discover that the stock consistently exceeds expected demand or that reorders arrive when a significant amount of merchandise still remains in stock. Knowing what to look for, you can test the poor stock turnover hypothesis by reviewing inventory records and interviewing the purchasing agent.

FIGURE 2.7
If the expected secondary symptoms are observed, the hypothesis might be true.

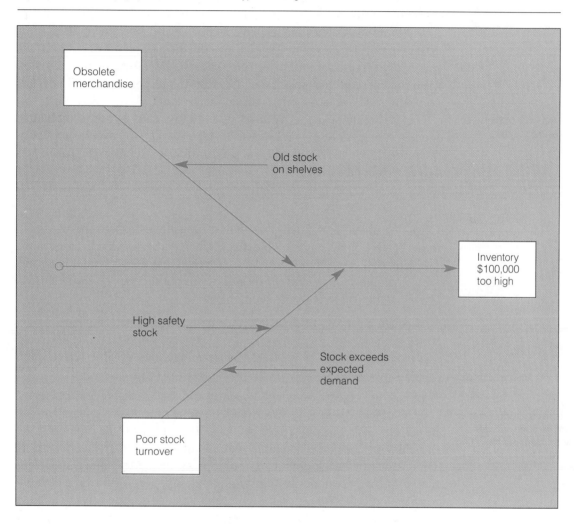

Note the process. First you observe symptoms and postulate causes. Next, you isolate one cause and list secondary symptoms that should be present if the hypothesis is true. Then you look for the secondary symptoms. If interviews with the responsible people and a review of the existing system uncover the expected symptoms, the theory might be correct. If the secondary symptoms cannot be observed, the hypothesis is rejected. You then consider another possible cause, test it, and continue until you feel confident that you know what caused the problem.

Your intent is to find causes, not to fix blame.

Finally, remember that your intent is to find causes, not to fix blame. Identifying and defining problems is much easier if you have the active cooperation of the user, and you will not get that cooperation if you are perceived as an enemy.

Defining Objectives

Once a problem is defined, the analyst typically expresses the causes in terms of a set of measurable **objectives** which, if met, are likely to solve the problem. Symptoms and causes are negative; they suggest what is wrong. Objectives are positive and thus less likely to put the user on the defensive. For example, you might state such objectives as:

> Reduce inventory by $100,000 by eliminating obsolete stock.
> or
> Reduce inventory by $100,000 by reducing safety stock to a level sufficient to cover expected reorder time plus five days.

Note that the objectives reflect the cause and that they are measurable.

Objectives specify *what* must be done, not *how* the problem will be solved.

The objectives specify *what* must be done, not *how* the problem will be solved. Test your objectives by visualizing at least three different ways of achieving them. For example, you might be able to reduce inventory safety stock by developing a computer-based inventory management system, improving communications with your suppliers, or hiring a consulting firm to do the job for you. If you can't imagine several ways to achieve the objective, then you are describing solutions, not writing objectives.

The problem definition represents the analyst's *preliminary* sense of the problem. It is an initial informed guess that might be wrong. Settling on a specific solution during the problem definition stage can be dangerous because you do not yet know enough to make that determination. Pay attention to what your intuition tells you, but don't let it direct the analysis process. Think first. Then act.

Think first. Then act.

PROFESSIONAL POINTER   ■

Keep an Open Mind

An analyst postpones defining a physical solution because once the solution is selected, objectivity ends. Instead of testing hypotheses, the analyst begins justifying a prior decision. Instead of seeking causes, the analyst begins planning implementation details. To be effective, you must study problems with an open mind, and you cannot do that if you have already decided on the solution. Avoid being prematurely physical.

Does that mean the analyst never thinks of possible physical solutions during the problem definition phase? Of course not. One way to understand a problem is to visualize possible solutions, and an experienced analyst would be foolish to ignore his or her experience. The key is keeping an open mind. If you can visualize a solution and then set it aside as but one possibility, fine, but if you always run with your very first idea, perhaps you should not be an analyst.

The Problem Statement

Once the problem is defined, the analyst's hypothesis and an initial sense of the problem's resource implications must be communicated to the user, to management, and (perhaps) to the technical people. Generally, this communication takes the form of a written **problem statement,** sometimes called a statement of scope and objectives, a user needs assessment, an operations concept document, or a mission statement. The precise form varies from organization to organization, but the intent is the same. A good problem statement lists the symptoms, suggests the problem's likely causes, and estimates the resources needed to solve the problem.

> **A good problem statement lists the symptoms, suggests the problem's likely causes, and estimates the resources needed to solve the problem.**

Problem Statement Contents

A good problem statement starts with a list of the observed symptoms in measurable form (Figure 2.8). The more specific the symptoms, the more likely it is that the problem will be solved.

The second element of a problem statement is a list of suspected causes stated as measurable objectives. There is a fine line between defining clear, measurable objectives and suggesting a physical solution to the problem (Figure 2.9), so it is important to remember that the intent of problem definition is to specify what must be done, not how to do it. You do not yet understand the problem well enough to solve it. Avoid being prematurely physical.

> **Avoid being prematurely physical.**

FIGURE 2.8
A good problem statement lists the symptoms, suggests likely causes, and estimates the resources needed to solve the problem.

A. THE PROBLEM	A list of symptoms.
Examples:	Inventory value is $100,000 too high.
	Our competitor can process a sales order in one day, but we need three.
B. THE OBJECTIVES	The likely cause or causes, usually stated in the form of objectives.
Examples:	Reduce average stock time by two days.
	Reduce inventory cost by $100,000 by eliminating obsolete inventory.
	Reduce inventory cost by $100,000 by reducing safety stock to a level sufficient to cover expected reorder time plus five days.
	Reduce sales order processing time to one day by improving paperwork flow.
C. RESOURCE IMPLICATIONS, or SCOPE	A sense of the problem's magnitude, often stated as a preliminary cost estimate.
Examples:	The cost of this system will not exceed $10,000.
	The estimated cost of this system is $10,000 plus or minus 25 percent.
	Preliminary estimates suggest that a team of three analysts/programmers will need six months to solve this problem.

A good problem statement also includes a preliminary estimate of the problem's resource implications, or **scope** (Figure 2.8). The scope represents the analyst's sense of the problem's magnitude. For example, one or two people might be able to quickly develop an inventory system for a small retail store, but integrating inventory information into a corporate-wide decision support system or developing a complete small-business accounting system are much bigger tasks. In most cases, the best way to communicate a sense of scope is to include a preliminary cost estimate. To the user, the cost estimate *is* the scope.

Verification

To minimize errors, you should always **verify** your work (Figure 2.10). Start with the symptoms. Go through them one by one and identify the objective or objectives that solve each problem. If you find a symptom that is not addressed by the objectives, then you have overlooked something.

FIGURE 2.9
There is a fine line between defining clear, measurable objectives and suggesting a physical solution to the problem.

Not Measurable	Reduce inventory cost.
Good	Reduce inventory cost by $100,000 by reducing safety stock to a level sufficient to cover expected reorder time plus five days.
Too Physical	Install a microcomputer system that will reduce inventory cost by $100,000 by reducing safety stock to a level sufficient to cover expected reorder time plus five days.

FIGURE 2.10
To minimize errors, verify your work.

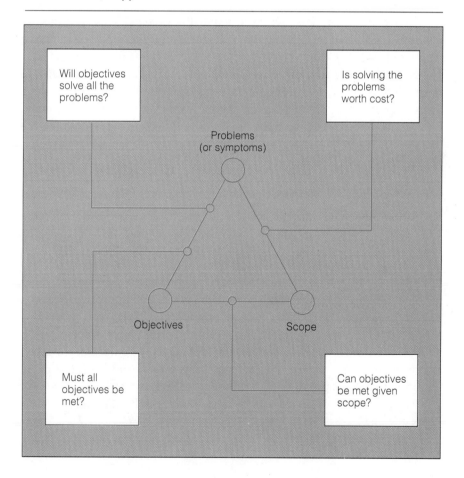

Next, move to the objectives, go through them one by one, and identify the symptom or symptoms that each one cures. If you discover objectives that do not address a symptom, either you have overlooked a symptom or you have added superfluous features to the proposed system.

The scope represents the analyst's sense of what it might cost to solve the problem. Ask the user if solving the problem is worth the cost. Ask the technical people if they can achieve the objectives given the scope. Ask management if adequate resources are available. The combination of the symptoms, the scope, and the objectives allows users, management, and technical personnel to independently determine if the problem is worth solving.

What if the user feels that the scope is too high? Reducing the scope probably means cutting back on at least some of the objectives. Is the project still worth doing? Ask the user.

What if the technical people feel that the objectives cannot be met within the scope? You have two choices: Increase the scope or cut back on the objectives. Either choice changes the user's view of the project.

We never have enough time to do the job right, but we can always find the time to do it over.

Balancing scope and objectives takes time, but it is time well spent. An incomplete problem definition increases the risk that the analyst will solve the wrong problem. There is an old saying: We never have enough time to do the job right, but we can always find the time to do it over. Take the time to do it right.

User Sign-off

The last step in the problem definition process is user sign-off (more accurately, customer sign-off). Generally, it takes the form of a letter or a notation on the problem statement indicating that the user has read the problem definition, understands it, agrees with it, and authorizes work to begin. If the user is to be billed for any work performed, the sign-off process will probably be more formal, but the intent is the same.

No matter how good a system might be, it is likely to fail unless the user accepts it.

User sign-off is crucial. The user, by definition, is the person or group experiencing the problem. At this stage the user is the expert, and attempting to solve a problem without the user's agreement is a mistake. No matter how good a system might be, it is likely to fail unless the user accepts it.

The problem definition must be written for the user, not for the analyst's technical peers. If the user does not understand the problem statement, then the analyst (not the user) is at fault. *At this stage the user is the expert.*

PROFESSIONAL POINTER   ■
_____

Be an Effective Interviewer

Interviewing is one of the analyst's most important sources of information during the early phases of the system development life cycle. A good course in interviewing techniques is recommended for any future systems analyst.

Effective interviewing demands careful preparation. Do your homework first. Learn something about the application. Read available documentation. Decide what you hope to gain from the interview. Then develop a list of questions and follow-up questions.

Start the interview by identifying yourself and your purpose. Then get to the point. Ask a relatively broad, open question first and let the interviewee talk. Avoid complexity. Ask one clear question at a time. Some people tend to wander, so use follow-up questions to focus the interview as necessary. Perhaps the most important rule is to listen. People sometimes answer questions you didn't ask, and you might learn something.

Think of your prepared questions as a guideline, not a script. Remember, the interviewee is the expert, and there may be a very good reason for answering questions in an order different from the one you planned. Before the interview ends, review the prepared questions and make sure they were all answered.

Unless you have an excellent memory, take notes, but don't overdo it; you cannot listen to the answers or ask intelligent follow-up questions if you are taking dictation. As soon as possible after the interview ends, transcribe your notes and fill in any missing details. If necessary, make a follow-up telephone call or schedule a second interview. Finally, offer to share your summary with the subject. It's good public relations, and it provides an opportunity for correcting misunderstandings.

The Feasibility Study

Developing a new system is a form of investment. Any investment carries a certain risk, and it makes sense to investigate the likelihood of success before committing resources. Thus, problem definition is often followed by a feasibility study aimed at determining quickly and at a reasonable cost if the problem can be solved and if it is worth solving.

At least three different types of feasibility are considered:

1. *Technical feasibility*. Is it possible to solve the problem using existing technology? Typically, the analyst proves technical feasibility by citing existing solutions to comparable problems. Prototypes, physical models, and analytical techniques such as simulation are also effective.

2. *Economic feasibility*. Do the benefits outweigh the cost of solving the problem? The analyst demonstrates economic feasibility through cost/benefit analysis.

3. *Operational feasibility*. Can the system be implemented in the user's environment? Is the proposed system consistent with the organization's strategic business plan? Perhaps a union agreement or a government regulation constrains the analyst. There might be ethical considerations. Maybe the boss suffers from computer phobia. Such intangible factors can cause a system to fail just as surely as technology or economics. Some analysts call this criterion *political* feasibility.

As part of the feasibility study, the analyst might consider several alternative solutions to the problem. Note that some alternatives might prove more feasible than others.

Assuming that one or more feasible solutions exist, the analyst prepares a feasibility study report (Figure 2.11) that outlines several alternatives and recommends a course of action. This document becomes the basis for a go/no go decision. One option is to drop the project. Another is to commit the resources needed to complete it. Because of the work done during the feasibility study, management has the information to make an informed decision.

The point of the feasibility study is to determine, at a reasonable cost, if the problem is worth solving. Thus the cost of the feasibility study should represent a small fraction of the estimated cost of developing the system. For example, if a given company's rule of thumb is to allocate roughly 10 percent of the scope to the feasibility study, a $10,000 system would call for a $1,000 study. Similarly, the "feasibility study" for a $1,000 program modification might consume a lunch hour and be documented on the back of a napkin, while you can easily justify spending $100,000 to determine the feasibility of a $1,000,000 system.

Note that the feasibility study is optional. On some small or "obvious" projects it represents a waste of time. Other jobs simply must be done. For example, if federal income tax rates change, your firm has no choice but to update its payroll system. Fixing a bug in a critical program is another

The point of the feasibility study is to determine, at a reasonable cost, if the problem is worth solving.

FIGURE 2.11
An outline for a typical feasibility study report.

A. TITLE PAGE	Project name, report title, author(s), date.
B. CONTENTS	A list of report sections with page numbers.
C. EXECUTIVE SUMMARY	A clear, concise, one-page summary of the feasibility study, the results, and the recommendations. Include authorizations, sources, alternatives considered, and alternatives rejected. Describe the costs, benefits, constraints, and time schedule associated with the recommended alternative.
D. PROBLEM DEFINITION	A one-page description of the problem. Some analysts use the most current problem statement.
E. METHOD OF STUDY	(two to three pages) A description of the work that was done during the feasibility study. The intent of this section is to demonstrate that you followed reasonable procedures and did your homework. Outline your steps and account for your time. Mention your sources and references, identify key people, and briefly describe the existing system. Explain *why* you did what you did and *how* you arrived at your conclusions. Much of the detail belongs in the appendix; include only those facts that are directly relevant to the study.
F. ANALYSIS	(one to two pages) A description of the logical system. If appropriate, include a high-level logical model. Identify interrelationships with other systems. List your final system objectives and explain why meeting those objectives will solve the problem.
G. ALTERNATIVES CONSIDERED	(two to three pages) For each alternative include a description, proof of its technical, economic, and operational feasibility, and a rough estimate of the resources needed to implement it. (Show your cost/benefit analysis here.) Be thorough, but don't overdo it; much of the detail belongs in the appendix. You should normally include at least three alternatives.
H. RECOMMENDATIONS	(one to two pages) Clearly state and justify your recommended course of action. Explain why you selected this alternative. If your recommendation conflicts with the results of the cost/benefit analysis, be prepared to justify your choice in greater detail.
I. DEVELOPMENT PLAN	(one to two pages) Assuming that the recommended course of action is adopted, include a projected schedule and projected costs for each step in the system development life cycle.
J. APPENDIX	Charts, graphs, statistics, interview lists, selected interview summaries, diagrams, memos, notes, references, key contacts, acknowledgements, and so on. In short, the details that support the study. Rather than making multiple copies, you might make the appendix available on a demand or need-to-know basis.

example. There is little point trying to prove feasibility when the problem *must* be solved (although you might want to investigate the relative feasibilities of alternative approaches). However, doing a feasibility study should be the default, and the burden of proof should be on the one who decides to skip this step.

The tools and techniques used to conduct a feasibility study are the same ones that support analysis and design. You will learn how to use those tools in subsequent chapters, so it makes little sense to cover the feasibility study in depth at this time.

The Go/No Go Decision

The feasibility study report is the basis for a go/no go decision. In a small firm, this decision is usually made by the user or the customer, but large organizations often assign this responsibility to a **steering committee** composed of representatives from each department or function that uses management information systems (MIS) services. The steering committee's job is to evaluate all pending projects that require MIS support (Figure 2.12). Because there are not enough resources to solve all the problems, the committee is expected to reject some projects and prioritize the others. Subsequently, as resources become available, the MIS manager assigns people to projects in priority order.

■   **PROFESSIONAL POINTER**

Negotiate When Necessary

Steering committees are influenced by political pressures. Each member of the committee represents a department or function that uses MIS services, and you can safely assume that they all consider their own department's projects crucial. If they can find a good "objective" reason to reject your project, they will because fewer projects increases the odds that their project will be funded. If your work is rejected because other projects are more important to the organization, fine. If your work is rejected because you wrote a sloppy report, then you didn't do your job.

Technically trained people tend to consider politics a dirty word. It isn't. Political negotiation is simply the way our society resolves conflicts.

FIGURE 2.12
The steering committee evaluates pending projects, rejects some, and prioritizes the others.

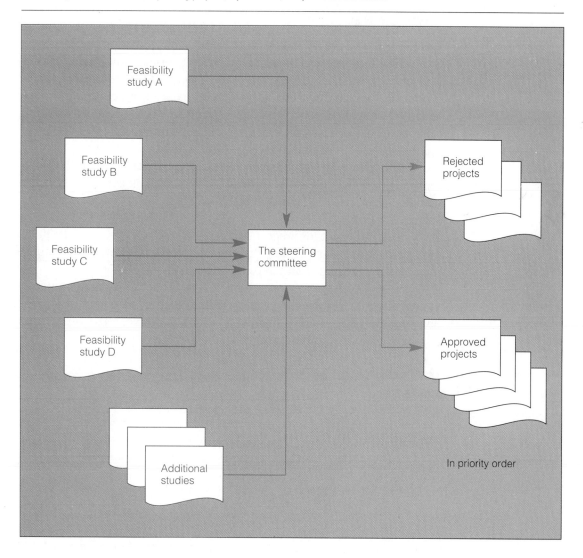

An Inventory Problem

Identifying Symptoms

Imagine that you are an analyst working as a consultant for The Appliance Store. Tina Temple owns the local franchise of this national chain that sells refrigerators, washers, dryers, television sets, sound systems, and similar products. A recent audit by the parent company suggested that inventory levels are roughly $50,000 too high given the store's sales. In response, Tina has asked you to look into the problem; a brief summary of your initial interview with her can be seen in Figure 2.13.

At first glance the problem seems obvious. Inventory is $50,000 too high, so you must find a way to reduce inventory. You can do that by discarding (selectively, of course) $50,000 worth of appliances. Problem solved. Or is it?

Note that the auditor's report said ". . . inventory levels are $50,000 too high *given* sales." Is it possible that the real problem is low sales? Perhaps increased advertising would be a better solution.

Move on to the second paragraph. Tina thinks a personal computer system might help solve the problem. Based on that statement, you might be tempted to implement a microcomputer-based inventory system. After all, that's what the customer wants. Isn't it?

FIGURE 2.13
A brief summary of an initial interview with the store manager concerning the inventory problem.

INTERVIEW WITH: Tina Temple, The Appliance Store

DATE: April 1, 1994

SUBJECT: Inventory

A recent audit indicated that inventory levels were $50,000 too high given sales. We must bring those inventory costs down.

Tina recently saw a demonstration of a personal computer system and feels that it might be the perfect solution.

This is a particularly important project because Tina's cousin, Ted Temple, who has been responsible for the store's stock since it opened five years ago, just announced his retirement effective in 30 days. Since no one else really understands his inventory system, it is essential that we "pick his brain" before he leaves.

People tend to state problems in terms of solutions. If you call a service station to report a dead battery, you might be wrong, but at least you give the mechanic a sense of the problem (in effect, a set of symptoms). The car is acting as if the battery is dead. There is probably nothing wrong with the brakes, the steering, or the exhaust system. There are still many possible causes, but at least you have narrowed them. Unfortunately, if you tell an incompetent (or dishonest) mechanic that your battery is dead, a new battery will probably be part of the solution. After all, you said you wanted one.

People tend to state problems in terms of solutions.

Does Tina really need a computer? Maybe? Would a computer solve her problem? Perhaps; it is a plausible solution. But if Tina was a computer expert, she wouldn't need your help.

Note the third paragraph in the interview summary. Tina's cousin, Ted Temple, her inventory expert, is retiring in 30 days and she wants you to capture at least some of his expertise before he leaves. Considering all three paragraphs, you might be tempted to write a program to automate Ted's inventory system on a personal computer, but would that solve the problem? If Ted's system is so good, why is inventory $50,000 too high? Is it possible that *he* is the problem? If Ted is the problem, and you agree to solve the problem by automating Ted's system, your solution will almost certainly fail. Automating a bad system makes it faster, not better.

Automating a bad system makes it faster, not better.

Defining Objectives

At this point, you might have an inventory problem or you might have a sales problem. The best way to be sure is to ask. (Tina might not be a computer expert, but she *is* the expert when it comes to running her store.) Ask her if sales have been as good as expected. Ask about sales personnel turnover. If the problem is really low sales, you should get some feedback consistent with that hypothesis. If you don't, the problem is probably inventory.

Could the store be carrying obsolete inventory? Once again, ask Tina. If old inventory is the problem you should be able to find some. Other possible clues might include poor record keeping, a sloppy warehouse, or a simple lack of knowledge on the part of the responsible people.

Assume, however, that Tina responds to your questions by showing you her inventory aging reports and explaining how she relies on frequent sales to move old inventory. A subsequent tour of the warehouse reveals a reasonably efficient, clean operation. The obsolete inventory hypothesis is probably wrong.

That still leaves a host of possible causes. Maybe merchandise is ordered before it is really needed. Maybe it takes too long to process a reorder when it arrives. Perhaps the time between a customer order and delivery could be reduced. Solving these problems is a bit more complex than discarding some obsolete appliances.

Imagine that, after additional study, you are able to define the following two objectives:

1. Reduce store inventory by $50,000 by providing accurate, daily inventory status data to support reorder and sale item decisions.
2. Maintain the new inventory level (as a percentage of sales) into the future.

The first objective suggests that the present system does not provide Tina with the timely information she needs to make good reorder decisions or to identify merchandise that should be put on sale. The second one clearly indicates that the solution is not to be a one-time, quick fix.

Did you notice that the analyst in this scenario knew a bit about inventory management and relied on that knowledge to suggest possible causes? A good analyst is more than a technical specialist. A reasonable understanding of the application is essential to problem definition because you cannot solve a problem you don't understand. Detailed knowledge of every aspect of the organization is impossible, but an effective analyst must be broadly trained in the key functional areas of his or her customer's business.

■ **PROFESSIONAL POINTER**

Understand the Application

A young, foreign-born student was having difficulty with a class project involving a general ledger system. After several minutes of one-on-one explanation, the instructor asked her if she had any more questions. She paused briefly and then asked, "Who is this General Ledger, anyway?"

Her problem was obvious. Raised and educated in a communist country, she had never been exposed to the American business practices we sometimes take for granted. After a brief overview of some basics, she did fine. However, her confusion clearly illustrated a basic principle: You can't solve a problem you don't understand. The analyst must know the application.

Estimating Scope

Estimating scope is difficult for beginners. The objective at this early stage is to gain a ballpark sense of the project's magnitude. Although you don't yet know enough to estimate precisely, you should be able to accurately gauge the system's order of magnitude size. For example, there is a clear difference between a $1,000 system, a $10,000 system, and a $100,000 system.

Perhaps the best way to estimate a problem's scope is to answer two questions: What is a solution worth? What will a solution cost? Start with the first one. What is the value of reducing inventory by $50,000? The obvious answer, $50,000, is wrong. Most firms finance their inventory by borrowing money, so the real cost is the interest paid on that loan. For example, at 1 percent per month, a $50,000 inventory reduction means a savings of $500 per month in interest charges. That's about $6,000 per year.

Tina could expect some savings in inventory carrying cost, too. With less value in inventory, insurance rates might drop. Given more space, fewer scratched and dented appliances might be expected. There would be an impact on the first year's income tax as well, so solving the inventory problem might be worth $6,000 to $7,000 per year. Anytime the cost of a project can be recovered through cost savings within a year or two, that project is a good investment, so solving the problem is easily worth $10,000, but there is no way Tina could afford to pay $100,000. This is roughly a $10,000 project.

Tina's suggested solution provides another clue. She thinks a personal computer might be the answer. Tina is not a computer expert, but she's not stupid, either. It is reasonable to assume that she knows what a personal computer costs. If she is willing to purchase one, then she is willing to spend at least a few thousand dollars to solve her inventory problem. That number has the same order of magnitude as the first estimate.

What would a solution cost? The answer, of course, depends on the solution, but, based on the analyst's experience, a personal computer is almost certainly powerful enough to track inventory for a store the size of Tina's. If a computer is not required, the solution will probably cost even less, so $10,000 should be plenty.

If the user feels that solving the problem is worth the scope and the technical people feel that it is possible to achieve the objectives given the scope, then the scope and the objectives are balanced. That suggests a good problem definition. If the scope and the objectives are not balanced, then one or both must change. If the scope and the objectives cannot be balanced, then the project should be dropped.

If two or more estimates derived from different perspectives verify each other, the analyst's confidence in that answer is greatly enhanced.

Note that the analyst estimated the scope not once but several times. A single estimate might be wrong, but if two or more estimates derived from different perspectives verify each other, the analyst's confidence in that answer is greatly enhanced. However, if the answers are *not* comparable, then something is wrong with the problem definition.

Writing the Problem Statement

Figure 2.14 shows a problem statement for the inventory project. (View the format as typical; there is no standard.) Read through it. The first three lines identify the document. Next comes a list of symptoms; note that it paraphrases Tina's initial problem statement. The objectives indicate what the analyst plans to do to solve the problem. Note that they *imply* a cause.

Take a few minutes to verify the problem statement. Inventory cost is too high. Is there at least one objective that promises to solve the problem? Yes, they both do. Next, read the two objectives and relate them to the symptoms. Do they both relate to high inventory cost? Yes. The symptoms and the objectives might not be right, but at least they are consistent with each other.

The scope sets an upper limit on the system's cost. If Tina had envisioned a $1,000 solution to her problem, she would react negatively to the $10,000 preliminary estimate. The time to catch misunderstandings is early in the process, before much money has been spent.

The next entry is as much political as technical. Tina suggested a personal computer system. The preliminary idea tells her that the analyst heard her and will consider her suggestion.

Don't promise what you can't deliver.

Why are the preliminary ideas and key contacts listed separately instead of being merged into the objectives? The objectives represent the analyst's promises. A computer might not be required. Trying to duplicate Ted's inventory system might conflict with the real objectives. As a general rule, don't promise what you can't deliver.

Although the problem statement estimates a system cost of $10,000, the customer is being asked to commit only 10 percent, or $1,000, at this time. During the feasibility study, the analyst will develop a much more accurate

FIGURE 2.14
An initial problem statement for The Appliance Store's inventory problem.

PROJECT PROPOSAL:	April 2, 1994
PREPARED BY:	W. S. Davis
THE CLIENT:	Tina Temple, The Appliance Store
THE PROBLEM:	A recent audit indicated that inventory is $50,000 too high, given sales.
OBJECTIVES:	1. To reduce store inventory by $50,000 by providing accurate, daily inventory status data to support reorder and sale item decisions. 2. To maintain the new inventory level (as a percentage of sales) into the future.
SCOPE:	The cost of this system will not exceed $10,000.
PRELIMINARY IDEAS:	A microcomputer-based inventory system.
KEY CONTACTS:	Tina Temple; Ted Temple.
FEASIBILITY STUDY:	In order to more fully investigate this project, a feasibility study lasting approximately two weeks and costing no more than $1,000 is suggested. The cost of the study is included in the scope. Following the feasibility study, the client will have the option of continuing with or terminating the project.

ACCEPTED BY:_____   DATE: _____

estimate of the system's cost, and that estimate will serve as a basis for a go/no go decision. If the study indicates that the objectives cannot be met within the specified scope, Tina can choose to commit more money or to kill the project.

The final step is user sign-off; note the space for a signature near the bottom of the problem statement (Figure 2.14). It is essential that Tina agrees to the scope and objectives in writing. Without a formal agreement, future misunderstandings are almost inevitable. The idea is not to "twist the user's arm," but to be certain that the user and the analyst are thinking about the same problem.

In this case, assume that Tina agrees with the problem definition and signs the problem statement. Assume further that the feasibility study confirms the problem definition and that Tina approves further work. Thus, it's on to analysis.

■   **MANAGEMENT'S PERSPECTIVE**

Manage Problem Definition

Problem definition is the most difficult system life cycle phase to manage and control. The scope gives management a sense of how much the feasibility study should cost. Subsequent steps in the life cycle can be scheduled and budgeted. But there is simply no basis for creating a budget or a schedule before the problem is defined. The fact that problem definition is a creative activity further complicates things because creativity, by its very nature, is difficult to manage.

Problem definition is necessary overhead. Think of it as seed money. Some problems will eventually be solved, but others will be classified as not worth solving. If you focus on the rejected projects, you see wasted effort, but if the analyst does his or her job, the problems that are solved are likely to be the right ones.

One technique used to define problems is called one-minute goal setting. This technique is described by Kenneth Blanchard and Spencer Johnson in their classic book *The One Minute Manager*. A key step is to write out each of your goals on a single sheet of paper that can be read in a minute or so. Their one-minute goal document was a model for the statement of scope and objectives described in this chapter.

When you assign a problem to an employee, ask him or her to write a one-page statement of scope and objectives and give you a copy. Then read it. You will know almost immediately if the employee misunderstood the problem, and quick feedback can save a great deal of wasted effort.

Summary

A problem is a difference between things as desired and things as perceived. Problem recognition is the first step in problem solving. Problem definition is concerned with identifying the problem's cause. A cause-and-effect diagram can be used to suggest or to document possible causes and secondary symptoms.

The problem statement lists symptoms, identifies objectives, and indicates the problem's scope. The problem statement can be verified by comparing the symptoms to the objectives and making sure the scope and the objectives are in balance. The problem definition phase ends with user sign-off.

Problem definition is often followed by a feasibility study. The idea is to determine if the project is technically, economically, and operationally feasible. The feasibility study report is the basis for a go/no go decision. In large organizations, this decision is often made by a steering committee.

Suggestions for Additional Reading

Blanchard, Kenneth, and Spencer Johnson. 1982. *The One Minute Manager*. New York: William Morrow and Company, Inc.

Gause, Donald C., and Gerald Weinberg. 1990. *Are Your Lights On? How to Figure Out What the Problem REALLY Is*. New York: Dorset House Publishing.

Paulos, John Allen. 1988. *Innumeracy*. New York: Vintage Books.

Pirsig, Robert M. 1974. *Zen and the Art of Motorcycle Maintenance*. New York: William Morrow and Company.

Walton, Mary. 1986. *The Deming Management Method*. New York: The Putnam Publishing Company.

Exercises

1. Distinguish between problem recognition and problem definition.

2. "You cannot solve a problem unless you know what caused it." Do you agree or disagree? Why?

3. A good analyst will consider several possible causes before writing the problem definition. Why? How does the analyst go about testing possible causes (hypotheses)?

4. Problems and objectives should be measurable. Why?

5. What is the purpose of a formal problem statement? What information should the problem statement contain? Why?

6. Briefly explain the value of verification.

7. What is the purpose of a feasibility study?

8. Large organizations sometimes assign the project go/no go decision to a steering committee. Why?

9. A small firm called The Print Shop has recently experienced significant growth. Listed below are several growth-related problems that were uncovered during an interview with the owner, Carl Jones. Prepare a problem statement for each one.

   a. When The Print Shop was a small, 10-employee company, orders were simply entered in a log book by the office secretary and crossed off as they were completed. Today, with the increasing volume of orders, the old system has broken down. On at least one occasion, an order was lost. If this problem continues, it could begin to cost the firm some business or even damage its reputation. Perhaps a computerized order entry system is needed.

   b. With the increase in sales, the volume of customer billings threatens to overwhelm the two billing clerks. If customers don't get their bills on time, payment will be delayed and interest that might be earned on that money will be lost. Would computerized billing help?

   c. As sales volume has increased, it has become necessary to keep more supplies in inventory, and keeping track of that inventory is a problem. For example, just last week the purchasing department ordered a very expensive maroon ink. Two days later a stock clerk discovered that the ink was already in stock. The firm cannot afford to continue spending money on things it doesn't need.

    d. The accounting department currently maintains a set of ledgers in which all The Print Shop's incomes and expenditures are reported. The two clerks are having trouble keeping up with the paperwork. Before a third clerk is hired, should moving the ledger to the computer be considered? A related problem is that the information recorded in the present ledgers is simply not accessible to management.

10. The following notes summarize an interview with the owner of a local clothing store. Based on this information, develop a formal problem statement.

Jan Tompson recently purchased the Campus Threads clothing store from a well-known national chain. Formerly, much of the record keeping for the business was done by the parent company. Jan plans to operate the store as a local business, so she will require local data processing capability.

    She would like us to help her install a microcomputer system to keep her books. She is particularly concerned about inventory control. Current fashion is trendy, so she must know exactly what she has in stock and must be able to identify shortages and process reorders on at least a daily basis. Additionally, she knows the computer can help with payroll, accounts receivable, accounts payable, general ledger, income taxes, and a host of other small business bookkeeping tasks.

The chain that previously owned Campus Threads had a credit system. Jan would like to install a credit system of her own. An option is to accept one or more of the standard bank credit cards, but the fees are high (at least 3 percent of sales), and these cards do not encourage customers to return to her store. She wants her charge system to be warm and personal.

11. The following notes summarize an interview with the owner of a local automobile dealership. Based on this information, develop a formal problem statement.

Bill Barnett is the owner of a small-town automobile dealership. He employs three salespeople, six service technicians, a service manager, a parts manager, a secretary, and a business manager. In an average week he sells three to four new cars and two to three used cars. Parts and service represent about half of the dealership's net profit.

    Lately, the business manager's position has become a problem. Two years ago, the woman who held that position since Bill founded the dealership retired. Her replacement resigned to accept a better job after less than a year. Last week, the current business manager announced that he will resign at the end of the month and return to school.

    When the business manager changes the result is chaos. First, the new person must be recruited, and this takes time. Then comes a training period. Meanwhile, Bill must somehow find time to interview candidates, train the new person, do the business manager's job, and still run the dealership.

    Complicating matters is the fact that each business manager seems to have his or her own way of doing things. Consequently, once the new business manager takes over, there is an initial period of confusion as everyone adjusts to the new regime. As a result, following both turnovers the business has experienced problems with payroll, sales commissions, customer orders, spare parts orders, training schedules, and other critical aspects of the business. At least one skilled service technician has left in disgust, and several customers have complained. A small dealership cannot afford dissatisfied customers or employees.

Bill has basically resigned himself to continued turnover in the business manager's position, claiming that "You just can't get good help these days." He wants to define a set of standard business procedures and implement them on a microcomputer. That way, the system will provide the continuity, and all he will have to do is find someone to run it.

The business manager is currently responsible for preparing the payroll, processing sales orders, computing sales commissions, maintaining data on the new and used car inventory, posting entries in the general ledger, paying bills, collecting payments, taking care of taxes, and numerous other accounting tasks. Additionally, each time a car is sold the business manager sits down with the customer to explain the financial details and verify payment.

12. Perhaps your instructor can arrange for you to conduct a class project with a local small business concern. Another source of possible class projects is your school. Potential problem areas include scheduling, preparing grade reports, tracking library circulation, billing student charges, and many others. With your instructor's permission, prepare a problem statement for a small business or school problem.

The GARS Project:

3

Defining the Problem

The Sports, Ski, and Concert Information Service (SSCIS)

Eight years ago, Tom Bowa and Mary Lewis graduated from college, married, and began working for different companies in the Boston area. They shared two hobbies: personal computing and sports.

Seldom do people have an opportunity to transform their hobbies into a full-time job, but it happened. Tom and Mary were attending a party, and the subject turned to baseball. A good natured argument ensued and, in mock frustration, someone suggested that the computer be asked to settle the issue.

Why not? Tom and Mary knew both baseball and computers. Developing a computerized baseball information system might be fun. So they did.

Much to their surprise, it became a commercial success. Then, success itself became a problem. The baseball information service was consuming so much time that they had to make a decision—abandon their hobby, or devote full time to it. They decided to strike out on their own.

The number of baseball enthusiasts around a major league city may seem endless, but the market for a baseball information service is limited. If Tom and Mary were to make a real success of their idea, they had to broaden its appeal, so football, basketball, and ice hockey were added to the service. This helped, but not enough.

Then Mary had an idea. Why not add ski information? If the on-line service included up-to-date ski conditions, subscribers could decide after work on Friday to schedule a minivacation for that same weekend and make last minute reservations through their personal computers or terminals. People would pay for that service, and resorts, ski lodges, and motels might be willing to pay for the right to be listed. With a computer-based service, even a last minute cancellation could be converted into an occupied room.

The ski information service was an immediate success. In fact, it was so successful that ski lodges from other parts of the country began to enquire about expanding the service. For this, Tom and Mary would need help, so they turned to THINK, Inc., a leader in the information services field.

Tom and Mary could not have approached THINK, Inc., at a better time. While the company was certainly successful, management had begun to question the growth potential of its specialized legal, medical, and news information services. After all, there are only so many doctors, lawyers, and newspapers.

The real potential for generating revenue lies in mass marketing, and the Bowa/Lewis Ski Service had potential. THINK could market the product nationally, so a deal was struck. THINK purchased rights to the ski and the sports information services, and hired both Tom and Mary as technical advisors. Concert information was added to the service, and the new system was christened SSCIS (pronounced SSS-KISS), for Sports, Ski, and Concert Information Service.

A year later, SSCIS was an established success and management was once again in a mood to gamble. The existing products generated a consistent, dependable revenue base. Money was available to support a somewhat risky venture with the potential for a large payoff, and management was actively looking for such a project.

The GARS Project

Genesis

Sometimes, innovative ideas are born in a flash of insight or intuition. Sometimes the germination of a new idea can be traced to an accident. That is how the games and recreation system got its start.

Tom and Mary were having lunch in the company cafeteria with two of their colleagues, and the conversation turned to video game parlors. They are obvious money-makers. "Perhaps," suggested Tom, "THINK should take a serious look at the electronic games market."

As the discussion continued, a few more people joined the little group. Someone mentioned the Space Raiders game that had been written by several THINK programmers and was available on virtually all the company's computers. Reluctantly at first, but then with increasing enthusiasm, everyone admitted to long hours spent in front of a display screen trying to save the earth from the evil Betas. Clearly, computer-literate people enjoyed playing electronic games. Maybe there really was a market for a games and recreation service.

One of the technical people was skeptical. She found playing the games boring, and preferred writing them. In her opinion, many "real" programmers felt the same way, and "real" programmers, as disproportion-ate buyers of personal computer systems, represented a significant part of the potential market for any at-home computer service. Why not develop a system that would give the subscriber a choice of playing or *writing* com-puter games? Perhaps royalties might be paid to successful game authors.

The conversation quickly became animated, with everyone throwing out thoughts and suggestions. The idea sounded good. Later that after-noon, Tom and Mary outlined the concept to the marketing manager, who was equally excited.

The idea began to snowball. With Mary as the sponsor and driving force, meetings were held and memos were written. Gradually, some sense of a viable project began to emerge. Finally came a decision: Let's look into it. The video games system was no longer just an idea.

The Analysis Team

Imagine that you, an experienced analyst, have been assigned to lead a three-member team to work on the new Games and Recreation System (GARS) project. Your assistants are two young, recently hired analysts, both of whom own personal computers and enjoy video games. During a brief-ing by Mary, your team was given an overview of the GARS concept (Fig-ure 3.1). Your immediate job is to prepare a formal problem definition.

Problem Definition   The first step is to interview key people. Young analysts often feel most comfortable discussing technology, so you assign your as-sistants to conduct interviews with the technical people who participated in the initial conversation and with a randomly selected group of other THINK employees. Figure 3.2 summarizes their findings.

The fact that the technical people suggested three languages, a set of in-terface standards, and an electronic mail network does not necessarily mean that these specific components must be part of the final system. Given an idea, technical people almost naturally think of how they might

FIGURE 3.1
The GARS concept.

THINK, Inc., plans to develop a Games and Recreation System (code-named GARS), perhaps as an added feature of the existing Sports, Ski, and Concert Information Service (SSCIS). Subscribers will access the system via standard telephone lines or through a cable television network. Once on-line, they will select a game or an information service from a standard menu.

Existing and internally developed electronic games, such as Space Raiders, will be used to establish a base for this project. The option of purchasing licenses to distribute selected popular commercially available games is another possible source for the GARS library.

As an added feature, subscribers will be encouraged to develop original games. When a subscriber completes an original game, he or she will place a note in a "customer comments queue." THINK personnel will monitor the queue, evaluate new games and accept or reject them. If a game is accepted, it will be added to the GARS library and made available to other GARS subscribers. Authors will be paid a royalty when other users play their games.

Customers, including game authors, will be responsible for maintaining their own terminals or personal computer systems and for paying their own telephone and cable television bills. THINK's responsibility begins and ends at the front end.

If GARS does as well as is hoped, it will grow rapidly, so provision must be made for rapid growth.

---

implement it. (In effect, they conduct a quick technical feasibility study in their own minds.) The analyst must recognize these preliminary thoughts for what they are: preliminary thoughts.

While your assistants are collecting information from the technical people, you are conducting interviews with key people in several equally important functional groups. Finance, as expected, is concerned with financial matters such as fee structures, billing, and payments (Figure 3.3). The nature of GARS creates several potential legal problems, so you touch bases with the legal department and the auditing department to discuss security, legal, and auditing concerns (Figure 3.4).

The first negative note (surprisingly) is voiced by the marketing department (Figure 3.5). They like the idea and they think GARS could be a substantial source of future new revenue, but they have no way of predicting how much revenue it might generate. The economic justification for the system is to be new revenue, so unless marketing can confidently forecast future income, the project cannot be economically justified.

Problem Statement   Additional interviews are conducted, the documentation for several comparable systems is reviewed, and a problem statement is written (Figure 3.6). Technical feasibility can almost be assumed; the people

FIGURE 3.2
GARS technical features.

GARS will support Visual BASIC, Pascal, and C++. There will be no charge (beyond the standard hourly usage fee) for subscribers who use an interpreter or a compiler to create a game. THINK, Inc., will need a set of interface standards, and games that do not conform to the standards will be rejected. One suggestion is to create a Windows-like user interface for accessing all games. Also, all games will require an on-line help window that displays clear playing rules. Several people suggested providing game authors with a standard user interface and/or a standard set of objects for constructing games.

For on-line marketing purposes, GARS will need an information module (like a help feature) that contains brief descriptions of approved games, a clear statement of game playing charges, and similar material. It should be a layered, menu-based interface that allows potential game players to quickly find games of possible interest. This module will be part of the system overhead; there will be no charge (other than the standard hourly usage charge) for accessing it.

Each GARS subscriber/author will be assigned a standard amount of disk work space. Subscribers who need more will be assigned more space at an extra charge.

Management will require a variety of reports, including: usage by game and by service, usage by customer, royalties by subscriber, and a series of more general usage, royalty, and exception reports. Popular games should be identified for possible purchase; unpopular games should be purged. Subscribers who earn high royalties should be identified as potential future employees.

The customer comments queue is an important feature of this system. Subscribers will be encouraged to write on the queue suggestions, complaints, original game notices, and similar messages to our staff and to other customers. By using their name or a user number, they should be able to retrieve system and personal messages from the customer comments queue. What is envisioned is essentially an electronic mail network limited to subscribers. Messages should be free form and limited to a single 80-character by 25-line screen.

FIGURE 3.3
GARS financial matters.

GARS fees will resemble the existing sports, ski, and concert information services fees. There will be a one-time membership fee of about $25 before a user is issued a user number and password. An initial log-on fee will be charged for accessing the system. A basic hourly usage fee will also be charged. Each time a user plays a game, an extra charge (perhaps 25¢ per play) will be assessed. The traditional information services will continue to be charged at the present rates. It has not yet been determined if GARS customers will automatically be members of the existing on-line information services (or vice versa).

Customers will be billed at the end of each month. A standard monthly billing program will be needed. All charges and all royalties must be itemized. Credit decisions must be made on customers, and those who do not pay their bills must be denied access to the system.

Authors will be paid a royalty (perhaps 5¢) each time their game is played. The royalty will appear as a credit on the subscriber's system usage bill. Net credit bills will be accompanied by a check for the net royalty amount. Note that it is possible for a nonsubscriber (a previous subscriber) to receive royalty payments.

It will also be necessary to track usage of licensed games. License fees resemble royalty payments, but it will still be necessary to account for royalties and license fees separately.

FIGURE 3.4
GARS security, legal, and auditing concerns.

Access to user number and password lists must be strictly controlled, and THINK, Inc., must be able to quickly change a user number or a password (or both) if security is violated. Each transaction processed by the system is to be logged.

System work areas, standard services, and games are to be backed up on-line. User work areas should be backed up daily. Users must not be allowed to access material in another user's work area without permission. To help avoid program theft, it should be impossible for anyone but the author or an authorized agent of THINK to obtain a source listing of any game or program on the system library.

According to the legal department, the entire royalty, not just the net royalty, must be reported to the internal revenue service as annual income. To report royalties, we must store each author's social security number. Note that THINK may eventually owe royalties to nonsubscribers.

Because royalties are involved, GARS must incorporate clear audit trails for game creation activities and for game playing fees. Before they are allowed to access an interpreter or a compiler, potential game authors must sign a waiver assigning publishing and distribution rights to THINK, Inc.

Safeguards and audit trails must be built into the system to ensure that copyright laws are not violated as games are developed and played. All game development activities and all THINK game reviews must be logged by date. Independent accounting and auditing procedures for licensing fees must also be built into the system.

FIGURE 3.5
GARS marketing concerns.

Marketing's reaction to the GARS project is mixed. They are excited by the idea, and see it as a potential source of new revenue, but they are reluctant to forecast revenue without additional information.

Subscribers to the existing SSCIS system average roughly $30 per month in billed services. Game authors are likely to use the system more intensively, but how much more are they likely to spend? Also, what percentage of existing SSCIS subscribers are likely to upgrade to GARS to access video games, and how much would their billed time increase?

To answer these (and other) questions, marketing recommends that we develop and test a prototype system.

at THINK have developed similar systems before, and they can do it again. Operational feasibility is another given. An on-line games and recreation system fits the company's image, and Tom and Mary are sponsoring it.

The only real concern is with economic feasibility. Development costs and future revenues are difficult to predict at this point, so the analysis team recommends that $250,000 be allocated to fund the development of a prototype system. The preliminary cost estimate is based on the firm's

FIGURE 3.6
A problem statement for the GARS project.

PROBLEM STATEMENT

Games and Recreation System (GARS)
July 18, 1994

THE PROBLEM:	To provide THINK, Inc., with a new, mass market source of revenue.
OBJECTIVES:	To develop an on-line games and recreation system to:

1. Support customers playing video games.
2. Support authors writing original video games.
3. Provide a communication link with customers.
4. Bill customers.
5. Pay authors royalties.
6. Pay necessary licensing fees.
7. Generate necessary management reports.

The proposed system must be designed for rapid growth. It must incorporate appropriate security, back up, and auditing procedures. It might be integrated with the present SSCIS information services. It might be accessed via telephone line or cable television network.

SCOPE:	The system development cost is difficult to estimate at present, but it will certainly exceed $1,000,000.
RECOMMENDATION:	We believe that GARS is technically and operationally feasible, but economic feasibility cannot be demonstrated without additional information. Thus we recommend that a prototype system be developed and tested at a cost not to exceed $250,000. The prototype will allow THINK, Inc., to estimate revenue potential, establish a realistic scope for the project, and evaluate economic feasibility.

---

experience with similar projects. The prototype will allow marketing to estimate the revenue potential. Given the experience of developing the prototype, the analysis team will be able to accurately estimate the cost of the project. Given those two values, economic feasibility can be determined.

Management agrees with your recommendation but adds one constraint: The prototype must be completed in 18 months. Given a commitment, work on the GARS project can now begin.

Exercises

1. The idea for the GARS project evolved from a lunchtime conversation. Is that realistic? How do you think innovative ideas get started?

2. Distinguish between an idea and a project. The answer is not in the book, so think about it.

3. Reread the interview summaries in the chapter. Identify the implied solutions and pick out the real system requirements. Relate them to the problem statement.

4. Have you ever attempted to define a technical problem by suggesting a solution? Is it possible that the analyst might read such implied solutions as system requirements? Why is that a problem?

5. Why is it so important that the analyst share a written summary of his or her understanding of the problem with management?

6. Explain the function of a problem statement.

7. A GARS prototype will be developed to help demonstrate economic feasibility. Does that make sense to you? Why, or why not?

PART III

Requirements Analysis

Until you know what to do, there is little point worrying about how to do it.

4

Information Gathering

When you finish reading this chapter, you should be able to:

—Explain what happens during analysis.

—Identify a system's logical elements.

—Create a data dictionary.

—Document processes.

—Briefly explain how CASE supports analysis.

Defining a System's Logical Elements

The objective of analysis is to determine *what* the system must do.

The objective of analysis is to rigorously define and verify the system's requirements; in other words, to determine *what* the system must do. Until you know what to do, there is little point worrying about how to do it.

The word *analyze* means (roughly) to study something by breaking it down into its constituent parts. The process is summarized in Figure 4.1. The analyst starts with the existing physical system, constructs a logical model, and then manipulates the model to create a new, improved logical model. The new model, in turn, is the basis for designing an improved physical system.

FIGURE 4.1
The analyst starts with the existing physical system, constructs a logical model, and then manipulates the model to create an improved, new logical model. The new model, in turn, is the basis for designing an improved physical system.

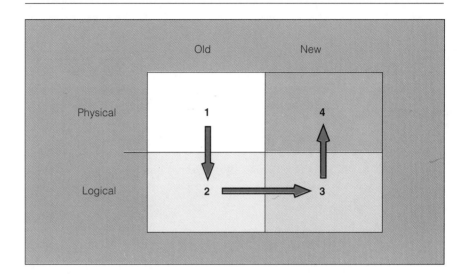

Studying the Present System

The old physical system is the starting point for analysis. Because it exists, you can study it. You can assume it is flawed, but it is not worthless. It must be performing a necessary function, or management would not have authorized you to fix it.

Often, the problem with the old system is not what it does but how it works. For example, consider a retail credit system in which customer invoices are handwritten, bills are prepared on a typewriter and distributed by mail, and payments are posted by hand. As the store grows, the paperwork will eventually overwhelm the system, prompting the owners to investigate improvements. The new system might be quite different from the old one, but it will still perform the same basic functions. Every retail credit system, no matter how technically sophisticated it might be, must process transactions, generate bills, distribute bills, and accept payments.

The first step in analysis is to extract the system's logical essence by separating *what* the existing system does from *how* it works. Unfortunately, that logical essence is often buried under mounds of detail. The problem, to borrow a few well-worn cliches, is to separate the wheat from the chaff, to distinguish the forest from the trees, or to find the needle in the haystack. The solution is to **partition** the problem into subproblems by focusing on such basic logical building blocks as data elements, processes, boundaries, and objects.

Start by conducting interviews with key user personnel. Ask what functions the system performs. Ask the user to identify key input and output documents. Find out who prepares the input and who uses the output, and interview those people. Then talk to the people who maintain the system and ask them to explain the existing documentation. When you finish an interview, write a summary. For example, Figure 4.2 summarizes an interview with Ted Temple, The Appliance Store's inventory expert.

Given a set of interview notes, you can begin to extract lists of the system's basic logical elements. As you will discover when you begin to analyze those logical elements, you are likely to miss quite a few, but the analysis tools you will learn to use in subsequent chapters are designed to highlight missing pieces. Once you discover what you do not yet know, you can schedule follow-up interviews with the appropriate people. Like problem definition, analysis is a cyclic process.

> **The first step in analysis is to separate *what* the existing system does from *how* it works.**

> **Analysis is a cyclic process.**

PROFESSIONAL POINTER   ■

Involve the User

Although most of the analysis work is done by the analyst, the user shares the responsibility for seeing that the requirements are defined correctly. For example, imagine a traveler climbing into a New York City taxi and telling the driver to take him to the airport. Thirty minutes later, they arrive at JFK. If, on checking his ticket, the traveler discovers that his flight departs from La Guardia, that is not the taxi driver's fault. User involvement is important throughout the life cycle, but it is *crucial* during analysis.

Identifying Processes

People tend to visualize systems in terms of the things they do, so the **processes** are often the easiest components to identify. In an information system, a process is an activity that transforms data in some way. Within a given process data might be collected, recorded, moved, manipulated, reformatted, sorted, computed, summarized, and so on.

> **People tend to visualize systems in terms of the things they do.**

FIGURE 4.2
A summary of an interview with Ted Temple.

INTERVIEW WITH:	Ted Temple, The Appliance Store
DATE:	April 4, 1994
SUBJECT:	Inventory

When a shipment arrives, a two-part form is filled out for each appliance. The sticky-back copy, called the price sticker, is attached to the appliance. The other copy, called the price tag, serves as the inventory control card and is kept in a filing cabinet in stock number order. Stock numbers are assigned sequentially, so the inventory file is also in date order. The inventory clerk notes the supplier of the item on the price tag before filing it.

When an appliance is sold, the sales clerk fills out a sales receipt. One copy goes to the customer. The price sticker is removed from the appliance and attached to a second copy of the sales receipt. At the end of the day, the inventory clerk collects these sales receipts and pulls the matching price tags from the inventory file.

At the end of the week the pulled price tags are used to prepare a sales report that summarizes sales by appliance type and by manufacturer. The original cost is obtained from the supplier's invoice, which is filed by supplier and by date. (The inventory clerk notes the range of stock numbers assigned to the appliances in an order before filing the supplier's invoice.)

The sales report tells Tina what appliances are selling. She uses it to help her decide what merchandise to order. The inventory clerk gets a list of merchandise to order from Tina, types the order forms, and sends them to the suppliers. He gets the mailing addresses from the old invoices.

Once a month the inventory clerk compiles a list of appliances that have been in inventory for more than 120 days. The fact that the inventory records are in date order simplifies this task. Tina uses the list to identify slow-moving items and decide on sales and discounts.

Every other month the inventory clerk performs a physical inventory, counting the number of appliances of each type both on the showroom floor and in the warehouse. He uses the physical inventory as a base for tracking the number of items in stock. As merchandise sells he subtracts sales from the count; as reorders arrive he adds the new units. These are daily tasks. He uses this information to prepare a weekly estimated stock level report. Tina uses this report, along with the sales report, to make reorder decisions. The next physical inventory serves to check the accuracy of the counts and becomes a new starting point.

A process is an activity, so read through the documentation and <u>look for verbs.</u> For example, the first paragraph in Figure 4.2 mentions *Fill out price tag, Attach price sticker,* and several other tasks. You can see a list of processes in Figure 4.3.

In addition to the interview notes, you should also review the objectives from the problem definition. There must be a way to achieve each one, so the objectives suggest processes, too. If you discover that your interviews have not yet identified at least one process that deals with each objective, you have not yet finished interviewing.

FIGURE 4.3
A list of the present inventory system's components.

Processes	**Data**
Fill out price tag	Price tag/sticker
Attach price sticker	Inventory file
File price tag	Sales receipt
Assign stock number	Sales report
Note supplier on price tag	Supplier invoice
Sell appliance	Merchandise to order
Fill out sales receipt	Order form
Give receipt to customer	Old inventory report
Remove price sticker	Physical inventory
Collect sales receipts	Stock level report
Match tag to inventory	
Prepare sales report	**Boundaries**
Retrieve supplier invoice	Customer
Note stock number on invoice	Supplier
File supplier invoice	Manager
Reorder stock	Financial system
Type reorder	
Get mailing address	
Prepare old inventory list	
Identify sale items	
Perform physical inventory	
Update stock levels	
Prepare stock level report	

Identifying Fields

After listing the processes, go through the documentation again and look for references to data (Figure 4.3). At this stage, you are likely to identify such physical entities as documents, forms, screens, reports, and files. For example, in this system the data to support reorder decisions are derived from a stock level report and a sales report. In another system, the necessary data might be derived from a single exception report or from an online database. The present system's documents, forms, screens, reports, and files are a function of its physical design. Those components can be changed, so you have not yet reached the system's basic logical building blocks.

Although the physical form of the data might change, the fields generally do not. For example, reorder decisions will still be made by comparing

FIGURE 4.4
Collect samples of the existing forms, reports, and other data structures mentioned in the interviews.

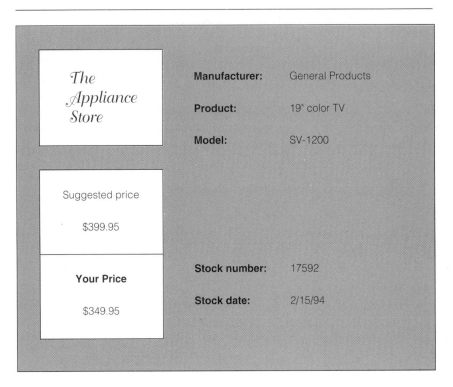

a stock level to a reorder point no matter how the data are presented. The best way to identify the logically necessary data is to list the fields that appear on the present system's documents, files, and other data entities. Later, you can recombine those fields to create the new system's data entities.

Start by obtaining copies of existing documents, forms, and reports (Figure 4.4). Get descriptions of existing computerized files, too. Then list their fields. For example, the price sticker contains such fields as *Manufacturer name, Product description, Model code, Stock number, Stock date, Suggested price,* and *Selling price.* Figure 4.5 lists the fields that appear on each of the forms, reports, and files identified by Ted.

FIGURE 4.4
Continued

The
Appliance
Store

Customer: _____

_____

_____

_____

Invoice number 123456

Date of sale _____

Stock number	Description	Quantity	Unit price	Item total

Subtotal _____
Sales tax _____
Total due |

FIGURE 4.5
A list of the fields that appear on existing forms and reports.

Price tag/sticker
Inventory file (same data)
    Manufacturer name
    Product description
    Model code
    Stock number
    Stock date
    Suggested price
    Selling price
      (Your price)

Sales receipt
    Customer name
    Customer street
    Customer city
    Customer state
    Customer zip code
    Customer phone
    Invoice number
    Date of sale
    Stock number
    Description
    Quantity
    Unit price
      (Selling price)
    Item total
    Subtotal
    Sales tax
    Total due

Supplier invoice
    Invoice number
    Invoice date
    Salesperson
    Order date
    Customer number
    Ship weight
    Routing
    Terms
    Date shipped
    FOB
    Sold name
    Sold address
    Sold city
    Sold state
    Sold zip code
    Sold attention
    Ship name
    Ship address
    Ship city
    Ship state
    Ship zip code
    Ship attention
    Order number
    Supplier order number
    Item code
    Quantity
    Product description
    Quantity shipped
    Unit price
    Amount due
    Total due

FIGURE 4.5
Continued

Sales report
  Report date
  Product type
  Manufacturer
  Model
  Weekly sales
  Unit cost
  Product cost
  Selling price
  Revenue
  Margin
  Total product sales
  Total product cost
  Total product revenue
  Total product margin
  Total weekly sales
  Total weekly cost
  Total weekly revenue
  Total weekly margin

Order form
  Order number
  Supplier name
  Supplier address
  Supplier city
  Supplier state
  Supplier zip code
  Order date
  Delivery date
  Ship via
  FOB
  Terms
  Model
  Product description
  Quantity
  Unit price
  Item amount
  Purchasing manager

Old inventory report
  Product type
  Manufacturer
  Model
  Old stock count

Physical inventory
  Product type
  Manufacturer
  Model
  Showroom stock
  Warehouse stock
  Total stock

Stock level report
  Report date
  Product type
  Manufacturer
  Model
  Start week stock
  Sales
  Received
  End week stock

■   **PROFESSIONAL POINTER**
_____

Question Every Item

Think back to the forms you completed when you applied for admission to a college, applied for a job, or filed your income tax. Did you ever wonder what possible use anyone might have for the answer to a particular question, or why you had to repeat the same information on form after form? Chances are you never asked those questions because you were reluctant to risk annoying the people who might admit you, hire you, or audit you, but you probably wondered.

As the responsible analyst, it is your job to question every item on every existing form or report. Those documents might be good. Then again, they might reflect a bad system. Decompose them, and let the analysis and design tools suggest the best way to reassemble the data. If something like the old form emerges, fine. If analysis suggests a new form, that's fine, too. In either case, you will know that you have the right form.

Identifying Boundaries

Most systems are components of larger systems.

Most systems are components of larger systems. The inventory system is but one part of the store's information system. Tina's store, in turn, is associated with a chain of appliance stores, the chain is part of the national economic system, and our economic system is part of an international economic system. To carry the point to an extreme, you can keep going through the ecosystem, to the solar system, to the universe, and so on.

It makes little sense to worry about how The Appliance Store's inventory system affects or is affected by the solar system because there is not a great deal Tina can do to influence what happens at that level. Ted (or his successor), on the other hand, is part of the inventory system and thus subject to its control.

Picture an imaginary circle drawn around the inventory system (Figure 4.6). Everything inside that circle (including Ted Temple) is subject to the inventory system's control. Everything outside that circle (including the solar system) is independent of the inventory system. The circle represents the inventory system's **boundaries**. Trying to control what lies outside the boundaries is, by definition, futile. Failing to control what lies inside the boundaries leads, at best, to an incomplete solution. You can see a list of the inventory system's boundaries in Figure 4.3.

A system's boundaries can be defined by identifying those people, organizations, and other systems that lie just outside the target system but communicate *directly* with it. For example, consider suppliers. Orders and payments flow from the store to the suppliers, and merchandise

FIGURE 4.6
Every system has boundaries.

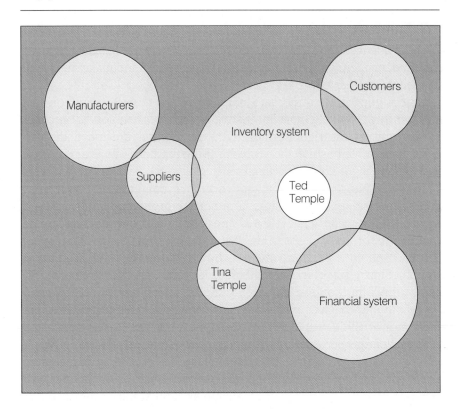

flows back to the store, but the store has little or no control over what happens inside a given supplier's organization. The suppliers lie on a boundary.

Why not include the appliance manufacturers? Were it not for them there would be no appliances to sell, but The Appliance Store deals with the manufacturers only *indirectly*, through the suppliers. Thus the manufacturers lie outside the inventory system's boundaries.

Consider the customers next. The Appliance Store cannot survive without them. Their purchases change stock levels, so they directly affect the inventory system. But the customers are independent. They come and go as they please, and the store has very little control over their actions. They are an independent entity that directly affects the system, so they lie on a boundary.

Next consider Ted and Tina. Ted is in charge of inventory, but his function is (or should be) largely clerical. In a well-designed system, clerks are constrained by the system because they are part of the system. Tina, on the other hand, is the responsible manager. Some of her actions will be influenced by the system, but (as the owner) she has the authority to act independently. Consequently, she (at least in her managerial capacity) defines another boundary.

Unless you define a system's boundaries, there is no way you can question them.

Unless you define a system's boundaries, there is no way you can question them. Only by questioning the boundaries can you be sure you are working on the right system. If the boundaries are too wide, you might not be able to solve the problem. If the boundaries are too narrow, the problem might not be worth solving.

For example, imagine that students have complained about your school's course registration system. A narrow problem definition might focus on registration-day activities and lead to a decision to hire more part-time registration clerks. If the real problem is insufficient sections of high-demand courses, that solves nothing. A broad problem definition might include within the system boundaries such factors as faculty workloads, admission policies, research policies, and school financing, and the debate alone would take years. Somewhere between those two extremes is a solvable problem that is worth solving.

Consider another example. Although Ted did not discuss The Appliance Store's financial system, it clearly shares some data with the inventory system. Customer transactions change inventory stock levels and they also represent cash flows, so it is reasonable to argue that the financial system lies on a boundary (Figure 4.6).

Now, question that boundary. One possibility is independent inventory and financial systems that share some data and nothing more. An option is an integrated system that includes *both* finance and inventory. For simplicity we'll keep them separate, but merging the inventory and financial management systems might be a better solution.

Check the supplier next. A big company might take over an important supplier and thus bring the supplier's organization inside its own inventory system, but that option would be unrealistic for a business the size of The Appliance Store. The supplier clearly lies on a boundary.

Relating Processes, Data, and Boundaries

Data imply processes and processes imply data.

Data imply processes and processes imply data. If a report exists, that report must be generated. If a form exists, the data on that form must be processed. If a process exists, it must have inputs and outputs. As you study the data, you will discover previously overlooked processes. As you study the processes, you will discover previously overlooked data. The new data and the new processes might change your view of the system. Analysis is an iterative task.

There is a similar relationship between data and boundaries. A boundary is a person, group, organization, or other system that lies just outside the target system but communicates directly with it. Communication normally implies the exchange of data. Source input data often come from (or describe) a boundary. Output data that are not subsequently input to other processes often flow to a boundary. New boundaries might imply new data; new data might imply new boundaries; in either case you might find it necessary to reevaluate at least part of the system. Once again, analysis is an iterative task.

Identifying Objects

Given the increasing complexity of today's hardware, software, and applications, many organizations are turning to object-oriented systems. The basic building block of an object-oriented system is called an object. An object incorporates both processes and data. Objects communicate with other objects through signals. The process of defining objects and signals begins during analysis.

The object-oriented approach is a bit different from traditional systems analysis and design, so further discussion of objects will be postponed until Chapter 9.

The Data Dictionary

As you begin to identify the system's logical elements, you can quickly generate an incredible mass of details. Making sense of all those details is difficult (at best), so the next step is to organize them by documenting them in a data dictionary.

☆ Data element
✶ Data structure
✓ Data transform

Key Terms

A **data dictionary** is a collection of data about the data. Its purpose is to rigorously define each and every data element, data structure, and data transform. The contents of the data dictionary are sometimes called metadata.

A data dictionary is a collection of data about the data.

Data dictionaries were first developed to support database management systems, and several key terms are derived from database theory. An **entity** is an object (a person, group, place, thing, or activity) about which data are stored. An **occurrence** is a single instance of an entity; for example, a particular 19-inch color television set is a single occurrence of the entity called inventory. An **attribute** is a property of an entity; for example, such attributes as stock number, description, and stock on hand might be associated with inventory. Generally, the same set of attributes is associated with each occurrence of an entity, so every part in inventory can be expected to have a stock number, a description, and a stock on hand. A **data element** is an attribute that cannot be logically decomposed. A set of related data elements forms a **data structure** or a **composite** data item.

The **key** to an entity is the attribute or group of attributes that uniquely distinguishes one occurrence from all other occurrences. A **foreign key** is a key to some other entity; for example, a supplier code might be associated with the inventory data. Keys can be used to define **relationships** that link data structures or entities.

Physically, data elements are stored as **fields**. The set of fields associated with an occurrence of an entity forms a **record**. Records, in turn, are grouped to form **files** or **databases,** or both, while relationships might be represented as indexes or pointers.

Defining Data Elements

The data dictionary defines each data element, specifies both its logical and physical characteristics, and records information concerning how it is used. Figure 4.7 summarizes the information that might be recorded in the data dictionary for each data element. Figure 4.8 shows a few data dictionary entries. Note that the relationships have not yet been defined.

The first step in preparing a data dictionary is to compile a list of fields such as the one pictured in Figure 4.5. If a field can be decomposed or partitioned into smaller units, break it down until you have identified the data elements. Assign each data element a meaningful name that suggests its purpose; ask the user for suggestions. Follow a consistent naming standard; for example, you might use the rules imposed by your primary pro-

FIGURE 4.7
Information that might be recorded for each data element in a data dictionary. Note that not every entry is relevant to every data element.

General
Data element name
Aliases or synonyms
Definition

Format
Data type
Length
Picture
Units (meters, pounds, etc.)

Control Information
Source
Change authorizations
Access authorizations
Security
Authorized users
Date of origin

Usage Characteristics
Range of values
Frequency of use
Input/output/local
Conditional values
Repetitive limits

Relationships
Parent structures
File or database
Data flows
Processes
Reports
Forms
Screens

gramming language, database management system, data dictionary software, or CASE product.

The next step is to define each data element. A good definition precisely indicates the element's purpose and clearly distinguishes it from the system's other data elements. Examples are useful, particularly for identifying exceptions to a general rule. Figure 4.8 shows definitions for several inventory system data elements.

The purpose of these definitions is to ensure that everyone means the same thing when they use the same term. For example, consider the number of students attending a school. Instead of a simple head count, administrators often use a different value computed by dividing total student credit hours by the standard full-time student load (typically, 15 hours). Note that the *Head count* and the number of *Full-time equivalent students* (as computed by the algorithm) can be quite different. The fact that two people can discuss something as obvious as the number of students attending a school and have very different ideas in mind underscores the need for clear data definitions.

> The fact that two people can discuss something as obvious as the number of students attending a school and have very different ideas in mind underscores the need for clear data definitions.

FIGURE 4.8
Some typical data dictionary entries.

Stock number

Alias:	UPC, Product ID, Product code
Definition:	A key field that uniquely identifies an item of merchandise. Assigned, in sequential order, by the inventory clerk when shipment arrives.
Type:	Character; picture X(5)
Relationships:	

Product description

Alias:	Description
Definition:	A brief verbal description of a product. For example, "Zenith 21-inch color TV" or "GE 19-cubic-foot refrigerator".
Type:	Character; picture X(40)
Relationships:	

Unit price

Alias:	Retail price, Customer price, Selling price, Your price
Definition:	The amount of money a customer pays for a single unit of merchandise.
Type:	Numeric; picture 9,999.99
Relationships:	

Once a data dictionary entry has been prepared for each data element, study the definitions for consistency and completeness. A good test is to ask the user to suggest a value that violates the definition. For example, many retail stores use the Universal Product Code (a preprinted bar code) as a product identifier, but simply defining *Stock number* as the UPC code would be wrong if the store also sells unmarked products. (Note that The Appliance Store does not use the UPC code as its stock number.)

Check the definitions for redundancy, too. Some data elements are known by two or more names. This often happens when different groups use the same data for different purposes or when several analysts work concurrently on the system. For example, data names *Unit price, Selling price, Retail price, Customer price,* and even *Your price* might refer to exactly the same value depending on who you are interviewing.

If you find yourself using virtually the same words to define two data elements, one name is probably an **alias** for the other. Rather than creating redundant data dictionary entries, clarify any differences in the definitions of those equivalent data elements, merge them, and record the alias name on the primary description.

If two clearly different data elements have similar names, change at least one of them because similar names can be confusing. For example, imagine that the purchasing department uses *Cost* to mean the amount the supplier charges the store while the sales department uses *Customer cost* to mean the amount the customer pays. *Wholesale cost* and *Selling price* are better names because they more clearly distinguish the data elements.

Sometimes you discover data elements that are virtually unused. For example, sales invoices sometimes include a box for defining shipping terms. That makes sense when the product in question will be shipped in bulk, but the field is meaningless on a typical retail sales transaction. Maybe the old system adopted a generic invoice. If the users cannot define the field or they openly admit that they don't use it, why include it in the new system?

As a new application is being developed, the analyst should check the required data elements against the organization's central data dictionary (if there is one). Using established names and definitions saves work. Failing to cross reference the existing data dictionary can introduce redundant data into the system, and that can affect data integrity.

FIGURE 4.9
This Warnier-Orr diagram shows how data structures are defined by partitioning them into data elements and lower-level data structures.

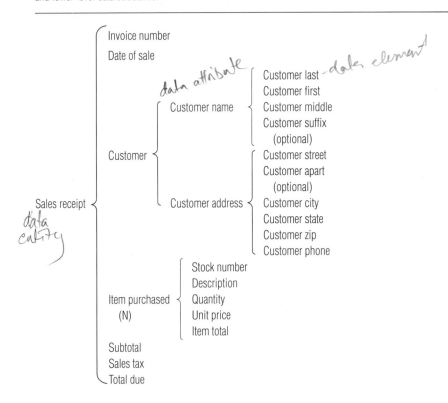

Defining Data Structures

In the data dictionary, data structures, also called group or composite data items, are defined by showing the data elements and substructures that compose them. For example, Figure 4.9 is a **Warnier-Orr diagram** that identifies the data elements recorded on a typical sales receipt.

The primary data structure, *Sales receipt*, is noted at the left. Moving to the second column, *Invoice number*, *Date of sale*, *Subtotal*, *Sales tax*, and *Total due* are data elements. *Customer* and *Item purchased* are composite items that are further decomposed. *Customer* consists of two lower-level composite items called *Customer name* and *Customer address*. Note that those lower-level composite items are decomposed into their constituent data elements.

One of the data elements that compose *Customer name* is called *Customer suffix*. It holds conditional data; an entry such as Sr., Jr., or III might or might not be present. Under *Customer address*, the field named *Customer apart* (an abbreviation for customer apartment) is another conditional data element.

A given sales transaction might represent the sale of several different products, so *Item purchased* is a repetitive data structure that consists of one or more sets of the data elements *Stock number, Description, Quantity, Unit price*, and *Item total*. The letter N in parentheses under *Item purchased* indicates that the substructure is repeated an unknown number of times. If the number of repetitions is known, the upper limit, the lower limit, or both can be noted in the parentheses.

Note that Figure 4.9 shows at least two data elements (*Customer suffix* and *Customer apart*) that did not appear on the list of fields in Figure 4.5. Often, as you begin to study the existing system in greater depth, you discover previously overlooked components.

Warnier-Orr diagrams are excellent tools for visualizing a data structure, but they take up considerable space, so many analysts use the symbols pictured in Figure 4.10 to document composite items. Figure 4.11 shows how the *Sales receipt* data structure and its substructures might be defined in a data dictionary. Note that a data structure can contain both composite items and data elements. In the data dictionary, composite items are decomposed or partitioned down to the data element level, and each data element is fully defined (as described earlier).

In the data dictionary, composite items are decomposed or partitioned down to the data element level, and each data element is fully defined.

Grouping the attributes associated with a customer makes sense, but data structures are not always so obvious. A key objective of many analysis

FIGURE 4.10
These symbols can be used to describe or document a data structure.

Symbol	Meaning
=	Contains, or is composed of
+	And
[]	Selection
¦	Separator
()	Optional
{}	Repetition

tools is to identify the data structures that are implied by the system's requirements. Consequently, the act of grouping data elements to form data structures is typically postponed until near the end of the analysis stage.

■   **PROFESSIONAL POINTER**

Be Patient

Creating a data dictionary is an iterative process. You will almost certainly *not* identify one data element, completely describe it, and then move on to the next one. You should not expect to compile a complete list of data elements, either. Instead, your data dictionary will evolve. As you study the system, previously overlooked data elements will emerge. Data element names and definitions can usually be specified near the beginning of analysis, but data groupings and relationships are not apparent until later, and a data element's *physical* characteristics may not be known until design begins.

The bottom line is: *Be patient.* Do not try to tell the system what the data structures should be. Instead, let the system's requirements tell *you* what those data structures *must* be. Learn to postpone decisions that have physical implications until those decisions must be made.

Data Dictionary Software

Compiling a complete set of data definitions is time consuming, even for a small system. Data dictionary software can help. Most data dictionary programs are designed to simplify data entry, and many prompt you through the process of defining a data element. Some can prepare at least part of the data dictionary from source code, a valuable option when existing files must be converted to database form. You might even be able to generate source code from your data descriptions. If possible, use data dictionary software to complete your class assignments.

Some data dictionary programs are associated with a specific database management system. If your organization has settled on a standard database package, use its data dictionary facility. Many CASE tools support a data dictionary and automatically extract key information from a logical model. Stand-alone data dictionary programs are commercially available, and some firms have written their own custom data dictionary software.

Not every school has access to an acceptable program, but products such as Hypercard, dBASE, and the Windows Cardfile accessory can be used to simulate a data dictionary. Even a word processor will do. If computer access is a problem, use index cards. The key is having one

FIGURE 4.11
Partitioning the *Sales receipt* data structure.

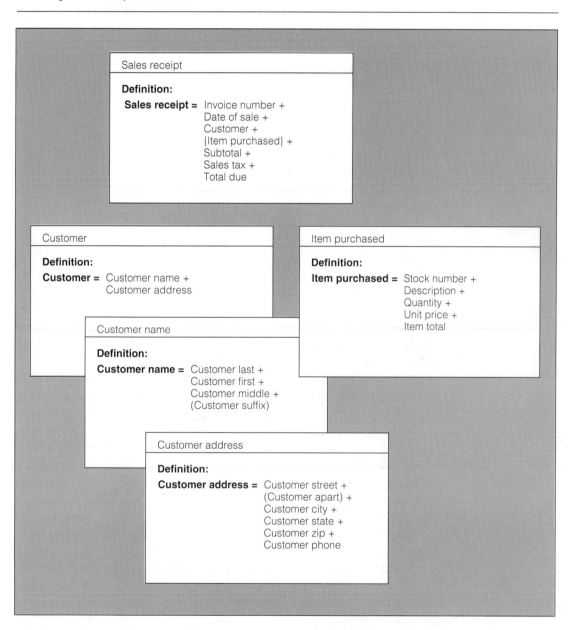

independent record for each data element and for each composite item so you can sort, index, group, or cross-reference the entries.

Describing Processes

In addition to documenting the system's data elements, you should also document its processes. For example, one of the processes listed in Figure 4.3 is *Fill out sales receipt*. You might begin analyzing that process by talking with the people who actually perform the task (in this case, with the salespeople). Ask someone to walk you through the process or observe someone actually performing the job, and note each step. Then do the same thing with someone else. You should quickly begin to sense the steps in that process. If that sense never develops, either you or the responsible people do not understand the process. Unclear processes are common sources of error.

Unclear processes are common sources of error.

You can learn a great deal by observing a process. For example, because sales receipts are filled out only as part of a sales transaction, *Fill out sales receipt* must be part of a more general sales transaction process. *Give receipt to customer*, another process from Figure 4.3, is also part of that larger process. By grouping related processes, you reduce the number of entities that must be accounted for, and that simplifies analysis.

Figure 4.12 lists the steps for processing a sales transaction using a form of **structured English**. There are several different standards for writing structured English, but the basic idea is to consistently use simple object-verb-subject or verb-subject sentences. Note that the **trigger event** (the event that starts the process) is listed first; in this case, handling a sales transaction begins with the arrival of a customer. The other entries describe the primary steps in the process, identify who is responsible for each step, and list key inputs and outputs. You can find several of those steps in Figure 4.3.

Another way of documenting a process is to prepare a **process flowchart** that shows graphically the flow of logic, control, and data through the process. Figure 4.13 identifies several common flowcharting symbols, and Figure 4.14 is a flowchart for the sales transaction process. Many other tools can be used to document processes; follow your own organization's internal standards.

FIGURE 4.12
The steps in a sales transaction.

1. Trigger event: Customer enters store.
2. Customer selects merchandise.
    a. Sales clerk helps customer.
3. Sales clerk writes sales receipt.
    a. Record date of sale, customer name, and customer address.
    b. For each item purchased:
        (1) Record stock number.
        (2) Record description.
        (3) Record quantity.
        (4) Read unit price from price tag.
        (5) Record unit price.
        (6) Compute and record item total.
    c. Compute and record subtotal.
    d. Compute and record sales tax.
    e. Compute and record total due.
4. Sales clerk accepts payment.
    a. Cash.
    b. Credit card.
    c. Check.
5. Sales clerk marks sales receipt paid.
6. Sales clerk removes price sticker from appliance.
7. Sales clerk attaches price sticker to sales receipt copy 2.
8. Sales clerk files sales receipt copy 2.
9. Sales clerk gives sales receipt copy 1 to customer.
10. Sales clerk gives merchandise to customer.
    a. Small items.
    b. Large item pick-up.
    c. Schedule delivery.

When you study the processes, it is easy to become bogged down in details. Some details are important. For example, if the sales clerk skips recording certain data on the sales receipt during busy periods, there must be a reason, and understanding the reason might prove useful. Other details are irrelevant. It probably doesn't matter that some clerks use ball-point pens and other clerks use pencils. It probably doesn't matter if the clerk block-prints or writes cursively.

How do you know which details are important and which details can be ignored? There is no easy answer to that question, but it helps to

FIGURE 4.13
Process flowcharting symbols.

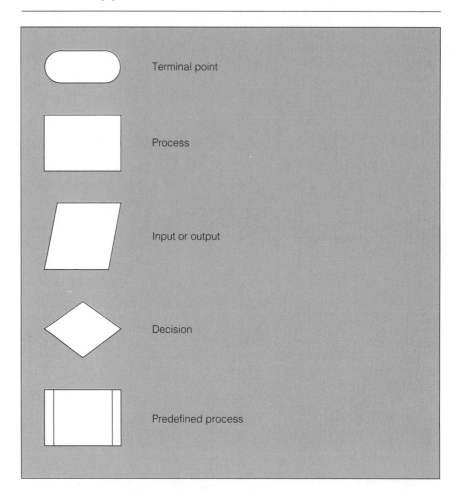

remember that the real objective is to understand what happens during a process, not exactly how it happens.

You may have noticed that the list of steps in Figure 4.12 is more detailed than the flowchart in Figure 4.14. The decision to drop certain details was made by considering each step and asking if it represented some task that must be performed or merely explained how a given task was performed.

FIGURE 4.14

93
A flowchart for the sales transaction process.

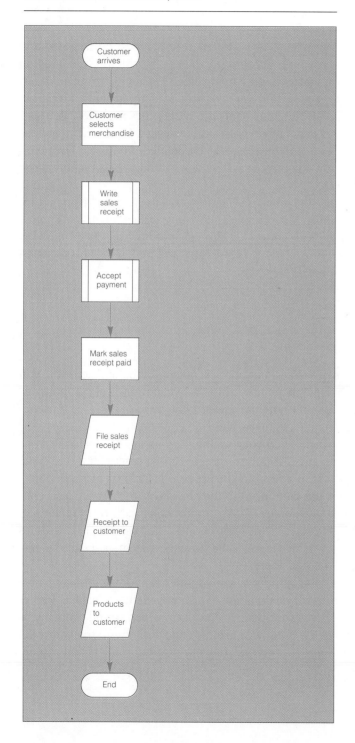

For example, in *any* retail sales system, receipts must be prepared and payments must be accepted. Receipts can be hand-written or prepared on a computer, but you must still prepare receipts. Payments can be made by cash, check, or credit card, but you must still accept payments. Preparing sales receipts and collecting payments are basic processes. How you perform those processes depends on your system design. Consequently, those two steps are shown in the flowchart as predefined processes. They contain details about how the present system works, and you can ignore those details for now.

Note also that the flowchart in Figure 4.14 was prepared using a limited number of symbols. For example, an existing system might incorporate manual procedures and computer programs. Showing them both as "processes" helps you generalize the system, and that helps you focus on what rather than how.

Using CASE

Given the system's processes, boundaries, objects, and data elements, you can begin to investigate the relationships between its logical components. Except for relatively small systems, however, the task of analyzing those relationships is too complex to do by hand, so consider using CASE.

Once you have completed your preliminary analysis, your definitions of the data elements, processes, and objects can be entered into the CASE repository. Many CASE systems include provisions for listing system objectives (from the problem definition) in the repository, too. As analysis continues, you can take advantage of CASE prototyping tools or use the CASE product's graphic interface to develop models. Software can be used to cross-reference and verify the models because the system's logical elements are all recorded in the repository.

Many different CASE products are commercially available, and new products and improved versions are constantly being released. Rather than tying this book to a specific CASE product (which would probably be obsolete by the time the book was printed), the author and the editor decided to focus on the tools that underlay most CASE products and explain how those tools can be implemented. Specific examples help, however, so

Chapter 10 will show you how analysis might be performed using a CASE product called Excelerator.

Focus on Managing

Following analysis, the system will be designed and developed. Additional personnel will be added to the project, and costs will begin to increase dramatically. Knowing this, some managers worry a bit too much about technical details.

Micromanagement is a mistake. Competent technical professionals resent managers who insist on influencing technical details, and the manager who focuses on those details can easily overlook resource implications. The analyst's job is to analyze the system. The manager's job is to manage.

Summary

The objective of analysis is to rigorously and completely define and verify the system's logical requirements. The first step is to partition the problem into subproblems by focusing on such basic logical building blocks as processes, data, boundaries, and objects.

Once the existing system's data are identified, they are defined in a data dictionary. An entity is an object (a person, place, thing, or activity) about which data are stored. An occurrence is a single instance of an entity. An attribute is a property of an entity. A data element is an attribute that cannot be logically decomposed. A set of related data elements forms a data structure or a composite.

The key to an entity is the attribute or group of attributes that uniquely distinguishes one occurrence from all other occurrences. A foreign key is a key to some other entity. Keys can be used to define relationships that link data structures. Physically, data elements are stored as fields. The set of fields associated with an occurrence of an entity forms a record. Records, in turn, are grouped to form files or databases, or both.

In the data dictionary, each field is assigned a unique name, but a given field might also be known by an alternate name, or alias. Data elements are grouped to form data structures. A data structure can be partitioned by creating a Warnier-Orr diagram or by using symbols to indicate how the data are joined. Creating a data dictionary takes time, but data dictionary software can help.

Processes can be documented by using a form of structured English or by drawing a process flowchart. The trigger event (the event that starts the process) should be identified.

Given a list of processes, boundaries, objects, and data, you can begin to investigate the relationships between these logical elements. Except for relatively small systems, the task of analyzing those relationships is too complex to do by hand, so consider using CASE.

Suggestions for Additional Reading

Boillot, Michel H., et al. 1985. *Essentials of Flowcharting.* 4th ed. Dubuque, IA: Wm. C. Brown Company.

Dickinson, Brian. 1989. *Developing Quality Systems: A Methodology Using Structured Techniques.* New York: McGraw-Hill Book Company.

Eliason, Alan L. 1990. *System Development: Analysis, Design, and Implementation.* 2d ed. Glenview, IL: Scott Foresman/Little Brown Higher Education.

Flaatten, Per O., et al. 1989. *Foundations of Business Systems.* Chicago: The Dryden Press.

McDermid, Donald C. 1990. *Software Engineering for Information Systems.* Oxford, UK: Blackwell Scientific Publications.

Wurman, Richard Saul. 1989. *Information Anxiety.* New York: Bantam Books.

Exercises

1. What is the purpose of analysis?

2. A common problem-solving technique is to partition a big problem into smaller problems and then attack those smaller problems. Does that make sense to you? Why, or why not?

3. The first step in systems analysis is to extract the present system's "logical essence." Briefly explain how the analyst goes about that task.

4. A system's basic logical components include processes, data elements, and boundaries. Define each of those terms, and explain why each one can be viewed as an elementary building block.

5. What is a data dictionary? Why is a data dictionary so valuable?

6. Briefly describe the contents of a typical data dictionary. Distinguish between a data element and a composite item.

7. Compile a preliminary data dictionary for the data elements listed in Figure 4.5. Include, where appropriate, group or composite items. Look for redundant sets of data on the various forms and reports, and account for them in the data dictionary.

8. Document each of the processes listed in Figure 4.3. Use structured English, process flowcharts, or both. Note that some of the processes can be grouped to form larger, more basic processes. Why would you want to group subprocesses at this point?

9. Systems analysis is an iterative process. Explain what that statement means. Use several examples to illustrate your answer.

10. Chapter 2 introduced projects for The Print Shop, Jan Tompson's Campus Threads clothing store, and Bill Barnett's automobile dealership. Prepare a preliminary data dictionary and document any known processes for one or more of those projects or for your own project.

Data imply processes and processes imply data.

5

Logical Modeling

When you finish reading this chapter you should be able to:

—Identify a system's processes, sources, destinations, data stores, and data flows.

—Explain the difference between logical and physical data flow diagrams.

—Draw a level-0 data flow (or context) diagram.

—Draw a level-1 data flow diagram.

—Complete process descriptions for each of the processes in a data flow diagram.

—Add each data element and data composite that appears on a data flow diagram to the data dictionary.

—Verify a logical model.

Structured Analysis

In Chapter 4, you developed a list of the inventory system's data elements and processes. Then you started compiling a data dictionary and a set of process descriptions. The next step is to construct a logical model of the system so you can sense how the components fit together. One technique,

FIGURE 5.1
Data imply processes and processes imply data.

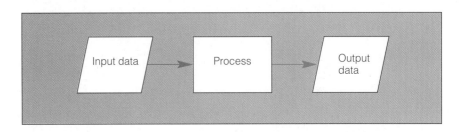

structured analysis, uses data flow diagrams, a data dictionary, and process descriptions to build the model.

The key to structured analysis is the relationship between data and processes.

The key to structured analysis is the relationship between data and processes (Figure 5.1); you probably learned about that relationship in your very first computer course. At this point it is unlikely that you have identified all the system's processes and all its data, but data imply processes and processes imply data. Consequently, as you develop the model, the data you do have will suggest unknown processes and the known processes will suggest unknown data.

■   **PROFESSIONAL POINTER**

Document for a Reason

Not too long ago, flowcharts were considered the standard form of program documentation. Although useful for describing processes, flowcharts are not good program planning tools, so they were typically prepared after the code was written and only if management insisted. (In fact, special programs were available to generate flowcharts from the source code.) Because the flowcharts merely echoed the code, most programmers found the code a better source of documentation, so the flowcharts were rarely maintained. In effect, they were useless.

You are about to begin studying a methodology that calls for preparing a data flow diagram. A data flow diagram is a planning tool. Like a program flowchart that merely echoes the source code, a data flow diagram prepared after design decisions have been made is a waste of time and effort. The point of creating a data flow diagram is not to create a data flow diagram but to develop a better system. Documentation for the sake of documentation is pointless.

Getting Started

Grouping Processes

The first step in creating a logical model is to prepare a list of the present system's boundaries, data, and processes. Figure 5.2 shows the components you identified in Chapter 4.

The problem with Figure 5.2 is that the list is too long. A diagram showing 23 processes, 10 data entities, and 4 sources or destinations would be difficult to follow because there is a limit to the amount of detail a human being can grasp. Numerous studies suggest that the number seven (plus or minus two) is significant because most people can keep track of between five and nine discrete "things." That suggests a target. For

FIGURE 5.2
A list of the logical elements that compose the present inventory system.

Processes
Fill out price tag
Attach price sticker
File price tag
Assign stock number
Note supplier on price tag
Sell appliance
Fill out sales receipt
Give receipt to customer
Remove price sticker
Collect sales receipts
Match tag to inventory
Prepare sales report
Retrieve supplier invoice
Note stock number on invoice
File supplier invoice
Reorder stock
Type reorder
Get mailing address
Prepare old inventory list
Identify sale items
Perform physical inventory
Update stock levels
Prepare stock level report

Data
Price tag/sticker
Inventory file
Sales receipt
Sales report
Supplier invoice
Merchandise to order
Order form
Old inventory report
Physical inventory
Stock level report

Boundaries
Customer
Supplier
Manager
Financial system

For clarity, a data flow diagram should contain between five and nine processes.

clarity, a data flow diagram should contain between five and nine processes or, more conservatively, symbols.

To achieve that target, it is necessary to merge related components. Consider the processes first. (As you may recall, you already merged several low-level processes when you defined the *Sales transaction* process in Chapter 4, so this step might already be done.) One useful key is the trigger event. Processes that are triggered by the same event (or by related events) might be related, but processes that are triggered by unrelated events usually cannot be combined.

For example, several tasks, including *Fill out price tag*, *Attach price sticker*, *File price tag*, *Assign stock number*, *Note supplier on price tag*, *Note stock number on invoice*, and *File supplier invoice*, are performed when a shipment arrives from a supplier (Figure 5.3). Defining a single process named *Process shipment* that contains all of those subprocesses reduces the number of logical components without losing any functions.

The point is to identify the tasks the system must perform, not to plan a program to perform those tasks.

Note the subprocesses are not necessarily listed in execution order; for example, *Note supplier on price tag* will almost certainly be done before *File price tag*. At this stage the point is to identify the tasks the system must perform, not to plan a program to perform those tasks.

Several of the high-level processes identified in Figure 5.3 are triggered by time. Certain tasks are performed at the end of the day. Others are performed at the end of the week, the month, or the quarter. Tasks that are performed at approximately the same time are often related. Visualize their trigger event as an alarm clock.

The fact that two processes occur at approximately the same time does not necessarily mean that they can be combined, however. For example, reorders and pay checks are both prepared weekly, but those processes are clearly not related. Even related processes must sometimes be kept separate. For example, security or auditing requirements might call for an incoming shipment to be independently evaluated by two different people, and that means two different processes.

Read through the remaining groups in Figure 5.3; they should make sense. If there is a logical reason why a particular subprocess cannot be part of the group, move it to its own group. The burden of proof is on moving the subprocess, however. The objective is to minimize the number of processes.

Note that these preliminary process groupings are just that—*preliminary*. Derived from the present system, they represent a starting point, and nothing more. As your logical model evolves, your initial judgments might

FIGURE 5.3
Group logically related processes to reduce the number of process symbols to a reasonable level.

Process	Trigger Event	Contains	Process Name
1	Shipment arrives	Fill out price tag Attach price sticker File price tag Assign stock number Note supplier on price tag Note stock number on invoice File supplier invoice	*Process shipment*
2	Customer makes purchase	Sell appliance Fill out sales receipt Give receipt to customer Remove price sticker	*Sell appliance*
3	End of day	Collect sales receipts Match tag to inventory Update stock levels	*Update inventory*
4	End of week	Prepare sales report Retrieve supplier invoice Reorder stock Type reorder Get mailing address Prepare stock level report	*Reorder stock*
5	End of month	Prepare old inventory list Identify sale items	*Identify sale items*
6	End of quarter	Perform physical inventory	*Perform physical inventory*

be proven wrong. Some processes will move; others will change; still others will disappear. The act of logically combining related processes is still valuable, however. For example, when you begin thinking about a general process such as *Sell appliance*, it is much easier to ignore the details associated with *Fill out sales receipt*.

Incidentally, not all analysts accept the "magic number seven" as a target. Indeed, it might be impossible to reduce a complex system to between five and nine processes. A data flow diagram is a bit like a road map. When you study a map, you focus on one small segment at a time, and the fact that the map itself contains hundreds of roads, towns, and other symbols is irrelevant. Still, the idea of reducing a data flow diagram to the minimum possible number of symbols is a good one.

Grouping Data

Look for data groupings that contain the same data elements.

Figure 5.2 lists 10 data entities. Perhaps some of them could be combined, too. Start by listing the data elements in each group (Figure 5.4). Then look for data groupings that contain the same data elements.

For example, because *Price tag* and *Inventory file* are taken from the same two-part form, they hold exactly the same data elements. Unless there is a good, logical reason to keep them separate, they can be merged. *Old inventory report*, *Merchandise to order*, *Physical inventory*, and *Stock level report* also contain the same data elements, so they can all be logically combined to form a single set of data about inventory (Figure 5.5).

Consider the sales data next. The number of appliances sold affects inventory, but the *Sales receipt* also holds the customer's name and address, the sales tax, and other data that are irrelevant to inventory. It might make sense to logically merge the *Sales receipt* and the *Sales report* data (Figure 5.5), but you cannot combine them with the inventory data. Logically, sales data are different from inventory data.

That leaves the *Supplier invoice* and the *Order form*. They contain such data elements as *Unit price* and *Description*, so you might consider combining them with *Inventory*. Other data elements describe the supplier, however, and they are not necessary for inventory management. Consequently, a third data group is needed to hold data about suppliers (Figure 5.5).

Consider the data from a slightly different perspective. Database theory defines an entity as a person, place, thing, or activity about which data are stored. In this example there are three entities: data are stored about inventory, about sales, and about suppliers. That suggests three data stores. (Later, you will learn to use more formal techniques to define your data entities.)

Drawing the Data Flow Diagram

Data Flow Diagram Symbols

A data flow diagram shows the flow of data through a system.

A **data flow diagram** shows the flow of data through a system using four basic symbols (Figure 5.6). **Sources** and **destinations** (or sinks) are represented by squares or rectangles. Each one stands for a person, organization, or other system that supplies data to the system, gets data from

FIGURE 5.4
A list of the data elements that appear on existing forms and reports, with related data sets grouped.

Inventory Data

Price tag/sticker
Inventory file (same data)
  Manufacturer name
  Product description
  Model code
  Stock number
  Stock date
  Suggested price
  Selling price
    (Your price)

Old inventory report
  Product type
  Manufacturer
  Model
  Old stock count

Merchandise to order
  Stock number
  Description
  Reorder quantity

Physical inventory
  Product type
  Manufacturer
  Model
  Showroom stock
  Warehouse stock
  Total stock

Stock level report
  Report date
  Product type
  Manufacturer
  Model
  Start week stock
  Sales
  Received
  End week stock

Sales Data

Sales receipt
  Customer name
  Customer street
  Customer city
  Customer state
  Customer zip code
  Customer phone
  Invoice number
  Date of sale
  Stock number
  Description
  Quantity
  Unit price
    (Selling price)
  Item total
  Subtotal
  Sales tax
  Total due

Sales report
  Report date
  Product type
  Manufacturer
  Model
  Weekly sales
  Unit cost
  Product cost
  Selling price
  Revenue
  Margin
  Total product sales
  Total product cost
  Total product revenue
  Total product margin
  Total weekly sales
  Total weekly cost
  Total weekly revenue
  Total weekly margin

FIGURE 5.4
Continued

Supplier Data

Order form	Supplier invoice
Order number	Invoice number
Supplier name	Invoice date
Supplier address	Salesperson
Supplier city	Order date
Supplier state	Customer number
Supplier zip code	Ship weight
Order date	Routing
Delivery date	Terms
Ship via	Date shipped
FOB	FOB
Terms	Sold name
Model	Sold address
Product description	Sold city
Quantity	Sold state
Unit price	Sold zip code
Item amount	Sold attention
Purchasing manager	Ship name
	Ship address
	Ship city
	Ship state
	Ship zip code
	Ship attention
	Order number
	Supplier order number
	Item code
	Quantity
	Product description
	Quantity shipped
	Unit price
	Amount due
	Total due

FIGURE 5.5
Reduce the number of data sets by combining those that contain the same data elements.

Data About	Contains
INVENTORY	Price tag
	Inventory
	Old inventory report
	Merchandise to order
	Stock level report
	Physical inventory
SALES	Sales receipt
	Sales report
SUPPLIERS	Supplier invoice
	Order form

FIGURE 5.6
Data flow diagram symbols.

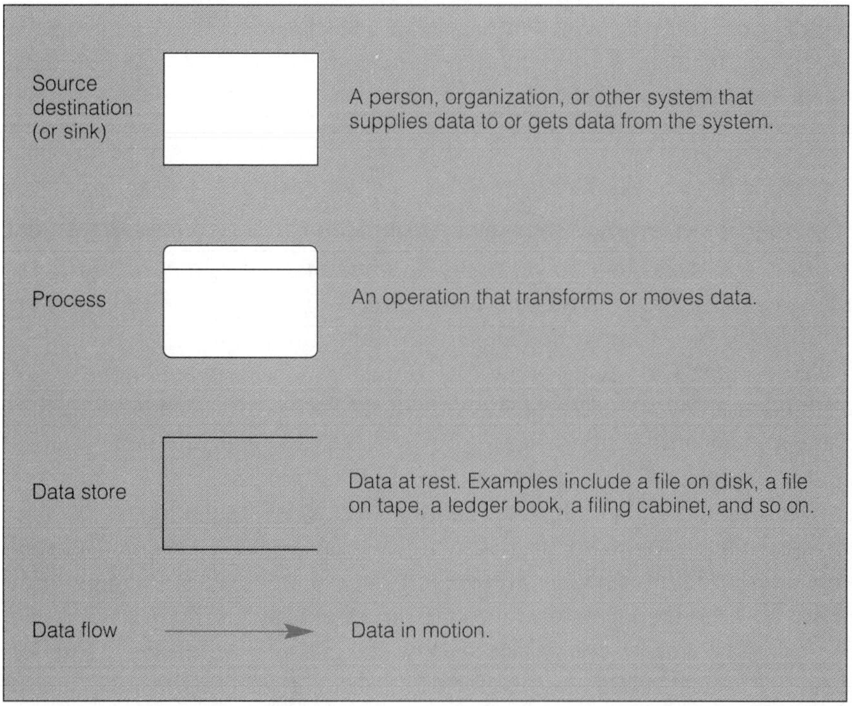

Source destination (or sink)		A person, organization, or other system that supplies data to or gets data from the system.
Process		An operation that transforms or moves data.
Data store		Data at rest. Examples include a file on disk, a file on tape, a ledger book, a filing cabinet, and so on.
Data flow	⟶	Data in motion.

the system, or both. They define the system's boundaries. A process, or **transform,** (a round-cornered rectangle or a circle) identifies an activity that changes, moves, or otherwise transforms data. A **data store** (an open-ended rectangle) represents data at rest and implies that the data are held between processes. A **data flow** (an arrow) represents data in motion.

A process is an activity that changes or moves data. An implication of that definition is that data cannot move *without* a process. Thus, data cannot legally flow directly from a source to a destination or between a source/destination and a data store unless they pass through an intermediate process. All data flows must begin or end (or both) with a process (Figure 5.7).

A data store implies that data must be held between processes for some *logical* reason. Most often, the data store is needed because the processes occur at different times, but that is not always the case. For example, consider a price tag. The price is associated with a product, so it might make sense to merge the price tag data into a common inventory data store. However, if your state has a law that requires a price tag on every item, then you have a logical reason to maintain separate inventory and price tag data stores. (Granted not all state laws are logical, but let's not quibble.)

Logical and Physical Models

Data flow diagram symbols describe logical, not physical, entities.

Note that the data flow diagram symbols describe logical, not physical, entities. A process might eventually be implemented as a computer program, a subroutine, or a manual procedure. A data store might represent a database, a file, a book, a folder in a filing cabinet, or even notes on a sheet of paper. Data flows show how the data move between the system's components, but they do *not* show the flow of control. The idea is to create a logical model that allows you to focus on what the system does while disregarding the physical details of how it works.

Some analysts like to begin studying the present system by preparing a **physical data flow diagram** that identifies the system's specific physical processes and physical data stores. For example, one data store might represent a printed report while a second data store is identified as a file on a 3.5-inch diskette. A **logical data flow diagram,** in contrast, does not suggest physical references. A given logical data store might represent a

FIGURE 5.7
All data flows must begin or end with a process, or both.

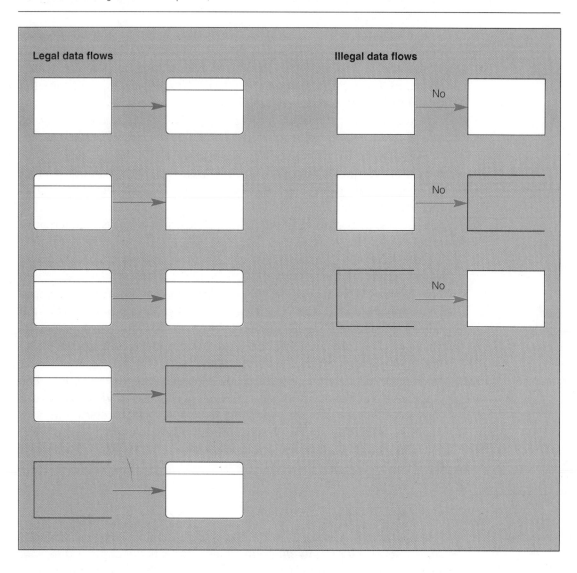

report, a disk file, a database, a filing cabinet, or notes on a sheet of paper. A physical model shows how the system works; a logical model shows what the system does.

For example, if a manager uses an inventory report to support stock re-ordering decisions, a physical data flow diagram would show that report as a data store and the activities associated with making that decision would appear as a process (a manual procedure). The physical model shows the relationship between the system's physical components.

Given a physical model, you can study the processes and data stores and generalize them using guidelines much like the ones described earlier in this chapter. By stripping away the physical attributes associated with the processes and the data stores, you convert the physical model to a logical data flow diagram. The logical model then becomes the basis for further analysis. A physical data flow diagram can also be used at the end of analysis (or the beginning of design) to define a specific physical alternative (see Chapter 13).

The decision to prepare a physical data flow diagram is a personal one. Some analysts find that preparing a physical model helps them understand how the present system works. Also, a clear sense of how existing components are related can suggest logical data and process groupings. On the other hand, a data flow diagram is easier to prepare after the components have been logically grouped, and spending too much time documenting the present system can bias subsequent analysis.

You are just beginning to learn how to create data flow diagrams. The Appliance Store's inventory system is relatively easy to visualize, and a physical data flow diagram showing all its existing processes and data might be confusing, so no physical model will be prepared at this time. Physical data flow diagrams will be reconsidered in Chapter 13 after you learn how to interpret them.

The Level-0 Data Flow (Context) Diagram

Given a list of processes, data, sources, and destinations, the next step is to draw a **level-0 data flow diagram,** sometimes called a **context diagram**. Figure 5.8 shows a context diagram for the *Inventory system*. The system itself is shown as a single process. It provides data to the FINANCIAL SYSTEM. It both provides data to and gets data from MANAGER, SUPPLIER,

FIGURE 5.8
A level-0 data flow diagram (or context diagram) shows the sources and destinations that define the system's boundaries.

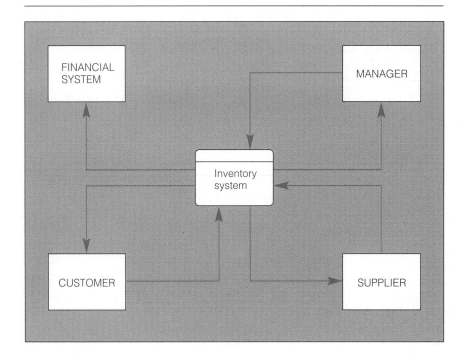

and CUSTOMER. By convention, the names of the sources and destinations are capitalized to distinguish them from the processes.

A context diagram documents the system's boundaries by highlighting its sources and destinations. By definition, a source or destination is outside the system's boundaries and thus not subject to the system's control.

A context diagram documents the system's boundaries.

A common mistake is to assume that people, by their very nature, are sources or destinations. That is not necessarily the case; some people are, and others are not. For example, the sales clerks and the inventory clerks are part of the system. Their activities are controlled by the system; they follow procedures. CUSTOMER, on the other hand, clearly lies outside the system because there is no way the system can control the customers' actions.

FIGURE 5.9
These four rules apply when you create or verify a data flow diagram.

_NB!!_

1. Any data element that flows out from a data store must first flow into that data store.
2. Any data element that flows into a data store must eventually flow out from that data store.
3. Any data element that flows out from a process must either be input to that process or generated by an algorithm within that process.
4. Any data element that flows into a process must either be output by that process or used by an algorithm within that process.

Another common mistake is to assume that all sources and destinations must be people. Again, that is not necessarily true. For example, FINANCIAL SYSTEM is another system that gets data from the inventory system, and SUPPLIER is another organization.

The FINANCIAL SYSTEM could be (perhaps should be) at least partially integrated with the inventory system. For one thing, those two systems share sales data, and design decisions affecting the structure of the inventory-related sales data might affect the financial system. Independence will be assumed to simplify the text example, but that would probably not be a good assumption in the real world.

The Level-1 Data Flow Diagram

A **level-1 data flow diagram** shows the system's primary processes, data stores, sources, and destinations linked by data flows. The secret to creating one is to take advantage of the four rules listed in Figure 5.9. Read them carefully. In essence, they say that every data element comes from somewhere (there are no miracles), and every data element that enters the system must be used (there are no black holes).

There are no miracles. There are no black holes.

Starting Your Data Flow Diagram   Because of the relationship between data and processes, you can start developing your data flow diagram with almost any component. It is best to start with the data that flow out to a destination, however, because a system's output defines its minimum content. Any data that flow out from a system must either flow into the system or be generated by the system.

Any data that flow out from a system must either flow into the system or be generated by the system.

FIGURE 5.10
The data elements that make up a customer receipt flow from the system to destination CUSTOMER.

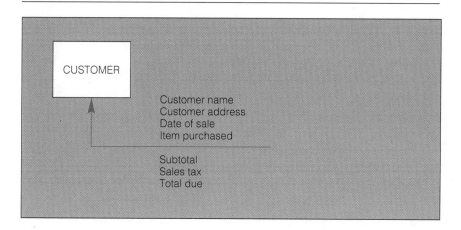

For example, a copy of the sales receipt flows to CUSTOMER. Earlier you compiled a list of the data elements and composites found on a sales receipt (Figure 5.4); the appropriate outputs are listed on Figure 5.10. (By convention, only the first letter of a data flow name is capitalized.) The idea is to find the source of each of those data elements.

Every data flow must start and/or end with a process, so look through the list of processes in Figure 5.3. The second group is the most likely source of a customer receipt, so it is reasonable to assume that the data flow to CUSTOMER from *Sell appliance* (Figure 5.11). (By convention, a process name consists of a verb followed by a noun.)

Customer name, *Customer address*, *Date of sale*, and *Quantity* (one of the data elements in *Item purchased*) originate with CUSTOMER (Figure 5.12), so they are listed on a data flow from CUSTOMER. The other data elements that compose *Item purchased* (*Stock number*, *Description*, and *Unit price*) are found on the price tag. The price tag is associated with the inventory data, so those three data elements probably flow from data store INVENTORY (Figure 5.12). The last three output data elements, *Subtotal*, *Sales tax*, and *Total due*, are computed by algorithms within the process called *Sell appliance*.

Every data flow must start and/or end with a process.

FIGURE 5.11
Every data flow must start and/or end with a process.

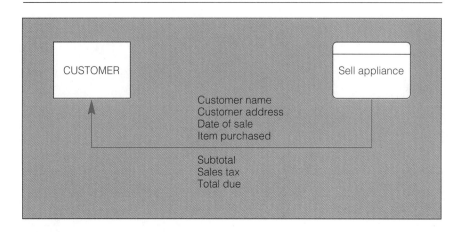

Describing Processes   As you define a process, note its input and output data elements and composites in a **process description** (Figure 5.13). Then briefly describe the tasks or activities it performs. Start by listing the lower-level processes you combined to form *Sell appliance* (Figure 5.3). Add a task to control each input or output data flow. Finally, list the algorithms you just identified (*Compute subtotal, Compute sales tax,* and *Compute total due*). Don't worry about the sequence of operations just yet because that is a design consideration.

The act of creating the data flow diagram uncovers previously overlooked tasks.

Note that the original list of processes was incomplete; the act of creating the data flow diagram uncovered previously overlooked tasks. Note also that *Remove price sticker* has been deleted from the list of tasks in Figure 5.13. It is implied by a more general task, *Accept inventory data*, and removing a price tag suggests a specific physical implementation that might change in a new, improved inventory system.

Tracing Data Flows   There is more to this system than just the three symbols shown in Figure 5.12, of course. For example, focus on data store IN-VENTORY. It sends data elements *Stock number*, *Description*, and *Unit price* to *Sell appliance*. A data store is simply a repository for data, so any data element that flows out must first flow into that store from a process. A

FIGURE 5.12
Any data element output by a process must either be input to the process or generated by the process.

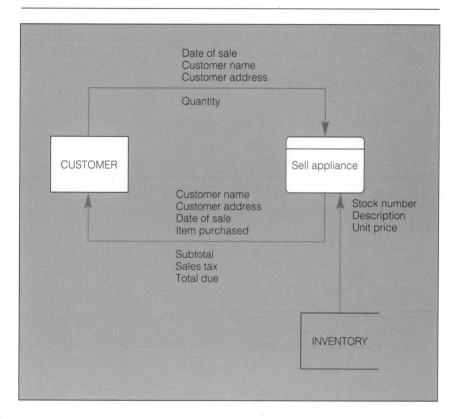

glance at the list of processes (Figure 5.3) should convince you that the first one, *Process shipment*, is the likely source of those three data elements (Figure 5.14).

If those three data elements flow from *Process shipment*, they must either flow into *Process shipment* or be generated by an algorithm within *Process shipment*. Consider *Description* first. It is reasonable to assume that it comes from SUPPLIER. You have reached a source, so there is no need to trace this data element any further.

The *Unit price* and the *Stock number* are a bit different. Although suppliers often suggest a selling price, the owner of the store can choose to

FIGURE 5.13
As you define a process, note its input and output data elements and briefly describe the tasks it performs.

PROCESS DESCRIPTION

SYSTEM: Inventory
PROCESS: 2, Sell appliance
DATE: April 12, 1994

Data in
Customer name
Customer address
Quantity
Date of sale
Stock number
Description
Unit price

Data out
Customer name
Customer address
Quantity
Date of sale
Item purchased
Subtotal
Sales tax
Total due

Tasks or activities
Fill out sales receipt
Give receipt to customer
~~Remove price sticker~~
Accept data from customer
Accept inventory data
Send data to financial system
Record sales data
Compute subtotal
Compute sales tax
Compute total due

Note
This process is triggered by
the arrival of a customer.

FIGURE 5.14
By tracing each data element back to its source, you define the logical relationships between the system's components.

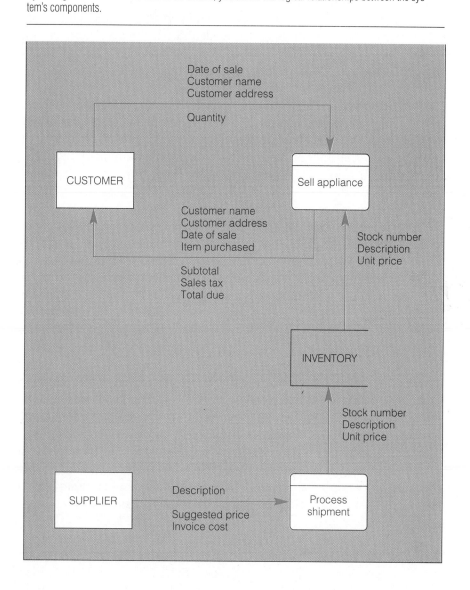

ignore it. Consequently, *Unit price* must be determined by an algorithm within *Process shipment.*

A similar argument can be made for *Stock number.* Although most appliance manufacturers assign a unique identifier called a universal product code (UPC) to each of their products, The Appliance Store assigns its own *Stock number*, so *Process shipment* must contain another algorithm.

Defining Algorithms   To identify the data elements that drive the newly discovered algorithms, you might have to ask the store owner for clarification. For example, assume that the manufacturer's *Suggested price* and the *Invoice cost* (the amount the store pays the supplier) are both considered in assigning a *Unit price.* Those two values come from SUPPLIER (Figure 5.14). Because the data elements that generate *Unit price* are both provided by SUPPLIER, you have traced *Unit price* back to its source.

Trace each data element back to its source.

The *Stock number* might be generated by concatenating (linking together) portions of the model code, the manufacturer's name, and the store's product classification code. If so, you would have to trace each of those data elements back to its source. For simplicity, let's assume that The Appliance Store's stock number is a simple sequential number assigned by the inventory manager; in other words, the source of *Stock number* is a counting algorithm. You now know enough to start a process description for *Process shipment.*

Considering Timing   Note that the two processes in Figure 5.14 are separated by a data store. When you link processes with a data flow, you imply that data move directly from the first to the second and are *immediately* processed. Clearly, *Sell appliance* and *Process shipment* occur at different times, so immediate processing is impossible. Avoid linking processes with data flows unless the data *must* move immediately from one to the other. Because processes linked by flows happen (by definition) at essentially the same time, they can usually be merged to form a single process, particularly at level 1.

When you link processes with a data flow, you imply that data move directly from the first to the second and are *immediately* processed.

Finishing the Level-1 Diagram   Continue following the same procedure until you complete the data flow diagram. Start with a destination. Identify the data elements that flow to it, trace them back to their sources, and move on to the next destination. After you have considered all the destinations, check the level-0 diagram and make sure you have accounted for all the data inflows from all the sources. Finally, make sure that each of the processes and each of the data stores you identified earlier appears in the data flow diagram.

Figure 5.15 shows an almost finished level-1 data flow diagram. (Page space is limited, so not all the data flows are listed.) Data store name VENDOR was selected to distinguish it from source/destination SUPPLIER.

By convention, the processes are numbered 1, 2, 3, and so on. The numbers do not imply sequence; they are for reference only. (In this case, they match the order in which the processes were listed in Figure 5.3.) Many analysts use the letter D followed by a number to identify the data stores; for example, INVENTORY might be D1, SALES might be D2, and so on.

Some components (for example, CUSTOMER and process 2) are linked by two data flow lines, while others (MANAGER and process 4) are joined by a two-headed arrow. Either form is acceptable. Some analysts use two flow lines when the input and output data flows are different and a single two-headed arrow when they are the same. For example, a process that gets data from a store, updates the data, and then sends the same data elements back to the store calls for a two-headed arrow.

Data store VENDOR and source/destinations SUPPLIER and MANAGER appear twice in Figure 5.15. You can repeat symbols if doing so makes the diagram easier to read. In this case, the only way to avoid duplicate symbols is to draw lengthy or crossing data flow lines, and that would be less clear. Duplicate symbols are usually marked in some way; for example, in Figure 5.15 the source/destinations are marked with a slash in the lower-left corner, and the data stores are marked with an extra vertical line.

You can repeat symbols if doing so makes the diagram easier to read.

Note how the data flow diagram summarizes details and gives you an overview of the entire system. Too many details means that you can't see the forest for the trees. The data flow diagram is a map of the forest.

The data flow diagram is a map of the forest.

Some Final Notes   Perhaps the most common beginner's mistake is confusing data flow diagrams with process flowcharts. The data flows do not necessarily imply sequence, nor do they imply a flow of control. For example, process 1 can logically access INVENTORY data before, after, or concurrently with process 3. In fact, it is theoretically possible to perform *all* the

FIGURE 5.15

The level-1 data flow diagram shows the sources, destinations, primary processes, and primary data stores linked by data flows.

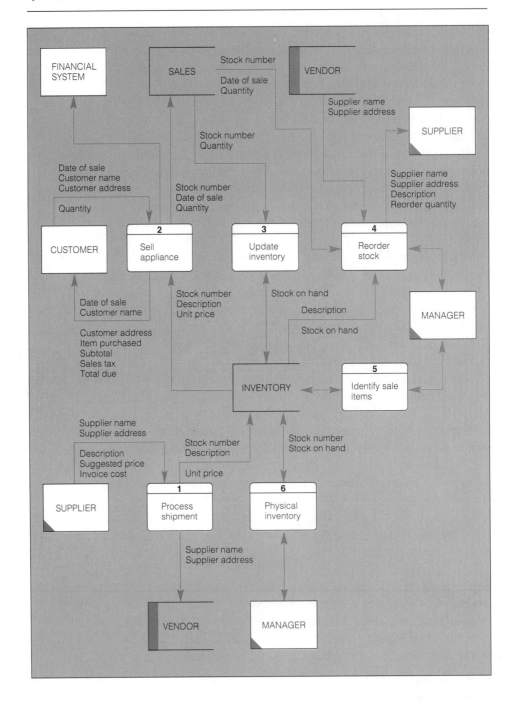

processes in Figure 5.15 concurrently. View each process as an *independent* activity. The data flows show how those activities are related.

Incidentally, the fact that all the processes in Figure 5.15 are separated by data stores contributes to their independence. Using data flows to link processes implies sequence. If you find yourself linking processes with data flows, you are probably drawing a flowchart using data flow diagram symbols.

Note that Tina (the MANAGER) is listed as a source/destination but that Ted is not. Sources and destinations are *outside the system's boundaries* and thus not subject to the system's control. Tina is the owner. Her decisions are based on data supplied by the system, but she can choose to ignore the data and act independently. Ted, on the other hand, is *part* of the system; he performs clerical functions that are defined by the system. A person is a source or destination if, and only if, he or she can act independently.

Note also that the FINANCIAL SYSTEM is identified as a destination. It is a related system that gets data from process 2, but it lies outside the boundaries of the inventory system. It might make sense to move inside the financial system and specify how several accounting tasks are performed. (In fact, you might suggest an integrated inventory and financial management system as one alternative solution.) But that would mean expanding the system beyond the stated problem, and the analyst cannot change the problem without the user's permission.

The data flow diagram is a logical model of the system. You can use it to visualize the entire system rather than just the individual components. The processes indicate what the system does. The data stores and data flows identify the data processed by the system. The sources and destinations define the system's boundaries.

The CASE Graphic Interface

Most CASE products include a graphic interface that simplifies creating a data flow diagram. Once the diagram is stored electronically, the CASE graphic interface makes it relatively easy to add, delete, and modify elements. Perhaps the most important advantage of CASE graphics is the ability of the software to trace the ripple effects that result from changes to the model and adjust the diagram as necessary.

If you find yourself linking processes with data flows, you are probably drawing a flowchart using data flow diagram symbols.

A person is a source or destination if, and only if, he or she can act independently.

The analyst cannot change the problem without the user's permission.

If at all possible, use CASE tools or some other graphics software to prepare your data flow diagrams. After you leave school and begin working as a systems analyst, you *will* use CASE. The specific CASE product will probably be different from the one you learned in college, but if you understand the modeling technique you should have little trouble adjusting.

■   **PROFESSIONAL POINTER**

Make Changes Easy

Several years ago, before graphic interfaces were widely available, an instructor divided each of two classes into small groups, presented the necessary background material for a logical model, and charged each group with developing an appropriate data flow diagram. The groups in class A were told to sketch their diagrams in pencil. The groups in class B were expected to use pen and ink and a template. In both classes, the best data flow diagram was to be selected and used by all the groups as the basis for subsequent work.

A week later, the two classes met (independently) to review their diagrams and select the best one. The discussion in class A was lively. Initially, each group defended its own work, but after a time they began to listen to each other. The class emerged at the end of the hour with a consensus data flow diagram that was significantly better than the one produced by any one group.

Class B was different. It too began with each group defending its own work, but the discussion never moved past that point. Instead of listening for good ideas, the students looked for weak points in the other groups' presentations. Their objective was not to find the best data flow diagram but to have their own diagram accepted by the class because that meant less work for them. The point is that people are naturally reluctant to scrap already completed work, and the more difficult the work is to change, the less willing they are to change it.

Analysis is an iterative process. Your understanding of the system *will* change. If the model is difficult to modify, you will fight making the necessary changes. The danger is that you will force the system to fit your model instead of changing the model to fit the system. If changes are easy to make, that problem disappears. Ease of change is one of the most powerful arguments for using CASE.

Documenting the Logical Model

The Data Dictionary

As you identify data elements, record them in the data dictionary. As work progresses, the data elements that occupy the same data store or share a data flow form composite items or data structures. For example, *Supplier name*, *Supplier address*, *Description*, *Reorder quantity*, and other data elements flow to SUPPLIER from process 4 and form a data structure that might be called *Reorder*. Record composites in the data dictionary by listing the data elements or substructures they contain (see Chapter 4). Then note on each data element the structures to which it belongs.

Review those logical data structures with the user. Ask specific questions. Do the fields in this structure *always* go together? Are any fields missing? How often does this data structure occur? When this data flow enters the system, how quickly must it be processed? How often do data enter the system via this data flow? What data element or elements do you use as a key for accessing this data structure? Record the answers in the data dictionary because you will need this information during system design.

Process Descriptions

In addition to recording data elements and data composites in the data dictionary, you should also prepare a process description for each process. Like the data descriptions, process (or data transform) descriptions are often recorded in the data dictionary.

After you define the process, review your definition with the user. Ask questions about the event that triggers the process. Ask how often the process is performed (continuously, daily, weekly) and how quickly the process must be completed. Ask about process volume, too. A good approach is to ask the user to distinguish between normal rates and peak rates. For example, an appliance store's sales might average a dozen appliances per day, but the majority of those sales might occur on Saturday. Be prepared to correct your process descriptions based on the user's comments.

The CASE Repository

When you use a CASE package, the data descriptions and process descriptions are both stored in the repository. With everything in a central place, the CASE software can keep track of the links and relationships between the processes and the data. It is the repository that allows CASE software to adjust for the ripple effects caused by a change to a part of the model.

Verifying the Model

The point of verification is to ensure that the model is complete and internally consistent.

Once the level-1 data flow diagram is finished, verify it both technically and with the user. The point of verification is to ensure that the model is complete and internally consistent. CASE is particularly valuable when the time comes to verify the model.

■   **PROFESSIONAL POINTER**

Verify

Measure twice, cut once. That old adage was popularized on the public television show *This Old House*. It clearly and succinctly states the point of verification.

Finding Missing Algorithms

Creating and documenting a data flow diagram does not necessarily reveal all the system's algorithms. Clearly, a model with missing components cannot be considered complete, so the first step is to look for missing algorithms.

One useful test is to compare a given process's input data to its output data. If they are different, that process must contain an algorithm because, by definition, any data element that flows out from a process must either flow into or be generated by that process. The data flow diagram might not define the algorithm for you, but the process of creating the logical model highlights missing components and that, in turn, tells you what questions to ask. When you discover an algorithm, add it to the appropriate process description, and remember that the new subprocess might imply new data elements.

The process of creating the logical model highlights missing components.

Decisions are particularly difficult to find. Sometimes you can spot a decision algorithm by studying a process and asking if every set of data elements that flows in subsequently flows out. If only *some* inputs generate outputs, a decision must be made within the process.

For example, process 1, *Process shipment*, is activated by the arrival of a shipment from a supplier (Figure 5.15). Because all shipments must be processed, outputs are generated for each set of input data, so no selection is made. Process 4, *Reorder stock*, is different, however. Sales and inventory data enter the process, but only *some* of the input data generate a reorder. A selection algorithm makes the reorder decision. Once you identify that selection algorithm, you can account for the input data that drive it.

Logical Verification

If the logical model dictates a particular physical solution, then that solution is not likely to be challenged in subsequent steps. Consequently, before you move on to more formal verification, you should take a few minutes to convince yourself that the data flow diagram does not limit you to a specific physical implementation. A good strategy is to visualize a manual solution and a computer-based solution and then make sure that both are compatible with the data flow diagram. If something in the model makes either alternative impossible, then the diagram is not sufficiently general and it should be changed.

> **If the logical model dictates a physical solution, then that solution is not likely to be challenged in subsequent steps.**

For example, imagine that the model contains a process named *Scan UPC code*. Almost certainly, the analyst who created that model was thinking of a bar code scanner like the ones supermarkets use. That's too physical. There are other ways to identify products, so you might change the name of data element *UPC code* to *Product code*. There are other ways to capture product information so you might change the process name to *Capture product information*. Can you see how those simple changes make the model more general?

Syntax Checking

You begin formal verification by performing a few syntax checks. Every data flow must have at least one arrowhead to define the direction of data movement. Every data flow must begin and/or end with a process. Every process and every data store must have at least one input and at least one output data flow. If the inflow is missing, the source of the data is unknown. If the outflow is missing, that process or store acts like a black hole. In either case, something is wrong. Most CASE packages include a syntax-checking routine.

Other syntax checks involve a bit of judgment. Process names should imply their function. Component names should be unique because redundant names are confusing. Review the names you assigned and, if necessary, change them. For example, in Figure 5.15, one data store was named VENDOR to distinguish it from source/destination SUPPLIER.

Tracing Data Elements

Rigorously trace each data element from its destination back to its source.

The next step is to rigorously trace each data element from its destination back to its source using the four rules outlined in Figure 5.9. For example, the data elements that flow to SUPPLIER from process 4, *Reorder stock* (Figure 5.15, right side), include *Supplier name*, *Supplier address*, *Description*, and *Reorder quantity*. (There might be more data elements on that data flow, but those four are enough to illustrate verification.)

Any data element output by process 4 must first enter process 4. Consider *Supplier name* first. It must come from data store VENDOR because it makes little sense to store a supplier's name in SALES or INVENTORY.

If *Supplier name* comes from VENDOR, it must first flow into VENDOR. Move to the bottom left of Figure 5.15 and find the duplicate symbol for data store VENDOR. Data enter VENDOR only from process 1, so *Supplier name* must come from *Process shipment*. Because data enter process 1.0 only from SUPPLIER, *Supplier name* must come from SUPPLIER, and that makes logical sense. You have found the first data element's source. Follow the same path for *Supplier address*.

Consider *Description* next. It flows to SUPPLIER from process 4. Because it describes a product in inventory, it makes sense to get it from data store INVENTORY. Three different processes put data into INVENTORY, but *Process shipment* is the most likely source of *Description*. Consequently, it too must come from SUPPLIER.

Reorder quantity is a bit different because it is generated by an algorithm within *Reorder stock*. Assume that the algorithm is based on sales per unit of time and the stock on hand for a given product. That means data elements *Stock number*, *Quantity*, *Date of sale*, and *Stock on hand* must flow into process 4 to drive the algorithm.

Clearly, the first three come from data store SALES. *Stock on hand* comes from INVENTORY, and it is computed by an algorithm in *Update inventory*. To compute *Stock on hand*, you need the *Stock number* and the *Quantity* purchased or returned, and those data must come from SALES. They enter SALES from *Sell appliance*. As an exercise, trace *Stock number*, *Quantity*, and *Date of sale* back to their sources.

In a larger organization, the algorithm for computing the reorder quantity might be more complex, requiring such data elements as inventory carrying cost, order processing cost, the suppliers' price breaks, and many others. The principle is the same, however. Start with a destination and trace each data element back toward its source. When you encounter an algorithm, identify the *algorithm's* input data elements and trace *them* back to their sources.

Identify the *algorithm's* input data elements and trace *them* back to their sources.

If you can find the source of *every* data element, your data flow diagram is internally consistent and you can be reasonably confident of its accuracy. If you cannot find the source of one or more data elements, then something is missing and you need a follow-up interview. Creating a logical model does not automatically define all the system's components, but it does suggest the questions you might ask.

Manually tracing data elements is tedious, time consuming, and error prone. In fact, if the system is even moderately large, it probably won't be done. At best, selected data *structures* will be traced and, because the data structures might be accidents of an earlier physical design, that defeats the purpose of verifying the data flows. Most CASE products include routines that automatically trace data flows.

Cross-referencing

The final verification step is to cross-reference the data flow diagram, the data dictionary, and the process descriptions (Figure 5.16). Start with the data flow diagram. Each data element, data store, and data flow must appear in the data dictionary, and each process must have a matching process description. If anything is missing, add the necessary documentation.

Cross-reference the data flow diagram, the data dictionary, and the process descriptions.

Then move to the data dictionary. Each logical data structure must match a data flow or a data store, and each data element must appear at least once on the data flow diagram. Additionally, each data element and each logical data structure must appear in the input or output list of at least one process description. There are two possible explanations for unused data elements: Either they are not needed by the system, or the analyst overlooked them.

Finally, consider the process descriptions. Each one must match a process on the data flow diagram, and the input and output lists must match the data flows. Every data element entering or leaving a process must appear in the data dictionary. Unused processes might have been overlooked when the data flow diagram was created. If not, they are unnecessary.

FIGURE 5.16
The final verification step is to cross-reference the data flow diagram, the data dictionary, and the process descriptions.

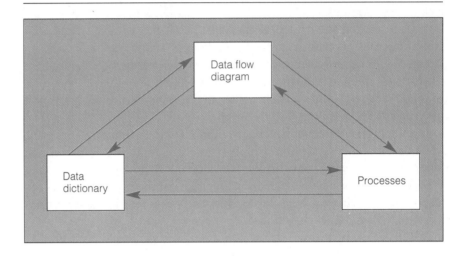

Note how the data flow diagram, the data dictionary, and the process descriptions cross-check each other. The data dictionary defines the data. The process descriptions define the processes. The data flow diagram graphically defines the relationships between the processes and the data. Verification is time consuming and tedious, but if anything is missing from the logical system design, the analyst will probably catch it. Once again, CASE verification software can help. For all practical purposes, you cannot properly verify a logical model without CASE.

For all practical purposes, you cannot properly verify a logical model without CASE.

Tracing Objectives

You cannot verify what isn't there.

Note that if a significant feature of the system was overlooked, verification will not necessarily find the error. (You cannot verify what isn't there.) Consequently, you should always check the logical model against the system objectives and identify the process or processes that contribute to meeting each one. If an objective cannot be matched with at least one process, you probably missed something. If a process cannot be matched with at least one objective, that process might be unnecessary. Many CASE products include facilities to trace objectives.

User Verification

The final test is to review the data flow diagram with the user, perhaps by conducting a **walkthrough**. A good technique is to start with an un-marked data flow diagram and add the sources, destinations, processes, data stores, and data elements as you simulate tracing the flows. As you work your way through the diagram, ask the user to try to break the system by suggesting situations it cannot handle. You simply cannot define the system's logical requirements without user involvement.

You cannot define the system's logical requirements without user involvement.

MANAGEMENT'S PERSPECTIVE   ■

Define and Enforce a Standard

The problem definition and feasibility study phases are usually brief and involve relatively few peo-ple. As analysis begins, however, more people are working on the project, and they must communi-cate with each other. Also, because the work might be spread over several months, turnover is al-most inevitable, and new project team members must be trained.

Communication and training are simplified if everyone uses the same tools and follows the same methodology. Many different analysis tools and CASE products are available. They all have their strengths and weaknesses, and it is difficult to decide which one to select as your organization's standard, but the fact that you have a standard (*any* standard) may be the real key.

Management should allow its technical people to define a standard and then enforce that stan-dard. If the analyst can demonstrate that a nonstandard tool is a better choice for a particular project, substitution should be possible, but the burden of proof should rest with the analyst who wishes to deviate from the standard.

Summary

This chapter introduced a logical modeling technique called structured analysis. The first step in this process is to identify the system's sources, destinations, processes (or transforms), data stores, and data flows. These components are then combined to form a data flow diagram.

A physical data flow diagram identifies the system's physical processes and physical data stores. A logical data flow diagram, in contrast, does not suggest physical references. The level-0 data flow diagram (or context dia-gram) documents the system's boundaries. The level-1 diagram shows the relationships that link the primary sources, destinations, processes, and stores. Data elements are defined in the data dictionary, and processes are documented in process descriptions.

The analyst verifies the logical model by checking syntax, tracing data flows, and cross-referencing the data flow diagram, the data dictionary, and the process descriptions. Making sure that all the objectives have been met provides a link back to the problem definition. Further verification is achieved by conducting a walkthrough with the user.

Suggestions for Additional Reading

DeMarco, Tom. 1978. *Structured Analysis and System Specification*. New York: Yourdon, Inc.

Gane, Chris. 1987. *Rapid System Development*. New York: Rapid System Development, Inc.

Gane, Chris, and Trish Sarson. 1979. *Structured Systems Analysis: Tools and Techniques*. Englewood Cliffs, NJ: Prentice-Hall, Inc.

Ince, Darrel, and Derek Andrews. 1990. *The System Life Cycle*. London: Butterworths.

Miller, George A. The magical number seven, plus or minus two, some limits on our capacity for processing information. *The Psychological Review* 63(2).

Thayer, Richard H., and Merlin Dorfman. 1990. *System and Software Requirements Engineering*. Los Alamitos, CA: IEEE Computer Society Press.

Yourdon, Edward, and Larry L. Constantine. 1979. *Structured Design*. Englewood Cliffs, NJ: Prentice-Hall, Inc.

Exercises

1. The first step in this chapter was to group related processes and data sets. Why?

2. Sketch and define each of the symbols used to prepare a data flow diagram. Those symbols are logical, not physical. What does that mean? Why is that distinction important?

3. Explain the difference between a physical data flow diagram and a logical data flow diagram.

4. What is a context diagram? Why is a context diagram useful?

5. Briefly explain the process of creating a level-1 data flow diagram.

6. Processes imply data and data imply processes. How does that simple fact help you create a data flow diagram?

7. Explain how to document a data flow diagram's components.

8. Briefly explain the process of verifying a logical model. Why is verification necessary?

9. The purpose of many analysis tools is to investigate the relationships between a system's logical elements. Explain how a data flow diagram helps the analyst achieve that objective. Why is understanding relationships important?

10. Chapter 2 introduced projects for The Print Shop, Jan Tompson's Campus Threads clothing store, and Bill Barnett's automobile dealership. Prepare fully documented level-0 and level-1 data flow diagrams for one or more of those projects or for your own project.

If the only tool you have is a hammer, pretty soon everything starts to look like a nail.

6

Data Modeling

When you finish reading this chapter you should be able to:

—Distinguish between a data flow diagram and an entity-relationship diagram and explain the relative strengths and weaknesses of both.

—Define entities, occurrences, attributes, and relationships.

—Explain cardinality.

—Explain why one-to-one relationships can often be merged.

—Explain why many-to-many relationships are often converted to one-to-many relationships.

—Prepare an entity-relationship diagram.

—Develop a set of logical data structures from an entity-relationship model and document them in an inverted L chart.

—Distinguish between first, second, and third normal forms.

—Transform a set of preliminary logical data structures to third normal form.

Entity-Relationship Diagrams

Why Model Data?

The output generated by a single tool can be misleading.

Every tool has its strengths and weaknesses. Every tool is based on certain assumptions about the general nature of the problem it is intended to solve, and those assumptions subtly influence the nature of the solution. Consequently, the output generated by a single tool can be misleading.

A data flow diagram is an excellent logical modeling tool because it shows the relationships between processes and data. However, a data flow diagram tends to focus your attention on the *processes,* and unless you fully understand those processes you will have trouble completing the model. Also, although processes do imply data, it is easy to miss key data when your attention is focused on the processes.

In this chapter, you will learn how to prepare an **entity-relationship diagram** that stresses the data and shows how the system's primary data entities are related. Note, however, that entity-relationship diagrams do not *replace* data flow diagrams. The idea is to prepare both because they complement each other. A data flow diagram gives you a good sense of the processes and a somewhat superficial view of the data. An entity-relationship model focuses on the data and often reveals details that were not apparent in the data flow diagram.

■   **PROFESSIONAL POINTER**

Use Multiple Tools

Perhaps you have heard the old story about the five blind men who were asked to describe an elephant. One touched the trunk and announced that the animal was snakelike. Another touched a leg and compared the elephant to a tree; to another, the tail suggested a rope, and so on. The point of the story is that if you only have part of the picture your conclusions can be very wrong.

Analysis and design tools are a bit like those five blind men. Each tool has its strengths and weaknesses. Some emphasize processes, while others emphasize data. Some give you a system overview; others precisely define details. That is why the analyst uses multiple tools. If you attack a problem from different perspectives you are likely to develop an accurate picture. On the other hand, if the only tool you have is a hammer, pretty soon everything starts to look like a nail.

Entities and Relationships

Entity-relationship diagrams were first proposed as a means of quickly obtaining, with minimum effort, a good sense of the structure of a database. Consequently, several key terms are taken from database theory. Before you begin working with entity-relationship diagrams, briefly review several key terms that were defined in Chapter 4.

An entity is an object (a person, group, place, thing, or an activity) about which data are stored. An occurrence is a single instance of an entity; for example, a particular 19-inch color television set is a single occurrence of the entity called inventory. An attribute is a property of an entity; for example, such attributes as stock number, description, and stock on hand might be associated with inventory. Generally, the same set of attributes is associated with each occurrence of an entity, so every part in inventory can be expected to have a stock number, a description, and a stock on hand. The set of attributes associated with an entity can be visualized as a table or a record.

A data element is an attribute that cannot be logically decomposed. A set of related data elements forms a data structure or a data composite; for example, the set of attributes associated with each occurrence of an entity is a data structure. The key to an entity is the attribute or group of attributes that uniquely distinguishes one occurrence from all other occurrences. A foreign key is a key to some other entity; for example, a supplier code might be associated with the inventory data.

A relationship links two entities and is shown by drawing a line between them (Figure 6.1). Logically, the relationship can be stated in the form of a sentence with a verb linking the two entities; for example,

Sales transactions are composed of *Products*.

or

Products make up *Sales transactions*.

The act of creating such sentences is a good test of the relationship's validity; if you can't express the link it might not exist. In cases where the relationship is unclear, the sentence might be written alongside the relationship line as shown in Figure 6.1.

FIGURE 6.1

A relationship between two entities is shown by drawing a line between them.

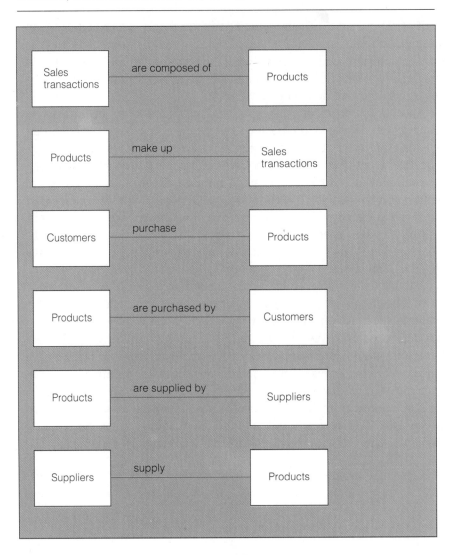

FIGURE 6.2

In a one-to-one relationship, each occurrence of entity A is associated with one and only one occurrence of entity B, and each occurrence of entity B is associated with one and only one occurrence of entity A.

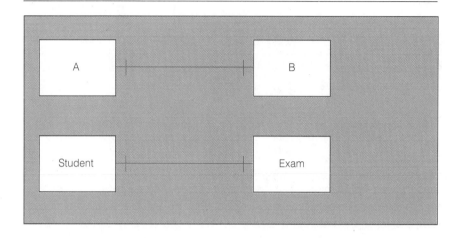

Cardinality

For a variety of reasons, some relationships are more stable and easier to maintain than others. (A detailed discussion of the underlying database theory is beyond the scope of this book.) **Cardinality,** a measure of the related entities' relative number of occurrences, is an important predictor of the strength of the relationship.

In a **one-to-one relationship** (Figure 6.2), each occurrence of entity A is associated with one and only one occurrence of entity B, and each occurrence of entity B is associated with one and only one occurrence of entity A. For example, imagine an instructor who maintains examination data on each student. There are two entities: *Students* and *Exams*. For each *Student* there is one and only one *Exam,* and for each *Exam* there is one and only one *Student.* Graphically, a one-to-one relationship is described by drawing short crossing lines at both ends of the line that links the two entities.

In a **one-to-many relationship** (Figure 6.3), each occurrence of entity A is associated with one or more occurrences of entity B, but each occurrence of entity B is associated with only one occurrence of entity A. For example, your grade in most courses is based on numerous grade factors (exams, papers, projects). A given *Student* has several different *Grade*

Some relationships are more stable and easier to maintain than others.

FIGURE 6.3

In a one-to-many relationship, each occurrence of entity A is associated with one or more occurrences of entity B, but each occurrence of entity B is associated with only one occurrence of entity A.

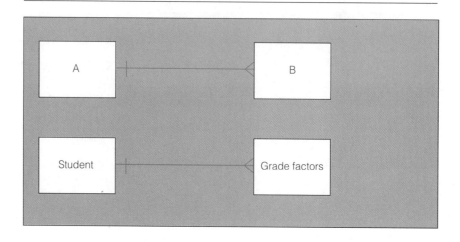

factors, but a given *Grade factor* is associated with one and only one *Student.* Graphically, a one-to-many relationship is shown by drawing a short crossing line at the "one-end" and a small triangle (sometimes called a crow's foot) at the "many-end" of the line that links the entities.

In a **many-to-many relationship** (Figure 6.4), each occurrence of entity A is associated with one or more occurrences of entity B, and each occurrence of entity B is associated with one or more occurrences of entity A. For example, your end-of-term *Grade report* can list several *Courses,* and a given *Course* can appear on many students' *Grade reports.* Graphically, a many-to-many relationship is shown by drawing a crow's foot at both ends of the line that links the entities.

Other types of relationships are possible. Sometimes entities are mutually exclusive, with A linked to either B or C, but not both. In a mutually *inclusive* relationship, if A is linked to B it must also be linked to C. Zero cardinality implies that an occurrence of A means *no* occurrence of B. Cross-links and loops can exist, too, but this chapter will focus on one-to-one, one-to-many, and many-to-many relationships.

FIGURE 6.4
In a many-to-many relationship, each occurrence of entity A is associated with one or more occurrences of entity B, and each occurrence of entity B is associated with one or more occurrences of entity A.

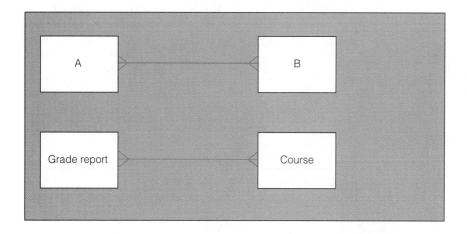

Analyzing Relationships

One-to-many relationships tend to be the most stable. Consequently, a primary objective of entity-relationship modeling is to convert one-to-one and many-to-many relationships into one-to-many relationships.

One-to-many relationships tend to be the most stable.

One-to-One Relationships

One-to-one relationships can often be collapsed by merging them. For example, Figure 6.5 shows a one-to-one relationship linking a set of employee data with that employee's address. You might be able to imagine an application in which it makes sense to keep the home address separate from the other employee data, but it seems reasonable to treat *Address* as an attribute of *Employee*. Generally, entities that share a one-to-one relationship should be merged unless there is a good reason to keep them separate.

One-to-one relationships can often be collapsed by merging them.

Note that not all one-to-one relationships can be collapsed. For example, imagine a relationship between athletes and drug tests. There is

FIGURE 6.5
One-to-one relationships can often be collapsed by merging them.

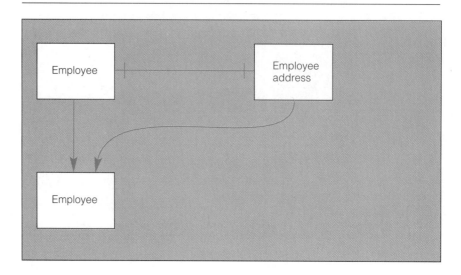

one *Drug test* per *Athlete* and one *Athlete* per *Drug test,* so the relationship is clearly one-to-one. You might argue that *Drug test* is an attribute of *Athlete,* but what if the law requires that drug test data be kept confidential? Because merging the data would make it relatively easy to link a specific person to a specific test result, merging them would probably violate the law, so there is a good logical reason to maintain separate entities.

Many-to-Many Relationships

Many-to-many relationships can cause maintenance problems. For example, Figure 6.6 shows a many-to-many relationship between *Inventory* and *Supplier.* Each product in *Inventory* can have more than one *Supplier,* and each *Supplier* can carry more than one product. If you were to store a list of suppliers in *Inventory,* adding or deleting a supplier might mean updating several *Inventory* occurrences. Likewise, listing products in *Supplier* could mean changing several *Supplier* occurrences if a single product were added or deleted.

FIGURE 6.6
A many-to-many relationship can often be converted to two one-to-many relationships.

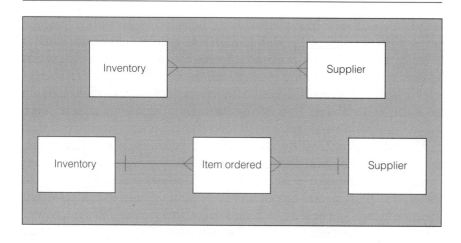

One solution is to create a new entity that has a one-to-many relationship with *both* original entities. For example, imagine a new entity called *Item ordered* (Figure 6.6). If you need 100 television sets, you might order 50 from supplier A, 25 from supplier B, and 25 from supplier C, so a given product in *Inventory* can appear on several active *Items ordered*. However, each *Item ordered* is for one and only one product. Likewise, a given supplier can appear on several active *Items ordered*, but each *Item ordered* lists one and only one supplier. Note that a given *Item ordered* links a specific product in *Inventory* with a specific occurrence of *Supplier*. The many-to-many relationship has been converted to two one-to-many relationships.

Convert a many-to-many relationship to two one-to-many relationships.

How does that affect data maintenance? Imagine that *Inventory*, *Item ordered*, and *Supplier* are three files. The file called *Item ordered* holds product codes and supplier codes, and it is indexed on both fields. Detailed information on products and/or suppliers can be obtained by accessing the *Inventory* file or the *Supplier* file, as appropriate. Dropping a product affects *Inventory* and *Item ordered*, but not *Supplier*. Adding a supplier affects *Supplier* and *Item ordered* but not *Inventory*. Because *Item ordered* is indexed on both keys, it is easy to maintain.

Defining Logical Data Structures

Once the entities have been identified, you can record each one in the data dictionary as a data composite and define the attributes (or data elements) each contains (see Chapter 4). If you prefer a graphical representation of the entity's contents, use an **inverted L chart** such as the ones pictured in Figure 6.7. The entity name appears at the top of the imaginary upside-down letter L. Attributes are listed under the entity name; some analysts like to include the data type or a picture clause for each attribute. Note that the key field (or fields) is clearly marked.

The entity's links are listed below the attributes. For example, note the link *Supplied by supplier* under *Inventory*. Move down to the second inverted L chart and find the link that reads *Supplies inventory*. The same link appearing in inverse form under two entities defines the relationship between them. Some analysts add cardinality limits to the links; the greater than (>) symbol implies a "many to" relationship. The completed inverted L charts represent a preliminary set of logical data structures.

> The completed inverted L charts represent a preliminary set of logical data structures.

Creating an Entity-Relationship Diagram

The Sales Data

In Chapter 5, a quick analysis of the data elements derived from the existing system's forms and reports suggested that data were collected about three entities: *Sales, Inventory,* and *Supplier*. Those three entities were subsequently treated as primary data stores on the level-1 data flow diagram (Figure 6.8). Why are *Sales, Inventory,* and *Supplier* entities? Did your preliminary analysis miss any entities?

Start with the definition of an entity: an object (a person, group, place, thing, or activity) about which data are stored. Then imagine that you have just finished a preliminary study of the present system. As part of that study, you collected lists of data elements from the existing forms and reports (Figure 6.9). Those lists are a good starting point for identifying the system's entities because they identify objects about which the current system is collecting data.

Start with the sales data. Several of the sales receipt's fields describe a customer. A customer is an object. Data are collected about that object, so

> An entity is an object about which data are stored.

FIGURE 6.7
An inverted L chart is used to document the attributes associated with an entity.

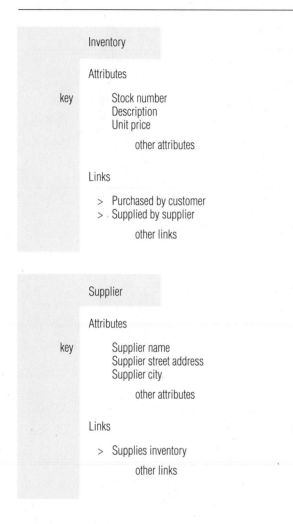

Inventory

Attributes

key   Stock number
             Description
             Unit price
                  other attributes

Links

          > Purchased by customer
          > Supplied by supplier
                  other links

Supplier

Attributes

key   Supplier name
             Supplier street address
             Supplier city
                  other attributes

Links

          > Supplies inventory
                  other links

Customer is probably an entity. (We missed that one in Chapter 5.) To put it another way, if *Customer* is not an entity, then there is no point collecting each customer's name and address.

Other data elements (*Stock number, Description,* and *Unit price*) describe a product in inventory, so *Inventory* must be a second entity and *Customer purchases Inventory* defines their relationship (Figure 6.10).

FIGURE 6.8
The data flow diagram from Chapter 5 shows three data stores, each of which is a likely entity. The data flows have been deleted from this model to make it easier to focus on the data stores.

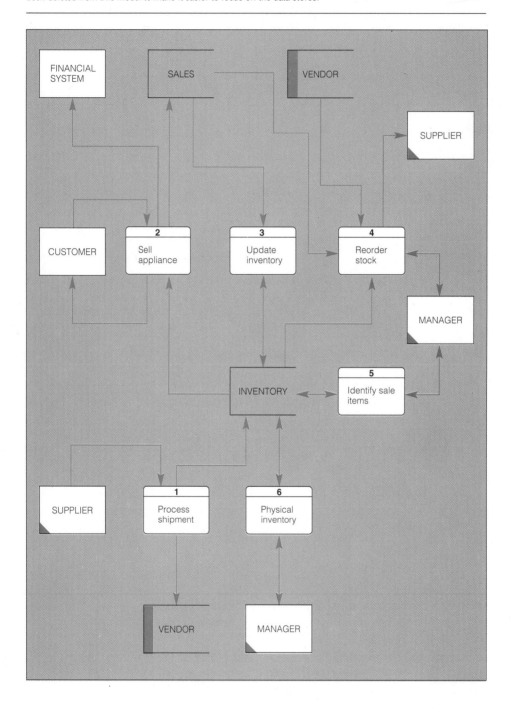

FIGURE 6.9

A list of the data elements that appear on the existing forms and reports.

Inventory Data

Price tag/sticker
Inventory file (same data)
   Manufacturer name
   Product description
   Model code
   Stock number
   Stock date
   Suggested price
   Selling price
     (Your price)

Old inventory report
   Product type
   Manufacturer
   Model
   Old stock count

Merchandise to order
   Stock number
   Description
   Reorder quantity

Physical inventory
   Product type
   Manufacturer
   Model
   Showroom stock
   Warehouse stock
   Total stock

Stock level report
   Report date
   Product type
   Manufacturer
   Model
   Start week stock
   Sales
   Received
   End week stock

Sales Data

Sales receipt
   Customer name
   Customer street
   Customer city
   Customer state
   Customer zip code
   Customer phone
   Invoice number
   Date of sale
   Stock number
   Description
   Quantity
   Unit price
     (Selling price)
   Item total
   Subtotal
   Sales tax
   Total due

Sales report
   Report date
   Product type
   Manufacturer
   Model
   Weekly sales
   Unit cost
   Product cost
   Selling price
   Revenue
   Margin
   Total product sales
   Total product cost
   Total product revenue
   Total product margin
   Total weekly sales
   Total weekly cost
   Total weekly revenue
   Total weekly margin

FIGURE 6.9
Continued

Supplier Data

Order form	Supplier invoice
Order number	Invoice number
Supplier name	Invoice date
Supplier address	Salesperson
Supplier city	Order date
Supplier state	Customer number
Supplier zip code	Ship weight
Order date	Routing
Delivery date	Terms
Ship via	Date shipped
FOB	FOB
Terms	Sold name
Model	Sold address
Product description	Sold city
Quantity	Sold state
Unit price	Sold zip code
Item amount	Sold attention
Purchasing manager	Ship name
	Ship address
	Ship city
	Ship state
	Ship zip code
	Ship attention
	Order number
	Supplier order number
	Item code
	Quantity
	Product description
	Quantity shipped
	Unit price
	Amount due
	Total due

Since one customer can purchase many products and a given product can be purchased by many customers, the relationship is many-to-many.

That accounts for several of the data elements on the old sales receipt, but *Invoice number, Date of sale, Quantity, Item total, Subtotal, Sales tax,* and *Total due* are clearly not attributes of *Customer* or *Inventory.* Instead, they describe the sale itself, so *Sales* must be another

FIGURE 6.10

The sales receipt holds data that describe a customer, one or more items from inventory, and the sale itself.

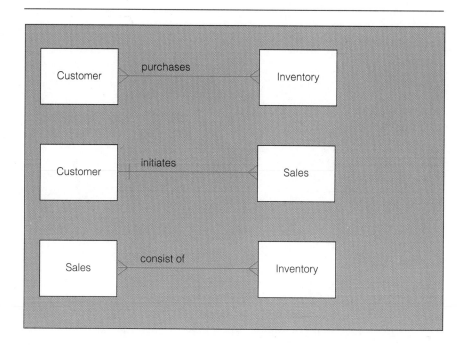

entity. The *Sales* entity is related to both *Customer* and *Inventory*. A quick review of the other sales-related documents should convince you that most of their fields describe a product in *Inventory*, are derived from *Sales*, or are computed on demand, so the existing data suggest no additional entities.

As Figure 6.10 shows, the *Sales* entity is related to the other two, as follows:

> *Customer* initiates *Sales*.
> *Sales* consist of *Inventory*.

The first relationship is one-to-many (Figure 6.11). A given *Customer* can have many *Sales* transactions, but a given *Sale* is associated with one and only one *Customer*. The second relationship is many-to-many because a

FIGURE 6.11
Customer has a one-to-many relationship with *Sales*. The relationship between *Sales* and *Inventory* is many-to-many, however, so this model is incomplete.

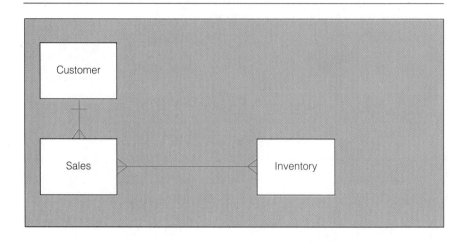

given *Sale* can include several products from *Inventory* and a given product in *Inventory* can appear in many *Sales*.

To resolve that many-to-many relationship, create a new entity, *Item sold*, that has a one-to-many relationship with both *Sales* and *Inventory* (Figure 6.12). A given *Sales* transaction can list many *Items sold,* but a given *Item sold* is associated with one and only one *Sales* transaction. A given product in *Inventory* can appear in many *Items sold,* but a given *Item sold* lists one and only one product. (Think of an *Item sold* as one line in a list of products purchased on a sales invoice.)

Note that the set of relationships described in Figure 6.12 also resolves the many-to-many relationship between *Customer* and *Inventory*. Those two entities are related through *Sales* and *Item sold,* and each of the intermediate relationships is one-to-many.

There is one possible source of confusion about the *Inventory* entity that might need clarification. A specific 19-inch color television set is an example of a single occurrence of that entity, but *Inventory* might hold 100 or more virtually identical television sets. For inventory control purposes, tracking television sets (a *class* of occurrences) is probably good enough. However, the *Customer* purchases a *specific* television set (identified,

FIGURE 6.12
Resolving the remaining many-to-many relationship calls for a new entity, *Item sold.*

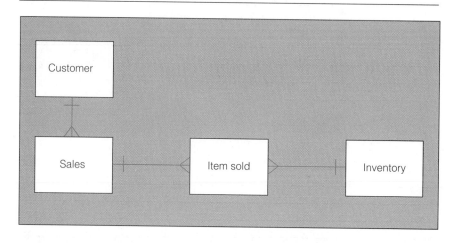

perhaps, by concatenating the serial number to the stock number). Thus a given *Item sold* lists one and only one occurrence of *Inventory.*

Once the model has been reduced to a set of one-to-many relationships, group the attributes by entity and document them as a composite item in the data dictionary (see Chapter 4). If you wish, prepare a set of inverted L charts, too.

The Supplier and Inventory Data

The supplier and inventory data (Figure 6.9) suggest a relationship between *Inventory* and *Supplier* (Figure 6.13). It is many-to-many because a given product can have many suppliers and a given supplier can supply many different products. Many-to-many relationships must be resolved, so add a new entity called *Item ordered* to the model (Figure 6.14). You now have two one-to-many relationships.

Check the relationships in Figure 6.14 and convince yourself that they really are one-to-many. Then go through the lists of data elements from the remaining documents and associate each attribute with the appropriate entity. Finally, make sure the data dictionary reflects the data structures.

Many-to-many relationships must be resolved.

FIGURE 6.13
The supplier data reveal a relationship between *Supplier* and *Inventory*.

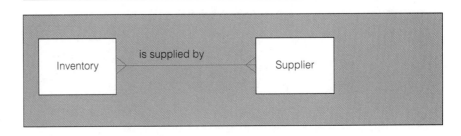

FIGURE 6.14
The many-to-many relationship can be resolved by creating a new entity called *Item ordered*.

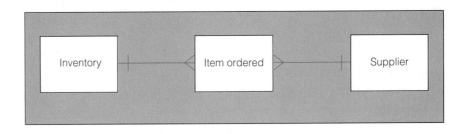

The entity called *Item ordered* will hold foreign keys that link a product to a supplier and a supplier to a product. Look for those keys as you compile the lists of attributes. *Supplier name* uniquely identifies a supplier. *Stock number* is The Appliance Store's internal inventory code, so it is probably not meaningful to the supplier, but you might concatenate *Manufacturer name* and *Model code* to uniquely identify a product. Those keys are rather clumsy, however, so ask the user if there is a product code (the UPC code might be a good one) and a supplier code. The codes might not appear on the various documents and reports, but they probably exist. The act of creating a model often tells you what questions to ask.

The act of creating a model often tells you what questions to ask.

FIGURE 6.15
The finished entity-relationship model.

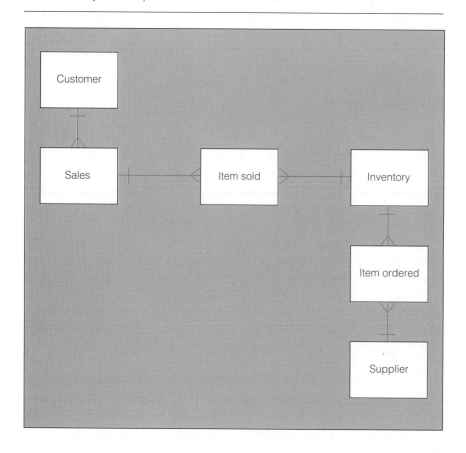

Completing the Model

The *Inventory* entity is related to both *Item sold* and *Item ordered*, so you can combine the two partial diagrams to form a single entity-relationship model (Figure 6.15). Note that the model reveals more detail about the data than the equivalent data flow diagram (Figure 6.8). Three entities (*Sales, Inventory,* and *Supplier*) appear as data stores in the data flow diagram, but *Customer* is identified only as a source/destination, and *Item sold* and *Item ordered* appear only as data flows (if at all). The entity-relationship model reveals details about the data that were not apparent when you created the data flow diagram.

Data Models and CASE

Many CASE products support both data flow diagrams and entity-relationship models. Because the data flows, data stores, entities, relationships, and data structures are all stored in the repository, you can often utilize information defined by one model as you build the other. Many CASE products also allow you to cross-reference the data flow diagram and the entity-relationship model to make sure they are consistent.

Some CASE products impose a methodology that *requires* both models. For example, as you will discover in Chapter 10, an Excelerator user creates a preliminary data flow diagram with a single data store, develops an entity-relationship model to identify the system's logical data entities, and then modifies the data flow diagram to include one data store for each entity.

If you know a great deal about the processes and very little about the data, then start with a data flow diagram. If you know a great deal about the data but not much about the processes, then start with an entity-relationship diagram. If your knowledge of both the processes and the data is sketchy, then consider starting with a prototype (see Chapter 8). In other words, start with the tool that best fits the problem, and don't try to force the problem to fit the tool.

Don't try to force the problem to fit the tool.

■   **PROFESSIONAL POINTER**

Ask Yourself Why

As you move through the system development life cycle, you will generate numerous documents and diagrams, and it is easy to become so obsessed with "dotting every i and crossing every t" that you miss the real point of the tool. The next time you are preparing documentation or constructing a model, stop and ask yourself why. If you think you are wasting your time, you are probably right. Either you don't understand the tool, or the tool is not appropriate to the application.

Data Normalization

First Normal Form

The data structures suggested by the data flow diagram and the entity-relationship diagram are preliminary. **Data normalization** is a formal technique for converting those preliminary data structures into easy-to-maintain, efficient data structures. Many CASE products include data normalization algorithms that operate on the information in the data dictionary or the repository.

The first step is to transform the preliminary data structures into **first normal form** by removing any repeating sets of data elements. Data in first normal form can be represented as one or more two-dimensional flat files that resemble simple spreadsheets (Figure 6.16). Each column holds one attribute and each row holds a single occurrence of the entity.

Data in first normal form can be represented as two-dimensional flat files.

FIGURE 6.16

If data are in first normal form, each entity can be viewed as a flat file with no repeating substructures.

	Attribute 1	Attribute 2	Attribute 3	. . .
Occurrence				
Occurrence				
Occurrence				
Occurrence				
Occurrence				
Occurrence				
Occurrence				
Occurrence				
Occurrence				

FIGURE 6.17
The *Sales* entity contains these data elements. The key field, *Invoice number,* uniquely identifies a single occurrence of this data structure.

Sales

Invoice number*
Date of sale
Customer name
Customer address
Item purchased (one or more)
   Stock number
   Description
   Quantity
   Unit price
   Item total
Subtotal
Sales tax
Total due
*The key field.

FIGURE 6.18
To put data into first normal form, move repeating substructures to new data structures.

Sales	***Item sold***
Invoice number*	*Invoice number**
Date of sale	*Stock number**
Customer name	Description
Customer address	Quantity
Subtotal	Unit price
Sales tax	Item total
Total due	
*The key field(s).	

For example, assume that Figure 6.17 is a list of the data elements associated with the entity *Sales*. (*Invoice number* is the key attribute.) A customer can purchase more than one item in a single transaction, so the set of data elements that describe an item sold might be repeated several times. To convert the sales data to first normal form, the repeating substructure must be moved to a new entity (Figure 6.18).

FIGURE 6.19
The *Inventory* entity contains these data elements.

Inventory

Stock number*
Description
Stock on hand
Reorder quantity
Reorder point
Unit price
Suppliers (one or more)
    Supplier code
    Supplier name
    Supplier address
    Reorder time
    Supplier price
*The key field.

Note that the new entity, *Item sold,* is keyed by both *Invoice number* and *Stock number.* (In other words, it has a concatenated key.) The first half of the key links the item sold to the invoice, and the second half identifies an item on that invoice, so the concatenated key uniquely identifies a specific item on a specific invoice.

The *Inventory* entity provides a second example (Figure 6.19). Its key is *Stock number.* (*Description* is another candidate key, but *Stock number* is a better choice because lengthy keys are clumsy.) Note that a given product can have more than one supplier, so the supplier data form a repeating substructure. To convert to first normal form, move the supplier data to a new entity (Figure 6.20). Key field *Stock number* appears in both entities and thus links them.

Second Normal Form

A data structure in first normal form can still cause maintenance problems if one or more data elements depend on only *part* of the key. To convert data in first normal form to **second normal form,** concentrate on those records with concatenated keys, check each nonkey attribute to see if it depends on the *entire* key, and move any data element that depends on only part of the key to a new entity.

To convert data in first normal form to second normal form, concentrate on those records with concatenated keys.

FIGURE 6.20

The *Inventory* data in first normal form.

Inventory	*Supplier*
*Stock number**	*Stock number**
Description	*Supplier code**
Stock on hand	Supplier name
Reorder quantity	Supplier address
Reorder point	Reorder time
Unit price	Supplier price
*The key field(s).	

FIGURE 6.21

The *Inventory* data in second normal form.

Inventory	*Item ordered*	*Supplier*
*Stock number**	*Stock number**	*Supplier code**
Description	*Supplier code**	Supplier name
Stock on hand	Reorder time	Supplier address
Reorder quantity	Supplier price	
Reorder point		
Unit price		
*The key field(s).		

For example, consider the data structures in Figure 6.20. The first entity, *Inventory,* has a single-attribute key, *Stock number,* so it is already in second normal form. The *Supplier* entity's key is formed by concatenating *Stock number* and *Supplier code.* Two of its attributes, *Reorder time* and *Supplier price,* depend on both keys. They are both attributes of a given product, and the *Reorder time* and *Supplier price* for a given item might vary from supplier to supplier, so they depend on *Supplier code,* too.

The other two attributes, *Supplier name* and *Supplier address,* depend only on the *Supplier code,* however, because *Stock number* does not uniquely define the supplier. A supplier might sell numerous products. If a given supplier moves to a new address, several different product/supplier records would have to be changed, and that creates a maintenance problem. Consequently, data that are unique to the supplier should be moved to a new entity (Figure 6.21).

FIGURE 6.22
The *Sales* data in second normal form. Note that the third data structure holds *Inventory* data.

Sales	**Item sold**	**Inventory**
Invoice number *	*Invoice number* *	*Stock number* *
Date of sale	*Stock number* *	Description
Customer name	Quantity	Unit price
Customer address	Item total	
Subtotal		
Sales tax		
Total due		

*The key field(s).

Consider the sales-related data next (Figure 6.18). The first data structure, *Sales,* has a single-attribute key, so it is already in second normal form. The second entity, *Item sold,* has a concatenated key (*Invoice number* plus *Stock number*), so study its data elements. *Quantity* and *Item total* are related to both *Invoice number* and *Stock number,* but *Description* and *Unit price* depend on *Stock number,* not *Invoice number.* Consequently, those two data elements must be moved to a third data structure (Figure 6.22). A quick check of Figure 6.21 should convince you that *Stock number, Description,* and *Unit price* are attributes of *Inventory.*

Third Normal Form

To be in **third normal form,** each data element in the structure must be a function of *the key, the whole key, and nothing but the key*. That definition lacks rigor, but it is easy to remember and it expresses the essence of third normal form. The process is simple: Review the structure's nonkey data elements, identify any that depend on an attribute other than the key, and move them to a new entity.

For example, consider the *Sales* data (Figure 6.22) and look at the first entity. *Customer address* depends on *Customer name,* but not on *Invoice number,* so the customer data should move to a new entity. Figure 6.23 shows the data in third normal form. *Customer code* and *Customer name* are both possible (candidate) keys for the new *Customer* entity, but the code is a better choice because two or more customers might have the same name. The fact that the *Customer code* appears in both *Sales* (as

To be in third normal form, each data element in the structure must be a function of *the key, the whole key, and nothing but the key.*

FIGURE 6.23
The data in third normal form. Note that *Description* and *Unit price* are associated with *Inventory* data.

Sales	*Customer*	*Item sold*
*Invoice number**	*Customer code**	*Invoice number**
Customer code	Customer name	*Stock number**
Date of sale	Customer address	Quantity
Subtotal		Item total
Sales tax		
Total due		

Inventory	*Item ordered*	*Supplier*
*Stock number**	*Stock number**	*Supplier code**
Description	*Supplier code**	Supplier name
Stock on hand	Reorder time	Supplier address
Reorder quantity	Supplier price	
Reorder point		
Unit price		

*The key field(s).

a foreign key) and *Customer* links a given sales transaction to a specific customer.

Quickly review the attributes associated with *Inventory, Item ordered,* and *Supplier* (Figure 6.23). In *Inventory,* all the attributes depend on the key, *Stock number,* and no attributes depend on other nonkey attributes, so no changes are necessary. In *Item ordered,* both *Reorder time* and *Supplier price* depend on the entire key and not on each other. In *Supplier,* it might be argued that *Supplier address* depends on *Supplier name,* but the code and the name are simply alternate candidate keys and the code is a better choice. These three entities are already in third normal form.

Compare Figures 6.15 (the entity-relationship model) and 6.23 and note that they identify the same six entities. Note also that the data models identify three data structures (*Customer, Item sold,* and *Item ordered*) that were not anticipated when the data flow diagram was created. Data models give you a rich understanding of the system's data requirements. You are now ready to modify the data flow diagram to reflect that understanding.

PROFESSIONAL POINTER   ■

Use Two Perspectives

When you prepare a data flow diagram, your primary focus is the processes and you build the logical data structures from the bottom up. When you prepare an entity-relationship diagram, your primary focus is the data and you build logical data structures from the top down. If you prepare *both,* you view the system from two different perspectives, and that helps to verify the models.

Data normalization is another bottom-up technique. In this chapter, you used an entity-relationship diagram to define a set of logical data structures from the top (the entities) down. Then you used data normalization to define those data structures from the bottom (a list of attributes) up. As a general rule, your confidence and understanding are enhanced any time you can reach the same conclusion from two different perspectives.

MANAGEMENT'S PERSPECTIVE   ■

Define Standards but Allow Flexibility

As a manager, should you require every analyst to use the same tools, or should you give your analysts the freedom to select the best tools for the job? The correct answer is—yes. Standards *are* important, but rigid standards are self-defeating. The idea is to define standards that everyone is *expected* to follow, but to allow some flexibility.

Be wary of the analyst who treats every job as a special case. Be equally wary of the analyst who *never* questions the standard and uses the same tools to attack every problem. Standards are important, but solutions are more important. The analyst's job is to find the right solution, not to complete the right paperwork.

If most projects seem to be nonstandard, then there really is no standard. Maybe the analysts need retraining. Maybe the standard should be scrapped and replaced by one that more analysts support. Generally, the best standards are the ones that are accepted willingly.

Summary

This chapter introduced entity-relationship diagrams. An entity is an object (a person, group, place, thing, or an activity) about which data are stored. An occurrence is a single instance of an entity. An attribute is a property of an entity. A data element is an attribute that cannot be logically decomposed. A set of related data elements forms a data structure or a data composite. The key to an entity is the attribute or group of attributes that uniquely distinguishes one occurrence from all others. A foreign key is a key to some other entity. A relationship links two entities.

Cardinality is a measure of the relative number of occurrences of two entities. In a one-to-one relationship, each occurrence of entity A is associated with one occurrence of entity B, and each occurrence of entity B is associated with one occurrence of entity A. In a one-to-many relationship, each occurrence of entity A is associated with one or more occurrences of entity B, but each occurrence of entity B is associated with only one occurrence of entity A. In a many-to-many relationship, each occurrence of entity A is associated with one or more occurrences of entity B, and each occurrence of entity B is associated with one or more occurrences of entity A.

One-to-many relationships tend to be the most stable. One-to-one relationships can often be collapsed by merging them. A many-to-many relationship can often be converted to two one-to-many relationships. Once the entity-relationship diagram is completed, an inverted L chart can be used to document the attributes associated with an entity. You should also record the entity in the data dictionary as a composite item.

Data normalization is a technique for designing easy-to-maintain, efficient logical data structures. The first step is to transform the preliminary logical data structure into first normal form by removing any repeating sets of data elements. To convert data in first normal form to second normal form, move any data element that depends on only part of a concatenated key to a separate entity. To be in third normal form, each data element in the structure must be a function of the key, the whole key, and nothing but the key.

Suggestions for Additional Reading

Chen, Peter. 1976. The entity-relationship model—towards a unified view of data. *ACM Transactions on Database Systems* 1(1):9–36.

Date, C. J. 1990. *An Introduction to Database Systems*. Vol. 1, 5th ed. Reading, MA: Addison-Wesley Publishing Company.

Dutka, Alan F., and Howard H. Hanson. 1989. *Fundamentals of Data Normalization*. Reading, MA: Addison-Wesley Publishing Company.

Martin, James, and Carma McClure. 1988. *Structured Techniques: The Basis for CASE*. Englewood Cliffs, NJ: Prentice-Hall.

McDermid, Donald C. 1990. *Software Engineering for Information Systems*. Oxford, U.K.: Blackwell Scientific Publications.

Exercises

1. Compare and contrast data flow diagrams and entity-relationship diagrams. How are they similar? How are they different? Why is it useful to know how to create both?

2. Define the terms *entity, attribute,* and *relationship*.

3. Explain cardinality.

4. Of the three types of relationships explored in this chapter, one-to-many relationships tend to be the most stable. Why do you think that is true? This question is only partially answered in the chapter, so think about it.

5. One-to-one relationships can often be collapsed by merging them. Why?

6. A many-to-many relationship can often be converted to two one-to-many relationships. Explain how. Why are the resulting one-to-many relationships considered better?

7. Compare the entity-relationship diagram (Figure 6.15) to the data flow diagram (Figure 6.8). How are they similar? How are they different? Explain both the similarities and the differences.

8. What is the purpose of data normalization?

9. Distinguish between first normal form, second normal form, and third normal form.

10. Chapter 2 introduced projects for The Print Shop, Jan Tompson's Campus Threads clothing store, and Bill Barnett's automobile dealership. Prepare an entity-relationship diagram and document the logical data structures for one or more of those projects or for your own project. Then convert the data structures to third normal form.

If the model is not consistent with reality, it is the model that must change.

7

Completing the Logical Model

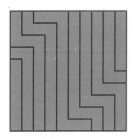

When you finish reading this chapter you should be able to:

—Modify a level-1 data flow diagram to incorporate new data stores and data flows.

—Verify the modified level-1 data flow diagram.

—Explode a process.

—Balance and verify an exploded process.

—Distinguish between global and local data.

—Define a functional primitive.

—Define the configuration item level.

—Explode a data flow diagram to the configuration item level.

—Balance and verify a complete logical model.

Modifying the Level-1 Data Flow Diagram

The entity-relationship model and the data normalization process you completed in Chapter 6 identified six data entities (Figure 7.1). Only three of those entities appear as data stores in the data flow diagram (Figure 7.2), so the three new entities (*Customer*, *Item sold*, and *Item ordered*) must be added to the logical model.

FIGURE 7.1

The data models you developed in Chapter 6 identified six data entities.

Sales	*Customer*	*Item sold*
Invoice number*	*Customer code**	*Invoice number**
Customer code	Customer name	*Stock number**
Date of sale	Customer address	Quantity
Subtotal		Item total
Sales tax		
Total due		

Inventory	*Item ordered*	*Supplier*
Stock number*	*Stock number**	*Supplier code**
Description	*Supplier code**	Suppler name
Stock on hand	Reorder time	Supplier address
Reorder quantity	Supplier price	
Reorder point		
Unit price		

*The key field(s).

The Customer Data

Consider the data associated with selling an appliance first (Figure 7.3). If you add a new data store called CUSTOMER DATA (to distinguish it from source/destination CUSTOMER) and accept a *Customer code* from CUSTOMER, *Customer name* and *Customer address* can be obtained from the new data store (Figure 7.4).

Any data that flow from a data store must first flow into that data store.

Any data that flow from a data store must first flow into that data store, so if CUSTOMER DATA exists there must be a source process. Analysis has not yet identified that process, so assume a new process called *Maintain customer* that creates, maintains, and deletes customer data (Figure 7.5). Note that if you link *Maintain customer* to CUSTOMER, you can trace *Customer name* and *Customer address* back to their source. Because the tasks performed by *Maintain customer* are unclear, you should plan follow-up interviews to more fully define it.

A quick review of the data flow diagram in Figure 7.2 should convince you that the customer data are not relevant to any of the remaining processes, so it might make sense to question the need for that new data store. If the data are simply collected and never used, perhaps the sales

FIGURE 7.2
The data flow diagram shows only three data stores.

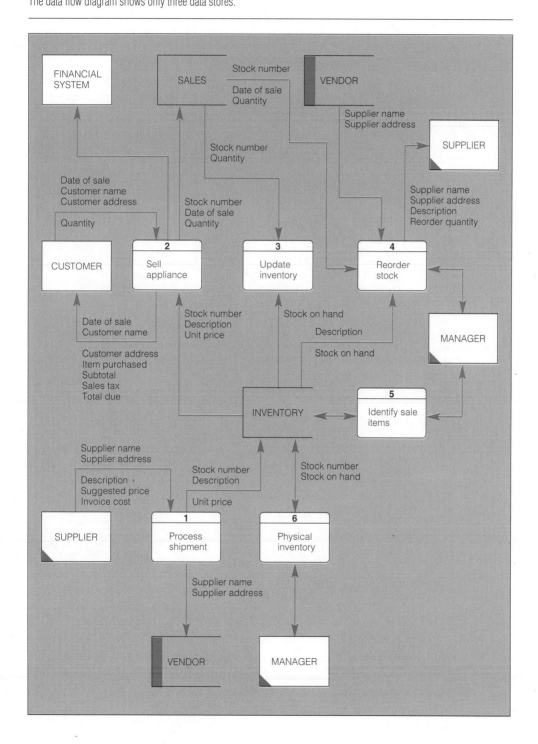

FIGURE 7.3
The data associated with selling an appliance.

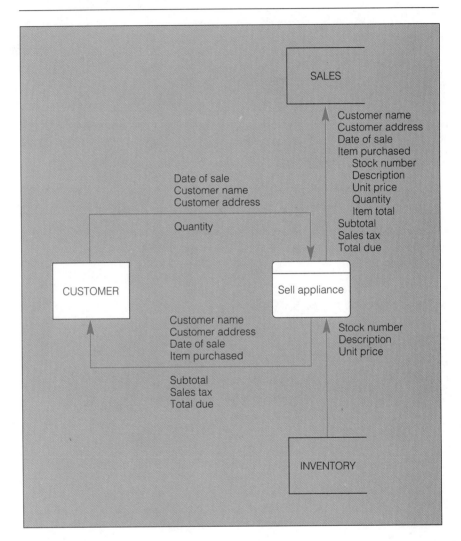

clerks can stop recording customer names and addresses. However, the fact that the data are collected suggests that they are probably necessary. Perhaps you missed yet another process. In any case, you have several more questions to ask in your next round of interviews.

FIGURE 7.4
Customer name and *Customer address* flow into *Sell appliance* from the new data store, CUSTOMER DATA.

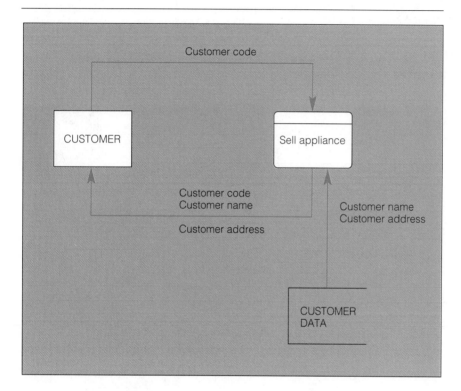

In this case, assume follow-up interviews reveal that the customer data are needed to verify returns and refunds and to address advertising mailers when The Appliance Store has a sale. Mailing advertising is a new activity that calls for a new process (Figure 7.6). Returns and refunds are part of the *Sell appliance* process, so make sure the appropriate tasks appear on the process description.

The Item Sold Data

Consider the data elements associated with *Item sold* next. Previously, all the sales data were held in SALES (Figure 7.7), but ITEM SOLD is a new data store that holds some of those data elements (Figure 7.8). Note that some of the sales data are obtained from INVENTORY, too.

FIGURE 7.5
The data that flow into CUSTOMER DATA originate with CUSTOMER.

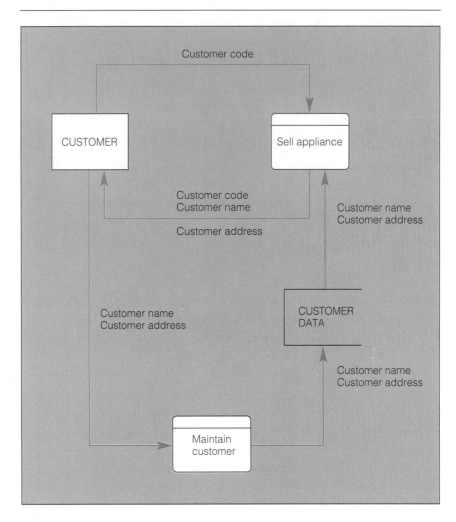

Data enter ITEM SOLD from *Sell appliance*, but where do those data elements go? One answer is back to *Sell appliance* to verify returns and refunds (Figure 7.9). A review of the data flow diagram reveals that data also flow from ITEM SOLD to two other processes, *Update inventory* and

FIGURE 7.6
Mailing advertising is a new activity that calls for a new process.

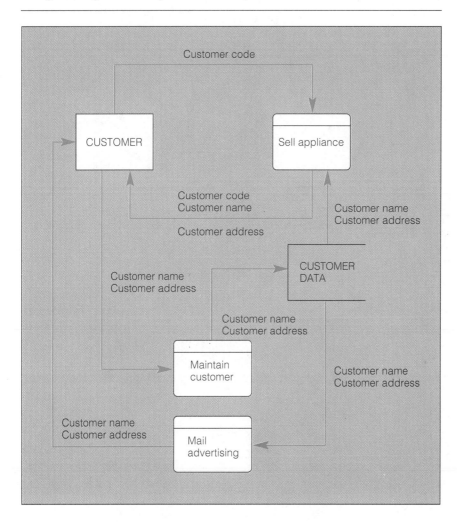

Reorder stock. Additionally, *Date of sale* flows from SALES to *Reorder stock*.

Figure 7.9 shows that all the data elements in ITEM SOLD are needed by other processes, but, except for verifying returns and refunds, *Date of sale*

FIGURE 7.7
Previously, all the sales data were held in SALES.

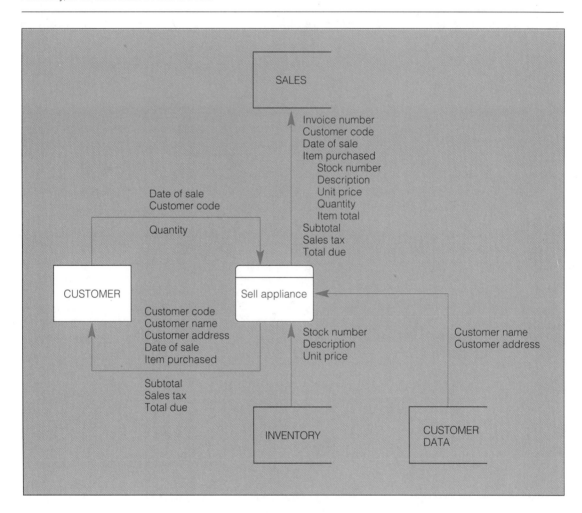

appears to be the only relevant SALES data element. Are there any other data flows from SALES?

Note that when the ITEM SOLD details are stripped from the SALES data, the remaining data structure resembles a cash flow, so the SALES

FIGURE 7.8
Item sold is a new data store that holds some of the sales-related data elements.

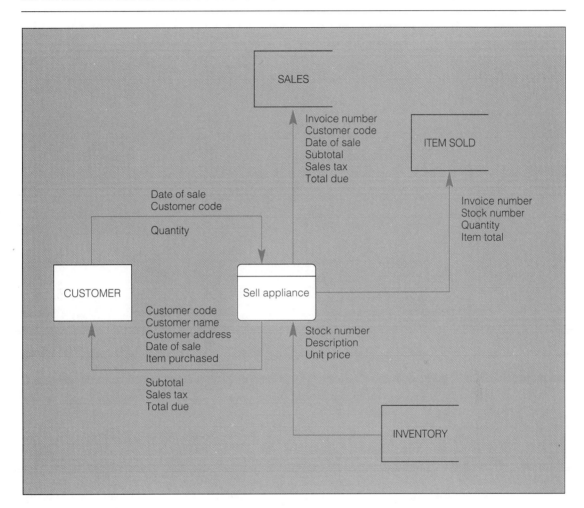

data probably flow to FINANCIAL SYSTEM. It is illegal for data to flow directly from a store to a destination, so you need an intermediate process (Figure 7.10). Defining that process might call for yet another round of interviews.

FIGURE 7.9
The data in ITEM SOLD flow to *Sell appliance*, *Update inventory*, and *Reorder stock*. The data in SALES flow to *Sell appliance* and *Reorder stock*.

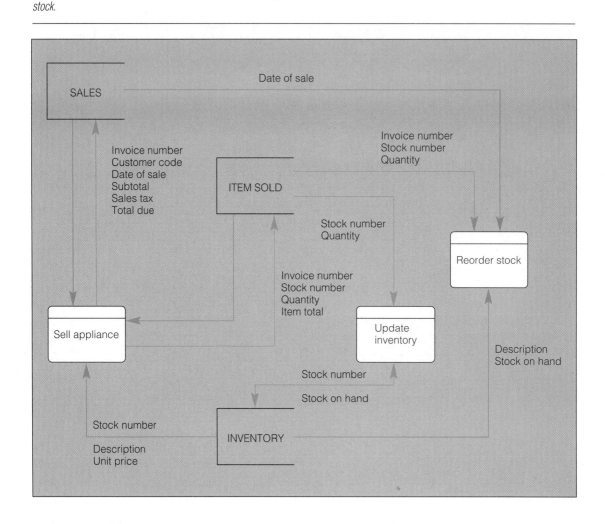

The Item Ordered Data

The new ITEM ORDERED data store lies between *Reorder stock* and *Process shipment* (Figure 7.11). It provides a link between the INVENTORY data and the VENDOR data from the time the order is placed to the time it is received by The Appliance Store, but follow-up interviews might be needed to fully define exactly how the data in ITEM ORDERED are used.

FIGURE 7.10
The SALES data flow to FINANCIAL SYSTEM through an intermediate process.

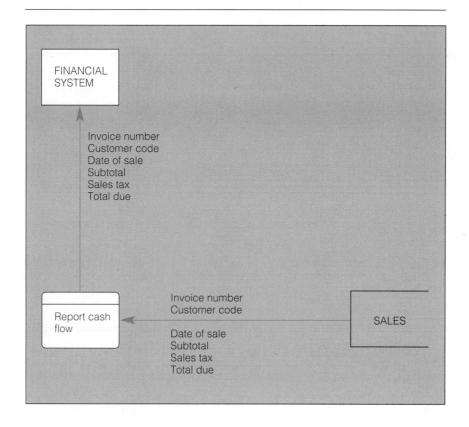

In this case, assume that Tina Temple, The Appliance Store's owner, is the interview subject and that your questions have prompted her to explain how she selects a supplier. She maintains a file of index cards that list the product, the supplier, and other key information for each item the store stocks. At reorder time, she identifies the supplier by pulling the product's index card. (The cards are filed by stock number.) Several products have more than one supplier, so she maintains a separate card for each supplier of each product. If she is dissatisfied with a supplier and decides to try a new one, she creates a new index card at reorder time based on information provided by the new supplier's sales associate.

FIGURE 7.11
The new ITEM ORDERED data store represents a pending order.

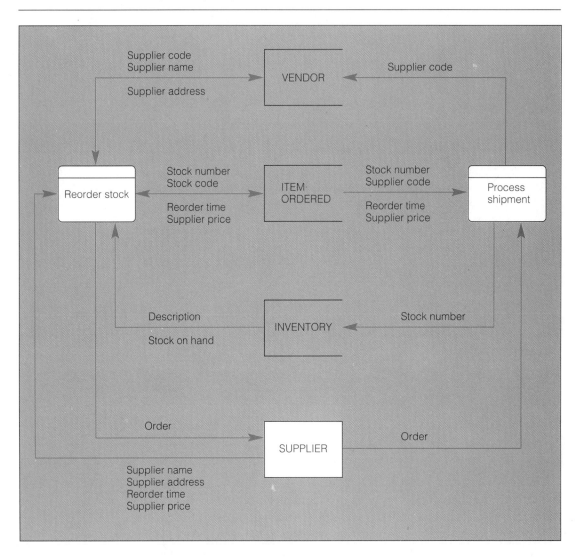

Tina's file of index cards holds much of the data in ITEM ORDERED; apparently this data store is more significant than you initially thought. The new system might make reorder decisions differently, but many of the tasks described by Tina will still be necessary. Figure 7.11 reflects your increased knowledge about reordering stock.

It is not unusual to discover new (or expanded) processes as a result of analyzing the data, nor is it unusual to discover new data as a result of analyzing processes. In this case, questions about the use of the data in ITEM ORDERED prompted your investigation. Another analyst might have observed that a given product can have several suppliers and asked Tina to explain how she selects a supplier. The answer probably would have revealed the need for something like the ITEM ORDERED data store. The questions that arise during analysis are just as important as the answers.

The questions that arise during analysis are just as important as the answers.

PROFESSIONAL POINTER   ■

Be Willing to Make Changes

Analysis is an iterative process. Unless you are incredibly skilled (or extremely lucky), your understanding of the system *will* change as you learn more about it. If you discover something about the system that is inconsistent with your model, it is the model, not reality, that must change.

If you are using CASE, the changes described in this chapter are relatively easy to make. If you prepared the model by hand, however, you might hesitate to scrap your old data flow diagram and draw a new one. The easier it is to make changes, the more willingly you will make them. To this point, using CASE may have seemed more trouble than it was worth. It is when you must change your model that you begin to sense the advantages of using software and graphical tools.

Verifying the Model

Figure 7.12 shows a modified level-1 data flow diagram that incorporates the new data stores, data flows, and processes. Assume that each of the new data elements, data composites, and processes has been recorded in the data dictionary or repository.

Any change to a model, no matter how minor, can have ripple effects, so it is important that you reverify the model. Start by searching for any missing algorithms. Once again, compare a given process's input data to its

Any change to a model, no matter how minor, can have ripple effects.

FIGURE 7.12
The modified data flow diagram.

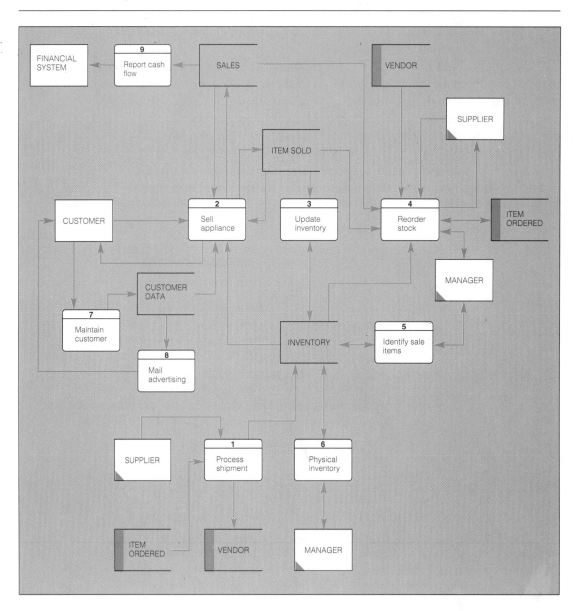

output data; if they are different, that process must contain an algorithm. Make sure the algorithm is documented in the appropriate process description. Remember that any new subprocess might imply new data elements.

Before you begin the formal verification process, make sure that the data flow diagram does *not* limit you to a specific physical implementation. A good strategy is to visualize a manual solution and a computer-based solution. If something in the data flow diagram makes either alternative impossible, then the model is not sufficiently general and it should be changed.

Formal verification comes next. Start by checking syntax. Every data flow must have at least one arrowhead and must begin and/or end with a process. Every process and every data store must have at least one input and at least one output data flow. If possible, use your CASE package's syntax-checking routine; it can save you a great deal of time.

Once again, rigorously trace each data element from its destination back to its source. If you can find the source of *every* data element, your data flow diagram is internally consistent and you can be reasonably confident of its accuracy. If you cannot find the source of one or more data elements, then something is missing. Data tracing is another task that is best performed by CASE software.

Data tracing is best performed by CASE software.

The final verification step is to cross-reference the data flow diagram, the data dictionary, and the process descriptions. Each data element, data store, and data flow must appear in the data dictionary, and each process must have a matching process description. Every data element and data composite in the data dictionary must appear in the data flow diagram and in at least one process description. Each process description must match a process on the data flow diagram, the input and output lists must match the appropriate data flows, and each input or output data element or composite must appear in the data dictionary. Finally, check the logical model against the system objectives and identify the process or processes that contribute to meeting each one.

As before, the final test is to review the data flow diagram with the user. This time, focus on the new components and ask the user about them. Often, you and the user will wonder how you missed those stores, flows, and processes the first time. Other changes seem to raise as many questions as they answer, however, so be prepared for yet another round of analysis.

Exploding the Processes

The Level-2 Data Flow Diagram

Each level-1 process consists of several subprocesses that are listed on the process description. Once the level-1 data flow diagram is completed and verified, the next step is to **explode** the processes. The basic idea is to draw an independent level-2 data flow diagram for each level-1 process. The act of exploding a data flow diagram is sometimes called **functional decomposition**.

For example, consider process 4, *Reorder stock*. A preliminary process description (Figure 7.13) lists 18 subprocesses. Some are the original tasks that were combined to form *Reorder stock* in Chapter 5. Each data flow represents at least one input or output operation, and those operations account for the next several subprocesses. The last three subprocesses were suggested by the interview with Tina. Assume that reorder decisions are made by computing the *Expected sales* (average sales per day times the supplier's *Reorder time*), subtracting that value from the current *Stock on hand*, and then comparing the result to the *Reorder point*.

Figure 7.14 shows how the subprocesses might be combined to form six primary tasks. The first one, *Communicate with manager*, provides data to the other five and contains little more than input and output instructions, so it belongs at a lower level. That leaves five major subprocesses. Figure 7.15 shows the level-2 data flow diagram for process 4. Note the numbering scheme. Processes 4.1, 4.2, 4.3, 4.4, and 4.5 are subprocesses of level-1 process 4.

The processes in Figure 7.15 are linked through data stores. You might have considered linking several of those processes with data flows because you can probably visualize writing a computer program in which you *Analyze sales data*, *Compute expected sales*, *Analyze inventory data*, *Make reorder decision*, and *Generate reorder*. There are other ways to perform these tasks, however, and placing stores between processes tends to produce a more general model. Note that the subsystem modeled in Figure 7.15 could be implemented as five independent batch processes, a single interactive program with intermediate data held in REORDER DATA, or even a series of manual procedures with notes written on a legal pad. Note also that ITEM ORDERED could be Tina's index card file.

To explode the processes, draw an independent level-2 data flow diagram for each level-1 process.

FIGURE 7.13   *179*

The inputs to, outputs from, and tasks performed by Process 4, *Reorder stock*.

Data in
SALES
  Date of sale
ITEM SOLD
  Invoice number
  Stock number
  Quantity
INVENTORY
  Description
  Stock on hand
  Reorder quantity
  Reorder point
VENDOR
  Supplier name
  Supplier address
ITEM ORDERED
  Supplier code
  Reorder time
  Supplier price
SUPPLIER (Source)
  Supplier name
  Supplier address
  Reorder time
  Supplier price

Data out
SUPPLIER
  (Destination)
  Supplier name
  Supplier address
  Description
  Reorder quantity
ITEM ORDERED
  Stock number
  Supplier code
  Reorder time
  Supplier price
VENDOR
  Supplier code
  Supplier name
  Supplier address

Local data
Expected sales
Sales per day

Tasks or activities
From Chapter 5:   1. Prepare sales report.
                   2. Retrieve supplier invoice.
                   3. Reorder stock.
                   4. Type reorder.
                   5. Get mailing address.
                   6. Prepare stock level report.
From data flows: 7. Get sales data.
                   8. Get item sold data.
                   9. Get inventory data.
                  10. Send reorder to supplier.
                  11. Communicate with manager.
                  12. Get item ordered data.
                  13. Create item ordered.
                  14. Create vendor data.
                  15. Get data from supplier.
New tasks: 16. Compute expected sales.
                  17. Make reorder decision.
                  18. Select supplier.

FIGURE 7.14
The tasks performed by process 4 can be combined to form six primary tasks.

Subprocess	Contains
Communicate with manager	Communicate with manager.
Analyze sales data	Get sales data.
	Get item sold data.
	Retrieve supplier invoice.
	Prepare sales report.
Analyze inventory data	Get inventory data.
	Prepare stock level report.
Make reorder decision	Make reorder decision.
	Get item ordered data.
	Create item ordered.
	Select supplier.
	Create vendor data.
	Get data from supplier.
Compute expected sales	Compute expected sales.
Reorder stock	Reorder stock.
	Type reorder.
	Get mailing address.
	Send reorder to supplier.

Local and Global Data

Data stores INVENTORY, SALES, SALE ITEM, and VENDOR appeared on the level-1 data flow diagram, but REORDER DATA did not. The new data store holds local data known only inside process 4, while the other data stores hold global data. That distinction is an important one.

Global data are shared by two or more higher-level processes. **Local data** are known within only one part of the system; intermediate computations are a good example. In this case, the data elements stored in RE-ORDER DATA (for example, *Expected sales*) are known only within the level-2 explosion of process 4 (and its subprocesses). Mistakes made while working with local data tend to be limited in scope, but global data errors can ripple throughout the system.

Local data elements should be recorded in the data dictionary and identified as local. If they already exist, they might not be local; perhaps a global data element was overlooked.

Mistakes made while working with local data tend to be limited in scope, but global data errors can ripple throughout the system.

FIGURE 7.15
A level-2 explosion of process 4.

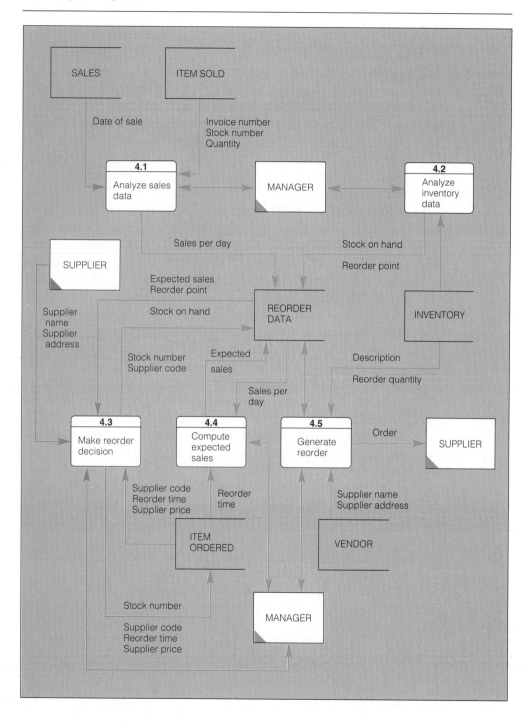

Balancing the Level-2 Explosion

An exploded data flow diagram must be **balanced**. An explosion is considered balanced if you can account for each input from and each output to the parent level. Start by moving up one level (in this case, from level 2 to level 1) and identify each data flow that enters or leaves the target process. For example, in Figure 7.12 data enter process 4, *Reorder stock,* from SALES, ITEM SOLD, ITEM ORDERED, INVENTORY, VENDOR, MANAGER, and SUPPLIER, and data flow from process 4 to MANAGER, SUPPLIER, and ITEM ORDERED.

Next move to the exploded data flow diagram (Figure 7.15) and list the data elements that compose each level-1 input and output data flow. Make sure every input global data element or composite is used by one or more subprocesses. Make sure every output global data element or composite is either input to the explosion or generated by an algorithm within a subprocess. Local data (by definition) are neither input to nor output from the level-2 data flow diagram, but you must be able to account for the algorithms that create and use them. Checking to ensure that an explosion is balanced is similar to tracing data elements from their destination (output) back to their source (input). Once again, CASE software can help.

Once the explosion is balanced, rewrite the level-1 process description for *Reorder stock,* replacing the several steps in Figure 7.13 with the five primary subprocesses (Figure 7.16). Then prepare process descriptions for 4.1, 4.2, 4.3 (Figure 7.17), 4.4, and 4.5. The act of defining those subprocesses may reveal local data elements and data components, and those data must be recorded in the data dictionary. When you finish documenting the explosion, cross reference the data flow diagram, the data dictionary, and the subprocess descriptions to make sure the model is internally consistent.

Exploding to Lower Levels

A **functional primitive** is a process (or transform) that requires no further decomposition. If the level-2 process descriptions are functional primitives, you have decomposed the data flow diagram far enough. The process description for a functional primitive is sometimes called a **mini-spec**.

It follows that if a given level-2 subprocess description is *not* a functional primitive you must explode it to level 3, but how do you identify a functional primitive? There are several tests you can use. If a given process

FIGURE 7.16
A process description for process 4, *Reorder stock.*

PROCESS DESCRIPTION

SYSTEM: Inventory
PROCESS: 4, Reorder stock
DATE: April 12, 1994

Data in
Date of sale
Invoice number
Stock number
Quantity
Description
Stock on hand
Reorder quantity
Reorder point
Supplier name
Supplier address
Supplier code
Reorder time
Supplier price

Data out
Supplier name
Supplier address
Description
Reorder quantity
Stock number
Supplier code
Reorder time
Supplier price
Supplier code
Supplier name
Supplier address

Tasks or activities
Analyze sales data
Analyze inventory data
Make reorder decision
Compute expected sales
Reorder stock

Local data
Expected sales
Sales per day

FIGURE 7.17
A preliminary process description for process 4.3.

PROCESS DESCRIPTION

SYSTEM: Inventory
PROCESS: 4.3, Make reorder decision
DATE: April 12, 1994

Data in
Stock number
Expected sales
Reorder point
Supplier name
Supplier address
Reorder time
Supplier price
Supplier code

Data out
Stock number
Supplier code
Supplier name
Supplier address
Reorder time
Supplier price
Stock number

Tasks or activities
Make reorder decision
Get reorder data (local)
Get item ordered data
Select supplier
Create item ordered
Get data from supplier
Create vendor data
Generate reorder data
Communicate with manager

Local data
Expected sales
Sales per day

description lists program instructions or simple sequence, decision, and repetitive logic blocks, you have probably gone far enough. If the sub-processes in the explosion are linked by data flows (rather than data stores), they communicate directly with each other and are probably part of the same routine. (Data flow diagrams are flexible, but there are better tools for designing programs.) If, on the other hand, one or more of the process description steps seems unclear, explode it. Note that there is some judgment involved. When in doubt, explode to the next level.

For example, Figure 7.18 shows an explosion of process 4.1, *Analyze sales data*. The level-3 subprocesses are identified by a digit in the hundredths position: 4.11, 4.12, 4.13, and so on. Subsequently, 4.12 might decompose into processes 4.121, 4.122, 4.123, and so on. In this case, however, the level-3 processes clearly represent discrete input, output, and processing steps, so they are functional primitives. (Indeed, process 4.1 may have been decomposed one level too far.)

The Configuration Item Level

The functional primitives and the data stores that appear at the lowest level of decomposition are called **configuration items**. A configuration item is a *composite* rather than a specific physical component; for example, a composite item might represent a program *and* the computer on which it runs or a database *and* the device on which it resides. If you decompose a configuration item, you move inside a specific hardware, software, or data component. You will deal with those components during design. Also, configuration items are general; you should be able to imagine implementing one manually or on a computer. In a complete logical model, all the processes are decomposed down to the **configuration item level**, an imaginary line that links the system's configuration items (Figure 7.19).

> If you decompose a configuration item, you move inside a specific hardware, software, or data component.

The Logical Model

A logical model consists of a complete set of leveled data flow diagrams (Figure 7.20), a data dictionary, and one process description for each process at each level down to the configuration item level. Note that some processes will be exploded only to level 2, others to level 3, and so on, so

FIGURE 7.18
A level-3 explosion of process 4.1, *Analyze sales data.*

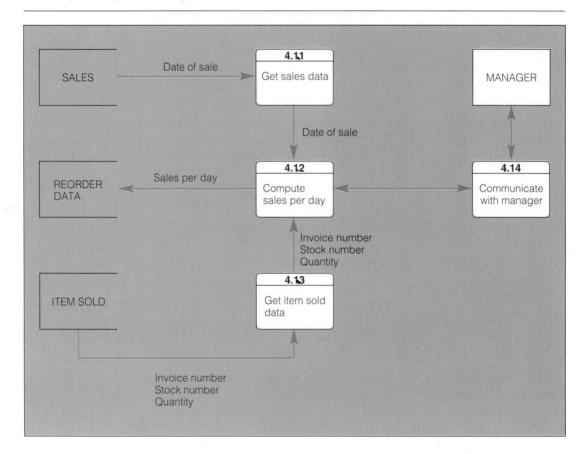

the configuration item level does not necessarily correspond to a single, consistent data flow diagram level. In Figure 7.20, a dashed line marks the configuration item level. Note that it moves back and forth between levels 2 and 3.

The documentation package for a large system can be quite lengthy. Processes above the configuration item level are purely logical, so their process descriptions consist of little more than lists of subprocesses. Those subprocesses can be obtained from the exploded data flow diagram, so

FIGURE 7.19
The configuration level defines an imaginary line that links the system's configuration items.

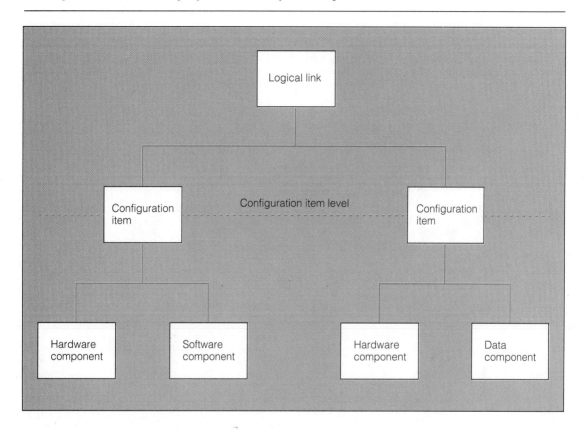

some organizations exclude process descriptions above the configuration item level from the finished model. The act of listing each process's data flows and subprocesses still helps you plan and verify the developing data flow diagram, however.

The configuration item level processes will become the system's programs and procedures. The data stores will become files and databases. The data flows will become reports, screens, forms, and dialogues. Above

The configuration item level processes will become the system's programs and procedures.

FIGURE 7.20
The logical model consists of a complete set of leveled data flow diagrams supported by a data dictionary and one process description for each process at each level.

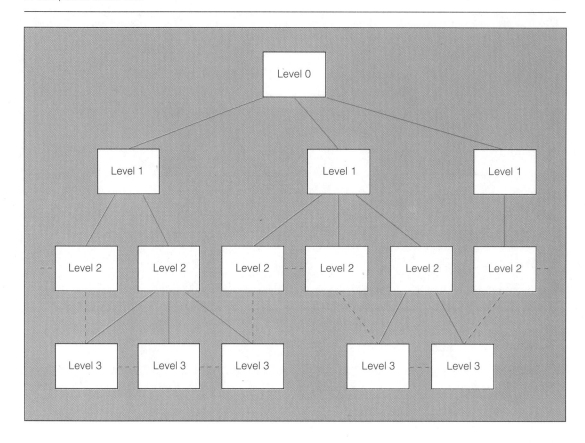

the configuration item level, the logical relationships between the components support planning, coordination, and control.

Once the complete logical model is finished, verify it. Work through the model once again and look for missing algorithms. Convince yourself one more time that the data flow diagram does *not* limit you to a specific physical implementation. Check the data flow diagram for syntax errors. Rigorously trace each level-1 data element from its destination back to its source, and carefully balance each lower-level process.

Then cross-reference the data flow diagram, the data dictionary, and the process descriptions, and identify the process or processes that contribute to meeting each objective. (If you have not yet learned to appreciate CASE, you will now.)

The final model is often subject to a more formal review called an **inspection**. The inspection is usually conducted by a team of technical personnel and (perhaps) user representatives who methodically work through the documentation looking for errors. The intent is to ensure that the work is technically sound and consistent with the system's objectives. A successful inspection certifies technical quality and helps to ensure that the component actually performs the necessary function.

A successful inspection certifies technical quality.

A walkthrough can be viewed as an informal inspection. In many organizations, programmers regularly "walk through" each others' code as a means of finding logical errors. Before presenting documentation to an inspection team or to management, many analysts, designers, and programmers conduct a walkthrough to fine-tune their presentation.

Inspections and walkthrough will be covered in greater detail in Chapter 19.

PROFESSIONAL POINTER ■

Good Tools Carry Over

The fact that the information in the data flow diagram, the process descriptions, and the data dictionary carries over from analysis to design is significant. Professional people resent preparing documentation that is simply reviewed and then discarded. Developing a complete logical model is hard work. The fact that the results can be used in subsequent steps makes the job a bit more palatable. Carry over from step to step is an attribute of a good tool.

MANAGEMENT'S PERSPECTIVE ■

Encourage Change

As the analysts learn more and more about a system, the logical model *will* change. As a manager, you might be tempted to ask an analyst preparing the third or fourth iteration of a data flow diagram why the job was not done right the first time. Avoid that temptation.

People tend to do things that earn rewards and to avoid things that bring criticism. If you criticize changes, your analysts will avoid making changes. If reality conflicts with the model, they will argue that reality, not the model, is wrong. They will defend their preliminary ideas rather than search for the user's requirements. They will find reasons to reject the user's suggestions because accepting these suggestions means changing the model. The result will probably be a bad system. If you want the job done right, find a way to reward change, not punish it.

Impediments to change discourage change. A graphical interface and software that can trace ripple effects makes it easy to change a model, and if changes are easy to make, they are more likely to be made. One of the most important things management can do to encourage good systems analysis is to provide the analysts with the right tools and the training to use those tools effectively. If your organization does not already use CASE, start planning the conversion now.

Summary

After you finish analyzing the data, revise the level-1 data flow diagram to reflect the new data structures and then reverify the model. The next step is to explode the model by preparing a level-2 data flow diagram for each level-1 process. The act of exploding a data flow diagram is sometimes called functional decomposition.

Global data are shared by two or more higher level processes. Local data are known only within one part of the system. An explosion is considered balanced if you can account for each input from and each output to the next higher level. A functional primitive is a process (or transform) that requires no further decomposition. The process description for a functional primitive is sometimes called a mini-spec. If a given level-2 subprocess description is *not* a functional primitive, explode it to level 3.

The functional primitives and the data stores that appear at the lowest level of decomposition are called configuration items. In a complete logical model, all the processes are decomposed down to the configuration item level. The final model is often subject to a formal review called an inspection. A walkthrough is an informal inspection.

Suggestions for Additional Reading

DeMarco, Tom. 1978. *Structured Analysis and System Specification*. New York: Yourdon, Inc.

Freedman, Daniel P., and Gerald M. Weinberg. 1982. *Handbook of Walkthroughs, Inspections, and Technical Reviews*. Boston: Little, Brown and Company, Inc.

Gane, Chris. 1987. *Rapid System Development*. New York: Rapid System Development, Inc.

Gane, Chris, and Trish Sarson. 1979. *Structured Systems Analysis: Tools and Techniques*. Englewood Cliffs, NJ: Prentice-Hall, Inc.

Ince, Darrel, and Derek Andrews. 1990. *The System Life Cycle*. London: Butterworths.

Thayer, Richard H., and Merlin Dorfman. 1990. *System and Software Requirements Engineering*. Los Alamitos, CA: IEEE Computer Society Press.

Yourdon, Edward, and Larry L. Constantine. 1979. *Structured Design*. Englewood Cliffs, NJ: Prentice-Hall, Inc.

Exercises

1. Why is it necessary to modify a preliminary data flow diagram to reflect the results of data analysis?

2. Even minor changes to a model sometimes cause ripple effects in other parts of the model. What are ripple effects? Cite some examples. Why are they important?

3. In the text, process 4, *Reorder stock,* was decomposed to level 2. Follow the same process to decompose process 2, *Sell appliance* (see Figure 5.13 for its process description).

4. Prepare process descriptions for one or more of the processes in Figure 7.12, and then decompose the process or processes to level 2. Choose processes other than 2 and 4.

5. Distinguish between global and local data. Why is that distinction important?

6. Explain what it means to balance a data flow diagram.

7. A logical model should be exploded to the configuration item level. Why? Exactly what is the configuration item level?

8. Describe the contents of a complete logical model.

9. Using Figure 7.17 as a guide, decompose process 4.3.

10. Chapter 2 introduced projects for The Print Shop, Jan Tompson's Campus Threads clothing store, and Bill Barnett's automobile dealership. In previous chapters you prepared a preliminary data flow diagram and a set of data models for one or more of those projects. Modify the data flow diagram to reflect the results of your data analysis. Then explode each of the processes to the configuration item level and complete the model documentation.

Most prototypes are written to be thrown away.

8

Prototyping

When you finish reading this chapter, you should be able to:

—Explain the prototyping process.

—Explain joint application development.

—Discuss bottom-up prototype development.

—Discuss the strengths and weaknesses of prototyping.

The Prototyping Process

It is not always possible to obtain all the information you need to create a complete logical model just by conducting interviews and studying the present system. Some processes are difficult to explain; for example, Tina might not be able to articulate precisely how her feel for the marketplace influences her reorder decisions. Another problem is that many people have difficulty conceptualizing their needs. Some are intimidated by technology. Others simply do not visualize things in cause-and-effect terms. Still others are so deeply immersed in details that they cannot see the patterns.

In such cases, **prototyping** is a powerful alternative or supplement to logical modeling. The basic idea is to build a reasonably complete, working, *physical* model (or **prototype**) of the system. As a minimum, the analyst can use screen painters, menu builders, and report generators to prepare a "slide show" of sample screens, dialogues, and reports. In a more complete prototype, preliminary versions of the system's programs are written in a fourth-generation language such as dBASE, FOCUS, or Lotus 1-2-3.

The user interacts with the prototype.

The prototyping process can be viewed as a loop (Figure 8.1). Following preliminary analysis, a first draft of the prototype is created. The user then interacts with the prototype and identifies its strengths and weaknesses. Assuming that the first draft is less than totally acceptable, the prototype is modified to reflect the user's suggestions and the user interacts with the new, improved version. The refine-and-test cycle continues until the user is satisfied.

The emphasis is on quick turnaround.

The emphasis is on quick turnaround, with changes made on the spot or within at most a few days. Instead of conceptualizing needs, the users work with and react to the prototype and the analyst observes and interprets their reactions. To many people, manipulating a working model seems more natural than answering questions in an interview. Prototyping is particularly valuable on projects with long development times because the user gets to see something physical.

Sometimes, the prototyping process continues until a finished system emerges (Figure 8.1). Usually, however, the purpose of the prototype is to clarify the system's requirements. The tasks and queries performed by the prototype demonstrate what the system must do; they translate into processes. Screens, dialogues, menus, reports, files, and databases represent the logical data structures. Once the requirements are defined, design begins and the prototype is thrown away.

Prototyping can replace logical modeling, but these two techniques are not mutually exclusive. At least some preliminary analysis must be done before the initial prototype can be developed, and the techniques for creating a logical model are an effective way to start. Also, prototyping can be used to define the contents of selected portions of a logical model when the interviews hit a dead end. In other words, prototyping is an analysis tool.

Many CASE products support prototyping. Screen painters, menu builders, report generators, fourth generation languages, and executable

FIGURE 8.1
Prototyping is a cyclic process.

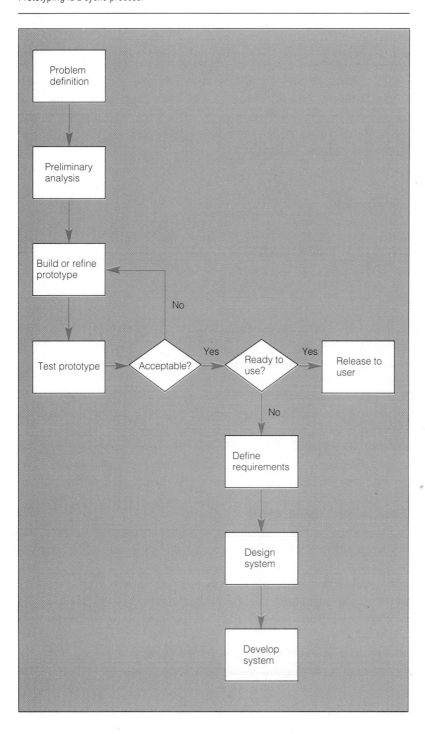

specification languages are popular tools. The primary advantage of CASE-based prototyping is derived from the repository. Given a logical model or a data model, data elements can be extracted from the repository and placed on a screen or inserted into a report. New data elements and processes suggested by the prototype can be recorded in the repository and later incorporated into a model. Because of the repository, all these analysis tools can support each other.

■   **PROFESSIONAL POINTER**

The User Is the Expert

Many years ago, an analysis team was assigned to develop an on-line labor data collection system. The primary user contact was an old timekeeper. He knew timekeeping inside and out, and there was no way the new system could have been created without him. Unfortunately, he knew very little about computers. The solution was to create a prototype.

A preliminary version of the data collection program was written and a selected group of employees began reporting their work through the on-line terminals. Most of the transactions were processed smoothly by the new system, but perhaps 10 percent were beyond the prototype. The exceptions were routed to the expert, and his corrections were captured and analyzed for patterns.

When a pattern was identified, the logic to handle that particular exception was added to the prototype. Gradually, fewer and fewer transactions slipped through the model. When the error rate dropped below 1 percent, the prototype was declared acceptable and the final version of the program was planned and written. The project was a success largely because the prototype allowed the analysts to capture the user's expertise in the user's own terms.

Joint Application Development

Interviewing is the weakest link in the traditional systems analysis process.

Interviewing is perhaps the weakest link in the traditional systems analysis process. For one thing, it tends to favor the most outspoken people. Interviews are usually conducted one on one, so users have no opportunity to interact with each other. Also, because the analyst drives the interviewing process, any bias he or she might have is likely to show up in the final specifications.

Joint application development, or **JAD,** is an alternative to traditional interviewing that is particularly valuable when a prototype is to be developed. The affected analysts and users attend an intense three- or four-day meeting. During this meeting, user needs are discussed, debated, and documented. Users can respond to other users and ask follow-up questions. When conflicting requirements call for trade-offs, the reasons are clear to all.

At the end of the JAD session, the participants sign a document summarizing the agreements they have reached. Some time later, when the prototype or the finished specifications are presented for approval, they can be linked to the JAD session. Consequently, there is a much better chance that the users will really understand the specifications.

Perhaps the most important advantage of joint application development is that it gives the users a sense of ownership in the system. They helped design it, so it reflects their needs. Even a mediocre system can be made to work if the users believe in it. Conversely, even an outstanding system can fail if the users reject it.

Creating a Prototype

The best way to grasp prototyping is through an example. The next several pages show portions of a prototype inventory system written in FOCUS, a fourth-generation language marketed by Information Builders Incorporated. The point of this discussion is to illustrate prototyping, *not* to teach you FOCUS, so many syntax details will be ignored. Still, you should be able to follow the sample code.

Bottom-up Development

The first step in creating a prototype is to conduct a preliminary analysis and define at least some of the key processes and data structures. You did that in Chapters 4 and 5; Figures 8.2 and 8.3 show the logical processes and data groupings that were used to prepare the level-1 data flow diagram.

Once preliminary analysis is complete, the prototype is developed **bottom up.** Start by viewing each function or process as a black box (Figure 8.4) and write an independent, single-task program for each one. Then ask

The prototype is developed bottom up.

FIGURE 8.2
The Appliance Store's inventory system performs these primary tasks.

Process	Trigger Event	Contains	Process Name
1	Shipment arrives	Fill out price tag Attach price sticker File price tag Assign stock number Note supplier on price tag Note stock number on invoice File supplier invoice	*Process shipment*
2	Customer makes purchase	Sell appliance Fill out sales receipt Give receipt to customer Remove price sticker	*Sell appliance*
3	End of day	Collect sales receipts Match tag to inventory Update stock levels	*Update inventory*
4	End of week	Prepare sales report Retrieve supplier invoice Reorder stock Type reorder Get mailing address Prepare stock level report	*Reorder stock*
5	End of month	Prepare old inventory list Identify sale items	*Identify sale items*
6	End of quarter	Perform physical inventory	*Perform physical inventory*

the appropriate users to test those small programs, collect their suggestions, improve the single-function prototypes, and test them again.

Eventually, you will reach the point where the users are satisfied with the functions. The next step is to write a control structure to combine functions to form a prototype system. Then you test the system until the users are satisfied with it.

Because most prototypes are designed to be thrown away, you can take several shortcuts. For example, error processing, data screening, and

FIGURE 8.3
The Appliance Store's inventory system stores data about these entities.

Data About	Contains
INVENTORY	Price tag
	Inventory
	Old inventory report
	Merchandise to order
	Stock level report
	Physical inventory
SALES	Sales receipt
	Sales report
SUPPLIERS	Supplier invoice
	Order form

exception handling account for a significant percentage of a production program's logic, but simply *recognizing* problems and printing or displaying error messages is often adequate in a prototype. If you can recognize an error or an exception, you can always add the logic to deal with it later.

Security checks and auditing procedures can also be streamlined. For example, a prototype's log-on routine might request a user number and a password but accept anything the user types, and a good way to simulate an audit trail is to print messages that identify key audit points. The idea is to build reminders of such requirements into the prototype but to postpone the detailed implementation until later. Remember that the objective is to define what happens. You can worry about exactly how to implement the functions later.

Most prototypes are designed to be thrown away.

Defining the Data Structures

Before you can begin writing the prototype, you must define your data. Figure 8.5 shows the data structures for the inventory and sales files as they might be coded in FOCUS. (The boxes were added to help you visualize key data groupings.) The field names are similar to dBASE, Pascal, or COBOL field names. A FORMAT specification defines each field's data type

FIGURE 8.4
Start by viewing each function as an independent black box.

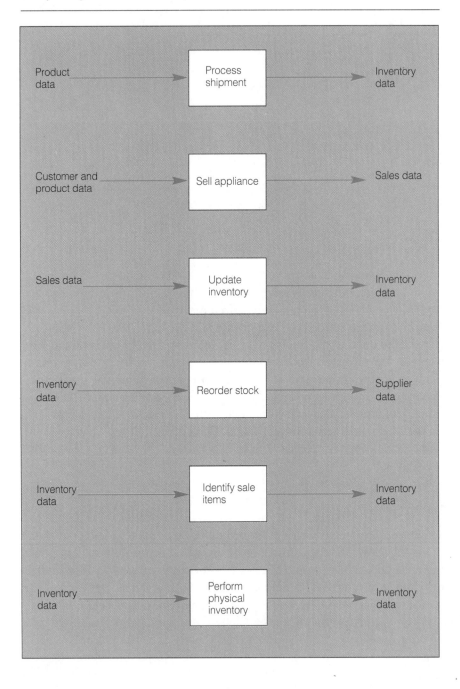

FIGURE 8.5
The first step in writing the prototype is to define your data.

```
FILE=INVEN, SUFFIX=FOC

  SEGMENT=PRODUCT,SEGTYPE=S1
    FIELD=PRODUCT_CODE     ,FORMAT=A10 ,INDEX=I    ,$
    FIELD=MANUFACTURER     ,FORMAT=A20            ,$
    FIELD=MODEL            ,FORMAT=A8             ,$
    FIELD=DESCRIPTION      ,FORMAT=A50            ,$
    FIELD=LIST_PRICE       ,FORMAT=P7.2           ,$
    FIELD=SELL_PRICE       ,FORMAT=P7.2           ,$
    FIELD=STOCK_ON_HAND    ,FORMAT=I3             ,$
    FIELD=REORDER_POINT    ,FORMAT=I3             ,$
```

```
FILE=SALES, SUFFIX=FOC

  SEGMENT=TRANS, SEGTYPE=S1
    FIELD=CUST_CODE        ,FORMAT=I6 ,INDEX=I     ,$
    FIELD=CUST_NAME        ,FORMAT=A20            ,$
    FIELD=SALESPERSON      ,FORMAT=A20            ,$
    FIELD=DATE_OF_SALE     ,FORMAT=A6YMD          ,$
    FIELD=SUBTOTAL         ,FORMAT=P8.2           ,$
    FIELD=SALES_TAX        ,FORMAT=P7.2           ,$
    FIELD=TOTAL_SALE       ,FORMAT=P8.2           ,$

  SEGMENT=SALE_ITEM, SEGTYPE=S1, PARENT=TRANS
    FIELD=PRODUCT_CODE     ,FORMAT=A10,            ,$
    FIELD=SELL_PRICE       ,FORMAT=P7.2           ,$
    FIELD=QUANTITY         ,FORMAT=I3             ,$
    FIELD=ITEM_TOTAL       ,FORMAT=P8.2           ,$
```

and length; type A means alphabetic, I stands for integer, and P designates a numeric field that contains a decimal point. The INDEX specifications define key fields. Parameters are separated by commas. Each field ends with a $ character.

Note (in file SALES) that the general invoice data (TRANS) and the set of fields that define a sale item have been grouped in separate segments. A given invoice can list numerous sale items, so the segment named SALE_ITEM should be a repeating data structure, but it is reasonable to assume one item per transaction to simplify testing the prototype. Segmenting or grouping the fields is a good way to remind yourself to add the repetitive structure later.

As you read through the field descriptions, it might occur to you that several fields are missing. As you and the user begin to test the prototype, those missing fields will become painfully obvious, and you will have to modify your data descriptions more than once. A good prototyping language makes it easy to change your code. Eventually, after several revision cycles, you will reach the point where the data structures begin to settle down. Given relatively stable data, you can normalize the data structures and modify the prototype to reflect the appropriate entities.

A good prototyping language makes it easy to change your code.

Loading Test Data

Once the data structures are defined, you can use programs similar to the one pictured in Figure 8.6 to load data into the files. (The boxes were added to help you visualize blocks of logic.) This program (or FOCEXEC in FOCUS terms) adds records to the master file named INVEN (the inventory file).

Read through the logic. MODIFY FILE must be the first command in any program that modifies the contents of a file; in this case it refers to file INVEN. The CRTFORM command creates a screen. (CRT stands for cathode ray tube, a key component in many display screens.) The strings enclosed in quotation marks define individual screen lines. The angle brackets enclose field names; you defined the fields in Figure 8.5. When you run the FOCEXEC, you will enter values for each of those fields.

The logic of this FOCEXEC begins with the MATCH command. After you enter a set of data for a given product, the input PRODUCT_CODE is checked against the database file. If the new value matches (ON MATCH) an existing record's PRODUCT_CODE, a message is displayed and the new

FIGURE 8.6
Use a program like this one to load test data into a file.

```
MODIFY FILE INVEN

CRTFORM
"        Enter values for the following fields:"
" "
"Product code          <PRODUCT_CODE>"
"Manufacturer name     <MANUFACTURER>"
"Model code            <MODEL>"
"List price            <LIST_PRICE>"
"Selling price         <SELL_PRICE>"
"Stock on hand         <STOCK_ON_HAND>"


MATCH PRODUCT_CODE
     ON MATCH TYPE "INVENTORY FILE ALREADY CONTAINS THIS PRODUCT"
     ON MATCH REJECT
     ON NOMATCH INCLUDE


DATA VIA FIDEL
END
```

data are rejected because the record already exists in the database. If there is no existing record with the PRODUCT_CODE you entered, the key word INCLUDE following ON NOMATCH adds the record to the database.

Near the end of the program, the line that reads

DATA VIA FIDEL

means that input data will come from the screen. (FIDEL is an acronym for FOCUS Interactive Data Entry Language.) The key word END marks the end of the FOCEXEC.

The File Update Routine

Given some data, you can write and test the single-function routines. Figure 8.7 shows a FOCEXEC that accepts data from a sales transaction and

FIGURE 8.7
This FOCUS logic updates the inventory file.

```
MODIFY FILE INVEN
```

```
      COMPUTE
          TRANS_TYPE/I1= ;
          QUANTITY/I3= ;
```

```
CRTFORM
" Enter the transaction type, where:"
"  "
"    1 = Subtract sales quantity from stock on hand."
"    2 = Add customer returns to stock on hand."
"  "
" Type 1 or 2 and then press the tab key:    <TRANS_TYPE/01>"
"  "
" Enter the product code:                     <PRODUCT_CODE>"
"  "
" Enter the quantity to be added or deleted:<QUANTITY/I3>"
"  "
" Press enter to complete the transaction."
```

```
IF TRANS_TYPE EQ 1 GOTO DECREASE
    ELSE IF TRANS_TYPE EQ 2 GOTO INCREASE
          ELSE GOTO ERROR;
```

updates (or modifies) the inventory master file. MODIFY FILE must be the first command in any FOCEXEC that changes the contents of a file. The COMPUTE command defines TRANS_TYPE and QUANTITY. Those two fields are not in the inventory file, but they will be input to the program.

The input data are read from the screen, so the next command is a CRTFORM. The strings enclosed in quotation marks define the individual

FIGURE 8.7
Continued.

```
CASE DECREASE
     ON MATCH COMPUTE STOCK_ON_HAND = D.STOCK_ON_HAND - QUANTITY
     ON MATCH UPDATE STOCK_ON_HAND
     ON NOMATCH TYPE "NO DATABASE RECORD FOR THIS PRODUCT"
     ON NOMATCH REJECT
ENDCASE
```

```
CASE INCREASE
     ON MATCH COMPUTE STOCK_ON_HAND = D.STOCK_ON_HAND + QUANTITY
     ON MATCH UPDATE STOCK_ON_HAND
     ON NOMATCH TYPE "NO DATABASE RECORD FOR THIS PRODUCT"
     ON NOMATCH REJECT
ENDCASE
```

```
CASE ERROR
     TYPE "ONLY TRANSACTION TYPES 1 AND 2 ARE VALID"
     TYPE "TRANSACTION REJECTED"
ENDCASE
```

```
DATA VIA FIDEL
END
```

screen lines. In this case, a two-line menu is displayed and the user is prompted to enter values for the three variables enclosed in angle brackets. Following the CRTFORM and the screen layout is an IF command that transfers control to one of three cases (DECREASE, INCREASE, or ERROR) depending on the transaction type. An error is recognized if a transaction type other than 1 or 2 is entered.

FIGURE 8.8
This FOCUS routine prints reorder requests.

```
DEFINE FILE INVEN
  R_SWITCH/I1 = IF STOCK_ON_HAND GE REORDER_PT THEN 0
               ELSE 1;
END
```

```
TABLE FILE INVEN
  PRINT PRODUCT_CODE MANUFACTURER MODEL
    IF R_SWITCH = 1
END
```

Below the IF block are the cases. Case DECREASE subtracts the input QUANTITY from the database STOCK_ON_HAND (the D. prefix references the current database value) and then updates STOCK_ON_HAND in the database. If there is no record in the database with the input PRODUCT_CODE (the INVEN file's key field), the transaction is rejected. Case INCREASE adds the input QUANTITY to STOCK_ON_HAND and then updates STOCK_ON_HAND. Case ERROR is executed if the user enters the wrong transaction code. As before, DATA VIA FIDEL means the input data will come from the screen, and END marks the end of the program.

Printing Reorder Requests

Figure 8.8 shows a different type of FOCEXEC that prints a report. In this case, the report is to be generated from the data in the INVEN file. The DEFINE block defines a reorder switch (R_SWITCH) that is set to 1 only if STOCK_ON_HAND is *not* greater than or equal to REORDER_POINT (the

ELSE condition); if you have ever worked with dBASE, the switch and the condition act much like a filter. Glance back at Figure 8.5 and verify that STOCK_ON_HAND and REORDER_POINT are in file INVEN.

The second part of the program prints a TABLE FILE from the data in INVEN. The condition

IF R_SWITCH = 1

limits the list to all the products in inventory for which the newly defined switch is 1. Because of the previous DEFINE block, R_SWITCH is 1 if (and only if) STOCK_ON_HAND is less than the REORDER_POINT.

TABLE FILE routines generate reports. MODIFY FILE routines change the contents of a database file. A similar TABLE FILE program might be executed before and after a MODIFY FILE program to show that the target record or records were actually changed. Such "before and after" reports are an excellent way to verify that the prototype is working correctly. You should generate such reports each time you change the prototype. If the results are wrong, the most recent change is the likely cause.

"Before and after" reports are an excellent way to verify that the prototype is working correctly.

The Remaining Single-Function Routines

Similar FOCEXECs are written for each of the system's primary functions. The user is then asked to test the FOCEXECs, one by one, and suggest changes. As part of this process, you and the user will identify missing data and missing procedures. Expect to modify each FOCEXEC and its associated data structures several times before you and the user are satisfied.

Building a System

Once the single-function routines are accepted by the user, you can combine them to create a system. The idea is not to simply merge all the single function routines, however. Instead, the objective is to put them together in a way that reflects the system's logical requirements.

Assume that the FOCEXECs and master files listed in Figure 8.9 have all been written and tested. Some of those functions can be performed by the sales clerks. Others, however, should be limited to management. For

FIGURE 8.9
Preliminary analysis might define these routines and master files.

Routines

FOCEXEC	Function
SELL	Handle and record sales transaction.
FIXERR	Correct an error on a sales transaction.
UPDATE	Update inventory based on sale.
MANAGE	Add, delete, or modify an inventory record.
REORDER	Identify products to be reordered from suppliers.
SHIPMENT	Update inventory based on shipment from supplier.
PURCHASE	Add, delete, or modify a supplier/vendor record.
SELECT	Identify sale items from inventory.
PI	Correct inventory file based on physical inventory.

Database Files

Master	Contents
INVEN	Stock on hand and inventory data by product code.
SALES	Sales transactions by customer code.
VENDOR	Supplier data by supplier name.

example, Tina would probably want to prevent the sales clerks from adding products to or deleting products from inventory.

In this case, it might make sense to group system functions into three major categories (Figure 8.10). The first set of functions can be accessed by the sales clerks or by management, but five other functions are limited to management. Because physical inventory is an annual task, the physical inventory routine is isolated in a third group.

The FOCUS dialog manager is used to combine single-function FOCEXECs to form a system. Figure 8.11 shows how the sales clerk functions might be organized. Dialog manager statements begin with a hyphen (-); otherwise they resemble FOCEXEC statements. The first command, -SET, defines a variable to hold a transaction code; the & prefix defines TRANS_CODE as a dialog manager variable. -CLERK is a label that marks the beginning of the dialog manager program. The -CRTFORM command defines a high-level system menu and prompts the user to enter a transaction code.

FIGURE 8.10
The prototype might be designed to restrict certain functions to management.

Sales Clerks	Management	Special
SELL	FIXERR	PI
UPDATE	MANAGE	
SHIPMENT	REORDER	
	PURCHASE	
	SELECT	

The user starts a transaction by typing 0, 1, 2, or 3 and pressing enter. The dialog manager then tests the code (the -IF command) and branches to the appropriate routine. For example, if you typed 1, control would flow to label -SALE where the commands that constitute the FOCEXEC named SELL are found. (To simplify the example, the actual FOCEXEC code is not shown.) The -RUN command tells the dialog manager to execute the FOCEXEC immediately. Finally, the -GOTO CLERK command sends the dialog manager back to the beginning of the program to await another transaction. Similar logic follows the labels -UP_INV and -SHIP. The routine called -ERROR displays an error message if an invalid transaction code is selected. The -SHUTDOWN label starts the logic that marks the end of the dialog manager program.

In this example, a similar dialog manager program, complete with its own high-level menu, will be written to incorporate all the managerial routines, while a third dialog manager program controls the FOCEXEC named PI (Figure 8.10). Along with the first dialog manager program, they form a complete prototype inventory system.

Other system designs are possible, of course. You might write a single dialog manager program to control access to *all* the single-function FOCEXECs. You might separate the sales, inventory management, and reorder functions and write three dialog manager programs. You might restrict the sales clerks to handling sales transactions, define a second set of procedures to be performed by an inventory clerk, and a third set of procedures to be performed by management. The best system design depends on the user's needs.

The best system design depends on the user's needs.

FIGURE 8.11
Under FOCUS, the dialog editor is used to link single-function FOCEXECS to build a system.

```
-SET &TRANS_CODE/I1= 0;


-CLERK
-CRTFORM
-"        Enter transaction code:"
-"  "
-"   0     End program."
-"   1     Complete sales transaction and print invoice."
-"   2     Update inventory based on sales transaction."
-"   3     Update inventory based on supplier shipment."
-"  "
-"    Type 0, 1, 2, or 3 and press enter: <&TRANS_CODE>"


-IF &TRANS_CODE=1 THEN GOTO SALE
     ELSE IF &TRANS_CODE=2 THEN GOTO UP_INV
     ELSE IF &TRANS_CODE=3 THEN GOTO SHIP
     ELSE IF &TRANS_CODE=0 THEN GOTO SHUTDOWN
     ELSE GOTO ERROR;


-SALE

 }     SELL FOCEXEC

-RUN
-GOTO CLERK


-UP_INV

 }      UPDATE FOCEXEC

-RUN
-GOTO CLERK
```

FIGURE 8.11
Continued.

```
-SHIP
    }
        SHIPMENT FOCEXEC
-RUN
-GOTO CLERK
```

```
-ERROR
-TYPE "ONLY CODES 0, 1, 2, AND 3 ARE LEGAL. TRY AGAIN."
-GOTO CLERK
```

```
-SHUTDOWN
-TYPE "PROGRAM SHUT DOWN."
```

PROFESSIONAL POINTER ■

First Ask What and Why

Functions are building blocks. A given set of functions can be combined or assembled in many different ways to create many different systems. When you choose to combine certain functions by listing them on the same menu or by referencing them from the same control structure, you are making an important design decision. Don't make it casually.

Most people who read this book know how to program, so you are probably inclined to implement the inventory system as one big modular program because that's what you did when you took COBOL or C. Systems analysis is different. The best design is the one that best meets the user's needs. Take the time to ask what and why before you decide how.

Defining Requirements

Although some prototypes are created to be used, completing the prototype does not normally mark the end of the system development life cycle. Think of the prototype as a first draft. *Most prototypes are written to be thrown away.*

Think of the prototype as a first draft.

The prototype demonstrates what the system must do. The master file formats, the CRTFORMS, and the reports define data structures that can be normalized and recorded in the data dictionary. The FOCEXECs define logical procedures and local data that can be formally documented. Given a FOCUS (or dBASE or Lotus) prototype, it is relatively easy to extract the system's requirements and, subsequently, write functionally equivalent, efficient software in a production language such as COBOL, C, or Ada.

Some Cautions

Creating a prototype can bias the systems analysis process. Prototyping is best for interactive applications.

Because it is a working model, people will inevitably think of the prototype as *the* solution. However, even if the prototype was created to be used and the prototyping language *is* the production language, much work remains to be done. As a minimum, someone must go back through the prototype, clean up the code, refine the screens and the file formats, add the necessary error processing, exception handling, security, and auditing procedures, document the system, and write a user's manual. Also, production data must be loaded into the files and the system must be thoroughly tested.

Creating a prototype can bias the systems analysis process in subtle ways. For example, because the prototype is developed on a computer, the system will almost certainly be implemented on a computer, and manual alternatives are unlikely to be even considered. Prototyping is best for interactive applications; in fact, the best use of prototyping may be to define the right user interface (see Chapter 18). A better option for a small inventory system might be to prescreen the data in batch mode, identify reorder candidates, and suggest only those products for the manager's approval. Given an interactive prototype, you might overlook that second option.

Another danger is that the system will never be developed because the prototype seems too good. Prototypes often lack security and auditing controls, and data integrity may be difficult to ensure. Additionally, prototypes are often inefficient and difficult to maintain. Economy of scale is another problem; models that test well sometimes fail when the number of users is dramatically increased. Don't forget that the prototype is just a first draft. In most cases it is designed to be thrown away.

Prototyping does not always work. Creating a large, complex system from the bottom up can be very difficult, and integrating subsystem prototypes can prove almost impossible because there is no clear way (short of a parallel top-down logical or data model) to visualize subsystem relationships. It is hard to trace the ripple effects that result from modifying a prototype, too, and that creates maintenance problems.

In spite of these limitations, prototyping is an excellent analysis tool, particularly when the user is a bit uncomfortable about technology. It should be part of every systems analyst's repertoire.

MANAGEMENT'S PERSPECTIVE   ■

Set Limits

Prototyping is an excellent choice in organizations that have moved to end-user computing. As users create and refine their own applications, their spreadsheets, databases, and macros represent a source of documentation for designing and developing more efficient versions of the software. In effect, the end users write prototypes and consequently do the preliminary analysis themselves.

One potential problem associated with managing a prototype development project is the nature of the process. A prototype is developed, tested, modified, and tested again, and that cycle continues until the user is satisfied. But what if the user is never satisfied? The vision of money and other resources flowing down a black hole is enough to give a manager nightmares. The solution is to impose reasonable time and resource limits on the process and to require regular status reports (or demonstrations). Also, you must be prepared to terminate projects that show little progress.

Summary

The basic idea of prototyping is to define a system's requirements by building and testing a reasonably complete, working model (or prototype) of the system. Joint application development (JAD) is an alternative to traditional interviewing that is particularly valuable when a prototype is to be developed.

Prototyping is a bottom-up process. Typically, key functions are identified, single-function routines are written, tested, and improved, and the single-function modules are combined to form a prototype system. Requirements are then extracted from the model, design begins, and the prototype is thrown away. The process was illustrated using FOCUS code.

Even if a given prototype was created with the intent of using it as a production system, considerable work remains before it can be released to the user. Creating a prototype can bias the systems analysis process. Prototypes often lack security and auditing controls, and data integrity may be difficult to ensure. Prototypes are often inefficient and difficult to maintain, and economy of scale is another problem. Creating a large, complex system from the bottom up can be very difficult. In spite of these limitations, prototyping is an excellent analysis tool.

Suggestions for Additional Reading

Boar, Berhard H. 1984. *Application Prototyping: A Requirements Strategy for the 80s.* New York: John Wiley & Sons.

Brathwaite, Kenmore S. 1990. *Applications Development Using CASE Tools.* San Diego: Academic Press, Inc.

Connell, John L., and Linda B. Shafer. 1989. *Structured Rapid Prototyping: An Evolutionary Approach to Software Development.* Englewood Cliffs, NJ: Yourdon Press.

Davies, Ian A. 1987. *An End-User's Guide to FOCUS.* Englewood Cliffs, NJ: Prentice-Hall.

Exercises

1. Briefly explain the prototyping process. Most prototypes are designed to be thrown away. Why?

2. Briefly explain joint application development.

3. Prototyping is a bottom-up process. Explain what that means.

4. Compare and contrast prototyping and logical modeling.

5. Explain how prototyping can be used to replace logical modeling as a requirements analysis technique.

6. Explain how prototyping can be used to supplement logical modeling.

7. Under what circumstances would you choose prototyping over logical modeling? Why? Under what circumstances would you consider actually using a prototype for production? Why?

8. Briefly describe the strengths, weaknesses, and limitations of prototyping.

9. Develop a prototype of The Appliance Store's inventory system using FOCUS, dBASE, or the programming language of your choice.

10. Chapter 2 introduced projects for The Print Shop, Jan Tompson's Campus Threads clothing store, and Bill Barnett's automobile dealership. Prepare a prototype system for one or more of those projects or for your own project.

Objects, data, methods, events, and signals are real things.

9

Object-oriented Analysis

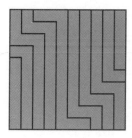

When you finish reading this chapter, you should be able to:

—Discuss the advantages and disadvantages of object-oriented software.

—Distinguish objects and object types and describe the contents of an object.

—Explain encapsulation and inheritance.

—Explain how objects communicate via signals.

—Explain polymorphism.

—Describe the goals of object-oriented analysis.

—Discuss the process of analyzing object structures and prepare an object-relationship diagram.

—Discuss the process of analyzing object behavior. Prepare a state-transition diagram, a network diagram, and an object flow diagram.

Software Complexity

A few decades ago, stand-alone, serial-batch programs were considered the state of the art. Today, we build highly integrated, user-friendly applications that hide their sophistication beneath layers of complex software. Modern networks and multiprocessing computers add parallelism to the equation, and virtual reality and multimedia applications are beginning to emerge.

When you first started to program, you were probably taught to "think like a computer" and visualize instructions being executed in sequence. However, the response time delays that result from testing control variables in strict sequence can cripple a multivariable, on-line, real-time program, and virtual reality applications simply cannot tolerate the unrealistic pauses and delays that result from reacting to events by considering options in a fixed order. As software becomes more complex, the old way of viewing logic becomes increasingly inadequate.

As software becomes more complex, the old way of viewing logic becomes increasingly inadequate.

New applications demand a different view of data, too. For example, the traditional character/field/record/file data structure does not fit word processing very well. Characters still exist, and it seems reasonable to treat a document as a file, but how do words, sentences, paragraphs, blocks, and sections map to fields or records? Graphics and multimedia present similar problems. Is a bit-mapped graphic image a field, a record, or a file? What about sound patterns and animations? Once again, the old model is inadequate.

If the old tools no longer work, we need new tools. The object-oriented approach to software (and system) development is a possible solution.

Objects and Object Types

An **object** is a thing about which you store and manipulate data. It might be a physical thing such as a person, a customer, a book, or an item in inventory. It might be an abstract thing such as a model, a concept, or a process. Unlike many technical terms, the word *object* means what you intuitively think it means.

The word *object* means what you intuitively think it means.

To avoid being swamped by the sheer number of objects, you group similar objects to form **classes** or **object types**. In biology you distinguish between mammals, birds, reptiles, and insects. In politics, you distinguish between Republicans, Democrats, and independents. Instead of separately tracking each item in an appliance store's inventory, the warehouse manager counts refrigerators, ranges, and television sets. Classifying or grouping objects makes it easier to keep track of them.

Classifying or grouping objects makes it easier to keep track of them.

An individual object is a single instance of an object class (or object type). For example, Figure 9.1 shows how a computer store might classify a personal computer. At the bottom, the object itself has a unique serial

FIGURE 9.1
An individual object is a single instance of an object class (or object type).

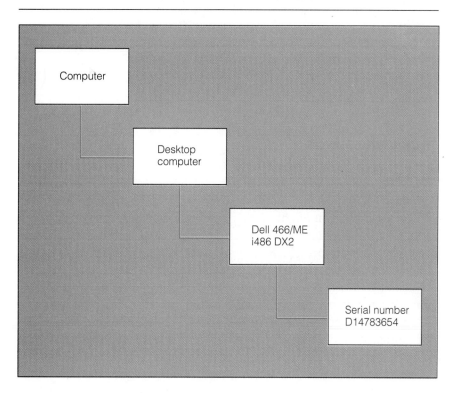

number. That particular computer is but one instance of a given model. Moving up the classification hierarchy, the store might distinguish between tower, desktop, laptop, and hand-held computers. Finally, computers, printers, boards, software, supplies, books, and services clearly represent different categories.

PROFESSIONAL POINTER ■

Binary Large Objects
Such difficult-to-classify entities as blocks of text, graphic images, and sound patterns have one thing in common: they can all be stored on a computer as binary patterns. In the object-oriented world, they are treated as binary large objects, or BLOBs.

Inside a BLOB, the rules imposed by a word processor or a graphics package might govern how the individual bits are manipulated, but other applications treat the BLOB as an independent object. For example, if you use a word processor to prepare text, a graphics program to prepare illustrations, and a spreadsheet program to prepare tables, you can subsequently use a desktop publishing program to integrate those elements by treating the text, the illustrations, and the tables as independent BLOBs and positioning them on a page. Imagine arranging individual pieces of furniture in a room, and you'll have a good visualization of the process.

Working with Objects

Encapsulation

Both **data** (attributes) and **methods** (processes) are associated with an object. For example, you might describe an item in inventory by listing such attributes as its product code, a brief description, its selling price, and so on. A method is a process that accesses an object. For example, associated with a given product are methods for placing it in inventory, changing one or more of its attributes, removing it from inventory, and so on. Methods define how the object's data are manipulated.

In an object-oriented program, the only way to access the data is through the object's own methods.

In an object-oriented program, each object's data and methods are bundled so that the only way to access the data is through the object's own methods. Hiding implementation details in this way is called **encapsulation.**

For example, Figure 9.2 pictures an inventory object. The inventory data form the core of the object. Surrounding it are methods that allow a user to create, maintain, update, delete, and perform a number of other operations on the data. The only way other objects can obtain inventory data is through one of the inventory object's methods.

Signals

Because the objects in a well-designed object-oriented system are encapsulated, they are isolated from each other and changes to one object cannot inadvertently affect others. Objects do not exist in a vacuum, however. They interact with other objects by transmitting and responding to **signals.**

Signals are generated by **events.** An event occurs when an object's **state** changes. A change in state usually implies a change in the value of one of

FIGURE 9.2
Encapsulation means that an object's data and methods are bundled so that the only way to access the data is through the object's own methods.

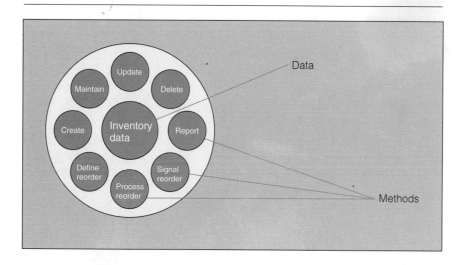

the object's attributes. The only way to change an attribute is through one of the object's own methods, so events imply methods.

Events imply methods.

For example, picture your car at a repair shop. When the service technician begins working on the car (an event), the car's state changes from *Waiting for service* to *Undergoing repairs*. When the technician finishes working, the object's state changes from *Undergoing repairs* to *Ready to go*. That event might prompt a telephone call (a signal) to let you (another object) know the car is ready. The data associated with these events are typically recorded on a service order. The procedures for completing the service order are methods.

Consider an inventory example. When a clerk completes a sale, he or she creates an object to hold sales data (Figure 9.3). Creating the object is an event (a change in state from nothing to something). Events generate signals. In some way (the exact mechanism will be determined later) that signal is recognized by a method within the *Inventory* object, and that method responds by adjusting stock on hand to reflect the sale.

Note that a given event does not direct its signal to a specific target object. Instead, the initiating event simply broadcasts the signal. Other

FIGURE 9.3
Objects interact with other objects by transmitting and responding to signals.

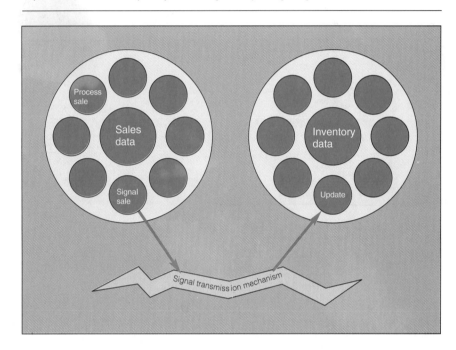

objects might respond to the signal or ignore it, but the source object neither knows nor cares. In this case, indifference implies independence.

Inheritance

A Mazda Miata can be described as a small, two-seat, sporty automobile. Because it is a *type* (subclass) of automobile, you can ignore all the attributes the Miata shares with other automobiles (four wheels, an engine, a cooling system, methods for propulsion, steering, and stopping) and focus on the attributes that make it unique.

Moving down another level, a specific Mazda Miata (an object) can be described in terms of the attributes that make *it* unique (red, convertible top, serial number), and the attributes it shares with other Miatas (small, two seats, sporty) can be assumed. In effect, each subclass borrows (or inherits) attributes and methods from its superclass. This concept is called **inheritance**.

Indifference implies independence.

Each subclass borrows attributes and methods from its superclass.

FIGURE 9.4
Objects inherit attributes and methods from their classes.

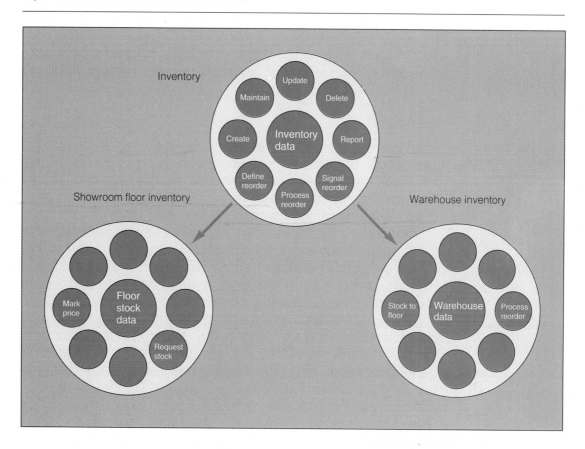

Consider an example (Figure 9.4). Start with a general class called *Inventory*. It defines such common attributes as product code, description, stock on hand, and reorder point. It also defines such general methods as create, maintain, and update.

Some objects are on the showroom floor and others are in the warehouse, so two subclasses can be defined. *Showroom floor inventory* inherits the contents of *Inventory*, so only those attributes and methods unique to an object on the showroom floor must be defined within the subclass. Likewise, *Warehouse inventory* inherits most of its attributes and methods from *Inventory*, so only those attributes unique to an object in the warehouse must be defined.

Move down to the individual objects. A specific television set on the showroom floor inherits all the attributes and methods from both *Inventory* and *Showroom floor inventory,* so very little remains to be defined at the object level. A specific refrigerator in the warehouse inherits all the attributes and methods from both *Inventory* and *Warehouse inventory,* so once again only those attributes and methods that are truly unique to the object remain to be defined.

Polymorphism

A key goal of object-oriented software is creating reusable code.

A key goal of object-oriented software is creating reusable code. The ability to inherit data structures and methods from a higher level helps. **Polymorphism** is another concept that leads to reusable code. A given operation or method is considered polymorphic if it produces similar results in different objects or at different levels.

For example, a customer sale, a customer return, the arrival of a shipment, and the completion of a physical inventory are all events that can change the value of stock on hand for a given object type. The general structure of the inventory update method might be inherited from the highest-level class and then customized for each of these special cases.

Now consider a different example. The completion of a sales transaction is an event that generates a signal. The *Inventory* object reacts to that signal by updating stock on hand. In an independent operation, the *Sales clerk* object might react to the same signal by noting certain details pertaining to the sale that are needed to compute a sales commission. The logic that recognizes the signal, defines the signal's structure, and activates the appropriate method is polymorphic because it can be used to support more than one task.

Some Examples

Object-oriented software is not just a dream that might be realized in the future; it is here today. Consider, for example, the pull-down menu common to so many microcomputer applications (Figure 9.5). You use standard methods to open, close, and select from the menu. The menu itself defines a structure for listing commands by name. Think of an empty menu as an object type and a menu that lists a specific application's commands as an instance of that object type. Because the instance inherits the common structure and the common methods, all you must do to customize the menu is to add the names of your commands.

FIGURE 9.5
A pull-down menu. This one is the WordPerfect 5.1 File menu.

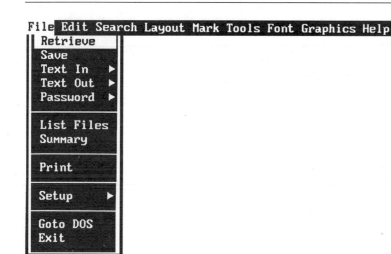

A Microsoft Windows or Apple Macintosh screen is another example (Figure 9.6). The graphic user interface defines a screen framework, buttons or icons, methods for navigating the screen, methods for initiating applications, and the rules for opening and closing windows. Because application programs inherit those methods and attributes, programmers do not have to re-create them each time they write a new program. Because those methods and attributes are common to most applications, the user sees a consistent interface that makes it easier to learn a new program.

Advantages of Object-oriented Software

The object-oriented approach offers many advantages over traditional software development. For one thing, it is intuitive. Objects are things that really exist, events are things that really happen, and real-world objects really do respond to something like signals. Consequently, it is much easier for users to define a system in terms they can understand.

The object-oriented approach is intuitive.

FIGURE 9.6
A Windows screen.

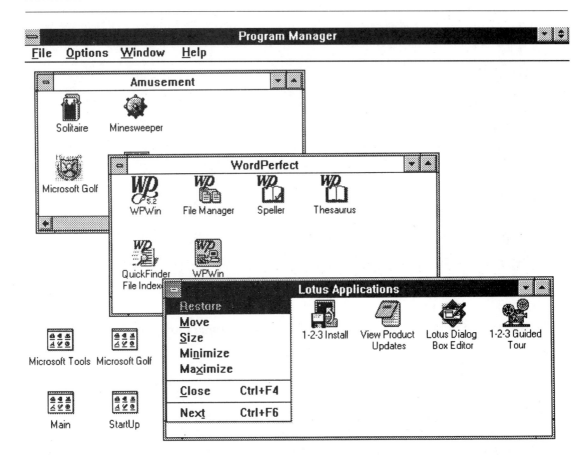

Object-oriented software is easier to change, debug, and maintain.

Object-oriented software is highly modular. Because the modules reflect natural classifications, they tend to be more independent and more stable than the somewhat arbitrary modules suggested by traditional structured programming techniques. Because data and methods are grouped in the same object, ripple effects are isolated and thus easier to trace. Consequently, object-oriented software is easier to change, debug, and maintain.

Reusable code is another advantage. The idea is not new; programmers have dreamed about reusable code for decades, and the discipline called reverse engineering is concerned with reviewing existing software and extracting reusable parts. However, the principle of reusability is imbedded in the theory that underlies object-oriented software, so that dream might finally be realized. Some experts believe that software development is evolving toward the hardware model and that we will someday be able to create applications by selecting off-the-shelf objects, assembling them, and writing a limited amount of application-specific code.

We will someday be able to create applications by selecting off-the-shelf objects and assembling them.

PROFESSIONAL POINTER   ■

Objects Are Objects

Sometimes it seems that every new technique or methodology comes equipped with its own vocabulary, and half the problem with learning the new approach is figuring out what the words mean. At first glance, the object-oriented approach seems to fit that pattern, but that first impression is misleading.

Granted, inheritance and polymorphism are difficult concepts, and you would probably not want to explain them to the typical user. The point is, you don't have to. They are important to the analyst, the designer, and the programmer, but the user can ignore them.

To the user, an object-oriented system comprises objects, data, methods, events, and signals. Those are real things that are found in real systems. People with little or no technical background can visualize those things and sense how they interact. The words mean pretty much what nontechnical people think they mean, so little is lost in translation when the user's observations are converted to technical terms.

Traditional systems and methodologies tend to reflect how the computer works, and few people have the technical training to understand why they work as they do. Object-oriented systems model reality, and you don't need technical training to understand how your own application really works. As a result, user involvement is easier to achieve. That might be the strongest argument in favor of creating object-oriented systems.

Disadvantages of Object-oriented Software

One disadvantage that is sometimes associated with object-oriented code is inefficiency. Supporting a signal transmission medium and other necessary system hardware and software *is* expensive and inefficient on a traditional single-processor computer, but the architecture of the near future will be quite different. Object-oriented software may actually be *more* efficient than traditional structured software on the parallel systems that are currently evolving.

In contrast to concerns with efficiency, programmer training is a real problem. Object-oriented programming is relatively new. Most practicing

Programmer training is a real problem.

FIGURE 9.7
To identify objects, read through the documentation and your interview notes, and look for nouns.

CUSTOMER
SALE
SALES INVOICE
SALES CLERK
INVENTORY
PRODUCT
INVENTORY REPORT
REORDER
SUPPLIER
SHIPMENT
MANAGER

programmers were trained to "think like a computer" and write structured programs in languages such as COBOL. Writing object-oriented code means learning a new language (such as C++) *and* learning a new way to conceptualize logic. That is a challenge. Until a critical mass of programmers is trained in the object-oriented approach, traditional programs will continue to dominate.

The availability of object-oriented development tools is another problem. C++ has become a de facto standard object-oriented programming language, but C (and its derivatives), though powerful, has its deficiencies. New software tools are constantly being developed, however, so expect this problem to take care of itself given time.

The Analysis Stage

Identifying Objects and Object Types

To identify objects, look for nouns.

In Chapters 4 and 5, you learned to extract processes by reading through the existing documentation and your interview notes and looking for verbs. To identify objects, review the same sources and look for nouns. For example, Figure 9.7 lists several objects that can be identified from the initial interview notes for The Appliance Store's proposed inventory system. Data entities, sources, and destinations are obvious examples, but objects can be abstract, too. For example a SALE might be inferred by the actions of a SALES CLERK and a CUSTOMER or by the existence of a SALES INVOICE. (Object names will be capitalized in this example to distinguish them from methods, events, and signals.)

Once you identify key objects, try to group them to form object classes. Start by trusting your intuition; certain objects just naturally fit together. Data structures form the core of most objects, so you can often group objects that share attributes. For example, PRODUCT clearly belongs to the more general class called INVENTORY, the data that comprise a SALES INVOICE have a great deal in common with a SALE, and the SALES CLERK object might inherit something from SALE, too.

Analyzing Object Structures

Given a list of objects and a sense of how they might be grouped to form object types or classes, the next step is to draw an **object-relationship diagram** (Figure 9.8). An O-R diagram resembles an entity-relationship diagram with objects replacing the entities. In this example, CUSTOMER purchases objects from INVENTORY, SALES CLERKS complete SALES INVOICES, and so on. Related objects either share the same class or communicate with each other, so relationships imply class structures or signals. The relationship between CUSTOMER and INVENTORY is many-to-many, but note that these two objects are also related through SALES INVOICE.

Analyzing Object Behavior

Objects hold data and methods and communicate by transmitting and responding to signals. An important part of analysis is determining what the key data, methods, and signals must be, and a good way to find out is to study object behavior.

Objects hold data and methods and communicate by transmitting and responding to signals.

Start with the individual objects, select one, and list all the things that can happen to it. (In other words, describe the object's life cycle.) One good source of ideas is to reread the documentation and look for verbs. For example, you might discover that a given television set is ordered, received from the supplier, accepted or rejected, stored in the warehouse, and so on (Figure 9.9). Note that each life-cycle activity suggests a method that changes the object in some way, and that each of those methods implies a signal.

An object is not ordered, stored, transferred, or sold by accident, so the next step is to identify the trigger event for each method. The trigger event

FIGURE 9.8
An object-relationship diagram for the inventory system.

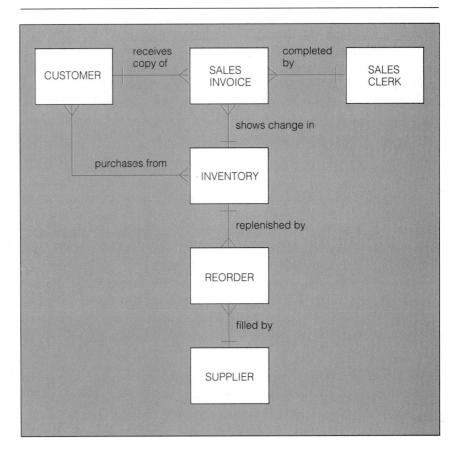

is the event that causes the indicated method to be carried out. For example, an object is ordered as the result of a management decision, and the trigger event for selling an object to a customer is a sales transaction. Trigger events imply signals.

Methods change objects.

Methods change objects, so the next step is to identify the object's state following the completion of each of those methods. For example, when a television set is ordered, its state changes from *Null* to *Pending*. Later,

FIGURE 9.9
The events and states associated with a specific object in inventory.

Method	Trigger Event	State After Method Completed
Order object	Management decision	Pending
Receive from supplier	Shipment arrives	Received
Accept shipment	Management decision	Accepted
Reject shipment	Management decision	Pending
Store in warehouse	Management decision	In warehouse
Transfer to showroom	Management decision	In showroom
Sell to customer	Sales transaction	Sold
Deliver to customer	Sales transaction	In transit
Accept by customer	Customer decision	Null
Return by customer	Customer decision	In showroom
Transfer to warehouse	Management decision	In warehouse
Return to supplier	Management decision	Null

when the object is sold, its state changes from *In showroom* to *Sold* (Figure 9.9).

It might be a good idea to separately compile lists of methods and states and then merge them. Extra methods mean you missed a state or two; extra states mean you missed some methods. Changes in state imply events, methods, supporting data, and signals. Trigger events imply signals and the methods that generate those signals. Events that cause similar changes in the object's state might suggest opportunities for reusable code. Events that are triggered by the same signal suggest related methods.

One way to model an object's state changes is to prepare a **state-transition diagram** (Figure 9.10). The states are listed inside boxes. Arrows show changes in state and the events that cause those changes are written alongside the arrows. A *null* state implies that the object does not exist in inventory. When the object is ordered, its state changes to *pending*. Subsequent events transfer the object to the warehouse, to the showroom, and eventually to the customer. Following customer acceptance or the return of the object to the supplier, it no longer exists in inventory so its state reverts to *null*.

When you finish creating the state-transition diagram for one object, repeat the steps just outlined for each of the others. Remember that each change in state implies a signal.

FIGURE 9.10
A state-transition diagram for an object in inventory.

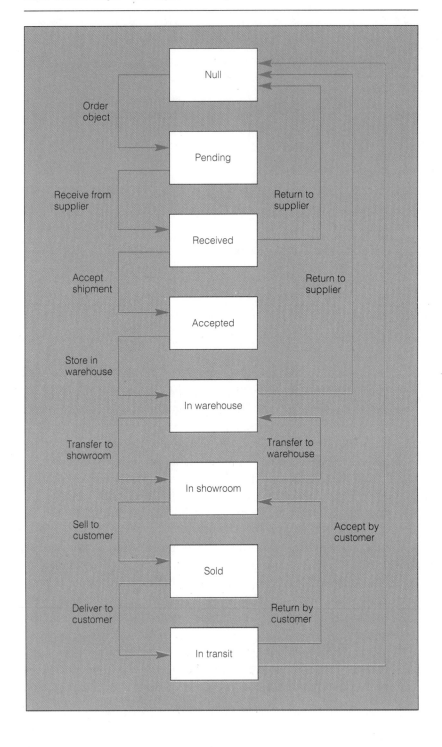

Modeling Object Interaction

When your attention is focused on a single object, it is difficult to sense how all the system's objects interact. One solution is to prepare a **network diagram** (Figure 9.11). In this partial example, a method within the IN-VENTORY object transmits a *Reorder requested* signal that is sensed by the REORDER object, and the SALE object transmits a *Sale completed* signal that is sensed by the INVENTORY object. The network diagram shows how the system's objects are linked. The exact nature of the signals has yet to be determined, but at least you know they exist.

A second way to model object interaction is to prepare an **object flow diagram** (Figure 9.12). An object flow diagram resembles a data flow diagram. The objects are represented by shaded rectangles. Methods (activities) that change or manipulate objects are represented by round-cornered rectangles. The flow lines represent any *thing* that passes between or through activities. The object flow diagram shows how methods interact with other methods. During design you will determine which object should hold each of those methods.

Methods interact with other methods.

Object-oriented CASE

The object-oriented approach is a natural for computer-aided software engineering. (In fact, many newer CASE products were themselves developed using object-oriented techniques.) Conceptually, there is little difference between storing processes, data entities, or objects on the repository. Object-oriented modeling techniques are comparable to traditional modeling techniques, and data and processes can be associated with objects just as easily as they can be linked to database files or program modules. Because the repository holds information that describes logical functions (rather than just code), CASE makes it relatively easy to identify reusable objects. Most CASE products incorporate object-oriented features or will in the near future.

The object-oriented approach is a natural for computer-aided software engineering.

Toward Design

Because the tools and techniques that support object-oriented design are essentially the same ones used in analysis, the transition from analysis to design is not as sharp as it is with the traditional process-oriented or data-oriented approaches. As you will discover in Chapter 21, the goal of object-oriented design is to define each object type's data structures, methods, and signals in enough detail to support programming.

FIGURE 9.11
A network diagram shows how objects communicate via signals.

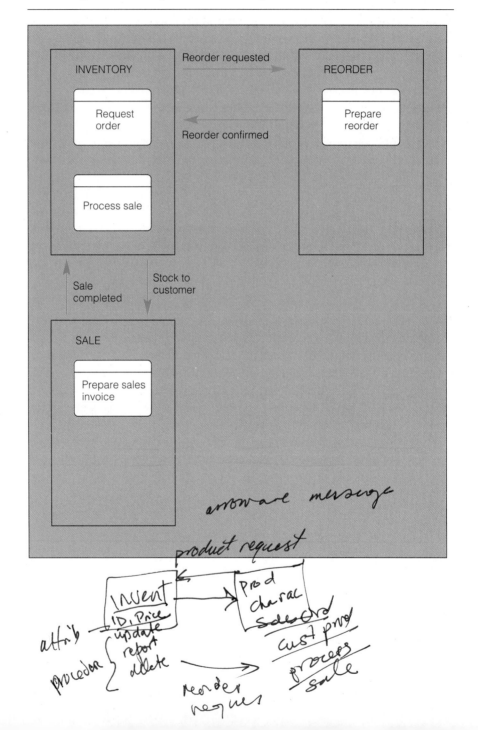

FIGURE 9.12
An object flow diagram for the inventory system.

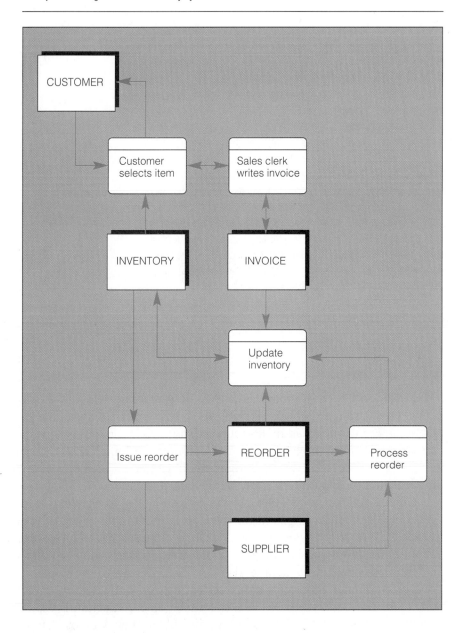

■ **MANAGEMENT'S PERSPECTIVE**

Object-oriented Software Is Coming

Two decades ago, management debated the wisdom of converting from traditional files to databases. The database approach promised significant advantages, but there were negatives, too. The cost of retraining personnel, purchasing database software, converting existing files, and rewriting existing programs was very high. Many of the advantages were derived from sharing data, so tangible benefits could not be realized until a critical mass of files and applications were converted. Faced with such imposing up-front costs, many organizations hesitated.

Today, a central database is the accepted standard, and organizations that have not yet converted find themselves at a competitive disadvantage. In retrospect, the real question was when, not if, the company should convert.

The object-oriented approach has many parallels. Getting started is expensive. Programmers and analysts must be retrained. New compilers and system development tools must be purchased and installed. Existing systems must be converted or at least wrapped in object-oriented shells.

The benefits are long-term, not near-term. Developing the first few object-oriented systems will probably take longer than usual as the technical people and the users learn the new approach. Reusable code will not be a factor until the organization has written several object-oriented programs. It might take years before the savings offset the initial investment. It will be difficult if not impossible to prove objectively that the benefits are worth the cost.

Before the turn of the century, those issues will probably be moot. Object-oriented software is coming, and your organization will eventually get on board. The question is when, not if.

Summary

The object-oriented approach is a promising technique for developing complex software. An object is a thing about which you store and manipulate data. Similar objects can be grouped to form classes or object types. In an object-oriented program, data and methods are bundled so that the only way to access the data is through the object's own methods. Hiding implementation details in this way is called encapsulation.

Objects interact with other objects by responding to signals that are generated by events. Events occur when an object's state changes. Each subclass inherits attributes and methods from its superclass. A given operation or method is considered polymorphic if it produces similar results in different objects or at different levels.

The Appliance Store's inventory system was used to illustrate several object-oriented analysis tools. An object-relationship diagram is used to study object structure. The analyst studies object behavior by defining states, the methods that cause changes in states, and those methods' trigger events. A state-transition diagram is then prepared for each object. Object interaction can be modeled by preparing a network diagram or an object flow diagram, or both.

Suggestions for Additional Reading

Budd, Timothy. 1991. *An Introduction to Object-Oriented Programming*. Reading, MA: Addison-Wesley Publishing Company, Inc.

Martin, James, and James J. Odell. 1992. *Object-Oriented Analysis and Design*. Englewood Cliffs, NJ: Prentice-Hall, Inc.

Winblad, Ann L., et al. 1990. *Object-Oriented Software*. Reading, MA: Addison-Wesley Publishing Company, Inc.

Exercises

1. Discuss the advantages and disadvantages of object-oriented software.
2. Distinguish between objects and object types. Describe the contents of an object.
3. Briefly explain encapsulation. If objects are encapsulated, how do they communicate with each other?
4. Briefly explain inheritance. How does inheritance contribute to the creation of reusable code?
5. Briefly explain polymorphism. How does polymorphism contribute to the creation of reusable code?
6. What are the goals of object-oriented analysis?
7. Briefly describe the process of analyzing object structure.
8. Briefly describe the process of analyzing object behavior.
9. Use object-oriented techniques to complete the analysis of The Appliance Store's inventory system.
10. Chapter 2 introduced projects for The Print Shop, Jan Tompson's Campus Threads clothing store, and Bill Barnett's automobile dealership.
    a. Explain how the object-oriented approach might be applied to these systems.
    b. Use object-oriented techniques to analyze these systems.

The objective of computer-aided software engineering is to automate key parts of the system development life cycle.

10

Using CASE Software

When you finish reading this chapter, you should be able to:

—Distinguish between traditional manual system development and computer-aided software engineering.

—Distinguish between a CASE tool, a CASE toolkit, and an analyst's workbench.

—Explain the advantages and disadvantages of using CASE.

—Briefly describe the Excelerator methodology.

Automating the System Development Life Cycle

Manual Analysis

It is certainly possible to prepare data flow diagrams, entity-relationship diagrams, and other logical models by hand, but (except on relatively small systems) few analysts have the time or the patience. The mechanics are tedious, mistakes are inevitable, and even minor changes can mean redrawing the model. Changes also introduce difficult-to-trace ripple effects that can affect seemingly unrelated components.

It is possible to prepare logical models by hand, but few analysts have the time or the patience.

Verification is particularly difficult to do by hand. Tracing data flows manually is a bit like looking up every word in a lengthy document to check the spelling. To save time, the analyst might assume a few key data structures and trace them through the diagram, but such assumptions defeat a key purpose of analysis. Preparing a data dictionary and a set of process descriptions takes time, too, and shortcuts are tempting to an analyst working under time pressure. The result is often no better than a rough draft of the logical model.

The CASE Approach

CASE can help. As you learned in Chapter 1, CASE is an acronym for Computer-Aided Software Engineering or Computer-Aided Systems Engineering (depending on whose book you read). The objective of CASE is to automate key parts of the system development life cycle.

Computer-aided software engineering is relatively new and still evolving, but the emerging definition implies software that enforces a specific system development methodology and supports the analyst and the designer across the life cycle. Even today, there are CASE products that at least partially automate and integrate problem definition, analysis, design, code generation, documentation, and testing. As this vision is realized, it may someday be possible to automatically generate the code for a complete software system from a graphical model.

Tools, Toolkits, and Workbenches

A **CASE tool** is a single tool (such as a chart generator or a form design program) that automates a single task. A **CASE toolkit** is an integrated set of tools that supports one life-cycle phase but does not necessarily provide bridges or links to prior or subsequent phases. An **analyst's workbench** contains a set of integrated tools that cut across life-cycle phases.

Figure 10.1 lists some typical CASE tools. In addition to the tools, most CASE products provide a graphical interface and other diagramming aids that simplify creating models. Routines that analyze a model are particularly valuable. They act much like compilers, checking the model for syntax, consistency, completeness, and flagging errors. Other routines automatically adjust for ripple effects when a model is changed.

The heart of most CASE products is an information repository that holds detailed information about the system's components (Figure 10.2).

FIGURE 10.1
Some CASE tools.

Problem Definition
Enterprise modeling
Requirements specification

Analysis
Data flow diagrams
Entity-relationship models
Data dictionary
State-transition diagrams
Action diagrams
Warnier-Orr diagrams
Prototyping tools

Design
Structure charts
Presentation graphics
HIPO
Warnier-Orr diagrams
Pseudocode
Structured English
Data normalization
Data structuring tools
Prototyping
Screen painters
Report design tools
Menu design tools
Data dictionary
4th-generation languages

Development
Code generators
JCL generators
Error message generators
Screen generators
Help screen generators
Documentation support
Test data generators
Form design tools
Project management
Library management
Data dictionary
4th-generation languages

Testing
Test data generators

Maintenance
Trace logic
Documentation maintenance
Library maintenance
Data dictionary

General
Graphical interface
Diagramming aids
Model analysis
Project management

The repository is something like a data dictionary, but it documents *all* the objects (not just the data) and defines how those objects are related. It is the key to integrating the tools both within a given phase and across life-cycle phases.

When data elements, processes, external entities, data flows, control flows, and relationships are first identified during analysis, references are added to the repository. When changes are made, the repository is updated to reflect them. When the logical model is complete, the repository holds the information needed to perform such tasks as cross-referencing components across levels or comparing a data flow diagram and an

The heart of most CASE products is an information repository.

FIGURE 10.2
The repository is the heart of most CASE products.

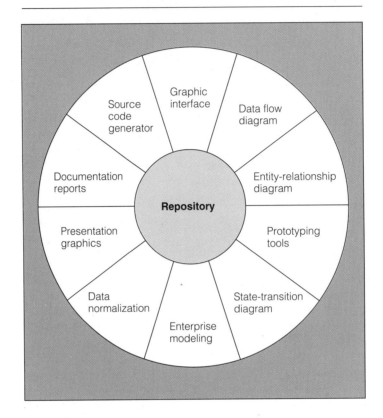

entity-relationship diagram for consistency. Later, during subsequent life-cycle phases, the CASE software can access the repository to extract information to support various tasks or to validate the analyst's work.

The fact that a given set of models is consistent and complete does not necessarily guarantee the best possible design. Most CASE products allow the analyst to perform what-if analysis on a model by changing assumptions and then using the software to modify the diagram and automatically adjust for ripple effects. This ability to manipulate and experiment with the model may be the most important benefit of CASE because it encourages the analyst to consider more alternatives.

What-if analysis may be the most important benefit of CASE.

Some CASE Products

Numerous CASE products are commercially available to run on a variety of platforms ranging from mainframes to microcomputers. Some of the better-known brand names include Excelerator (Index Technology), Foundation (Anderson Consulting), IEW (Knowledgeware), System Architect (Popkin Software & Systems, Inc.), Oracle (Oracle Corporation), and Application Factory (Cortex Corporation). This list is by no means complete, nor does it represent an endorsement of these products.

Several years ago, IBM announced plans for a broadly based CASE environment known as AD/Cycle. Rather than a specific set of tools, AD/Cycle is a **CASE framework** that defines a frame of reference for developing applications and suggests standards that allow different CASE products to communicate. AD/Cycle currently incorporates such existing products as Excelerator and IEW.

The Advantages of CASE

Many benefits have been attributed to CASE, but most advertising stresses improved productivity. Although some claims border on hype, there is little doubt that the proper use of a CASE product can significantly reduce development time. The reason is automation; replacing tedious manual procedures with even semiautomated tools can significantly reduce the time required to complete the models. Additionally, if the CASE product enforces a specific methodology, then documentation is more consistent. That means better communication between analysts and programmers *and* between projects, and that can save a great deal of time.

The proper use of a CASE product can significantly reduce development time.

Most experts believe that the real advantage of CASE is improved quality. With the software imposing a methodology, the analyst is much less likely to take shortcuts or to overlook details. As a result, the job is likely to be done properly, with complete, consistent diagrams, complete requirements specifications, and highly maintainable code.

The real advantage of CASE is improved quality.

The ability of a CASE product to adjust for ripple effects following a change to a model is particularly valuable. Because the analyst does not have to redraw the model to test a new assumption, he or she is more likely to try alternatives. Although the first feasible solution is sometimes the best choice, considering alternatives usually leads to a better system.

A CASE product does not *create* logical models or physical designs, so computer-aided software engineering cannot *replace* the analyst. Instead, CASE supports the analyst by performing much of the detail work. That allows the analyst to be more productive and more creative. If you plan to work as a systems analyst, CASE is in your future.

CASE is in your future.

■   **PROFESSIONAL POINTER**

CASE *Improves Quality*

I wrote my first textbook in the 1970s. I started by carefully outlining the chapters. Then I typed a first draft, marked corrections by hand, retyped the material, made a few more corrections, and submitted the manuscript to the publisher.

Word processing has changed the way I work. Because the software allows me to make corrections electronically, I can revise the manuscript several times before submitting it. The result (I think) is better quality in less time. CASE helps the analyst in much the same way word processing helps the author.

An Example

You encountered references to CASE throughout the first nine chapters. Perhaps the best way to sense how the individual tools are integrated by a CASE product is through an example. The next several pages show how a logical model of The Appliance Store's inventory system might be created using Excelerator/IS, a product of Index Technology Corporation. Before you begin, it is essential that you understand the underlying tools and modeling techniques used by Excelerator, so read Chapters 4 through 7 if you have not already done so.

Excelerator

Excelerator features a graphic interface for developing logical models, an XLDictionary that serves as a repository, prototyping tools, documentation tools, model analysis tools, and project management tools. Although

FIGURE 10.3
The inventory system's processes, data entities, and external entities.

External Entities	**Processes**
FINANCIAL SYSTEM	*Process shipment*
CUSTOMER	*Sell appliance*
SUPPLIER	*Update inventory*
MANAGER	*Reorder stock*
	Identify sale items
Data Entities	*Perform physical inventory*
SALES	
INVENTORY	
VENDOR	

selected tools can be used independently, Excelerator is designed to support and enforce a standard methodology.

The Excelerator methodology assumes that considerable preliminary analysis has been done before you begin creating the computer model. Figure 10.3 shows a list of the primary processes, data entities, and external entities (sources and destinations) for the inventory system.

Logging On

Before you can access Excelerator, the system manager or the project manager must assign you a log-on ID. On some systems you will also be assigned a password; on others you will be expected to select your own password. Logging on is straightforward; enter your log-on ID and your password and then select your project from a list. When you finish logging on, the Excelerator main menu will appear (Figure 10.4).

Building a Context Diagram

The first step in developing a logical model is to create a context diagram for the system. Select GRAPHICS from the main menu, and a second menu that lists the available graph types appears (Figure 10.5). Select *Data Flow Diagram* and, after a brief pause, a work screen appears (Figure 10.6). To the left of the screen is a list of commands. The graph itself is constructed in the open space to the right of the list. You select a command by pointing to it with the mouse and clicking the left mouse button.

For example, if you click on OBJECT, a list of object types appears just below the commands (Figure 10.7). Click on PROCESS, position the mouse

The first step is to create a context diagram.

FIGURE 10.4
The Excelerator main menu.

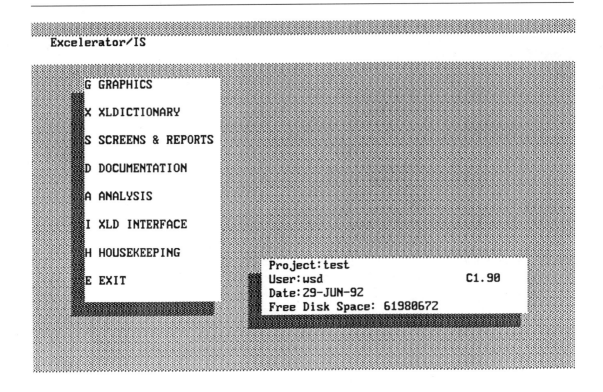

pointer near the center of the work space, click again, and a process symbol appears. Click on X-ENTITY (external entity), position the mouse pointer, click again, and an external entity symbol appears. Because X-ENTITY is the active object, you can position symbols for the remaining external entities on the work space without returning to the menu. Figure 10.8 shows the work screen with five symbols in place.

The next step is to connect the symbols. Select CONNECT from the menu. Then touch the source symbol, click the mouse, touch the target symbol, click the mouse, and a data flow will appear between them. (Note: You can control the path of the line by clicking on intermediate spots.) Use the PRO-FILE command to switch between single-arrow and double-arrow data flows.

FIGURE 10.5
This menu lists the available graph types.

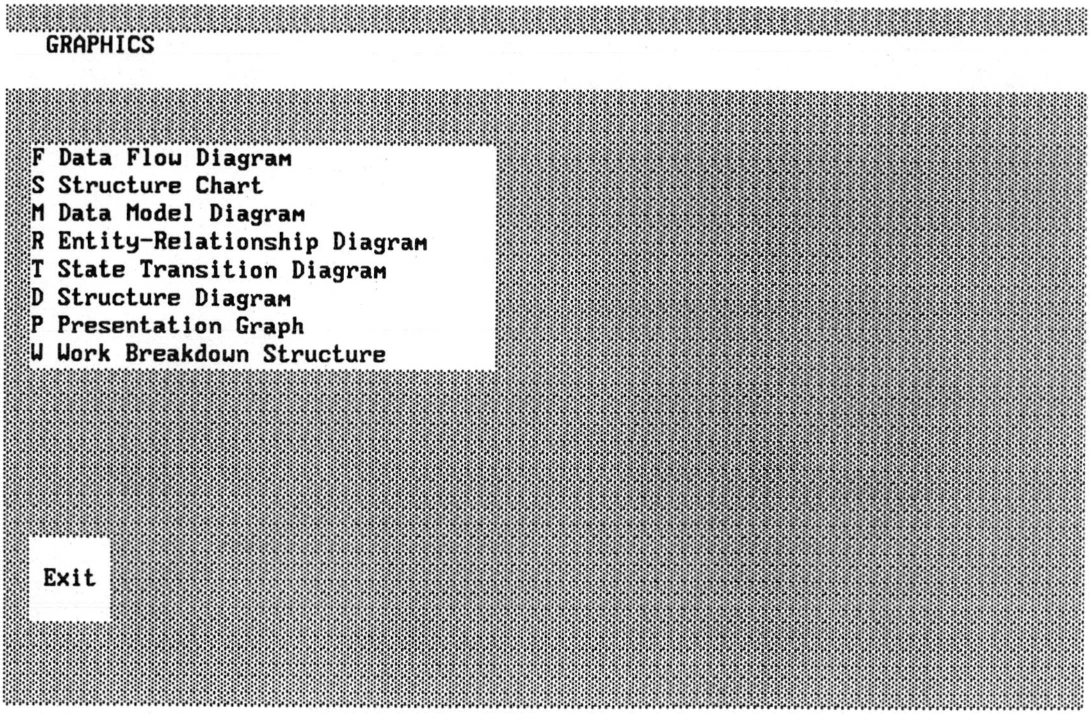

```
GRAPHICS

F Data Flow Diagram
S Structure Chart
M Data Model Diagram
R Entity-Relationship Diagram
T State Transition Diagram
D Structure Diagram
P Presentation Graph
W Work Breakdown Structure

Exit
```

Finally, define each of the context diagram's symbols to the XLDictionary by selecting DESCRIBE from the menu and then clicking on a symbol. If you select a process, Excelerator automatically assigns a level number. (You can override this convention if you wish.) Once you name the process, a process description screen will appear. Figure 10.9 shows the completed process description for *Inventory system*. Note that it explodes to a data flow diagram to be labeled LEVEL1.

When you exit the description screen, the entity you just described will be labeled. Continue describing the remaining symbols in turn. Figure 10.10 shows the finished context diagram. Use the ZOOM command to view selected portions in more detail.

FIGURE 10.6
The graph work screen.

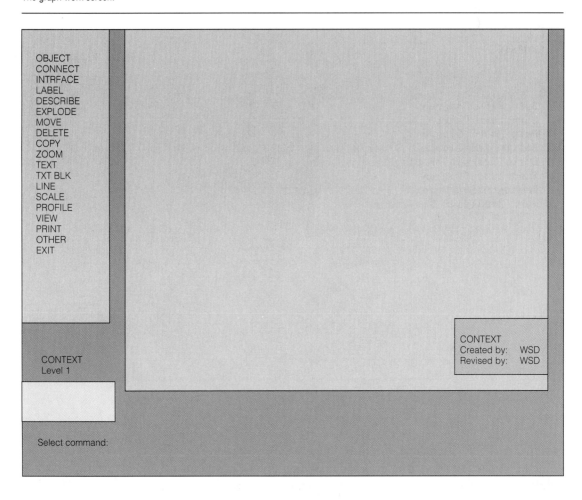

Creating the Level-1 Data Flow Diagram

Create the level-1 data flow diagram.

To create the level-1 data flow diagram, select EXPLODE from the menu. Then click on the process symbol labeled *Inventory system,* and a new work screen will appear. As before, you can use Excelerator's graphic interface to create the data flow diagram by selecting objects from the menu, connecting them, and describing them. Figure 10.11 shows a completed level-1 data flow diagram.

FIGURE 10.7
A list of available objects.

```
OBJECT
CONNECT
INTRFACE
LABEL
DESCRIBE
EXPLODE
MOVE
DELETE
COPY
ZOOM
TEXT
TXT BLK
LINE
SCALE
PROFILE
VIEW
PRINT
OTHER
EXIT
========
PROCESS
X-ENTITY
DAT STOR
CTL TRN
CTL STOR
OFFPAGE
```

Once the graph is finished, you can use Excelerator's analysis routine to check it for completeness and consistency. EXIT the work screen, return to the main menu (Figure 10.4), and select ANALYSIS. After you identify the graph to be analyzed, Excelerator will check the diagram and generate an analysis report (Figure 10.12).

Creating the Entity-Relationship Model

The next step in the Excelerator methodology is to create an entity-relationship model for the system. The idea is to use the data model to define the system's data entities and then represent them as data stores on the level-1 data flow diagram before you explode the processes.

Once again, select GRAPHICS from the main menu. When the secondary menu appears, select *Entity-Relationship Diagram*. When the work screen

The next step is to create an entity-relationship model.

FIGURE 10.8
The context diagram's objects.

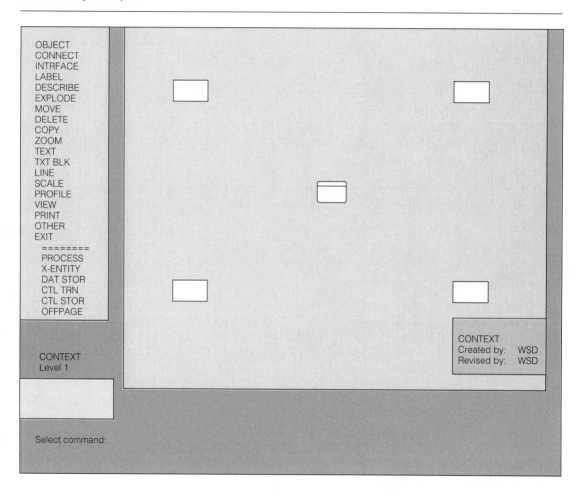

appears and you select OBJECT, two object types are listed: ENTITY and RELATION. You position, connect, label, and describe these objects just as you did with the data flow diagram. When you finish creating the entity-relationship model, you exit graphics and analyze the graph. For example, Figure 10.13 shows an analysis report run on the entity-relationship model before the entities were described to the XLDictionary. Note that it lists three errors.

FIGURE 10.9
This screen describes the *Inventory system* process to the xLᴅɪctionary.

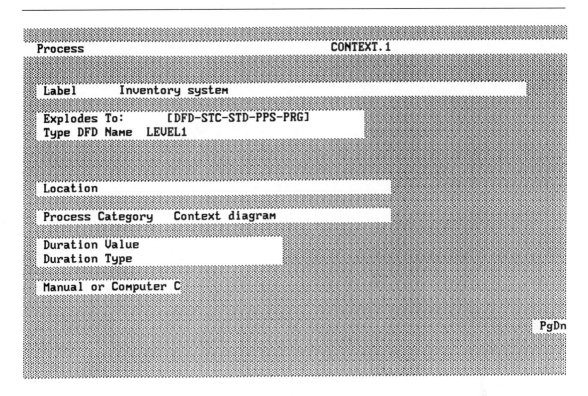

Exploding the Data Flow Diagram

After you add data stores for each of the entity-relationship diagram's entities to the level-1 data flow diagram, the next step is to explode each of the
processes. The Excelerator methodology suggests that you continue
exploding until the lowest-level processes can be described in roughly one
page of pseudocode. In most cases, that target will put you at or slightly
below the configuration item level.

**Explode each of the
processes.**

Verification

The last step is to verify the specification. The verification process includes
checking the data flow model for completeness and consistency across

Verify the specification.

252

FIGURE 10.10
The completed context diagram.

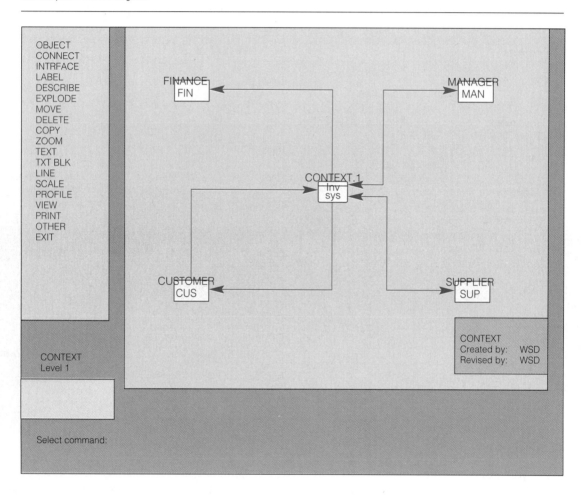

FIGURE 10.11
A level-1 data flow diagram for the inventory system.

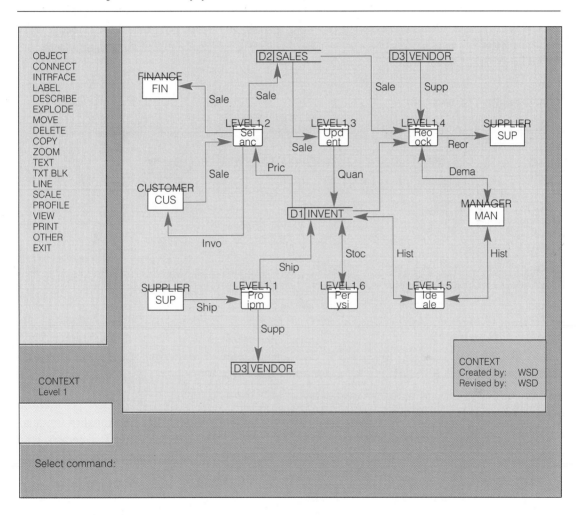

FIGURE 10.12
An Excelerator analysis report.

```
DATE: 29-JUN-92              DATA FLOW DIAGRAM                    PAGE        1
TIME: 15:01                                                 Excelerator/IS
PROJECT NAME: test


GRAPH NAME:   LEVEL1


    ------------------------------------------------------------------------
   |                                                                        |
   |              *** No errors were found for this report ***              |
   |                                                                        |
    ------------------------------------------------------------------------




Press ESC to exit.                      Use arrow keys, PgUp, PgDn to scroll output.
```

levels and cross-referencing the data flow and entity-relationship models. Once verification is completed, the analyst can use other Excelerator features to extract key information from the specification and lay the groundwork for design and development.

■   **PROFESSIONAL POINTER**

CASE *Is in Your Future*

Although computer professionals have long automated other people's work, until recently their own jobs have been largely untouched by automation. That is changing. Today's CASE products are far from perfect, but better versions are coming. The days when systems and programs were custom designed and constructed from scratch by technical artisans are behind us. If you are a computer professional, computer-aided software engineering is in your future.

FIGURE 10.13
This analysis report lists three errors

```
DATE: 29-JUN-92      UNDESCRIBED GRAPH OBJECTS AND CONNECTIONS       PAGE       1
TIME: 15:50                                              Excelerator/IS
PROJECT NAME: test


GRAPH TYPE:  Entity-Relationship Diagram
GRAPH NAME:  INVEN


The following objects are not described:

OBJ TYPE    LABEL
-----------------------------------------------------------------------------
|ENTITY   | Sales                                                            |
|ENTITY   | Inventory                                                        |
|ENTITY   | Supplier                                                         |
|                                                                            |

-----------------------------------------------------------------------------




Press ESC to exit.            Use arrow keys, PgUp, PgDn to scroll output.
```

Some Cautions

There are many CASE products on the market, and the odds are slim that your school and your employer will choose the same one. For now, focus on the underlying ideas and not just the syntax of a particular CASE product. If you know what CASE does, you can always learn a new set of rules for doing the same thing, but if all you know is how to use a tool, changing tools means starting over.

Before you begin developing CASE models, it is essential that you understand the underlying modeling techniques. (Drawing your first few data flow diagrams and entity-relationship models by hand is *not* a waste of time.) Trying to learn a CASE product and a modeling technique concurrently is a mistake because it is so difficult to separate diagramming errors from syntax errors.

Focus on the underlying ideas and not just the syntax. If all you know is how to use a tool, changing tools means starting over.

There is no universal tool.

Because most CASE products are based on a specific methodology, they force the analyst to follow the same basic procedures all the time. To an extent that is an advantage; a consistent methodology improves communication and control and helps ensure that nothing is overlooked. However, a methodology that is perfect for one application might be inappropriate for another. The analyst's job is to select the right tool for the application, not to force the application to fit the tool. There is no universal tool.

There is no substitute for skilled personnel.

Because CASE promises to automate at least portions of the analysis and design process, management sometimes sees CASE as a replacement for the analyst. Although CASE products do streamline many of the time-consuming details of systems analysis and design, they do little to help with the more subjective aspects of the job. There is no substitute for skilled personnel. The primary advantage of CASE is that it makes the systems analyst more productive.

■   **MANAGEMENT'S PERSPECTIVE**

Consider CASE

Computer-aided software engineering is attractive to management because it promises to increase productivity and improve information system quality. One problem is the cost of converting to CASE. The software itself is expensive, and it takes time (and money) to train analysts to use a new methodology. During training, other system development projects wait, and that represents an opportunity cost.

Complicating matters is the vast array of competitive, incompatible CASE products currently on the market. Business failures among software companies are common, and selecting the wrong CASE vendor could mean starting over in a few years. CASE is risky.

CASE software continues to evolve, and the product you purchase today is likely to change, but computer-aided software engineering is worth that cost. The idea that major portions of the system development life cycle can (and should) be automated is the real key. Organizations that continue to build custom systems by hand risk falling behind their competition. If your firm has not yet begun the transition to CASE, perhaps you should.

Summary

The acronym CASE stands for computer-aided software engineering or computer-aided systems engineering. The objective of CASE is to automate key parts of the system development life cycle. CASE helps to increase productivity and improve system quality.

A CASE tool automates a single task. A CASE toolkit is an integrated set of tools that supports one life-cycle phase. An analyst's workbench implies a set of tools that cut across life-cycle phases. The repository holds information on all the system's objects or components and serves to integrate the various models and phases. A CASE framework defines a frame of reference for developing applications.

To illustrate the CASE approach, The Appliance Store's inventory system was analyzed using Excelerator. It is essential that you understand the underlying methodology and modeling techniques before you begin to use a CASE product.

Suggestions for Additional Reading

Brathwaite, Kenmore S. 1990. *Applications Development Using CASE Tools*. San Diego: Academic Press, Inc.

Flaatten, Per O., et al. 1989. *Foundations of Business Systems*. Chicago: The Dryden Press.

Index Technology Corporation. 1989. *Excelerator/IS Application Guide*. Cambridge, MA: Index Technology Corporation.

Martin, James, and Carma McClure. 1988. *Structured Techniques: The Basis for CASE*. Englewood Cliffs, NJ: Prentice-Hall, Inc.

McClure, Carma. 1989. *CASE is Software Engineering*. Englewood Cliffs, NJ: Prentice-Hall, Inc.

Exercises

1. Few analysts have the time or the patience to analyze and design a complex system by hand. Do you agree or disagree? Why?

2. What is CASE? How does CASE differ from traditional systems analysis?

3. Distinguish between a CASE tool, a CASE toolkit, and an analyst's workbench.

4. Distinguish between a data dictionary and a repository. Briefly explain how the repository helps to verify models, link models, and link across phases.

5. What are the advantages of using CASE? What are some disadvantages or dangers?

6. Computer-aided software engineering will never replace the analyst. Do you agree or disagree? Why?

7. Briefly explain the Excelerator methodology.

8. Before you begin developing CASE models, it is essential that you understand the underlying modeling techniques. Why?

9. Prepare a data flow diagram and/or an entity-relationship model of The Appliance Store's inventory system using Excelerator or a similar CASE product.

10. Chapter 2 introduced projects for The Print Shop, Jan Tompson's Campus Threads clothing store, and Bill Barnett's automobile dealership. Prepare a logical model for one or more of those systems using Excelerator or a similar CASE product.

If it isn't in the specifications, it isn't a requirement.

11

Defining Requirements

When you finish reading this chapter, you should be able to:

—Explain why a requirements specification is necessary.

—Briefly describe the competitive procurement process.

—List and explain the characteristics of a good requirement.

—Explain and illustrate the various types of requirements.

—Prepare a requirements specification for a small system.

The Requirements Specification

The logical models and prototypes prepared during analysis are often less than adequate as a foundation for system design. They tend to be somewhat ambiguous and subject to interpretation. The customer might not understand the models, and communication among all affected parties is essential before key design decisions are made. Thus the final step in analysis is to write a formal requirements specification.

The requirements specification is a document that clearly defines the customer's logical requirements (or needs). It builds on the logical model.

FIGURE 11.1
The deeper you go into the system development life cycle, the more it costs to fix a requirements error.

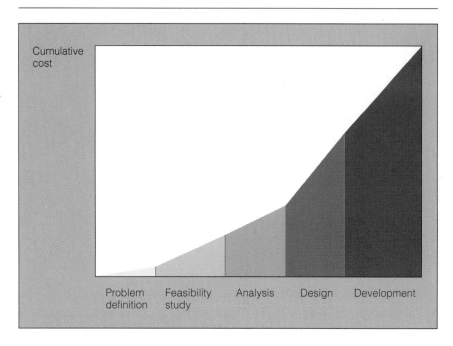

**The requirements speci-
fication clearly defines
the customer's logical
requirements.**

Where the model is ambiguous, the requirements specification gives the correct interpretation. Where the model is imprecise, the document adds the necessary details. Where the model is silent, the document supplements it. Finally, the requirements specification states the client's needs in such a way that it is possible to test the finished system to verify that those needs have actually been met.

Although a few pages might be enough to define a simple system's requirements, a complete requirements specification for a significant system can be quite lengthy. Preparing one is both time consuming and expensive, so why bother?

You know the least about the system at the beginning of the system development life cycle, so it is easy to misinterpret or overlook a requirement. As you complete analysis and move into design, that initial error will lead to subsequent design errors which, in turn, will lead to programming errors, and so on. All those errors must be undone before the original error can be corrected, so the deeper you go into the system development life cycle, the more it costs to fix a requirements error (Figure 11.1).

There is an old saying: We never have the time to do the job right, but we can always find the time to do it again. The point of a requirements specification is to ensure that the customer's needs are correctly defined before time, money, and resources are wasted working on the wrong solution.

> **We never have the time to do the job right, but we can always find the time to do it again.**

PROFESSIONAL POINTER ∎

Spend Extra Time on the Requirements

Perhaps you have seen the advertisement that features an automobile mechanic explaining how a simple oil change could have saved a customer an expensive engine job. The tag line goes something like, "You can pay me now or pay me later."

Think of that advertisement if you find yourself questioning the need for a requirements specification. People are not very good at catching things they previously overlooked, so if you miss a requirement there is a good chance you won't realize your error until you release the system to the user and start hearing complaints. Spending extra time on the requirements is much more cost effective than trying to make major changes to an operational system. In other words, you can pay now or pay (a lot more) later.

Competitive Procurement

Although a requirements specification should be prepared for all but the smallest system development projects, it is *essential* in **competitive procurement** situations. Not too long ago, competitive procurement was associated largely with government and Department of Defense projects. Today, however, the trend toward downsizing and outplacement has led to an increase in the number of firms that subcontract information system development projects. When work is subcontracted you cannot depend on informal lines of communication to correct errors and oversights, so a formal requirements specification is essential. Literally, if it isn't in the specifications, it isn't a requirement.

> **When work is subcontracted, a formal requirements specification is essential.**

Standards

There are several widely used standards for writing requirements. DOD-STD-2167A defines procedures for defense system software development. (DOD-STD is short for Department of Defense STandarD). DOD-STD-490

FIGURE 11.2
The system/segment specifications (sss), or A-specs, define major systems and subsystems at a conceptual level.

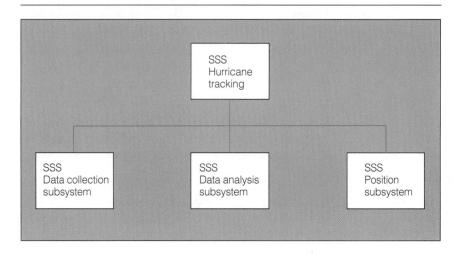

and DOD-STD-499 must be followed on most military contracts. Other standards, such as IEEE STD-729 (a glossary) and IEEE STD-830 are defined by civilian organizations (in this case, by the Institute of Electrical and Electronics Engineers), and many companies have their own internal standards.

Figure 11.2 shows a hurricane tracking system that consists of three major subsystems. The key elements of a DOD-STD-2167A requirements specification that might be prepared for such a system are described in the following sections.

The System/Segment Specifications   Sometimes called the project or mission requirements, the **system/segment specifications** (sss), or **A-specs,** identify major systems and subsystems at a conceptual level. For example, the highest-level system/segment specification for the system pictured in Figure 11.2 might identify such requirements as:

- Locate the position of the hurricane's eye within 500 meters every 15 minutes.

- Reproject likely landfalls every 15 minutes.
- Graphically display the hurricane's most current position and likely landfalls in a format acceptable to the television networks.

Note the nature of these requirements. They are logical. They describe what the system must do, not how the system must work. For example, the requirement that a hurricane's position be graphically displayed calls for both hardware and software, making it a hardware/software composite item. Clearly, it specifies more than a single physical component.

The system/segment specifications define the requirements down to, but not including, the configuration item level. A high-level mission requirement might be subdivided into several segments, and those segments might be further subdivided, so there can be several levels of system/segment specifications.

> The system/segment specifications define the requirements down to the configuration item level.

The system's physical components begin to appear at the configuration item level where you would, for the first time, find boxes that distinguish between hardware and software components. Chapters 5 through 7 explained the process of developing a logical model down to the configuration item level. Such a model might be used as a reference for creating the system/segment specifications.

The System/Segment Design Documents   The **system/segment design documents** (SSDD), or **B-specs,** define in black-box form the components that occupy the configuration item level. For example, you might prepare a system/segment design document for a program, but the routines that compose the program are below the configuration item level and so do not appear in the SSDD.

> The system/segment design documents (SSDD) define the components that occupy the configuration item level.

Figure 11.3 shows that the *Data collection subsystem* consists of a *Satellite segment*, an *Observation plane segment*, a *Data preparation segment*, and perhaps several other discrete, high-level, physical components. In this example, the *Satellite segment* is hardware and the *Data preparation segment* is software. If controlling the satellite calls for additional software, the appropriate program would appear as a separate segment. One system/segment design document is prepared for each configuration item. These documents summarize high-level design decisions, and they serve as a basis for defining the next lower level of requirements.

Like the system/segment specifications, the system/segment design documents are logical, not physical. Each one describes a discrete physical component, but they specify what that component must do, not how it

FIGURE 11.3
The system/segment design documents (SSDD), or B-specs, define the configuration item level components.

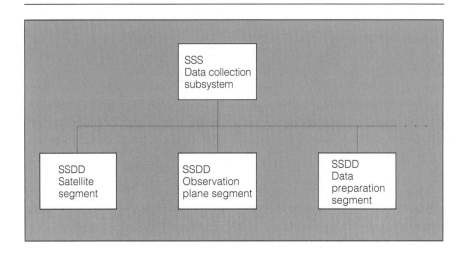

must work. For example, an SSDD for a microcomputer might specify such things as weight and size limitations, response time requirements, and the number of transactions that must be processed per unit of time, but it will not specify a particular model computer or distinguish between an IBM PS/2 and an Apple Macintosh.

The Software Requirements Specifications and Prime Item Development Specifications   The contents of each SSDD are further defined in a set of physical design specifications. Each subsystem that is to be implemented in hardware is called a **hardware configuration item** (HWCI) and is documented in a **prime item development specification** (PIDS). Each subsystem that is to be implemented in software is called a **computer software configuration item** (CSCI) and is documented in a **software requirements specification** (SRS).

The contents of each SSDD are further defined in a set of physical design specifications.

These documents consist of program or hardware design specifications. They are prepared after key design decisions have been made. Unlike the SSS and SSDD specifications, they define *how* the solution will be implemented. You will work at the physical design specification level in Part V of this book.

The Procurement Process

Figure 11.4 summarizes the competitive procurement process. Note that few organizations seek competitive bids at each stage, so the process is much more flexible than the flow diagram suggests.

The process begins with the government agency or the customer organization that is sponsoring the project. Based on a preliminary analysis of the problem, user experts define a set of needs and write the system/segment specifications (A-specs), which are then released for bids.

On a major system, several firms might be awarded contracts and charged with preparing competitive system/segment design documents (B-specs). The completed SSDDs are submitted to the customer and evaluated. The best set is then selected and once again released for bids. Sometimes, the firm that prepared the system/segment design documents is prohibited from participating in the next round.

Based on the competitive bids, a contract to generate a physical design and prepare a set of specifications based on the system/segment design documents is subsequently awarded to one or (perhaps) two companies. One PIDS (hardware) or SRS (software) is prepared for each SSDD. (In other words, one physical design specification is created for each configuration item.)

At the end of this phase, the PIDS and SRS documents are reviewed and approved. The best design specifications are then released for a final round of competitive procurement, with the winning firm getting a contract to build the system. Clearly, the organization that created the final specifications has an advantage, but there are no guarantees. Sometimes a backup supplier is awarded a portion of the contract.

The intent of this process is to solicit fair, impartial, *competitive* bids. Because the contract is typically awarded to the low bidder, the process tends to minimize cost. Also, multiple bidders bring different viewpoints to the process, and that means alternative solutions. Finally, the step-by-step nature of the process gives the sponsoring organization frequent opportunities to exercise control.

The intent is to solicit fair, impartial, *competitive* bids.

There are negatives associated with the procurement process, and almost anyone who has worked on government-sponsored projects can tell you a horror story or two. Preparing specifications and bids is expensive, and part of that cost is likely to be wasted because it is difficult (perhaps impossible) to prespecify every detail of a complex system that will be developed over several years. The process tends to be rigid; sometimes it seems that when the specifications conflict with common sense, the specifications take precedence. Requirements change over time, and procedures for dealing with changes are a major weak point.

Preparing and evaluating all those documents and all those bids is incredibly time consuming, and that is perhaps the biggest problem with traditional competitive procurement. In today's economy, firms that cannot react quickly to changing conditions find it difficult to compete, and the delays caused by frequent bidding cycles are simply intolerable. Consequently, most organizations that subcontract information system development work use a streamlined version of the competitive bidding process that sacrifices control to gain time.

Several years ago, a reporter asked an astronaut to describe the sense of danger he felt when riding a rocket into space. The astronaut responded by pointing out that every component of the spacecraft was supplied by the lowest bidder, and everyone laughed. The point was clear: Low bids do not always imply high quality. In an effort to improve quality, many organizations have significantly reduced the number of projects that go through the competitive procurement process and have chosen instead to establish long-term relationships with a limited number of subcontractors. Such relationships are a key element of total quality management.

Low bids do not always imply high quality.

■   **PROFESSIONAL POINTER**

Trust Reality

There is an old story, well known in engineering circles, that clearly illustrates the danger of interpreting specifications too rigidly. The story cannot be directly confirmed, so think of it as hypothetical.

Back when the government first started crash testing automobiles, a set of specifications was released requesting bids for crash test dummies with a limited range of neck motion. One bidder submitted a very competitive bid for dummies with more realistic necks. Clearly, had those dummies been used, the crash tests would have yielded much better data about the nature of the injuries a real person might have suffered, but the bid was rejected because the dummies did not match the specifications.

If a set of specifications or a model does not match reality, trust reality. If the procurement process does not include reasonable procedures for modifying specifications, then something is wrong with the process.

FIGURE 11.4
The competitive procurement process.

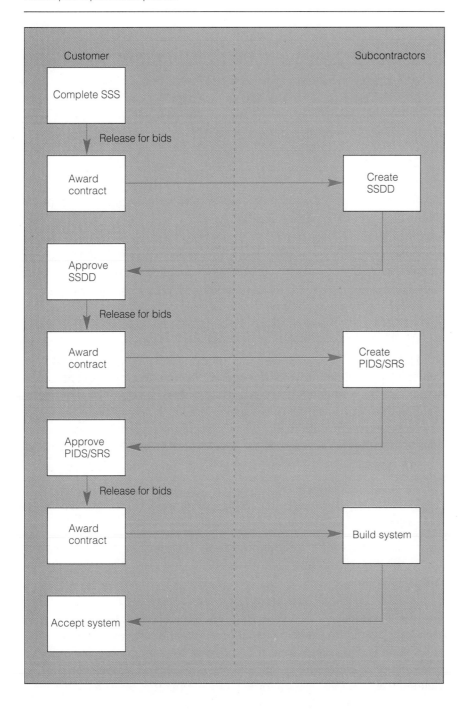

Requirements

In spite of the weaknesses just described, the competitive procurement process serves as a useful model for managing outplacement projects. Even if the bidding cycles are eliminated, the standards and guidelines that have evolved for writing requirements can prove extremely useful.

Characteristics of a Good Requirement

A good requirement is unambiguous, testable, consistent, correct, understandable, modifiable, and traceable.

A key objective of a requirements specification is to clearly define the system's requirements in enough detail to exclude multiple interpretations.

Unambiguous   A key objective of a requirements specification is to clearly define the system's requirements in enough detail to exclude multiple interpretations. In other words, a requirement must be **unambiguous.**

For example, the requirement

Reorders must be mailed at the end of the week.

contains several flaws. Is it essential that reorders be *mailed*? If so, such options as facsimile transmission and the telephone are unacceptable. To whom are they mailed? The obvious answer is the supplier, but the requirement does not say that. If a given reorder is ready *before* the end of the week, must it wait? Finally, what does "at the end of the week" mean? Friday morning? Friday afternoon? Saturday? Before Monday morning? Now consider an improved version:

All *Reorders* identified during a business week must be ready to send to the SUPPLIER no later than 3:00 P.M. on the last business day of that week.

Note that it allows for alternatives to mailing, clearly indicates who receives the reorders, allows for early reorders, and precisely defines the normal reorder time.

Requirements must be testable.

Testable or Verifiable   To ensure that requirements are actually met in the finished system, they must be **testable** or **verifiable.** In other words, when the system is completed, it must be possible to demonstrate, for a reasonable cost, that each requirement has been met. In effect, the specifications detail the acceptance criteria for each requirement.

FIGURE 11.5
A good requirement is testable.

Nontestable Requirement	**Testable Requirement**
The *Reorder quantity* is a one-month supply.	The *Reorder quantity* is computed by multiplying *Average sales per day* by 30, yielding a one-month supply.
The system must be able to handle emergency *Reorders*.	The system must be able to prepare an emergency *Reorder* ready to send to a SUPPLIER within one hour of the time the need is identified.
The *Reorder stock* process must be performed in a small room.	The space available for performing the *Reorder stock* process is limited to a 6-by-8-foot room.
The *Stock on hand* must be 100 percent accurate.	The *Stock on hand* must be accurate to within 1 percent for at least 99 percent of the products in inventory.
Inventory data must be maintained for every product in inventory.	Inventory data must be maintained for at least 1,000 different products with an average *Stock on hand* of at least 50 units per product.
The system must allow for growth.	The system must allow for a 50-percent growth in INVENTORY data over the next five years.

Figure 11.5 compares several testable and nontestable versions of the same requirements. Note that the testable versions include parameters that can be measured. Testable requirements are an excellent source for creating a test plan.

Consistent   Requirements must be **consistent**; in other words, they cannot conflict with each other. For example, suppose that the analyst had written

> All *Reorders* identified during a business week must be ready to send to the SUPPLIER no later than 3:00 P.M. on the last business day of that week.

Then suppose that a later requirement specified

> The system must be able to prepare an emergency *Reorder* ready to send to a SUPPLIER within one hour of the time the need is identified.

The designer would have to assume that the first requirement did not apply to emergency reorders. Otherwise, the two requirements could not coexist.

Correct   Requirements must be **correct.** In this context, the word *correct* means that every listed requirement must actually be a requirement.

Requirements cannot conflict with each other.

Every listed requirement must actually be a requirement.

Sometimes, consciously or unconsciously, unnecessary features or capabilities sneak into a system. If you cannot explain why a given requirement is necessary, perhaps it isn't.

Understandable   A key purpose of the requirements specification is to communicate system requirements to *all* interested parties. Not all readers will be technical experts, so the requirements must be written in such a way that they are **understandable** to the customer, the user, and other non-specialists.

Requirements must be understandable.

Modifiable   The analysis stage might take months or even years, and it is unreasonable to assume that the customer's needs will remain constant, so a well-written requirements document must be **modifiable.** There is little point to delivering the wrong system just because the requirements specification is so rigid that it cannot be changed.

Requirements must be modifiable.

Traceable   Finally, a good requirement is **traceable.** For any given requirement, you should be able to define its origin by tracing it back to a higher-level requirement, and you should also be able to identify the lower-level requirements that satisfy it. Look at the following examples:

Not Traceable
- The system will collect SALES data and use those data to update *Stock on hand* in INVENTORY.

Traceable
- The system will collect SALES data.
- The system will use SALES data to update *Stock on hand* in INVENTORY.

Each requirement should define a single system attribute.

To simplify traceability, each requirement should define a single system attribute. For example, read the "not traceable" requirement just given. It is possible (perhaps even likely) that the SALES data will be collected by one process and *Stock on hand* will be updated by a separate process. If *Stock on hand* is not correct, the problem might lie with either process, and that complicates testing.

Now consider the second alternative. If the SALES data are wrong, then the first requirement has not been met. If the SALES data are correct but *Stock on hand* is not properly updated, the problem clearly lies with the second requirement. If tests are devised for each requirement, the correct problem will be identified.

Types of Requirements

A **behavioral requirement** defines something the system does. In this category, a **functional requirement** identifies a task that the system or component must perform, for example:

- The system must track reorders that have been issued but have not yet arrived.
- The store MANAGER must approve all *Reorders* before they are sent to the SUPPLIER.
- A *Product* is considered for reorder when the *Stock on hand* falls below the *Reorder point*.

Also in this category, an **interface requirement** identifies a link to another system component:

- The *Reorder stock* process must generate *Reorder* forms ready to be sent to the SUPPLIER.
- The *Reorder stock* process must accept data flow *Inventory status* from INVENTORY.
- The *Reorder stock* process must accept data flow *Supplier status* from VENDOR.

More generally, behavioral requirements specify inputs, outputs, and algorithms.

Behavioral requirements specify inputs, outputs, and algorithms.

Nonbehavioral requirements define attributes of the system. For example, **performance requirements** specify such characteristics as speed, frequency, response time, accuracy, and precision:

- All *Reorders* identified during a business week must be ready to send to the SUPPLIER no later than 3:00 P.M. on Friday afternoon or no later than 3:00 P.M. on the last business day of that week.
- The system must be able to generate at least 50 *Reorders* per week.
- The system must hold data for at least 1,000 unique inventory items.

Other nonbehavioral requirements might define such parameters as portability, reliability, security, and maintainability.

Such constraints as physical size and weight, environmental factors, ergonomic standards, and the like are listed in **design requirements** or **constraint requirements:**

- The space available for performing the *Reorder stock* process is limited to a 6-by-8-foot room.

Quality requirements, often stated as an acceptable error rate, the mean time between failures, or the mean time to repair, are sometimes grouped with performance requirements, but many organizations list them separately. Firms that have adopted total quality management often include additional measures of quality.

Economic requirements specify such things as performance penalties, limits on development and operating costs, the implementation schedule, and resource restrictions. They are more common in Europe than in the United States. Occasionally, marketing and political requirements are added.

■   **PROFESSIONAL POINTER**

Know What You Need

Cathy Guisewite's "Cathy" is a popular comic strip about the trials and tribulations of a young, single woman. In one recent strip, the title character walked into a computer store to buy a personal computer. "What do you plan to do with it?" asked the clerk. Flustered, Cathy left the store. When her friend asked her why, she replied, "He got too technical."

The real problem was that Cathy had no idea why she wanted a personal computer. You cannot make intelligent decisions about technology unless you know what you want that technology to do. That, in a nutshell, is why you need a requirements specification.

Writing Requirements

The remainder of this chapter shows how a requirements specification might be written for The Appliance Store's inventory system.

Writing the High-Level System/Segment Specifications

The system/segment specifications identify the system and its major segments at a conceptual level. Typically they define key terms and identify broad, systemwide objectives and constraints. In some cases, the data dictionary is treated as an official part of the requirements specification so the data element, data composite, and data transform definitions can be used without rewriting them.

The problem definition is a good starting point. The problem definition (as modified by the feasibility study) is a good starting point for defining systemwide requirements because the ultimate test of any system's success or failure is how well it meets its objectives.

Starting with the objectives is also a good way to ensure that the objectives were not lost in the details of creating a logical model.

For example, two primary objectives were listed on The Appliance Store's inventory problem definition:

1. To reduce store inventory by $50,000 by providing accurate, daily inventory status data to support reorder and sale item decisions.
2. To maintain the new inventory level (as a percentage of sales) into the future.

The scope implied a third objective:

3. To meet objectives 1 and 2 for no more than $10,000.

At first glance, those objectives seem clear, but they leave several questions unanswered.

What exactly does it mean to "reduce inventory by $50,000"? Is the analyst to compare the absolute inventory values on two reference dates? If so, which dates? What if the store decides to reduce stock because of a recession, or increase stock because of a surge in demand? Should changes in inventory levels that have nothing to do with the new system be used to determine the system's success or failure?

What is meant by "improving the precision and timeliness of the inventory data"? How precise? How timely? In objective 2, what does "into the future" mean? One month? A year? Ten years? In objective 3, does the $10,000 limit refer to a one-time capital investment or does it include continuing operating costs?

Back when the problem was initially defined, it was difficult to state the objectives much more precisely. However, unless those questions are answered, it will be difficult if not impossible to determine if the finished system is a success or a failure. The point of the system/segment specifications is to answer precisely these kinds of questions.

A good way to start preparing the highest-level system/segment specification is to list the system's objectives and then define key terms. For example, read through the requirements listed in Figure 11.6. Note that, based on these criteria, once the December 31, 1994, sales and physical inventory data are compiled, the analyst and the customer will *know* if the new system is a success.

Incidentally, the numbers preceding the individual requirements in Figure 11.6 are for identification. Your organization might have different numbering standards.

■ **PROFESSIONAL POINTER**

A Word Is Worth a Thousand Pictures

Everyone knows that a picture is worth a thousand words, but sometimes a word is worth a thousand pictures. For example, when you hear the word *automobile* you might think of the old clunker you bought for a few hundred dollars back in high school. Other people might picture a sports car, a Rolls Royce, a minivan, a 4x4, a Toyota, a Saturn, and so on. In fact, you might discover that almost everyone you talk to associates a different image with the word *automobile*. If people can't agree on the precise meaning of a simple word, how can they possibly agree on the meaning of a complex requirement?

Once, many years ago, a young programmer was assigned to write a program to statistically analyze a set of punched card data. Before starting work, the programmer asked the user if the cards contained any special characters. The user said no, so the programmer didn't bother to check for nonnumeric data.

A few days later, a test run produced a boxfull of paper listing line after line of data-error messages, each one flagging a special character. When the programmer confronted the user with a few dozen cards containing @, #, and $ symbols, the user replied, "Those aren't special characters; they're on just about every card."

To the programmer, the term *special character* meant any punctuation mark except for a decimal point. To the user, a special character was an unusual symbol that appeared only under special circumstances. They were both right; they just weren't speaking the same language. Define your terms first. It saves a great deal of trouble.

Writing the Low-Level System/Segment Specifications

As you read the examples that follow, note that references to processes and data dictionary items are italicized and that sources and destinations are capitalized. Assume that those terms are defined elsewhere in the requirements specification. For example, the data dictionary and the logical model are often included in the requirements specification as an appendix. Finally, remember that system/segment specifications are prepared for each segment down to the configuration item level.

The level-1 data flow diagram for The Appliance Store's inventory system is reproduced as Figure 11.7. (To improve readability, the data flows are not listed.) It serves as a convenient outline for writing the specifications. Focus on process 4, *Reorder stock*. Figure 11.8 shows several logical requirements associated with that process (the number 1.4 indicates level 1, segment 4). Note that the requirements are logical; they do not specify or suggest a physical implementation.

FIGURE 11.6
A portion of the high-level system/segment specifications for the inventory system.

The system must:
1. Reduce store inventory by $50,000.
    1.1 The $50,000 target represents a reduction from inventory levels as determined by the physical inventory completed on March 30, 1994.
    1.2 A unique item in inventory is defined by a UPC code or by the item's manufacturer plus its model code.
    1.3 Stock on hand is defined for each item in inventory as the sum of the number of units in the warehouse plus the number of units on the showroom floor.
    1.4 The dollar value of inventory is computed by multiplying the stock-on-hand by the supplier invoice cost for each item in inventory and then adding those products.
    1.5 The criteria for meeting this objective are defined under requirement 3.
2. Improve the precision and timeliness of the inventory data.
    2.1 The stock on hand for each item in inventory must be updated and reported to the store manager at least once per day.
3. Maintain the new inventory level (as a percentage of sales) into the future.
    3.1 The base level of sales is defined as total sales for 1993.
    3.2 The target new inventory level shall be defined as inventory value on March 30, 1994, minus $50,000, divided by total sales for 1993.
    3.3 The inventory value on December 31, 1994, divided by total sales for 1994, shall be less than or equal to the target new inventory level defined in 3.2.

   Note also that the requirements are *not* independent. For example, it might be possible for a team of three or four clerks to manually generate up to 50 reorders per week (4), including up to five emergency reorders per day (5), but only if all those clerks and all their equipment can fit into a relatively small room (6). If a given solution violates any single requirement, then that solution is unacceptable.

Requirements are *not* independent.

Writing the System/Segment Design Documents

The system/segment specifications define the system down to the configuration item level. One system/segment design document is prepared for each configuration item. For example, assume that the analyst has decided to implement process 4, *Reorder stock,* on a computer. That design decision means that both hardware and software components must be specified. Figure 11.9 lists four SSDD requirements for the software component. Note that each requirement defines a *single* attribute of the system or the component.

Each requirement defines a *single* attribute of the system or the component.

FIGURE 11.7

A data flow diagram is a convenient reference for writing the requirements specifications.

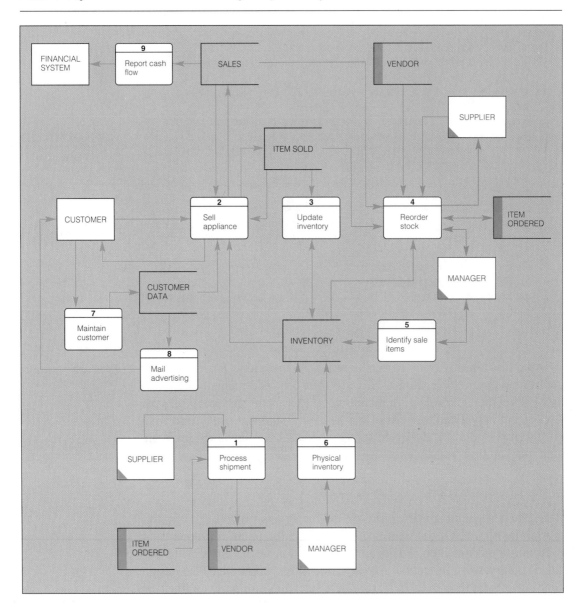

FIGURE 11.8
System/segment specifications (A-specs) for process 4, *Reorder stock.*

1.4   The system must support the store MANAGER's stock reorder decisions.
1.   Reorder decisions are made by the MANAGER based on sales and inventory data.
2.   All *Reorders* identified during a business week must be ready to send to the SUPPLIER no later than 3:00 P.M. on the last business day of that week.
3.   The system must be able to prepare an emergency *Reorder* ready to send to a SUPPLIER within one hour of the time the need is identified.
4.   The system must be able to generate at least 50 *Reorders* per week, including emergency reorders.
5.   The system must be able to generate as many as five emergency *Reorders* on any given business day.
6.   The space available for performing the *Reorder stock* process is limited to a 6-by-8-foot room.

FIGURE 11.9
Some examples of the inventory system's SSDD-level functional requirements.

2.4.1   A program will be written to support the store MANAGER's stock reorder decisions.
1.   To minimize the risk of redundant reorders, the system must track reorders that have been issued but have not yet arrived.
2.   The store MANAGER must approve all *Reorders* before they are sent to the SUPPLIER.
3.   The store MANAGER must be able to modify the *Supplier name*, the *Reorder quantity*, or any other parameters on a *Reorder* before approving it.
4.   *Reorders* must follow The Appliance Store's parent chain's standard reorder form.

Compare the requirements listed in Figure 11.9 to the ones described in Figure 11.8 and note the difference. The SSS (Figure 11.8) lists requirements that help the analyst decide if the *Reorder stock* procedure should be performed manually or on a computer. Once that decision has been made, the SSDD (Figure 11.9) identifies requirements that are important to writing the software, but not to selecting the hardware. Each system/segment design document holds the logical requirements for a *single* component—hardware or software, but not both.

Part IV of this book discusses the tasks the analyst performs between the end of analysis and the beginning of design. During that transitional phase, you will develop the information you need to complete the system/segment design documents.

Writing the Software Requirement Specifications and the Prime Item Development Specifications

The contents of each configuration item are defined in a set of prime item development specifications (hardware) and software requirements specifications (software). They consist of high-level design requirements, so they define *how* the solution will be implemented. Detailed specifications are easier to understand if they all follow the same general format, so a standard outline is often used for these specifications. Figure 11.10 shows the recommended outline for a software requirements specification prepared to meet DOD-STD-2167A.

Figure 11.11 shows a few software requirements specifications for a program that is to be written to support the stock reorder decision in the inventory system. Note that they specify key algorithms. Other requirements in the SRS might define input and output data structures and file formats, specify a programming language or a database management system, or define a high-level control structure. In short, the SRS should contain enough information for a programmer to start writing the program or for an analyst to select the appropriate commercial software.

The Complete Requirements Specification

Figure 11.12 pictures the structure of a complete requirements specification. At the top, a system/segment specification defines the primary logical requirements that refer to the entire system. Additional system/segment specifications list the requirements that are associated with major segments and subsegments down to the configuration item level.

At the configuration item level, one system/software design document defines the logical requirements for each component. Below the configuration item level, one primary item development specification (hardware) or software requirements specification (software) defines the high-level physical design requirements for the component. The logical model is sometimes added to the requirements specification as an appendix.

A complete set of requirements can be quite lengthy. The author must avoid the temptation to describe a preferred physical design, to define an implementation plan, or to write a novel. The idea is to specify exactly what the system must do. Period.

The idea is to specify exactly what the system must do.

FIGURE 11.10

An outline for a computer software configuration item (CSCI) software requirements specification (SRS).

1. Scope
   1.1 Identification
   1.2 Computer software configuration item overview
   1.3 Document overview
2. Application documents
   2.1 Government documents
   2.2 Nongovernment documents
3. Engineering requirements (for a CSCI)
   3.1 CSCI external interface requirements
   3.2 CSCI capability requirements
       3.2.1 Capability 1
       3.2.2 Capability 2

       3.2.*n* Capability *n*
   3.3 CSCI internal interfaces
   3.4 CSCI data element requirements
   3.5 Adaptation requirements
       3.5.1 Installation-dependent data
       3.5.2 Operational parameters
   3.6 Sizing and timing requirements
   3.7 Safety requirements
   3.8 Security requirements
   3.9 Design constraints
   3.10 Software quality factors
   3.11 Human performance/human engineering requirements
       3.11.1 Human information processing
       3.11.2 Foreseeable human errors
       3.11.3 Total system implications (e.g., training)
   3.12 Requirements traceability
4. Qualification requirements
5. Preparation for delivery
6. Notes (e.g., glossary, background information)
Appendices

FIGURE 11.11

Some software requirements specifications.

3.2.1 A *Product* is considered for reorder when the *Stock on hand* falls below the *Reorder point.*
3.2.2 The *Reorder point* is computed by multiplying *Average sales per day* for the *Product* by the selected *Supplier's Reorder lead time.*
3.2.3 The *Reorder quantity* is computed by multiplying *Average sales per day* by 30, yielding a one-month supply.

FIGURE 11.12
The structure of a complete requirements specification. The dashed line marks the configuration item level.

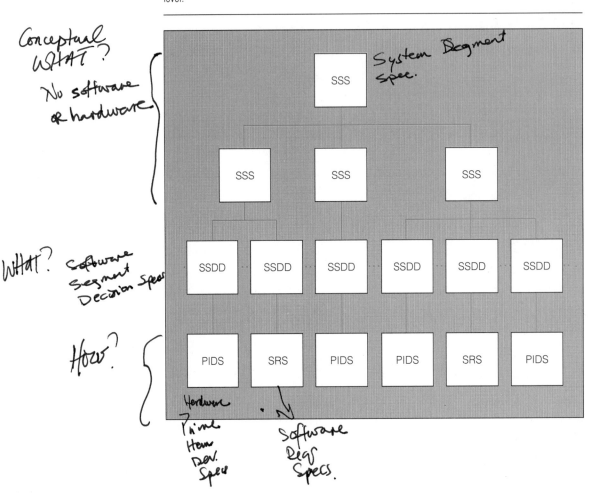

Handwritten annotations:

Conceptual
WHAT?
No software
or hardware

System Segment Spec.

WHAT?
Software
Segment
Decision Spec

How?

Hardware
Prime
Item
Dev.
Spec

Software
Reqs
Specs.

The Flowdown Principle

Each low-level requirement must be linked to a single high-level parent.

Within the requirements specification, the **flowdown principle** requires that each low-level requirement be linked to a single high-level parent (Figure 11.13). Note that parent requirements can be distributed downward to several different children, but each child requirement can have only one parent. Tracing requirements is a form of verification.

FIGURE 11.13
Good flowdown links each low-level requirement with a single high-level parent.

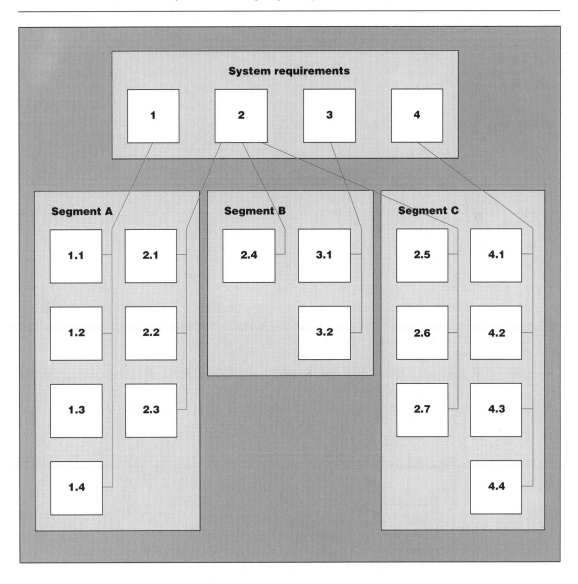

CASE and the Requirements Specification

During the latter stages of analysis, all the work associated with entering information to the CASE product begins to pay off.

The information stored in the CASE repository is an invaluable aid to creating a requirements specification. Functional and performance requirements can often be taken directly from the repository, and logical models suggest interface requirements. Perhaps most important is the ability of the CASE software to trace requirements and thus automate flowdown. During the latter stages of analysis, the system comes together, and all the work associated with entering information to the CASE product begins to pay off.

■   **MANAGEMENT'S PERSPECTIVE**

Insist on Well-Written Specifications

Many firms have begun subcontracting much of their technical design and development work, and the need for a clear requirements specification is doubly important when a subcontractor is involved. Inside your organization, a shared culture might allow separate groups to "understand" unstated requirements, but no such informal link exists with outsiders. If your firm subcontracts technical work, then you need a formal requirements specification procedure.

On the surface, subcontracting is simple: You develop requirements, submit them for bids, and accept the low bid. There is a great deal more to it, however. Subcontractors must be managed. Requirements *will* change because it is literally impossible to prespecify every aspect of a complex system, so you will need procedures for managing change.

Dealing with a subcontractor is a hopeless task when the specifications are poorly written. Take the time to do the job correctly. Insist that your technical people do the necessary analysis. Then have the specifications written and reviewed, and insist that the job be taken seriously. Remember, if it isn't in the specifications, it isn't a requirement.

Summary

The requirements specification is a document that clearly defines the customer's logical requirements (or needs). Competitive procurement calls for formal requirements specifications. Standards such as those defined by the Department of Defense are often used by those writing requirements. The system/segment specifications, or A-specs, define the system requirements down to the configuration item level. The logical requirements for each configuration item are defined in a set of system/segment design documents, or B-specs. High-level design requirements for each hardware configuration item are then defined in a prime item development specification, and design requirements for each computer software configuration item are defined in a software requirements specification.

A good requirement is unambiguous, testable or verifiable, consistent, correct, understandable, modifiable, and traceable. Behavioral requirements define something the system must do; examples include functional and interface requirements. Nonbehavioral requirements, such as performance requirements, define attributes of the system. Other types of requirements specify design, constraint, quality, and economic attributes. The flowdown principle suggests that each low-level requirement have a single high-level parent.

Suggestions for Additional Reading

Davis, Alan M. 1990. *Software Requirements: Analysis and Specification.* Englewood Cliffs, NJ: Prentice-Hall, Inc.

Gause, Donald C., and Gerald M. Weinberg, 1989. *Exploring Requirements: Quality Before Design.* New York: Dorset House Publishing.

Martin, Charles F. 1988. *User-Centered Requirements Analysis.* Englewood Cliffs, NJ: Prentice-Hall, Inc.

Thayer, Richard H., and Merlin Dorfman. 1990. *System and Software Requirements Engineering.* Los Alamitos, CA: IEEE Computer Society Press.

U.S. Department of Defense. *Military Standard, Defense System Software Development* (DOD-STD-2167A). Washington, D.C.: Department of Defense.

Exercises

1. Why are requirements specifications necessary?

2. What is the configuration item level? Why is it significant?

3. Distinguish between system/segment specifications, system/segment design documents, prime item development specifications, and software requirements specifications.

4. Briefly describe the competitive procurement process.

5. Explain how the logical model prepared during analysis is related to the requirements specification.

6. Briefly describe the characteristics of a good requirement and explain why each of those characteristics is important.

7. Distinguish between behavioral and nonbehavioral requirements. Distinguish between functional, performance, interface, and design requirements.

8. Explain the flowdown principle.

9. Write a set of system/segment specifications for The Appliance Store's inventory system.

10. Chapter 2 introduced projects for The Print Shop, Jan Tompson's Campus Threads clothing store, and Bill Barnett's automobile dealership. Prepare a set of system/segment specifications for one or more of those projects or for your own project.

The GARS Project:

12

Analysis

The Analysis Stage

The objective of analysis is to define what the system must do. You have been authorized to develop a prototype GARS system, and that objective does not change just because you are creating a prototype. Although the prototype's main purpose is to provide marketing with necessary information, it will also serve as a framework for designing the system, so it is essential that you plan a complete system.

The Logical Model

Identifying the System's Logical Elements

The first task for you and your team is to compile a preliminary list of the proposed system's logical elements. In this case there is no present system, but you know the prototype must be compatible with SSCIS. Additionally, you have interview notes and copies of relevant memos to provide a starting point for planning GARS.

Working independently, you and your assistants read through the documentation and extract lists of sources, destinations, processes, and data entities. After one of your assistants merges the three lists, a meeting is scheduled. During the meeting, the analysis team reads through the merged list, eliminates redundant entries, looks for missing entries, and finally agrees on a preliminary list of system elements (Figure 12.1).

Developing the Level-1 Data Flow Diagram

Next, one of the junior analysts uses the organization's CASE system to prepare a context diagram (Figure 12.2) and then adds the primary data stores to create a preliminary version of the level-1 data flow diagram (Figure 12.3). Copies of the two diagrams are distributed to the team and another meeting is held to discuss the data stores. One of your assistants suggests that CUSTOMER and CUSTOMER WORK might be merged, but the suggestion is rejected because, for security reasons, customers should not have access to billing and royalty information. After a time the team agrees that the partial data flow diagram shown in Figure 12.3 is a reasonable start.

FIGURE 12.1
A preliminary list of the GARS system's elements.

Source/Destination
Subscriber
Customer (same as subscriber)
Author (type of subscriber)
Internal revenue service (IRS)
Management
System manager

Processes
Access game
Access information
Access system information
Record charges
Access comments queue
Check security
Log activity
Generate royalty report
Generate management reports
Compile charges
Compile royalties
Prepare bills
Assign work space
Assign security
Backup system files
Backup user files
Record royalties

Data
Sports information
Games
Ski information
Concert information
Customer charges
Bills
Customer work space
Comments queue
Royalty
YTD royalty (IRS)
System information
Management reports
Credit information
Security information
Usage log
Customer access data
Game information
Information services
New game
Messages
Royalty information
Income statement
Reports (management)

The processes are the next topic for discussion. Figure 12.1 lists 17 of them, and a data flow diagram showing 17 processes would be difficult to follow, so your team sets about creating logical process groups. One way to group processes is by their trigger events. For example, some tasks, such as responding to a customer request or accessing the games file, must be performed interactively in response to customer actions (Figure 12.4), while others are performed monthly, annually, and so on. Note that the trigger events reflect legitimate system requirements.

Can any of the six logical groupings in Figure 12.4 be combined? Preparing management reports and backing up the system are both daily tasks, but they are clearly independent and thus should be kept separate. However, because system backup is the responsibility of the system

FIGURE 12.2
The context diagram.

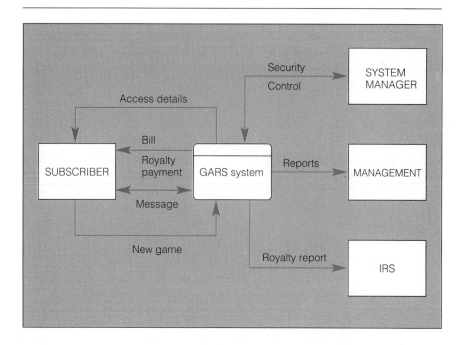

manager, it might make sense to combine those tasks with the system manager requests. That leaves five major processes. Given a set of reasonable process groupings, a level-1 data flow diagram is prepared (Figure 12.5) and the data elements, data composites, and data transforms are documented on the CASE repository.

Preparing a Data Model

The next step is to prepare a data model to more precisely define the data entities (Figure 12.6). Note that the relationship between *Customer* and *Customer work* is one-to-one. Normally, a one-to-one relationship suggests that the data entities be merged, but these two must be kept separate for security reasons.

FIGURE 12.3
The evolving level-1 data flow diagram with key data stores in place.

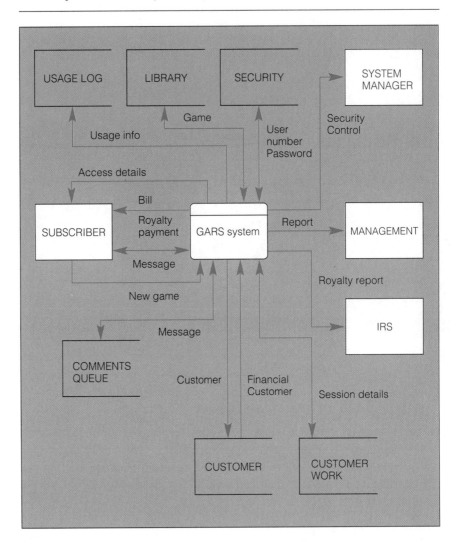

FIGURE 12.4
Processes can be grouped by their trigger events.

Customer Action (Interactive)
Access games
Access sscis information
Access system information
Record charges
Record royalties
Access comments queue
Check security
Log activity

irs Report (Annual)
Generate royalty report

Management Reports (Daily)
Generate management reports

Monthly
Compile charges
Compile royalties
Prepare bills

System Manager Request (As Required)
Assign security
Assign work space

Backup (Daily)
Backup user files
Backup system files

Three of the remaining data entities are linked by an intermediate entity called *Session*. In the context of the system, the *Session* entity is local to process 2, *Control system*. It is used to hold information on a given customer's activities from log on to log off.

Because the data are documented in the repository, there is no need to reenter details about already defined data elements and composites, but any new information revealed by the data model must be recorded. When the entity-relationship model is complete, you can use the CASE analysis software to cross-reference it against the data flow diagram. Because the two models are consistent, you can safely assume that your preliminary sense of the key data entities is reasonable.

Exploding the Data Flow Diagram

Figure 12.7 lists the functions performed by process 2, *Control system*. The tasks that were combined to form *Control system* are included in the list, but some of the subprocess names have been improved and a few functions that are common to on-line, interactive systems have been added. The list of subprocesses is the basis for documenting process 2 in the repository and for preparing a level-2 data flow diagram (Figure 12.8).

FIGURE 12.5

The level-1 data flow diagram. Because of page space limitations, the data flows are not labeled.

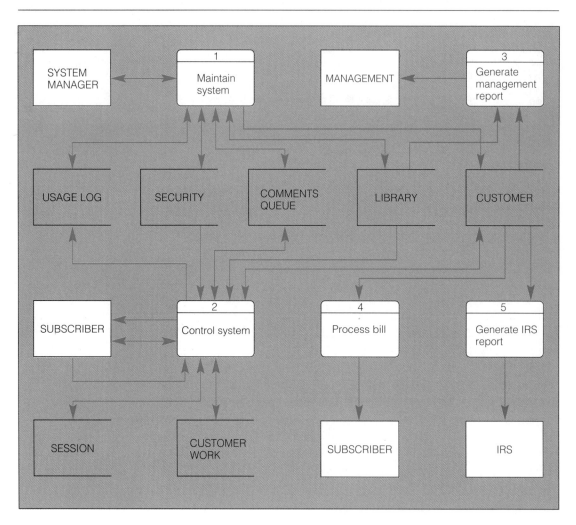

To check the explosion, you go back to the level-1 data flow diagram, compile a list of process 2's inflows and outflows, and make sure you have accounted for all of them. Subscriber or customer communication takes place through *Control user access*. All six global data stores communicate with process 2, and they all appear in the exploded diagram. The local

FIGURE 12.6
A data model for the GARS system.

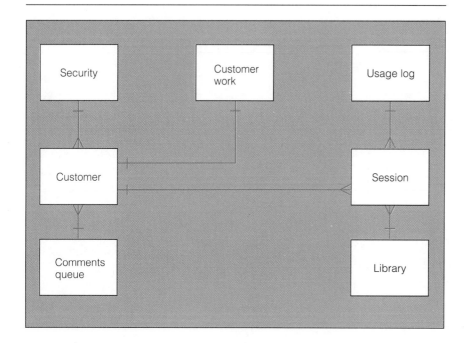

FIGURE 12.7
Process 2's subprocesses.

1. *Log transaction.*
2. *Access system information.*
3. *Access SSCIS information.*
4. *Access game.*
5. *Control user access.*
6. *Manage user work.*
7. *Add message to comments queue.*
8. *Retrieve message from comments queue.*
9. *Verify customer identity.*
10. *Record charges.*
11. *Record royalties.*

FIGURE 12.8

An explosion of process 2, *Control system.* Because of page space limitations, the data flows are not labeled.

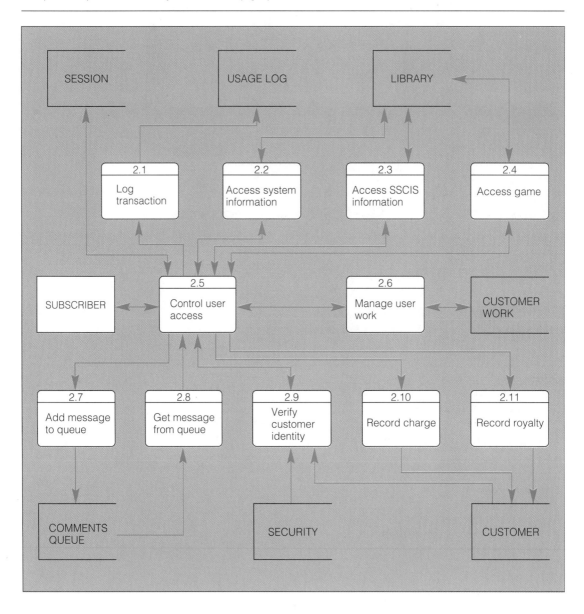

FIGURE 12.9
Some of the data that compose the data flow from CUSTOMER to process 2.9, *Verify customer identity.*

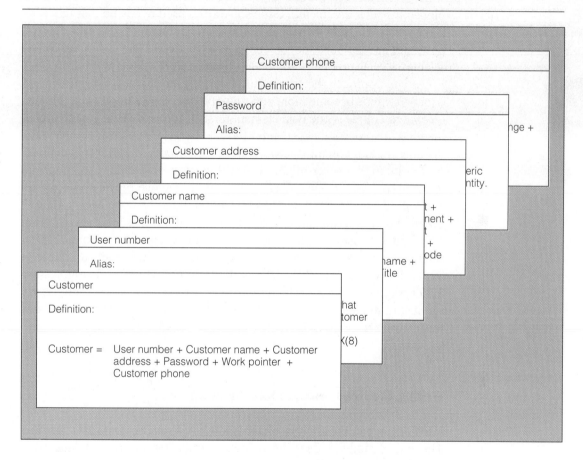

data store called SESSION is used by process 2.5, *Control user access*, to hold transient information for each user session. Note that, except for process 2.9, no single subprocess communicates with more than one data store (Figure 12.8). As you approach the configuration item level, the processes should become more and more specialized, so that seems reasonable.

As the exploded data flow diagram is prepared, its components are documented in the CASE repository. For example, Figure 12.9 identifies several of the data elements and composites that constitute the data flow from data store CUSTOMER to process 2.9, *Verify customer identity*. Once the exploded model is completed, CASE software is used to ensure that the level-2 data flow diagram is balanced. In a similar manner, the other level-1 processes are exploded, documented, and balanced. (The task of exploding selected level-1 processes will be left for an end-of-chapter exercise.)

As you approach the configuration level, your process descriptions and data definitions become more and more precise. For example, imagine that *Overhead charge* is one data element on a customer bill and you are documenting the process that generates those bills. Before you can complete the documentation, you must know exactly how *Overhead charge* is defined.

Marketing's answer might be $2.00 per hour of actual use, but what does "actual use" mean? Assume it is the difference between the log-on and log-off times. To what precision should that difference be calculated? Should you round up and charge $2.00 per hour or fraction thereof? If so, 1.25 hours of usage would cost $4.00. Should you simply round? That same 1.25 hours rounds to 1.0 integer hours and generates a charge of $2.00. Do you work to two digits of precision? If so, 1.25 hours times $2.00 per hour is $2.50. Which number is correct? The answer will have a significant impact on the revenue generated by the GARS system, and it is the analyst's responsibility to answer such questions.

Writing the Requirements Specification

The final step in the analysis phase is to write a requirements specification. The logical model defines the necessary processes and logical data structures and suggests their relationships. In this case, the GARS prototype will be developed internally, so the logical model is an acceptable definition for most of the functional and some of the interface requirements.

Other requirements can be borrowed from other systems. For example, the existing SSCIS specifications almost certainly include performance requirements for an on-line, interactive system and, because GARS must be compatible with SSCIS, there is no sense reinventing those specifications. Other standards might be borrowed from existing billing, auditing, security, and program development software requirements.

The requirements that are unique to GARS will have to be spelled out in more detail, of course. For example, subscriber work-in-progress is probably protected by copyright laws, so the system will have to limit access to the subscriber work space, log all transactions that access the work space, and so on. Royalty payments are another unique feature, so you will need requirements to define the royalty algorithm, protect the confidentiality of royalty data, identify auditing standards for reviewing royalties, and so on.

Finally, because the point of this prototype is to collect information to help marketing assess economic feasibility, you must define what marketing needs. For example, if one key statistic is the amount of time per day a typical GARS subscriber spends creating a new game, collecting the data to generate that statistic is a requirement. If marketing wants to know the percentage of GARS subscribers who actually create games, make sure the prototype counts subscribers by activity. If another key statistic is hours per day per subscriber *playing* games, you have another requirement.

Approval

Within THINK, Inc., requirements specifications are always subjected to a technical inspection. The purpose of the inspection is to ensure that the requirements and the logical model:

1. are complete and internally consistent,
2. are consistent with the objectives defined during problem definition, and
3. represent a reasonable basis for designing a system to solve the problem.

In this case we'll assume that after a few minor oversights are noted and corrected the requirements pass inspection.

A management review comes next. The system passed its inspection, so technical accuracy can be assumed and management can focus on resource issues. Will the proposed system give marketing enough information to estimate GARS revenue potential? Can MIS spare the necessary analysts and programmers, or are they needed to help on other, more crucial projects? Does Mary still believe in GARS? Can THINK continue funding the prototype?

Assume that the answer to each of those questions is "yes." Given a successful management review, the analysis team is authorized to prepare detailed cost estimates, a budget, and a schedule for the prototype GARS system.

Exercises

1. The first step in developing the level-1 data flow diagram was to group processes by their trigger events. Does this technique seem sensible to you? Why, or why not?

2. Why did the analysis team prepare an entity-relationship diagram when the data flow diagram already showed the key data entities?

3. In this chapter, the analysis team ran the CASE verification software following each explosion. Why is that a good idea?

4. In a good logical system design, configuration items should be specialized so that they directly access only one data store. Does this standard seem sensible to you? Why, or why not? How does it relate to structured programming?

5. Why was it so important that marketing be involved in defining the system requirements for the prototype?

6. Decompose *Maintain system*, process 1 on Figure 12.5.

7. Decompose *Generate management report*, process 3 on Figure 12.5. You might want to refer back to the problem definition to find necessary information.

8. Complete the data dictionary entries for the data elements referenced in Figure 12.9.

9. The data elements flowing to process 5, *Generate IRS report* (Figure 12.5), include the author's social security number and accumulated royalty earnings for the year. Trace these elements to their sources, and identify any needed algorithms.

10. The data elements flowing to process 4, *Process bill* (Figure 12.5), include a customer's identification number, name, address, total charges, total royalties, net amount due, hours of use, and available work space. Trace each of those data elements to its source. Identify any needed algorithms.

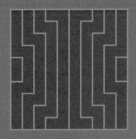

PART IV

The Transition from Analysis to Design

There are many hows but only one what.

13

Generating Physical Alternatives

When you finish reading this chapter, you should be able to:

—Discuss the tasks that must be performed during the transition from analysis to design.

—Explain why alternative solutions are necessary.

—Given a logical model of a system, show how alternative physical solutions can be generated.

—Use system flowcharts to document physical alternatives.

The Transition from Analysis to Design

During the design phase, your attention shifts to the system's physical components.

The logical requirements tell you what the system must do. The next step is to determine exactly how the requirements will be met. During the design phase, your attention shifts to the system's physical hardware, software, data, and procedural components.

The system development process is about to move into high gear. Designers, programmers, and other technical experts will soon be assigned to the project, and they will need disk space, computer time, and other resources to support their efforts. Estimated resource requirements, a clear sense of the project's costs and benefits, and a design and development plan must be communicated to management before those resources are committed.

During the transitional period between the end of analysis and the beginning of design, the analyst generates the information management needs by:

1. identifying several alternative high-level physical designs for meeting the requirements,
2. documenting each alternative,
3. estimating the costs and benefits for each alternative,
4. performing a cost/benefit analysis for each alternative,
5. recommending the preferred alternative, and
6. preparing a development plan for the preferred alternative.

Many CASE products incorporate tools to support these tasks.

Alternatives

There are many alternative solutions to The Appliance Store's inventory problem. You might install inventory software on an IBM PC or PS/2, a Macintosh, or any of hundreds of comparable microcomputers. Minicomputer or mainframe time might be rented from a service bureau. Several companies are in the business of providing data-processing support, and Tina could sign a contract with one of them. A manual system might be worth considering, too. Generating alternatives is easy. The problem is finding *realistic* alternatives.

Generating alternatives is easy. The problem is finding *realistic* alternatives.

A good strategy is to give the user three options. Start by recommending the alternative that best solves the problem *as you understand it*. A high-cost option (perhaps slightly more expensive than the scope) shows the user the additional benefits that might be realized by spending a bit more money. Adding a low-cost alternative gives the user a sense of the benefits that might be lost if not enough is invested.

It is important that the alternatives be realistic. If you cannot imagine the user actually selecting one of the suggested options, do not include it; the point of alternatives is to give the user a choice, not to list some magic number of alternatives. For example, given a project scope of $10,000, a $15,000 high-cost option might be reasonable, but a $100,000 "solution" is absurd. Presenting unreasonable, unrealistic alternatives damages your credibility.

You should also give the user alternatives that are clearly different. For example, if you simply list three identically equipped microcomputers that vary only in brand name, you are not really giving the user a choice. If, on the other hand, you suggest a manual system, a microcomputer-based system, and a contract with a service bureau, you give the user a sense of the variety of options that are available. Although your job is to recommend one of those alternatives, remember that the final choice must be the user's, not yours.

PROFESSIONAL POINTER   ■

Consider Unconventional Alternatives

Too many alternatives can be confusing, but adding an extra one is a good strategy when an unconventional solution is worth considering. For example, subcontracting work to a service bureau is an excellent, low-cost solution to many small-business information processing problems, but some people are uncomfortable with the idea of storing key operating information on another company's computer. Add the service bureau as an extra alternative and mark it "worth considering." If the user rejects it, nothing is lost. If the user expresses an interest in the service bureau, you can explore that alternative in more detail.

Defining Alternatives

Trigger Events and Response Times

The logical model is a good starting point for generating alternatives (Figure 13.1). The first step is to define the trigger events and response time requirements for each process because those parameters often suggest how processes can be combined.

The trigger event is the event that activates the process; for example, *Process shipment* is triggered by the arrival of a shipment and the activities associated with *Sell inventory*, *Update appliance*, and *Reorder stock* are all triggered by a sales transaction (Figure 13.2). Because the manager

The trigger event is the event that activates the process.

FIGURE 13.1
The logical model is a good starting point for generating alternatives.

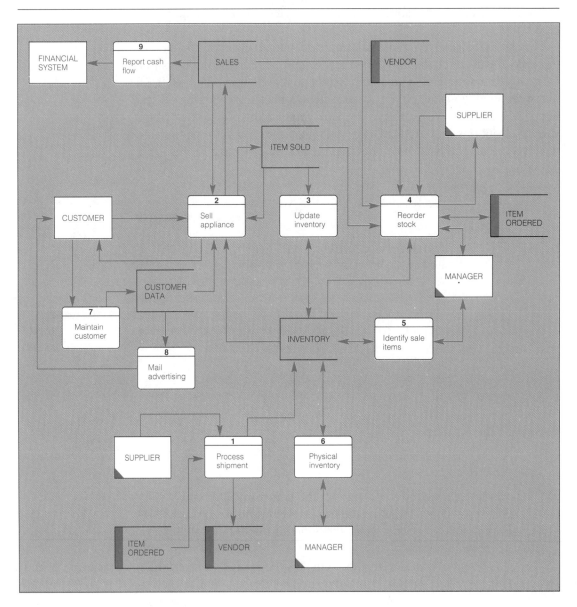

FIGURE 13.2
Define the trigger events and response time requirements for each of the processes.

Process	Trigger Event	Response Time
1 *Process shipment*	Shipment arrival	End of day
2 *Sell appliance*	Sales transaction	Minutes
3 *Update inventory*	Sales transaction	End of day
4 *Reorder stock*	Sales transaction	End of week
5 *Identify sale items*	End of week	End of week
6 *Physical inventory*	End of quarter	End of quarter
7 *Maintain customer*	Sales transaction	End of day
8 *Mail advertising*	End of month	End of month
9 *Report cash flow*	End of day	End of day

will almost certainly need a week's summary of sales to make decisions on sale items, *Identify sale items* is a scheduled (batch) end-of-week activity, and so on.

Response time is the maximum allowable time to complete the process once the trigger event has occurred. For example, *Sell appliance* is an interactive task that must be completed while the customer is in the store, so its response time is measured in minutes. The other processes in this system can all be performed in batch mode, so their response time requirements are identified as end of day, end of week, and so on. Note that the *maximum* allowable response time is listed. For example, it would be perfectly acceptable to update inventory within minutes of a sales transaction, but it would *not* be acceptable to put off selling appliances until the end of the day.

> **Response time is the maximum allowable time to complete the process once the trigger event has occurred.**

Automation Boundaries

Now that the trigger events and response time requirements have been defined, you can begin to generate alternatives by superimposing **automation boundaries** on the data flow diagram. An automation boundary is simply a line drawn around one or more processes. The idea is to group the processes enclosed by an automation boundary to form a single program or procedure. A set of automation boundaries defines a family of alternative solutions.

> **A set of automation boundaries defines a family of alternative solutions.**

FIGURE 13.3

In this example, each process occupies its own automation boundary.

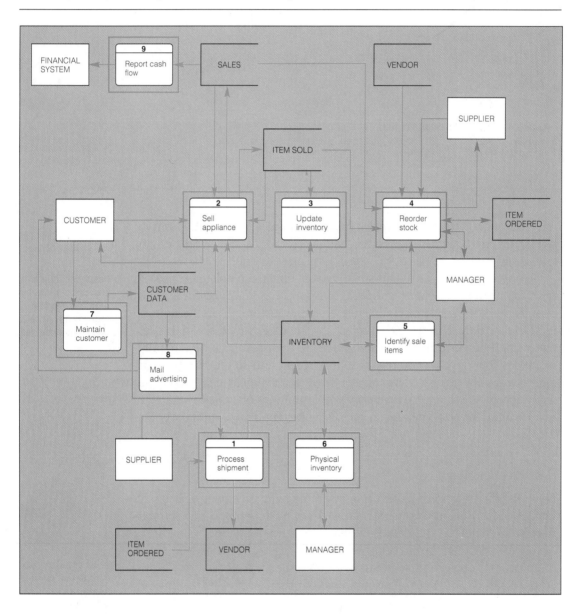

One possibility is to enclose each process inside its own automation boundary (Figure 13.3). In this family of alternatives, each process is implemented as an independent program or procedure. A manual system might incorporate procedures to *Process shipment, Sell appliance, Update inventory*, and so on. A second alternative might include nine programs, one for each process. A third alternative might call for a *Process shipment* program, a *Sell appliance* manual procedure, programs to *Update inventory* and *Perform physical inventory*, and manual procedures to perform the other tasks. Additional alternatives might be suggested by studying the level-2 data flow diagrams.

If you change the automation boundaries, you get a new family of alternatives. For example, Figure 13.4 includes an automation boundary that encloses processes 3 and 4. Because all the processes within a given boundary are implemented in a single physical component, the alternatives in this family contain a single program or procedure that performs all the functions associated with *Update inventory* and *Reorder stock*.

During analysis you treated the processes on the level-1 data flow diagram as independent entities. If the processes really are independent, how can you possibly combine them?

The point of analysis is to construct a general model of the system's logical requirements. Independent processes make the model more general simply because they can be combined to form numerous alternatives, so separating key processes was a legitimate analysis objective.

The point of design is to select a specific solution. The fact that processes *can* be performed independently does not necessarily mean that they *should* be. Unless there is a good reason why two processes cannot be combined, you can merge them and generate alternatives around the new process groupings. For example, you can often combine processes that share the same trigger event, and processes 3 and 4 are both triggered by a sales transaction.

The fact that processes *can* be performed independently does not necessarily mean that they *should* be.

When two or more processes are merged, the shortest response time applies to the new process. For example, Figure 13.2 shows that inventory must be updated *at least* daily and reorders must be issued *at least* weekly. Daily reorders are fine but weekly inventory updates are unacceptable, so if you merge processes 3 and 4 the resulting program or procedure must be executed at least daily.

Processes 2, 3, and 4 are all triggered by a sales transaction, so it might make sense to group them (Figure 13.5). One possible physical alternative

FIGURE 13.4

In this example, processes 3 and 4 are inside the same automation boundary, so each alternative in this family merges the functions performed by *Update inventory* and *Reorder stock*.

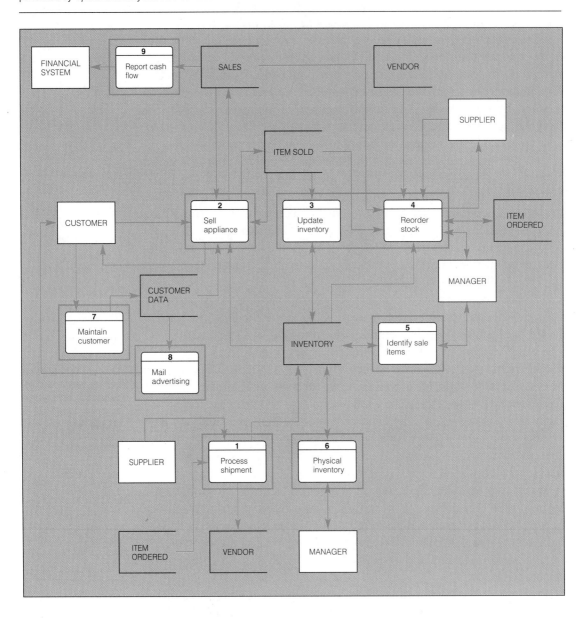

FIGURE 13.5
This example groups processes 2, 3, and 4.

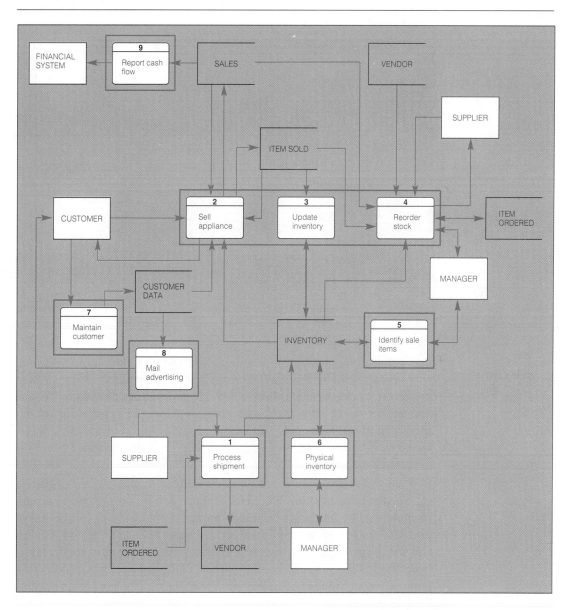

FIGURE 13.6
A checklist can suggest standard patterns or configurations.

		Microcomputer	Minicomputer	Mainframe	Network
In-house	Batch				
	Interactive				
	Real-time				
External	Batch				
	Interactive				
	Real-time				

_____ Service bureau

_____ Manual

within this family features a program to perform the functions associated with *Sell appliance*, *Update inventory*, and *Reorder stock*. In the present system, stock is reordered weekly and inventory is updated daily, but appliances are sold continuously as customers arrive. Because the tightest response time rules, the program would have to run continuously and respond to sales transactions in minutes. That, in turn, implies an on-line, interactive program.

Follow a systematic procedure to generate alternatives. Start by drawing a separate automation boundary around each process. Then try grouping processes by drawing a boundary around 1 and 2, then 1 and 3, and so on. Next, try sets of two processes each; for example, 1/2 *and* 3/4. Gradually, move up to groups of three, then groups of four, and so on until you have tried every possible combination. The limit is a single automation boundary containing all the processes. That limit might suggest an on-line, interactive program that does everything.

Given even a small data flow diagram, an amazing number of alternative solutions can be generated. Some, of course, will make no logical sense, so they can be eliminated quickly; for example, because physical inventory is performed quarterly, it would make no sense to combine processes *Sell appliance* and *Physical inventory*. The scope is another useful screen; alternatives that are likely to cost significantly more than the scope are not economically feasible. The idea is to identify two or three reasonable alternatives that are worthy of further study.

Some analysts use a **checklist** to suggest alternatives (Figure 13.6). A checklist guarantees that standard or "obvious" configurations are not overlooked and it can also be used to suggest alternatives within a given automation boundary. Brainstorming and the analyst's experience are other sources of alternatives.

Many CASE products include routines that allow you to graphically define automation boundaries on a data flow diagram. Some can even suggest alternatives comparable to the ones you might generate with a checklist.

Documenting Alternatives

Physical Data Flow Diagrams

During analysis, the process, data store, and data flow symbols were treated as logical entities, but there is no reason why they cannot be used to represent programs, manual procedures, files, databases, reports, screens, and other physical entities. Given appropriate documentation, a physical data flow diagram can be used to document alternative solutions.

System Flowcharts

A **system flowchart** is another tool for documenting a physical system. Each component is represented by a symbol that visually suggests its function (Figure 13.7). The symbols are linked by flowlines that represent data flows, control flows, and/or hardware interfaces. By convention, the direction of flow is from the top left to the bottom right, and arrowheads must

FIGURE 13.7
In a system flowchart, each physical component is represented by a symbol that visually suggests its function.

	Process	A program or some other automated procedure. The computer on which that program runs.
	Document	A printed document or paper form. Often implies a printer.
	On-line storage	Magnetic disk, diskette, or some other on-line medium. A file stored on such a device.
	Display	A keyboard/display unit or a display terminal. Implies the data displayed on the screen.
	Manual procedure	A process performed by manual means; for example, filling out a sales receipt.
	Predefined process	A subroutine, subsystem, or other system that is documented on another flowchart.
	Flowline	A flow of control and/or data between symbols. Often implies a hardware interface.

FIGURE 13.8
Presentation graphics software allows the analyst to substitute icons of real equipment for many flowcharting symbols.

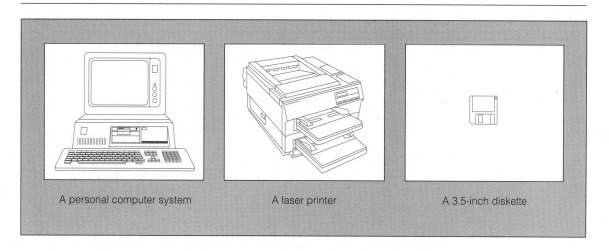

A personal computer system   A laser printer   A 3.5-inch diskette

be used when that convention is not followed. For clarity, all the flowlines in this book will have arrowheads.

The symbols shown in Figure 13.7 conform to ISO Standard 1028 and ANSI Standard X3.5-1970, but other symbols are used, too. Different organizations have their own special symbols, and analysts sometimes use presentation graphics software to substitute icons for the graphic symbols (Figure 13.8). System flowcharts and presentation graphics are common CASE tools.

Drawing a System Flowchart

The first step in drawing a system flowchart is to identify the system's physical components. For example, picture a program that communicates with a user through a keyboard and a display unit, updates a disk file, and prints a report. Figure 13.9 shows a system flowchart for this application. The rectangle represents the program. The display symbol stands for the keyboard/display unit, and the two-headed flowline implies both input and output. The file is stored on disk and the report is printed on a printer.

FIGURE 13.9
A system flowchart.

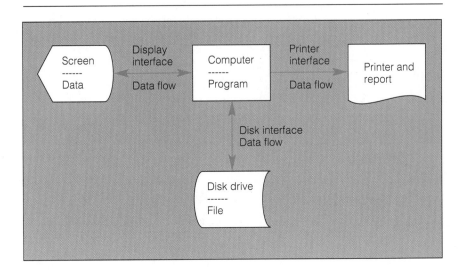

Note that each symbol represents both a discrete hardware component *and* either software or data. The rectangle represents both the computer and the program that runs on it. The on-line storage symbol represents both the disk drive and the file it holds. The printer symbol stands for both the printer and the report. The display screen represents both the display unit and the screen format. The flowlines represent both hardware interfaces and control and/or data flows. A system flowchart conveys a great deal of information in a highly compact form.

A system flowchart conveys a great deal of information in a highly compact form.

The Inventory System

Figure 13.10 shows a level-1 data flow diagram for the inventory system with processes 3, 4, 5, 7, 9 and part of 2 enclosed in an automation boundary. (To make it easier to visualize the boundaries, the data flows are not labeled.) *Update inventory*, *Reorder stock*, and *Identify sale items* are clearly related because the first process updates inventory and the other two react to changing inventory levels. *Maintain customer* and *Report*

FIGURE 13.10
This data flow diagram shows processes 3, 4, 5, 7, 9, and part of 2 grouped within the same automation boundary.

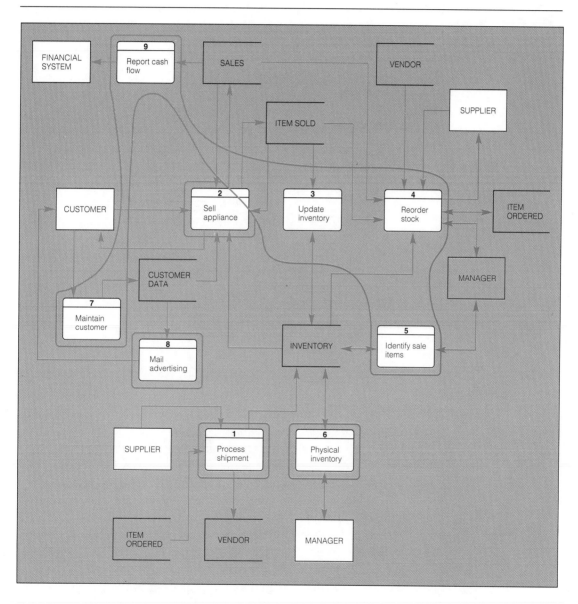

FIGURE 13.11
One set of components suggested by Figure 13.10.

Component	Implements
Manual procedure *Data access/entry* program	*Process shipment*
Manual procedure *Data access/entry* program	*Sell appliance*
Manual procedure *Data access/entry* program	*Physical inventory*
Manual procedure *Mail merge* program	*Mail advertising*
Program	*Update inventory* *Reorder stock* *Identify sale items* *Maintain customer* *Report cash flow*
Sales data file	SALES
Item sold file	ITEM SOLD
Vendor file	VENDOR
Item ordered file	ITEM ORDERED
Inventory file	INVENTORY
Customer file	CUSTOMER

cash flow rely on the same data that drives *Update inventory*, so merging these five processes seems reasonable.

Figure 13.11 lists one possible alternative suggested by that set of automation boundaries. Note that the first four boundaries incorporate both a manual procedure and a computer program. Because the processes either input data to or get data from computer files (or both) they cannot be implemented as pure manual procedures; a review of the exploded data flow diagrams should identify the manual and electronic subprocesses. In this case, it makes sense to move the data entry task from *Sell appliance* to inside the automation boundary that incorporates processes 3, 4, 5, 7, and 9. There is no rule that limits an automation boundary to a single level.

FIGURE 13.12
A partial system flowchart showing how process 1 will be implemented in this alternative.

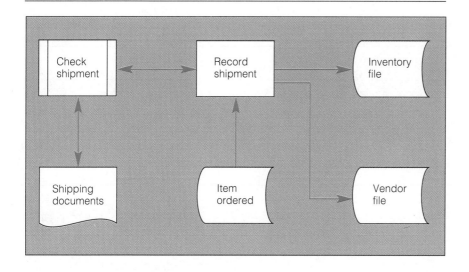

The next step is to document the alternative. The best way to develop a complex system flowchart is one automation boundary at a time, so start with the first process. Figure 13.11 lists both a manual procedure and a program for process 1, *Process shipment*. The flowchart in Figure 13.12 shows a predefined process (*Check shipment*), a program (*Record shipment*), the three files accessed by the program, and a set of *Shipping documents*. The manual procedure is shown as a predefined process because it is complex and a system flowchart that contains too many symbols is difficult to read.

Figure 13.13 is a flowchart of the predefined process. When a shipment arrives, it is inspected manually and either rejected or tentatively accepted. The appropriate data are then input via a keyboard/display unit to the *Record shipment* program (the link to Figure 13.12). Unless the program finds something wrong with the shipment, the newly arrived stock is released to the warehouse. If the shipment is rejected for any reason, the *Shipping documents* are marked and sent to the reorder process.

The best way to develop a complex system flow-chart is one automation boundary at a time.

FIGURE 13.13
A system flowchart for the predefined process named *Check shipment*.

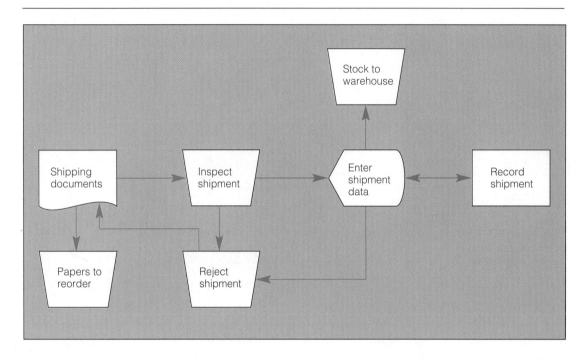

Consider another example. Figure 13.14 shows one alternative for implementing the automation boundary that includes data flow diagram processes 3, 4, 5, 7, 9, and part of 2. It starts at the top left with the input of data from sales transactions and rejected shipment documents. Most of the functions are performed by the *Inventory program* that communicates with all six files. A *Cash flow* report goes to the *Financial system*. Near the bottom right, an *Order* is sent to the supplier. Additionally, based on an analysis of how badly the merchandise is needed, rejected shipments might be returned to the supplier.

The finished system flowchart is shown in Figure 13.15. It graphically documents one *physical* alternative. Except for the predefined processes (which are flowcharted elsewhere), each symbol represents one of the

FIGURE 13.14
This system flowchart shows one alternative for implementing the automation boundary that incorporates data flow diagram processes 3, 4, 5, 7, 9, and part of 2.

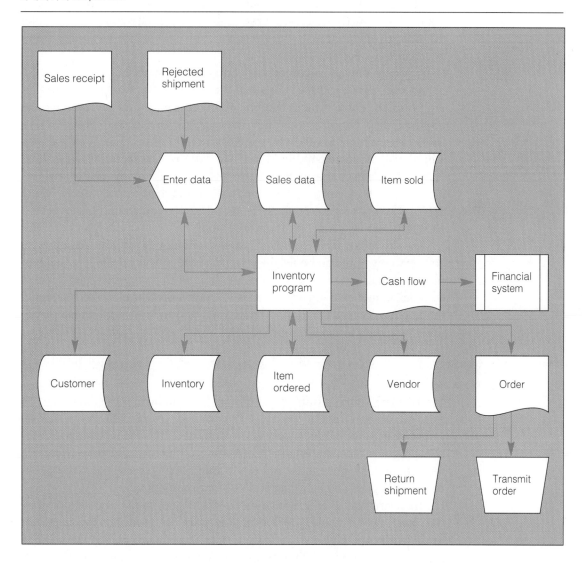

system's discrete components at a black-box level. The symbol numbers are for reference and the large boxes drawn around sets of components relate the system flowchart to the automation boundaries on the data flow diagram. Note how the data files serve to link the primary components. Take the time to read through the flowchart and make sure you understand what each symbol means.

A system flowchart can be misleading, so more documentation might be needed. For example, consider the six on-line storage symbols in Figure 13.15. Each of those symbols represents a file and each on-line file implies a disk. Does the alternative call for one disk to hold all six files, or six separate disks? Should you use 5.25-inch diskettes, 3.5-inch diskettes, a hard disk, or some combination? Two experts looking at the same flowchart might reasonably answer those questions differently, so the analyst's intent must be clearly documented in an attached set of notes (Figure 13.16). If you compare Figures 13.15 and 13.16, you should discover that all the system flowchart symbols are listed.

The flowchart for a complex system can be quite lengthy. An off-page connector symbol can be used to continue the flowchart on a subsequent page, but multiple-page flowcharts are difficult to read. When faced with a complex system, a good approach is to draw a high-level flowchart showing key functions as predefined processes and then explode those predefined processes to the appropriate level on subsequent pages.

Alternative Physical Designs

Figure 13.17 shows a different alternative for the inventory system. In this one, all or part of the logic associated with every data flow diagram process but *Physical inventory* is incorporated in a single *Manage inventory* program. Sales transactions, incoming shipments, and advertising still require manual procedures, but clerical personnel access the *Manage inventory* program to enter data and obtain information.

To verify that an alternative meets the system requirements, compare the data flow diagram to the system flowchart. Start with the logical model and identify the physical component that implements each process, data store, and data flow. In this example, the data stores appear as on-line storage symbols, the processes are incorporated in the program, in manual procedures, or in predefined processes, and the data flows appear as

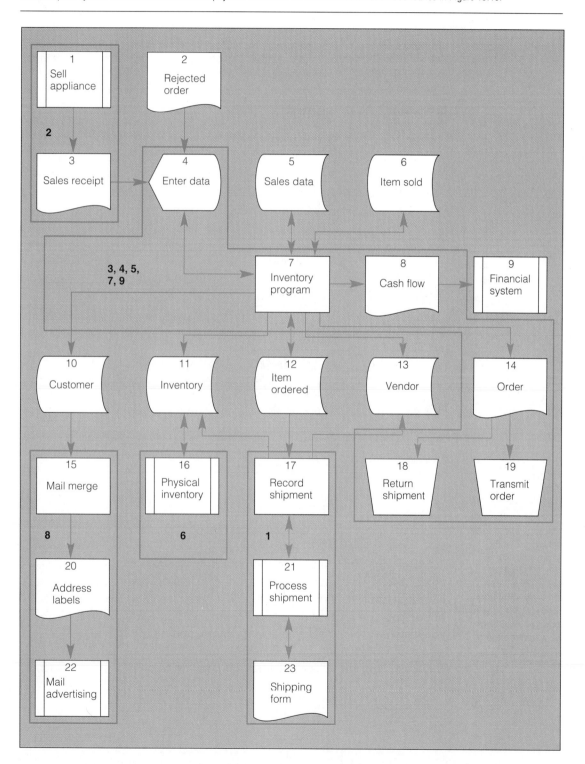

FIGURE 13.16
Clearly document the components associated with each alternative in an attached set of notes. This figure lists the components for the alternative pictured in Figure 13.15.

Component	Implements
Personal computer	7. *Inventory program*
	15. *Mail merge*
	17. *Record shipment*
Keyboard/display	4. *Enter data*
Laser printer	8. *Cash flow*
	14. *Order*
	20. *Address labels*
Hard disk	10. *Customer*
	11. *Inventory*
	12. *Item ordered*
	13. *Vendor*
Diskette drive	5. *Sales data*
	6. *Item sold*
Manual procedures	1. *Sell appliance*
	16. *Physical inventory*
	18. *Return shipment*
	19. *Transmit order*
	21. *Process shipment*
	22. *Mail advertising*
Paper forms	3. *Sales receipt*
External forms	2. *Rejected order*
	23. *Shipping form*
Other system	9. *Financial system*

If you cannot find a logical component in the system flowchart, you probably overlooked something. If you cannot find a physical component on the data flow diagram, you may have added an unnecessary component to the system.

flowlines. If you cannot find a logical component in the system flowchart, you probably overlooked something.

After you finish mapping the data flow diagram to the system flowchart, reverse the process. Start with the system flowchart and ensure that each flowchart symbol corresponds to at least one data flow diagram symbol. If you cannot find a physical component on the data flow diagram, you may have added an unnecessary component to the system.

Finally, document the components needed to support this alternative (Figure 13.18). If the sales transaction data are to be input as they occur,

FIGURE 13.17
A second alternative derived from the same logical model.

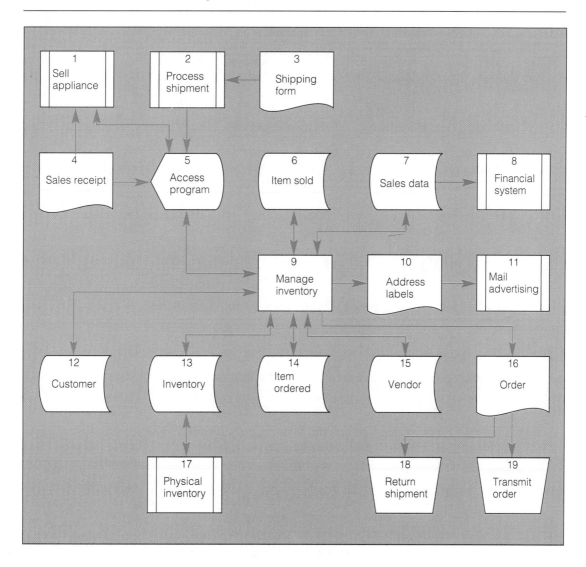

FIGURE 13.18
The components that support the alternative documented in Figure 13.17.

Component	Implements
3 Personal computers	1. *Sell appliance*
3 Keyboard/display	5. *Access program*
3 Dot-matrix printer	4. *Sales receipt*
1 Personal computer	2. *Process shipment*
1 Keyboard/display	5. *Access program*
1 Network server	9. *Manage inventory*
1 Hard disk	6. *Item sold*
	7. *Sales data*
	12. *Customer*
	13. *Inventory*
	14. *Item ordered*
	15. *Vendor*
1 Laser printer	10. *Address labels*
	16. *Order*
External forms	3. *Shipping form*
External system	8. *Financial system*
Manual procedures	1. *Sell appliance*
	11. *Mail advertising*
	17. *Physical inventory*
	18. *Return shipment*
	19. *Transmit order*

you must have several data entry stations for the sales personnel. (If you have ever been in a crowded supermarket with only one open checkout lane, you know why.) Because shipments arrive at the loading dock and the people who process them must have convenient access to the system, you will need another data entry station. If these data entry stations are to be linked to a common program, you'll need a network server and network software, too. This second alternative would provide faster service than the first one, but it would cost a great deal more. (In fact, it almost certainly exceeds the inventory system's scope and thus should not be presented as a realistic alternative.)

Compare the two inventory system flowcharts and review their components. Both are derived from the same data flow diagram, so they perform the same logical functions, but they are clearly different. Numerous other physical alternatives could be derived from the same logical model, and a separate system flowchart could be drawn for each one. There are many hows, but only one what.

PROFESSIONAL POINTER   ■

Document Each Symbol's Meaning

If no supporting documentation is available, a system flowchart can be misleading. It summarizes a great deal of information for those who know what the symbols mean, but if personnel change (and turnover is a problem in the information systems field), the new people might legitimately misinterpret the system designer's intent. As a result, the wrong system might be implemented.

For example, in an effort to show a need for system backup, the analyst might add a magnetic tape symbol to the system flowchart. There are many ways to backup files. The designer's intent might have been to imply backup to some "generic" magnetic medium, with the precise medium to be determined later, but a new designer inheriting the project might reasonably interpret the symbol as a requirement for magnetic tape. Take the time to document the meaning of each symbol on your system flowchart.

Advantages and Disadvantages

A data flow diagram is an abstract, logical model. A system flowchart is a concrete, physical model that identifies the system's discrete components. Programs and procedures replace generalized processes; files and databases replace data stores; reports and screens replace data flows. Given the flowchart, it is possible to visualize exactly how the system will be implemented. A system flowchart is particularly valuable as a presentation aid because it shows how the major components fit together. In effect, it acts as a system road map.

Other benefits accrue to the analyst. Using the flowchart as a guide, discrete units of work (such as writing a program or installing a new printer) can be identified, cost estimated, and scheduled. On large projects, the components suggest how the work might be divided into subsystems. Some analysts also use system flowcharts to help develop operating system command language specifications. For example, on an IBM mainframe each program symbol calls for an EXEC statement and each peripheral device implies one DD statement.

A system flowchart's symbols represent *physical* components.

A system flowchart's symbols represent *physical* components, and the mere act of drawing one implies a physical decision. Consequently, system flowcharts are poor planning tools because the appropriate time for making physical decisions is *after* planning has been completed. Use data flow diagrams or entity-relationship diagrams to plan a solution. Develop a prototype if necessary. Identify the system's requirements. Then choose one or more physical alternatives, and draw system flowcharts to *document* them.

■   **MANAGEMENT'S PERSPECTIVE**

Effective Management Requires Planning

Once design begins, the focus shifts to the system's discrete physical components. Consequently, progress is easier to measure and such traditional tools as budgets and schedules can be used to support project management. Most of the activities that take place during the transition from analysis to design are performed to support management. The project's costs, benefits, and resource needs are estimated, and those estimates, in turn, allow management to prioritize and schedule projects and allocate the resources needed to complete them.

Summary

During the transition from analysis to design the analyst generates and documents several alternatives, estimates costs and benefits and performs a cost/benefit analysis, and prepares a development plan for the recommended alternative. The data flow diagram is a good starting point for generating alternatives. The first step is to identify the trigger event and the maximum acceptable response time for each process. You then group processes by drawing automation boundaries on the data flow diagram. Each set of automation boundaries defines a family of alternatives. Some analysts use checklists to generate alternatives.

One way to document an alternative is to draw a physical data flow diagram. A system flowchart is another option. Because a system flowchart can be interpreted several different ways, it is necessary to document the components associated with each of the symbols.

Suggestions for Additional Reading

Boillot, Michel H., et al. 1985. *Essentials of Flowcharting.* 4th ed. Dubuque, IA: Wm. C. Brown Company.

Gane, Chris, and Trish Sarson. 1979. *Structured Systems Analysis: Tools and Techniques.* Englewood Cliffs, NJ: Prentice-Hall, Inc.

Gore, Marvin, and John W. Stubbe. 1988. *Elements of Systems Analysis.* 4th ed. Dubuque, IA: Wm. C. Brown Company.

Weinberg, Gerald M., and Daniel Weinberg. 1988. *General Principles of System Design.* New York: Dorset House Publishing.

Exercises

1. Briefly describe the tasks that are performed during the transition from analysis to design and explain why each of those tasks is necessary.

2. The analyst typically investigates several alternative solutions before detailed design begins. Why?

3. The real problem is not generating alternatives, but finding *realistic* alternatives. Do you agree or disagree? Explain why.

4. Briefly explain the process of generating alternative solutions by drawing automation boundaries on a data flow diagram.

5. Some analysts use a checklist to generate alternative solutions. What advantages are associated with using a checklist? How can a checklist be used with automation boundaries?

6. Why is a system flowchart such a useful tool for documenting a physical alternative?

7. It is sometimes necessary to attach notes to a system flowchart to explain what the analyst meant by each of the symbols. Why?

8. A system flowchart is *not* a good planning tool. Why?

9. Draw system flowcharts to document at least two alternative high-level physical designs for The Appliance Store's inventory system. Do *not* reproduce the system flowcharts from this chapter.

10. Chapter 2 introduced projects for The Print Shop, Jan Tompson's Campus Threads clothing store, and Bill Barnett's automobile dealership. Draw system flowcharts to document at least two alternative high-level physical designs for one or more of those projects or for your own project.

If the benefits do not exceed the cost, then the system is not worth developing.

14

Evaluating Alternatives

When you finish reading this chapter, you should be able to:
—Distinguish between development costs, operating costs, and benefits.
—Distinguish between tangible and intangible benefits.
—Explain how to estimate development costs.
—Explain how to select a platform for a given alternative.
—Explain how to estimate operating costs and benefits.
—Briefly explain the objectives of cost/benefit analysis.

Costs and Benefits

Cost/benefit analysis is the de facto basis for allocating resources.

Most organizations have a limited supply of capital and other resources, and cost/benefit analysis is the de facto basis for allocating those resources. The idea is to treat each project as a potential capital investment and select those projects that promise the highest return on investment. Much of the relevant terminology is borrowed from finance and cost accounting, so the results are meaningful to most managers.

FIGURE 14.1
The accuracy of the estimate improves as work progresses.

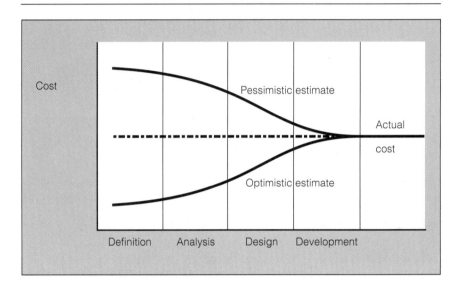

Development costs are one-time costs that occur before the system is released to the user. They include the labor and hardware costs associated with problem definition, the feasibility study, analysis, design, development, and testing. Estimated development costs also play a role in project management where they serve as targets against which actual progress can be measured.

The earlier costs are estimated, the more useful they are for planning.

The earlier in the life cycle development costs are estimated, the more useful they are for planning purposes. During problem definition the best you can do is make an informed guess about the system's likely order of magnitude cost; the actual cost of the system (a perfect "estimate") is usually not known until after the system is finished (Figure 14.1). However, reasonably accurate estimates can be made during the transitional period between analysis and design, and that is early enough to be useful.

Operating costs are those continuing costs that begin after the system is released and last for the life of the system. They include personnel, supplies, maintenance, utilities, insurance, and similar costs. New systems are developed to obtain **benefits. Tangible benefits** can be measured in financial terms and usually imply reduced operating costs, enhanced revenues, or both. **Intangible benefits,** such as improved morale or employee safety, are more difficult to measure, but they can be very important. Accurate estimates of costs and benefits are essential to cost/benefit analysis.

Accurate estimates of costs and benefits are essential to cost/benefit analysis.

PROFESSIONAL POINTER   ■

Take Cost Estimating Seriously

The computing profession has such a poor reputation for estimating costs and projecting schedules that "late and over budget" has become almost a cliche. To an engineer, being 2 percent over budget is embarrassing. To a programmer, coming within 20 percent of the target is considered pretty good. That must change.

The reason bad estimates are a problem is that few systems or programs are developed in a vacuum. Other groups make plans that assume the proposed new system will be delivered as promised. If the system is late or over budget, those plans must be adjusted, and people resent the fact that they cannot depend on the computer "experts."

This inability (or unwillingness) to accurately estimate cost and time hurts the profession's image. Better tools and methodologies can help, but there is no magic formula. Preparing a cost estimate is hard work, and the key is meticulous attention to detail. Perhaps if we began to pay as much attention to our cost estimates as we do to our code, the problem would be solved.

Cost-estimating Strategies

The first rule of cost estimating is to use a methodology. A methodical approach helps to ensure that nothing is overlooked and tends to produce more consistent estimates. Many organizations have developed internal cost-estimating standards, and numerous commercial methodologies are available. Two good examples are Barry Boehm's CONSTRUCTIVE COST MODEL (COCOMO) and the Putnam SLIM model. Once a cost-estimating methodology has been selected, it can be integrated into the organization's CASE product and subsequently enforced by the software.

Use a methodology.

Ideally, the responsibility for developing a cost estimate should be assigned to someone with no personal stake in the project because it is

It is difficult to be objective when you have a vested interest in the outcome.

difficult to be objective when you have a vested interest in the outcome. An experienced cost-estimating specialist or an outside consultant are good choices. The estimator's primary responsibility should be the accuracy of the estimate, not the delivery of the product.

It is difficult to directly estimate the cost of a complete system, so most analysts follow a "divide and conquer" strategy. The idea is to focus on the system's components or modules, independently estimate the cost of each of them, and then sum the component costs. This approach, called bottom-up estimating, is the basis for most of the more popular methodologies.

"Divide and conquer."

Most analysts estimate software costs indirectly by starting with such cost factors as programmer time, lines of code, number of modules, number of basic structures, and so on. For example, it is relatively easy to estimate the number of lines of code in a well-specified program module, and if you accumulate the individual module estimates, you get a good sense of the number of lines of code in the program. If you divide that sum by the number of lines of code produced per month by a typical programmer, you get programmer months. Multiply that quotient by a programmer's monthly salary and you get the program's expected cost.

Cost estimates should always be verified.

Cost estimates should always be verified. The best way to verify a cost estimate is to have two different groups independently prepare it. For example, an estimating team might use a bottom-up methodology to develop a precise, detailed estimate. Meanwhile, an experienced analyst might prepare a ballpark estimate based on his or her experience. If the results are comparable, the detailed estimate is probably good. If the numbers differ significantly, something is wrong and further study is needed.

Auditing is another way to verify a cost estimate. The auditor selects specific details from the estimate and asks the analyst to explain them. If the analyst can produce the appropriate documentation to support the selected values, there is reason to believe that the overall estimate is correct. If, on the other hand, the analyst cannot prove the details, the entire estimate loses validity.

One way to ensure that people take cost estimating seriously is to hold them responsible for the accuracy of their estimates. Perhaps the best way to evaluate estimates is to identify and explain differences between estimated and actual costs during a postrelease audit. Over time, these audits can help an organization fine-tune its cost-estimating standards and procedures.

Estimating Development Costs

Development costs are those costs encountered up to the time the system is released to the user (Figure 14.2). They include the costs associated with problem definition, the feasibility study, analysis, requirements specification, design, development, and testing. Any equipment purchased to support the new system is a development cost. The salaries of the analysts, designers, technical writers, programmers, and other personnel who work on creating the system are included along with the cost of the computer time and the supplies they use. During system release, the costs associated with training, testing, and fine-tuning are development costs.

Note that these are *one-time* costs. They start accumulating when work on the project begins and end when the finished system is released to the user. Contrast development costs with the operating costs that start when the system is released and continue for the life of the system.

Development costs are *one-time* costs.

Identifying the System's Components

The first step in estimating development costs is to compile a list of the system's physical components. Figure 14.3 shows a system flowchart that documents one alternative inventory system, and Figure 14.4 is a list of components derived from that flowchart. Given that list you can begin to estimate each component's cost.

Selecting a Platform

If the alternative being estimated includes a computer, the next step is to select a **platform**. A platform is defined by a specific set of hardware and an operating system. DOS, Windows, and OS/2 all run on IBM PS/2 and compatible microcomputers and represent three different platforms. Apple's Macintosh system is a non-IBM microcomputer platform. Other popular platforms include a DEC VAX running UNIX and an IBM mainframe running MVS. Once you select a platform, your choice of software and peripheral hardware is constrained by the platform.

Your choice of software and peripheral hardware is constrained by the platform.

The secret to selecting a platform is to express the system's requirements in terms of certain common measures of hardware performance (Figure 14.5). Consider cost first. A typical microcomputer system sells for

FIGURE 14.2
Development costs are encountered up to the time the system is released to the user.

Problem Definition
Analyst time
Meetings
Interviews

Feasibility Study
Analyst time
Meetings
Supplies
Interviews
Computer time
Inspections
Presentations
Reviews

Analysis
Analyst time
Meetings
Supplies
Computer time
Walkthroughs
Presentations
Interviews
Inspections
Reviews

Requirements Specification
Analyst time
Technical writer time
Meetings
Supplies
Computer time
Verification time
Presentations
Printing costs
Walkthroughs
Inspections
Reviews

Design
Analyst time
Designer time
Walkthroughs
Reviews
Meetings
Supplies
Computer time
Inspections

Development
Equipment costs
Equipment testing
Site preparation
Supplies
Coding time
Debug time
Documentation time
Technical writer time
Walkthroughs
Module testing
Program testing
Computer time
System testing

Release
Final test
User training
Database initialization
File initialization
Fine-tuning
Troubleshooting
Hand-holding

FIGURE 14.3
A system flowchart for one alternative inventory system.

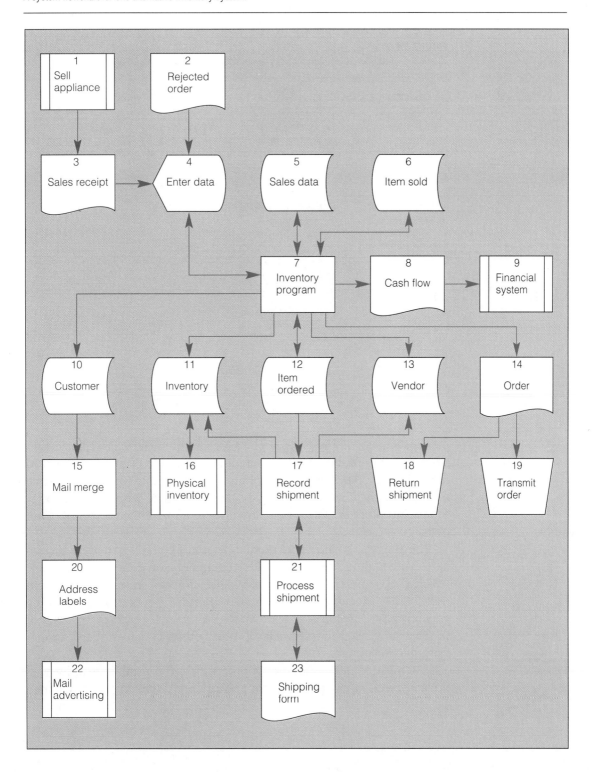

FIGURE 14.4
The components that compose a system can be extracted from the system flowchart.

Personal Computer
Keyboard/display
Laser printer
Hard disk
Diskette drive

Software
Inventory program
Mail merge program
Record shipment program

Reports and Forms
Cash flow report
Order form
Address labels
Sales receipt
Rejected order
Shipping form

Files
Customer
Inventory
Item ordered
Vendor
Sales data
Item sold

Manual Procedures
Sell appliance
Physical inventory
Return shipment
Transmit order
Process shipment
Mail advertising

Financial System

---

perhaps $2,500, and systems can be purchased for less than $1,000. Mini-computers are more expensive, ranging from a low of about $10,000 to more than $500,000, while mainframes range from $100,000 to several million dollars. Given the $10,000 scope associated with The Appliance Store's inventory system, a minicomputer or a mainframe is probably out of the question.

The ability to support concurrent operations is an important distinction between computer types. Most microcomputers are designed for a single user. Minicomputers, on the other hand, support scores of concurrent users, while a mainframe can deal with hundreds, even thousands, and a network provides at least one level of concurrency for each workstation. If the alternative calls for several levels of concurrency, you probably cannot use a microcomputer.

The most common measure of processor speed is millions of instructions per second, or MIPS. It is not always clear if the MIPS value claimed

FIGURE 14.5
Some common measures of hardware performance. The actual numbers change frequently, so the table values are for illustration only.

		Microcomputer	Minicomputer	Mainframe
Cost	LOW	$1,000	$10,000	$100,000
	TYPICAL	2,500	50,000	3,000,000
	HIGH	10,000	500,000	20,000,000
Concurrent Users		1	Scores	Hundreds
MIPS	LOW	1.0	1.0	3.0
	TYPICAL	2.0	4.0	10.0
	HIGH	4.0	6.0	30.0
Memory	LOW	2MB	512KB	4MB
	TYPICAL	4MB	40MB	50MB
	HIGH	16MB	1GB	1GB
Peripherals	LOW	3	10	20
	TYPICAL	4	50	100+
	HIGH	8	200	600
Secondary Storage	LOW	360KB	200MB	360MB
	TYPICAL	80MB	1GB	10GB
	HIGH	200MB	500GB	7,000GB
Physical Size		Desktop	Desk	Small room

for a given computer is based on clock speed (the theoretical limit), cycle time for a typical instruction mix (whatever that means), or benchmark performance, so comparing two computers based on MIPS is a bit like comparing apples and oranges. However, given estimates of a program's size (number of instructions), response time, transaction rate, and execution time, it is relatively easy to convert the speed requirements of the application to a MIPS equivalent, so the numbers are useful. If the processing speed required by a program exceeds a microcomputer's speed, you can't use a microcomputer. If a minicomputer is not fast enough, you need a mainframe.

Memory capacity is another important statistic. On most computers it is measured in 8-bit bytes, although some machines use words. On larger computers, the amount of *virtual* memory represents the effective limit on the address space. A program's memory requirements consist of space to hold the program's logic, active data, buffers, and control routines, so estimate the number of bytes required by each of those factors and sum them to get the necessary memory space. Once again, if the system's requirements exceed a microcomputer's capacity, you need a minicomputer, and so on.

Other measures of performance are concerned with peripheral devices. For example, secondary storage capacity affects the amount of data that can be accessed by a system, and the number of disk drives is limited by the number of peripherals a platform can support. A microcomputer is restricted by the number of available slots on the motherboard, so a screen, a printer, two or three disk drives, a modem, and perhaps three other peripheral devices is about all you can have. Minicomputers and mainframes use channels to significantly increase the number of peripherals.

To compute the system's secondary storage requirements, first identify its files and databases. For each data entity, study the data structure to determine the record size and multiply record size by the estimated number of records to be stored. Then sum the space requirements for all the data entities to get a rough estimate of the amount of secondary space you'll need. (Remember to include additional space for expansion.) Compare the answer to the limits imposed by a microcomputer, a minicomputer, and a mainframe and you'll know which platform to choose.

To estimate the number of peripheral devices required by the system, first determine the number of concurrent users. Each one will need a terminal or some other means of accessing the computer. Add the number of disk drives needed to hold the files and databases, and don't forget printers and other I/O devices. Once again, compare the result to the limits imposed by each platform and then make your decision.

Anything you can do on a microcomputer you can do on a minicomputer, and anything you can do on a minicomputer you can do on a mainframe, but the reverse is *not* necessarily true.

Note that you can use a microcomputer only if it is sufficiently powerful to support *every* requirement. If even one requirement exceeds a microcomputer's capacity, then you must use *at least* a minicomputer, and if any single requirement demands a mainframe's power, then the system requires a mainframe. Anything you can do on a microcomputer you can do on a minicomputer, and anything you can do on a minicomputer you can do on a mainframe, but the reverse is *not* necessarily true.

■   **PROFESSIONAL POINTER**

Define Standard Platforms

The microcomputer revolution resembled guerrilla warfare in many organizations. Often, the decision to use a personal computer was a reaction to poor MIS service, and the equipment was installed over the objections of the MIS staff. In the absence of a plan, people naturally selected the hardware and software they already knew how to use so, by the time MIS reacted, it found itself dealing with several platforms, numerous word-processing and spreadsheet programs, and incompatible data formats.

If your organization is to avoid that nightmare, you need standard platforms. You might choose DOS, Windows, OS/2, or the Apple Macintosh for your microcomputer systems. UNIX runs on several different hardware configurations. In recent years, the midsize IBM AS/400 running OS/400 has grown in popularity. MVS running on an IBM computer is the dominant mainframe platform, but many other options exist. (The great thing about standards is that there are so many to choose from.)

The choice can be difficult. It is tempting to postpone the decision until the marketplace or some standards group defines the *right* platforms, but that may never happen. Any reasonable standard is probably better than no standard at all because if change should prove necessary, at least you'll be able to change everything from the same base.

Estimating Hardware Costs

Given a platform, you can find reasonably current cost data for commercially available hardware in such sources as technical periodicals and newsletters, catalogs, vendor literature, and publications such as *The Auerbach Reports* and *The Datapro Reports*. If you don't have access to a library, any retail computer store should be able to give you current prices for the computers they carry, and minicomputer and mainframe vendors usually respond quickly to a request for a price quotation. The first several lines in Figure 14.6 list costs for the inventory system's hardware components.

One frequently overlooked aspect of hardware cost is site preparation. Apparently trivial things such as the size of a room or the width of a doorway become significant if the equipment does not fit. Vendors publish technical specifications for their hardware, and such parameters as size and weight are usually listed. Measure the available space and be certain each piece of hardware fits. If new space is needed, the cost can be factored into the decision-making process.

Check the equipment's power requirements, too. Attempting to run a computer with less than adequate power can lead to downtime or even damage the equipment and void your warranty. Rewiring might be necessary, particularly in older buildings. Finally, look into environmental requirements. Computers are designed to work best within fairly narrow temperature and humidity ranges, and additional air conditioning might be necessary. Planned expenditures are better than surprises.

Planned expenditures are better than surprises.

FIGURE 14.6
A cost estimate for the inventory system.

Cost Estimate

System: Inventory management   Date: May 8, 1994
Prepared by: W. S. Davis

Component	Cost	Total
Purchased hardware and software		
Acme 486 SX computer (or equivalent)	$2,600	
4MB memory		
1.44MB diskette drive		
120MB hard disk		
VGA interface		
Keyboard		
Apollo VGA display (or equivalent)	500	
JPC laser printer (or equivalent)	1,400	
Manage inventory program	450	
Mail merge program	120	
Site preparation and installation	500	
System test	1,000	$6,570
Professional time (at $250/day)		
Select hardware and software (1.5 days)	375	
Customize reports (1 day)	250	
Clarify manual procedures (1 day)	250	
Design files (4 days)	1,000	
Design *Record shipment* program (1 day)	250	
Write *Record shipment* program (1 day)	250	
Train clerical personnel (0.5 days)	125	
Train sales clerks (2 days)	500	
Train inventory manager (1 day)	250	
Train store manager (1 day)	250	3,500
Clerical time (at $100/day)		
Initialize *Vendor* file (1 day)	100	
Initialize *Customer* file (2 days)	200	
Initialize *Inventory* file (5 days)	500	800
Subtotal		10,870
Contingency (10 percent)		1,087
Total		$11,957
Consulting services		1,000
TOTAL ESTIMATED SYSTEM COST		$12,957

Purchased Software

Like hardware, the cost of purchased software can be obtained from technical publications, newsletters, vendor literature, and numerous other sources. Figure 14.6 lists two purchased programs: *Manage inventory* and *Mail merge*. Often the real problem is not finding appropriate commercial software but selecting a program from a host of alternatives. A good strategy is to develop a set of test procedures based on the requirements specifications and then use those procedures to screen the software.

Software Development

The cost estimate for the inventory system (Figure 14.6) includes two days of programmer time to design, write, and test the *Record shipment* program. To estimate the software development cost for a more complex program, decompose the program into modules, estimate lines of code for each module, sum the module estimates, divide by your organization's standard for lines of code per time period, and multiply the result by the appropriate programmer cost. Although few analysts can picture all the details associated with a complete program, modules are easy to visualize, so module estimates tend to be quite accurate.

Several more formal techniques can be used to estimate software development costs. For example, the COCOMO model uses the formula

$$K_m = 2.4 \, S_k^{1.05}$$

where: K_m represents programmer months, and
S_k represents thousands of lines of code.

The numbers 2.4 and 1.05 are constants derived from actual experience on scores of projects. Additional parameters can be used to adjust the formula for such attributes as project complexity, hardware constraints, analyst and programmer experience, and the use of modern programming practices. For more information see Barry Boehm's book, *Software Engineering Economics*. Some CASE products incorporate a formal cost-estimating methodology based on COCOMO or a similar model.

Often, in an effort to deliver the system more quickly, the work is assigned to a team instead of to a single analyst or programmer. If one person can write a program in six months, it might seem reasonable to assume that two can do the job in three months, but that is not always the case.

Some tasks cannot be subdivided.

Some tasks cannot be subdivided. (It takes nine months to have a baby no matter how many women you assign.) Other tasks *can* be subdivided, but not without added cost. For example, if one person can mow a football field in one hour, two people might be able to do the job in half an hour, but 60 people would need considerably more than one minute because it would take so much time to coordinate and manage them. The problem is compounded by the nature of the programming process. Creating software is inherently different from producing widgets (or automobiles or soft drinks), and the rules that apply to manufacturing such things are simply not valid when they are applied to software.

Unfortunately, there is no simple equation to adjust a cost estimate for the number of people involved. The amount of time required for management and coordination depends on such factors as the complexity of the job and the experience of the workers. The point is to be aware of these costs and to allow for them. One suggestion on small projects is to add an extra unit of work to each module for each person who shares the work. If the estimate is expressed in days, add one day per module per person; if it is expressed in months, add a month, and so on. On larger projects, use a formal methodology such as the COCOMO model.

We will return to this issue in Chapter 16.

Other Cost Factors

No matter how good a cost estimator you are, you will always miss some costs. For example, such tasks as hardware installation, user training, file and database initialization, software fine-tuning, parallel runs, testing, meetings, walkthroughs, reviews, postinstallation "hand-holding," and

Checklists are effective.

many others are easy to overlook. Checklists are perhaps the most effective tool for remembering them. In many organizations, the cost estimator starts with a standard list of potential cost factors and prepares a cost estimate for each one. If a particular cost factor does not apply to the project, the analyst is expected to explain why.

Verification

Bottom-up cost estimates tend to be precise, but, because the analyst focuses on the individual modules and components, it is easy to overlook interfaces, control structures, and even major components. Consequently, it is important that you verify your cost estimate in some way.

FIGURE 14.7
Using historical data, you can compile a typical life-cycle cost distribution and then use it to quickly estimate the ballpark cost of a new project.

Phase	Percent of Total Cost	Spent to Date	Estimated Cost
Feasibility study	10		
Analysis and requirements	25	$25,000	
Design	25		$17,858
Development	30		21,428
Testing and release	10		7,142
Total	100		$71,428

One simple **top-down** estimating technique is to compare the new
project's expenditures to a typical project. For example, imagine that Figure
14.7 represents the average breakdown of life-cycle costs for a number of
projects done over the past several years. Note that expenditures for problem definition and analysis represent 35 percent of the total system cost. If,
to cite an example, $25,000 has been spent through the analysis stage,
then, assuming the new system is typical, it should cost roughly $71,000 to
develop ($25,000 divided by 35 percent). Similar ratios can be used to es-
timate the cost of each life-cycle step.

The numbers in Figure 14.7 are for illustration only. There is no standard life-cycle cost breakdown, and it is doubtful that any single cost distribution will be valid for all projects. The best bet is for your firm to develop its own internal cost patterns from historical data. If you need help
getting started, Barry Boehm's *Software Engineering Economics* discusses
life-cycle cost distributions in some detail, and numerous other studies
have been published.

A second top-down technique is to estimate by analogy. The basic idea
is to compare the new system to similar projects that were completed in
the past. For example an analyst might sense that the inventory program is
comparable to the accounts payable program completed a year ago. If the
cost of the old program is known (and it should be), then that cost represents a pretty good ballpark estimate for the inventory program. Some ad-
justment for inflation or degree of difficulty might be necessary, but if the
analogy is reasonable, the estimate is usually reasonable.

If the bottom-up and top-down estimates are similar, they tend to verify each other.

If the bottom-up and top-down estimates are similar, they tend to verify each other. If they differ significantly, however, more work remains to be done. Perhaps the new project is not typical. If so, show where the bottom-up estimate differs from the top-down pattern. Maybe you missed a component or an interface. Maybe you made a computational error. If you can explain the differences, the two estimates can still be used to verify each other.

Top-down cost estimates can be surprisingly accurate, but because they tend to be somewhat subjective they lack precision and are difficult to audit or verify. They should be used primarily to validate a more precise bottom-up estimate.

Contingencies

Management must be given a sense of each project's level of risk.

There are risks associated with developing a new system. Management must be given a sense of each project's level of risk so that they can intelligently choose which ones to support and which ones to reject. One option is to add a **contingency factor** to the estimate to cover unanticipated costs.

Start by listing everything that could possibly go wrong with the project. Then estimate the cost associated with each problem. For example, if slipping the inventory system's release date by three months means $20,000 in extra programmer costs plus a $10,000 opportunity loss, the total cost of a three-month delay is $30,000.

Next, estimate the probability that each of those problems will occur and multiply that probability by the estimated cost. The result is the problem's expected cost. For example, imagine that there is a 10 percent chance of the inventory system being three months late. If that problem occurs, it will cost an extra $30,000. The expected cost of that problem is 10 percent of $30,000, or $3,000. The contingency factor is the sum of the expected costs of all the potential problems.

Some organizations prefer to assign a subjective risk factor (low, intermediate, high) to each project and then use the risk factor to select a contingency percentage. For example, low risk projects might call for a contingency factor equal to 5 percent of the total development cost, while intermediate risks carry a 10 percent contingency, and high risks carry a 20 percent contingency. Because the contingency factor is added to the development cost, it affects the cost/benefit analysis.

PROFESSIONAL POINTER   ■

Measure the Right Things

Once upon a time, a sawmill decided to pay its buzz saw operators based on the number of board feet of lumber they produced. Because of space limitations, it was necessary to move the lumber away from the saw as soon as it was cut, so by the time the boards could be counted they could no longer be associated with a specific operator.

An efficiency expert suggested a solution. As the logs were cut, sawdust was produced. More cuts meant more sawdust *and* more lumber, so pounds of sawdust could be converted into board feet of lumber by a simple formula. All that was necessary was to sweep the sawdust generated by each saw into a separate box, weigh the boxes, and compute each operator's daily production.

The plan made sense, so management decided to try it. A few months later, lumber production had declined a bit, but the output of sawdust was way up. Moral: If you measure people based on the amount of sawdust they produce, you will get a lot of sawdust.

The fact that you can measure something does not necessarily mean that it is worth measuring. Keep that idea in mind as you work with various cost-estimating factors. The numbers you use should make sense in the context of the application. If they don't, either they are wrong or you don't understand them.

Estimating Operating Costs and Benefits

Operating costs are those costs that begin when the system is released to the user and continue for the life of the system (Figure 14.8). Checklists are particularly useful for identifying relevant operating costs.

The operating costs associated with a new system are used to estimate benefits (Figure 14.9). A cost reduction is the difference between the new and the old systems' operating costs. Revenue enhancements are computed by subtracting the new system's marginal operating cost from new revenues. The key is the net change in cost, so ignore any cost factor that does not change.

For example, imagine replacing a manual inventory system with a new computer-based inventory system. The costs of operating the old system appear in various accounting reports, so they are known. The new system will add some new costs, such as operating and maintaining the computer, insurance on the new equipment, a maintenance contract, computer

FIGURE 14.8
Operating costs begin when the system is released to the user and continue for the life of the system.

Personnel
System operators
Data entry clerks
Report distribution
Software maintenance

Supplies
Paper
Disks
Forms
Postage

Utilities
Electric
Air conditioning
Heat

Computer Resources (Mainframe)
Processor time
Disk space

Hardware Maintenance
Personnel
Maintenance contracts
Replacement equipment

Backup
Hardware
Supplies; disk space
Emergency plan

Insurance

Security
Physical access
Code management

Lease and Rental Costs
Office space
Equipment

supplies, data entry, and several others. It might eliminate some existing costs; for example, it might be possible to get by with fewer inventory clerks. Finally, the new system might reduce the amount of money tied up in inventory. Sum the savings, subtract the new costs, and you get the net cost reduction.

The key to estimating operating costs is recognizing them.

The key to estimating operating costs is recognizing them. Go through a checklist and identify any cost factor that is likely to change as a result of the new system. Then estimate the costs associated with that factor in both the old and the new systems and compute the difference. Even apparently minor costs can accumulate quickly. For example, postage on a first-class letter seems insignificant, but if you multiply that cost by several thousand pieces of mail per month the annual cost of postage can be imposing.

Cost reduction and revenue enhancement are examples of tangible benefits that can be directly estimated in financial terms. Intangible benefits are more difficult to measure. For example, a new system that improves

FIGURE 14.9
Benefits are the advantages realized from a system.

Tangible Benefits

Cost reduction
  Personnel
  Overtime
  Job consolidation
  Supplies
  Paperwork
  Inventory
  Distribution
  Travel
  Utilities
  Hardware
  Software
  Maintenance
  Improved quality
  Production
  Materials
  Advertising
  Marketing
  Cost of money
  Subcontractor control
  Training

Revenue enhancement
  New products
  Time to market
  Improved quality
  Sales efficiency
  Product enhancements
  Advertising support
  Marketing techniques
  Advertising
  Bidding tools
  New markets

Intangible Benefits

Employee morale
Corporate image
Perceived quality
Time to market
Public relations
Environmental concerns
Reduced turnover
Health and lifestyle
Ethics
Legal concerns
Safety

work place safety *might* save money by reducing time lost to injuries, but there is no way to prove the injuries will actually happen if the new system is not installed. In most organizations, an economic analysis based on *tangible* benefits is the de facto standard for ranking alternative investment opportunities, and the burden of proof for justifying a project based on intangible factors generally rests with the analyst, the user, or the project's sponsor.

Cost/Benefit Analysis

Developing a new system is a form of investment.

Developing a new system is a form of investment. Funds must be committed throughout the life cycle. In return, future benefits are expected. If the benefits do not exceed the cost, then the system is not worth developing. The purpose of cost/benefit analysis is to give management a reasonable picture of the costs, benefits, and risks associated with a given system so they can compare one investment opportunity with others.

Following analysis, the analyst documents high-level physical designs for one or more alternatives and then prepares a cost estimate and a cost/benefit analysis for each one. The first step is to discount all costs and benefits to their present values.

The discounted values can be used to compute the project's payback period, the amount of time it takes for the accumulated benefits to equal the initial investment. The shorter the payback period, the sooner the organization begins realizing a profit. Another measure, net present value, is the difference between the accumulated present value of the benefits and the present value of the investment. The higher the net present value, the better the investment. The internal rate of return is analogous to the annual percentage rate that banks and financial institutions use when advertising an investment opportunity or a loan, so you can use the internal rate of return to compare or to rank in-house and external alternatives. The specific cost/benefit measures to be computed vary with the organization.

If you have ever taken a finance, cost-accounting, or engineering economics course, these cost/benefit measures are probably familiar to you. (If you have never taken such a course, perhaps you should.) Most spreadsheet programs include built-in functions to perform these computations; for example, check the Lotus functions named @NPV and @IRR. You will also find net present value and internal rate of return functions on many scientific and business calculators.

The Management Review

Given a set of alternatives and their associated costs and benefits, the analyst selects the best option, briefly explains why the others were rejected, and prepares an estimate of the resources needed to design and develop the recommended alternative (see Chapter 16). The complete package then goes through a technical inspection and a formal management review.

Following the review, management has several options. They can kill the project. They can postpone development. If the necessary resources are not available, they can subcontract work, hire temporary personnel, instruct the analysts to purchase the necessary software, or postpone work on other projects. The cost/benefit analysis and the proposed budget and schedule give management the information they need to make this decision. Once the project is approved and scheduled, detailed design can begin.

MANAGEMENT'S PERSPECTIVE   ■

Consider Intangible Costs Too

In the early 1980s, Japanese automobile makers focused on such factors as total quality and long-term customer relations. The benefits (if any) were intangible and long-term, but the costs were very tangible and very near-term. Clearly, their strategy worked. Surveys consistently suggest that people choose Japanese cars because of perceived quality.

Meanwhile, at least one domestic automobile maker, in an attempt to cut design and production costs, eliminated all but cosmetic differences between similar cars with different nameplates. (Remember the television ads that criticized the competition's look-alike models?) That decision was not made casually. Sharing production facilities and parts really does reduce costs.

Unfortunately, people did not like the new models. When quality problems surfaced, they affected all the company's nameplates, so people began to associate poor quality with the parent company rather than with one subsidiary. As a result, revenue losses more than offset the cost savings. It is easy (and not very fair) to criticize a decision after the outcome is known, but the American company clearly made a bad one.

In purely financial terms, the Japanese decision was difficult to justify. They accepted a tangible cost to achieve an intangible benefit, and that is risky. The Americans, in contrast, focused on tangible benefits and ignored intangible costs. That is conservative. In this case, the risk paid off and the safe decision proved disastrous.

Intangibles are important, so don't ignore them. Insist that your analysts prepare a cost/benefit analysis based on tangible costs, but insist that they identify intangible costs and benefits, too. Then ask some questions. What if those intangible benefits or those intangible costs are actually realized? How does that change the cost/benefit analysis, and how likely is it to happen? There is more to managing than watching the short-term bottom line.

Summary

Development costs are one-time costs that occur before the system is released to the user. Operating costs are those continuing costs that begin after the system is released and last for the life of the system. New systems are developed to obtain benefits. Tangible benefits can be measured in financial terms and usually imply reduced costs, enhanced revenues, or both. Intangible benefits, such as improved morale or employee safety, are more difficult to measure.

Use a methodology to estimate costs, work from the bottom up, focus on those factors that lead to the cost, and verify the estimate. Start with a high-level system design, independently estimate the cost of each discrete component, and then sum the estimates to get the development cost. The first step in estimating hardware costs is to select a platform. Top-down estimating techniques are useful for verifying an estimate. Add a contingency factor to allow for unanticipated costs and risk.

Operating costs affect benefits. A cost reduction is a net change in operating costs. Any increase in operating costs must be subtracted from new revenues to compute net revenue enhancement. Intangible costs and benefits should be considered where appropriate. Given estimates of development costs and benefits, you can compute such cost/benefit factors as payback period, net present value, and internal rate of return.

Suggestions for Additional Reading

The Auerbach Reports. Pennsauken, NJ: Faulkner Publishing, Inc. Updated frequently.

Boehm, B. W. 1981. *Software Engineering Economics*. Englewood Cliffs, NJ: Prentice-Hall, Inc.

Brooks, Frederick P., Jr. 1975. *The Mythical Man Month*. Reading, MA: Addison-Wesley Publishing Company.

The Datapro Reports. Delran, NJ: Datapro Research, a subsidiary of McGraw-Hill Publishing Company. Updated frequently.

Grady, Robert B., and Deborah L. Caswell. 1987. *Software Metrics: Establishing a Company-Wide Program*. Englewood Cliffs, NJ: Prentice-Hall, Inc.

Londeix, Bernard. 1987. *Cost Estimation for Software Development*. Reading, MA: Addison-Wesley Publishing Company.

Various technical publications, such as *Datamation, Computerworld, PC World, Mac World, PC Week*, and many others.

Exercises

1. Distinguish between development costs, operating costs, and benefits.

2. Distinguish between tangible and intangible costs and benefits.

3. Why is it so important that you follow a methodical approach when you prepare cost estimates?

4. What is bottom-up cost estimating? Why would you choose to estimate bottom up?

5. This chapter suggested that you use such measures as lines of code to estimate software development costs. Why is that a good idea?

6. How can you verify a cost estimate? Why would you want to?

7. What is a contingency factor? Why are contingency factors added to cost estimates? Explain how to compute a contingency factor.

8. The computing profession has a poor reputation for estimating a system's cost. Why do you suppose that is a problem?

9. Prepare a development cost estimate and a list of potential benefits for one of the alternative physical designs from Chapter 13.

10. Chapter 2 introduced projects for The Print Shop, Jan Tompson's Campus Threads clothing store, and Bill Barnett's automobile dealership. Prepare at least one development cost estimate and a list of potential benefits for one or more of those projects or for your own project.

The GARS Project:

15

The Transition to Design

Generating Alternatives

Your analysis team has been authorized to develop a GARS prototype. Because the prototype will serve as a framework for the system, your first task is to rough out a complete system design and then plan the prototype within that context.

Once again the team meets, this time to generate alternative physical designs. The data flow diagram is a good starting point (Figure 15.1). In this logical model, each process represents a group of tasks that share the same trigger event, so a first family of alternatives can be generated by using the CASE system to draw separate automation boundaries around each process.

A second family of alternatives can be generated by merging some hourly functions into process 2, *Control system*. Moving functions on-line usually makes the system easier or more convenient to use. However, adding functions makes the on-line program bigger, more complex, and more difficult to maintain, so the choice is not obvious.

The ultimate system would have all functions on-line. With such a system, customer bills could be compiled and printed on request or mailed throughout the month, customers would have the option of receiving end-of-year reports that correspond with a fiscal rather than a calendar year, and several other marketing advantages might be realized.

Figure 15.2 shows a system flowchart for one alternative. This system contains five programs. *System control* incorporates all the interactive functions including several system control functions (such as maintaining and backing up the system) that are accessed through the system manager's terminal. Three batch programs, *Management report generator, Earnings report generator,* and *Billing program,* perform obvious functions. The *Log analysis program* reads log tapes, generates a report, and allows the system manager to study the log data for security purposes. You should have little difficulty relating the data flow diagram to the system flowchart.

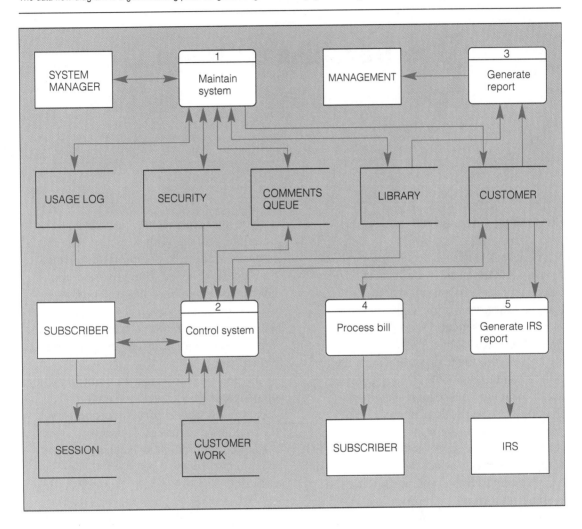

FIGURE 15.2
One alternative system flowchart.

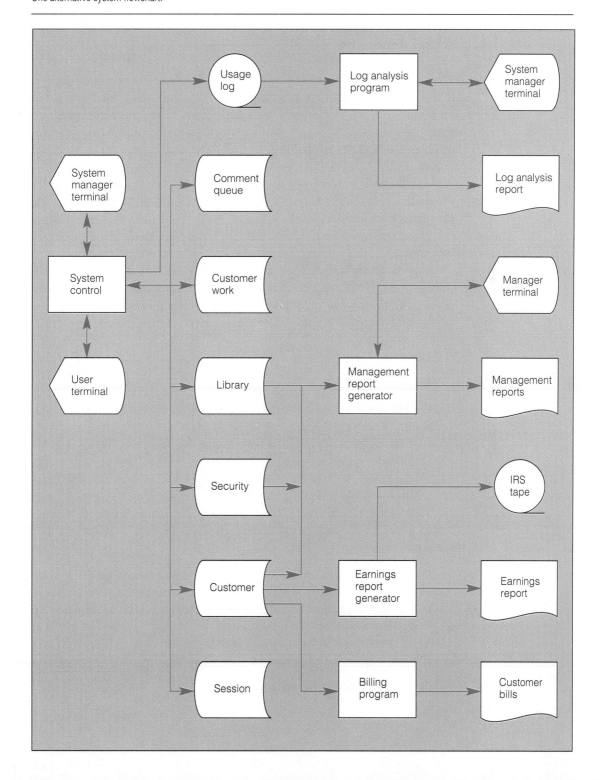

A First Alternative

The prototype must be created within the framework of the high-level system design. It can cost no more than $250,000 and must be completed in 18 months, so the next step is to determine how much of the proposed system design can be implemented given those constraints. Consider, for example, how a prototype might be defined for the system pictured in Figure 15.2.

It is difficult to estimate the cost and development time for a complex program such as *System control,* so its logic must be decomposed. Start by listing the routines that compose the equivalent data flow diagram process and its explosions; you should be able to extract them from the CASE repository.

A good technique for identifying additional functions is to "walk through" a typical user session. For example, start with the user log-on process. Checking a user number and a password implies reading the customer information file, and additional terminal identification logic might also be required.

Following log-on, the customer will request a service, so the system must respond to customer commands and access the various libraries. The user will need a work space, of course. With multiple users, security routines to keep one user from interfering with another must be implemented. Additionally, service charges and royalties must be accumulated and each transaction must be recorded on the usage log tape. Finally, customers might choose to add messages to or retrieve messages from the comments queue. Figure 15.3 summarizes a number of basic *System control* functions. You can prepare similar lists for the other programs.

Given a list of functions, you can begin to estimate their costs. For example, consider the task of checking a user number and a password. The log-on module must:

1. request the user number and the password from the user,
2. access the security file for the user's official password,
3. compare the password entered by the user to the password recorded on the security file, and
4. accept or reject the request for access.

You can visualize that logic. If someone asked you to estimate how long it would take to plan and write the log-on module, you could provide a

FIGURE 15.3
A list of *System control* functions.

Check user number	*Access work space*
Check password	*Implement internal security*
Access customer information	*Charge for service*
Check device identification	*Accumulate royalty*
Identify service requested	*Log usage*
Access games library	*Store comments*
Access sports/ski information	*Retrieve comments*
Access system information	

realistic estimate based on your own experience with similar programming problems. Given an estimate for development time, you can estimate the module's cost.

Figure 15.4 shows the estimated personnel time needed to plan and code each major function in the proposed system. The individual module estimates total 83 analyst months and 121 programmer months. At $3,000 per month for an analyst and $2,500 per month for a programmer, those estimates amount to $249,000 in analysis costs and $302,500 in programming costs for a total of $551,500. Add computer time, testing, management, and overhead, and the system cost clearly exceeds the prototype limit, so some functions must be cut.

Look at the problem another way. The target for completing the prototype is 18 months from project inception. Assume that 3 months have already passed, and that three analysts are assigned to the project. At $3,000 per month per analyst, you have already spent $27,000, leaving $223,000 to complete the prototype.

The three analysts have been assigned to the project for the duration. There are 15 months to go, and that represents 45 analyst months. At $3,000 per month, the analysts will cost an additional $135,000, leaving $88,000 to pay for programmers. If programmers earn, on average, $2,500 per month, you can pay for just over 35 programmer months. You need 83 analyst months to design the complete system, but you have only 45. You need 121 programmer months to implement the system but you can afford only 35. The prototype cannot incorporate all the processes.

Assume that, after extensive discussions with marketing, you are able to group the system's functions into three categories. Some are essential

FIGURE 15.4
Time estimates (in personnel months) by function.

Function	Plan	Program	Total	Cumulative
Overhead	24	0	24	24
System control				
Check user number	1	1	2	26
Check password	1	1	2	28
Access customer information	1	1	2	30
Check device identification	3	3	6	36
Identify service requested	6	6	12	48
Access games library	1	3	4	52
Develop new game	1	1	2	54
Access sports/ski information	1	1	2	56
Access system information	1	1	2	58
Access work space	1	1	2	60
Implement internal security	3	3	6	66
Charge for service	6	8	14	80
Accumulate royalty	6	18	24	104
Log usage	1	3	4	108
Store comments	2	4	6	114
Retrieve comments	2	4	6	120
Analyze log contents	6	18	24	144
Report generator				
Library usage	2	6	8	152
Analyze comments	2	6	8	160
Analyze customer information	2	6	8	168
Billing	4	8	12	180
Earnings report	4	8	12	192
Maintenance and backup	2	10	12	204
Totals	83	121	204	

(Figure 15.5); without them the prototype is not worth doing. Other functions are desirable but not absolutely essential (Figure 15.6); marketing can, reluctantly, live without them. The third list (Figure 15.7) contains "bells and whistles" that can be eliminated without jeopardizing the prototype. Note that some functions are partially implemented on more than one list.

The essential list (Figure 15.5) calls for 36 analyst months and 50 programmer months for a total of 86 personnel months. You and your assistants

FIGURE 15.5
Essential prototype system functions. Note that some functions are only partially implemented.

Function	Plan	Program	Total	Cumulative
Overhead	12	0	12	12
System control				
Check user number	1	1	2	14
Check password	1	1	2	16
Identify service requested	3	3	6	22
Charge for service	2	4	6	28
Log usage	1	1	2	30
Access games library	1	3	4	34
Access sports/ski information	1	1	2	36
Access system information	1	1	2	38
Develop new game	1	1	2	40
Access work space	1	1	2	42
Store user comments	2	4	6	48
Access customer information	1	1	2	50
Analyze log contents (basic)	2	6	8	58
Report generator (partial)				
Library usage	1	3	4	62
Analyze customer information	1	3	4	66
Billing	2	6	8	74
Maintenance and backup	2	10	12	86
Totals	36	50	86	

represent 45 analyst months that have already been assigned to the project, so you have plenty of analyst time. However, based on the computations you just completed, you can afford to pay for only 35 programmer months, and that's not enough. Even if you use the 9 extra months of analyst time to write some of the programs, you will still be 6 programmer months short. At $2,500 per month, that amounts to $15,000 over the $250,000 limit.

You have a total of 45 analyst months and you need only 36, so you could replace an analyst with a programmer for the last 9 months of the project. Programmers cost $500 per month less than analysts, so that would save $4,500 of the cost overrun, but it still appears that the prototype will exceed $250,000.

FIGURE 15.6
Desirable prototype system functions.

Function	Plan	Program	Total	Cumulative
Overhead	6	0	6	6
System control				
Identify service requested	3	3	6	12
Charge for service	2	2	4	16
Accumulate (fixed) royalty	2	4	6	22
Report generator				
Library usage (full)	1	3	4	26
Analyze customer information	1	3	4	30
Earnings report (basic)	2	2	4	34
Totals	17	17	34	

To further complicate matters, assume that marketing has decided to move two functions, fixed royalty payments and the associated basic earnings report, from the desirable to the essential list. That adds 4 planning months ($12,000) and 6 programming months ($15,000) to the total. Those numbers bring you to 40 analyst months and 56 programmer months. If you assign the analysts to do 5 months of programming you can get by with 51 programmer months, but you have enough money to pay for only 35. To implement this alternative, you will need $290,000 ($40,000 more than the amount authorized) to pay for 16 extra programmer months.

Additional Alternatives

Before you arrive at a recommended system design, your team investigates two more alternatives in similar detail. For each alternative you prepare a system flowchart, compile a list of functions to be performed by each physical component, develop a set of cost and time estimates, and identify the functions that will be included in the prototype. (Because the objective is

FIGURE 15.7
"Bells and whistles." In many case, these functions represent the completion of tasks already partially implemented.

Function	Plan	Program	Total	Cumulative
Overhead	6	0	6	6
System control				
Check device identification	3	3	6	12
Charge for service	2	2	4	16
Accumulate royalty	4	14	18	34
Log usage (full)	0	2	2	36
Implement internal security	3	3	6	42
Retrieve comments	2	4	6	48
Analyze log contents	4	12	16	64
Report generator				
Analyze comments	2	6	8	72
Billing (full services)	2	2	4	76
Earnings report (full)	2	6	8	84
Totals	30	54	84	

to create a prototype, a cost/benefit analysis is not necessary.) This information, along with your recommendation, is submitted to management for approval. In this case, assume that the system design outlined in the previous section is the recommended alternative.

Management's Reaction

It will cost $290,000 to develop a GARS prototype that performs the *essential* functions. It would make little sense to implement a prototype that did not include all those functions, so at this point management has two options: increase funding or drop the project. Assume that their decision is to increase funding to $290,000. You now have a good grasp of the functions to be performed by the prototype and sufficient resources to do the job, so you and your team can start to design the prototype.

Exercises

1. This chapter suggested that the prototype should be designed in the context of a system plan. Why?

2. Following system design, management faces an important go/no go decision. Why is it crucial that this decision be made now? Why not earlier?

3. Explain how functional decomposition can help simplify estimating costs.

4. Imagine that you have been asked to design a system to track library circulation. Walk through the process of circulating a book, and list the functions that are involved. In other words, what happens between the time you decide to check out the book, and the time that book is returned to the stacks by library personnel?

5. Explain the process of compiling a priority list of system functions. Why was this such an important step in defining the GARS prototype?

PART V

Physical Design

If the objectives are unrealistic, they will not be met.

16

Project Management

When you finish reading this chapter, you should be able to:

—Explain why systems are designed and developed from the top down.

—Identify a set of activities for a small project and prepare a Gantt chart.

—Define the events, activities, and activity durations for a small project and prepare a project network.

—Given a project network, compute the earliest and latest event times for each event, identify the critical path, and compute the slack time for each activity.

—Outline the contents of a project plan.

Design Strategy

As you begin physical design, the system's requirements are known. Alternative solutions have been investigated, and the preferred high-level design has been selected and documented, perhaps in the form of a system flowchart (Figure 16.1). In most cases, you also have a cost estimate for the recommended alternative (Figure 16.2).

Think of design and development as a top-down process.

Think of design and development as a top-down process (Figure 16.3). Systemwide factors that affect numerous components are defined first. For

FIGURE 16.1
A system flowchart for the recommended alternative.

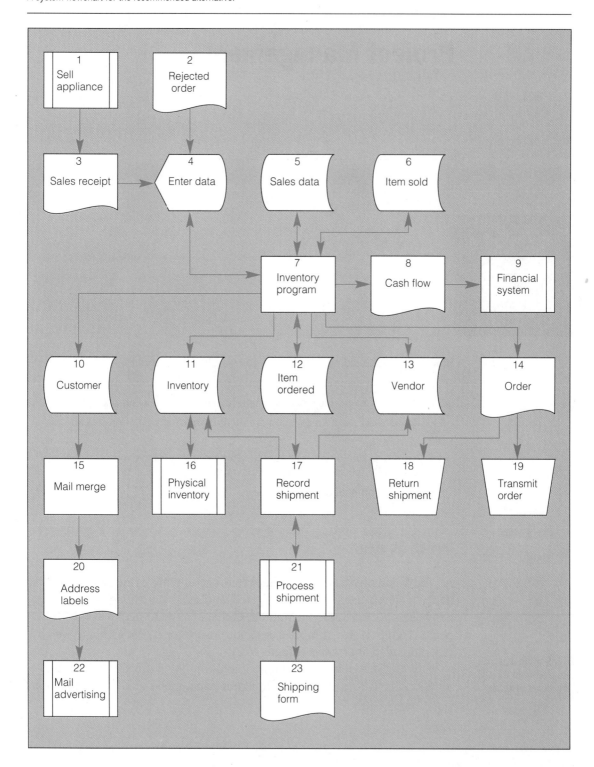

FIGURE 16.2
A cost estimate for the recommended alternative.

365

Cost Estimate

System: Inventory management   **Date:** May 8, 1994
Prepared by: W. S. Davis

Component	Cost	Total
Purchased hardware and software		
Acme 486 SX computer (or equivalent)	$2,600	
4MB memory		
1.44MB diskette drive		
120MB hard disk		
VGA interface		
Keyboard		
Apollo VGA display (or equivalent)	500	
JPC laser printer (or equivalent)	1,400	
Manage inventory program	450	
Mail merge program	120	
Site preparation and installation	500	
System test	1,000	$6,570
Professional time (at $250/day)		
Select hardware and software (1.5 days)	375	
Customize reports (1 day)	250	
Clarify manual procedures (1 day)	250	
Design files (4 days)	1,000	
Design *Record shipment* program (1 day)	250	
Write *Record shipment* program (1 day)	250	
Train clerical personnel (0.5 days)	125	
Train sales clerks (2 days)	500	
Train inventory manager (1 day)	250	
Train store manager (1 day)	250	3,500
Clerical time (at $100/day)		
Initialize *Vendor* file (1 day)	100	
Initialize *Customer* file (2 days)	200	
Initialize *Inventory* file (5 days)	500	800
Subtotal		10,870
Contingency (10 percent)		1,087
Total		$11,957
Consulting services		1,000
TOTAL ESTIMATED SYSTEM COST		$12,957

FIGURE 16.3
Think of design and development as a top-down process.

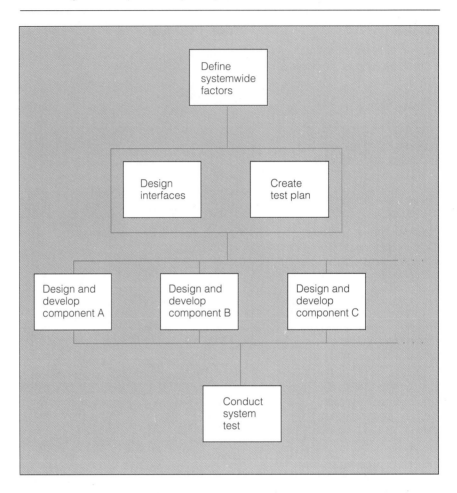

example, if the system is computer based, you cannot even begin to plan a program's logic or the physical structure of a database without first knowing what platform will be used.

Next, the interfaces defined by the system's operating environment are specified. For example, a given application program might communicate with an operating system, a database management system, data

FIGURE 16.4
An application program communicates with an operating system, a database management system, data communication software, and user interface software.

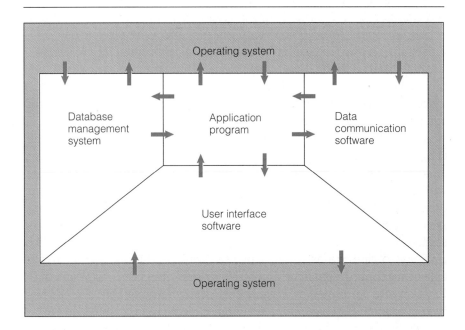

communication software, and user interface software (Figure 16.4). The system software defines an operating environment on a given platform. That environment affects hardware, software, data, and procedures, so it must be specified very early in the process.

Given a clear sense of the operating environment, you can turn your attention to the interfaces that are unique to the application. Look for entities that move between components. (In other words, focus on the arrows that link the system flowchart's symbols.) Control signals generated by one event often trigger other events, and those signals must be clearly specified. Dat . structures link components, so files and databases are an early design objective. Data move between programs and users in the form of screens and reports, so the application-specific user interface should be designed early, too. People must interface with the system, so the user's manual is another priority.

One more step remains before you begin to design the application software and the detailed operating procedures. The requirements specifications define the rules for accessing, protecting, and manipulating the data and specify such technical details as response times, data volumes, transaction rates, and so on. Those requirements affect the programs and the procedures, so the responsible personnel must be aware of them. An excellent way to express the requirements in a form that makes sense at the individual component level is to prepare a test plan. Given a test plan and a set of clearly defined interfaces, the technical experts will know what their components are expected to do.

Given clearly defined interfaces and a test plan, the individual system components can be designed and developed independently, in parallel. Not all features are equally important, however, so it is usually a good idea to work on the most significant ones first and then adjust the secondary features as necessary. To put it another way, as you design and develop the system's components you should focus your attention on the steak, not the sizzle.

Focus on the steak, not the sizzle.

Some organizations implement this principle by using a technique called **baseline design.** For any given system, roughly 80 percent of its functions are performed by roughly 20 percent of its components. The idea is to guarantee that a functional system is delivered on time and within budget by completing that key 20 percent first. Note that the baseline 20 percent might include partial implementation of most or all of the system's discrete components.

Keep these general design principles in mind as you read the balance of this section. This brief design strategy overview might help if you find yourself wondering how a particular design issue fits into the big picture.

■   **PROFESSIONAL POINTER**

Start with the User's Manual

In many organizations, one of the first steps in the design process is to prepare a preliminary user's manual. The user's manual typically defines access procedures and specifies the user interface. Given a first draft to review, the user can suggest changes before design decisions make those changes impossible or expensive. Given the user's manual, the technical people can design their software to be compatible with it (instead of vice versa). If the objective is to meet the requirements (and it certainly should be), starting with the user's manual makes a great deal of sense.

Preparing a Schedule

Managing a project in which several teams work concurrently on parallel tasks demands careful planning and coordination. Consequently, before design begins the analyst normally prepares a **project plan** for the balance of the life cycle.

Identifying Activities

The first step in preparing a project plan is to define a project **schedule.** Start by identifying the tasks or **activities** to be performed. The cost estimate pictured in Figure 16.2 is a good source of information because it identifies the billable time associated with key activities. Figure 16.5 lists the activities that can be derived from the cost estimate.

The next step is to estimate each activity's **duration.** The cost estimate can be misleading, so be careful. For example, Figure 16.2 shows 1.5 days of *billable* time for selecting and ordering hardware and software. In this

FIGURE 16.5
A list of the activities associated with the inventory system.

Activity	Duration (Days)
Select and order hardware and software	2
Shipment time	5
Prepare site and install	1
Customize reports	1
Clarify manual procedures	1
Design files	4
Design *Record shipment* program	1
Write *Record shipment* program	1
Write sales data entry program	1
Train clerical personnel	0.5
Train sales clerks	2
Train inventory manager	1
Train store manager	1
Initialize *Vendor* file	1
Initialize *Customer* file	2
Initialize *Inventory* file	5
System test	1

case, the analyst assumed that the order would be called in to the supplier near the end of the day, so Figure 16.5 shows 2 days of *elapsed* time for the first activity.

Some organizations use an algorithm to compute the estimated duration. Start by asking several experts for their best guesses and then plug the optimistic, mean, and pessimistic values into the following formula:

$$\text{Duration} = \frac{\text{Optimistic} + (4 * \text{mean}) + \text{pessimistic}}{6}$$

Group work presents a unique set of problems for the estimator. For example, if an activity's cost estimate is based on 6 programmer months of effort, two people might need only 3 months to do the job. Then again, they might need more time because there is more to subdividing work than just dividing personnel months by the number of people. Tasks like designing systems and writing programs are fundamentally different from digging ditches, and the failure to recognize this distinction is a common cause of planning error.

Tasks like designing systems and writing programs are fundamentally different from digging ditches.

Frederick Brooks considers this problem in depth in his classic book, *The Mythical Man Month;* if you have never read it, you should. The book was based on his work developing IBM's Operating System/360, at the time the biggest software project ever attempted. One of his conclusions is particularly significant. He discovered that if a given module is behind schedule, adding people only makes things worse. Consequently, generating accurate estimates and assigning the right number of people to each task is critically important because that is the only opportunity you have to assign the right groups in the first place. That is one reason why project planning is usually done by experienced analysts.

If a module is behind schedule, adding people only makes things worse.

PROFESSIONAL POINTER

Estimates and Measurements Are Different

Lines of code and similar approximations of program size are used to estimate time and cost because in general big programs take longer to write than small ones. The relationship tends to break down when you apply it to individual routines or individual programmers, however. Sometimes, the most difficult routines are small ones, and lengthy routines can reflect brute force programming instead of careful, thoughtful, elegant logic.

For example, back in the 1960s assembler language programs were often developed in two stages. During stage 1, the objective was to produce a program that worked. Once a working version of the software was released to the user, a second group of highly proficient hackers (a term of

FIGURE 16.6
A Gantt chart shows the schedule for all of a project's activities at a glance.

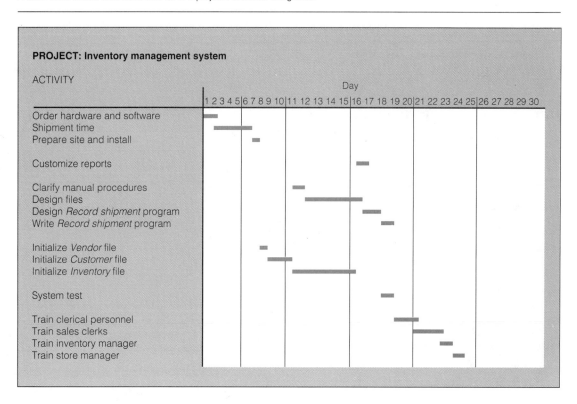

respect in those days) was assigned to produce an efficient version of the program by, among other things, *reducing* the number of lines of code. Note that during stage 2 there was an *inverse* relationship between lines of code and cost.

Lines of code is a useful tool for *estimating* software development time and cost, but using such statistics to measure actual performance can be dangerous. Such attributes as clarity, maintainability, precision, and elegance are better measures of a finished program than size. Tell a good programmer you plan to measure his or her performance based on lines of code, and you will probably get many, many lines of code.

Gantt Charts

A calendar might be all you need to schedule a simple project, but a **Gantt chart** (Figure 16.6) is often a better choice because it shows the whole

FIGURE 16.7
This Gantt chart shows the file initialization and programming activities being performed in parallel with shipping time.

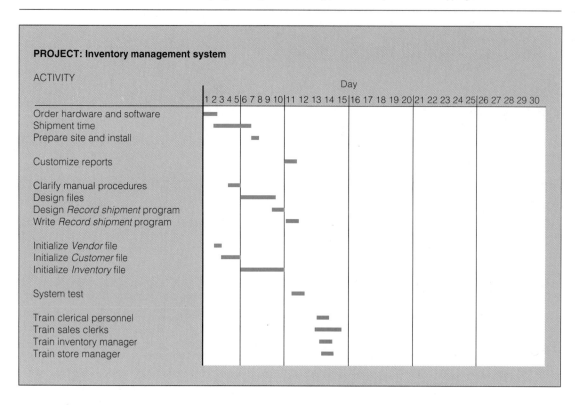

project at a glance. The activities are listed at the left. Time progresses across the top. Each activity is represented by a horizontal bar. The bar's left edge indicates when the activity begins and its length shows the activity's duration.

The Gantt chart in Figure 16.6 assumes that all work will be done on the customer's new computer. Consequently, file initialization cannot begin until the computer is installed, and programming must wait until after the files are initialized. Note, however, that such tasks as clarifying procedures and designing the record shipment program can be done in parallel with other activities.

Figure 16.7 shows a different Gantt chart for the same project. On this schedule, file initialization and programming are done on the consultant's computers while the customer's machine is being shipped. Note that the work is completed in significantly less time. Of course, using the consultant's computers will probably mean additional charges, but getting the system several days earlier might be worth the extra cost.

Project Networks

Events, Activities, and Durations

Gantt charts are useful on small projects with relatively few activities, but a **project network** is much better for tracking and managing a large project. Like a Gantt chart, it graphically depicts activities and their starting and completion times. Additionally, the project network shows how the activities are related.

In a project network (Figure 16.8), each activity (a line or an arrow) begins and ends with an event (a circle or a bubble). Activities are identified by the numbers of their beginning and ending events. *Order hardware and software* is activity 1-2. *Shipment time* (activity 2-5) begins with event 2 and ends with event 5. Note that events are points in time, while activities consume both time and (usually) resources.

Each activity's duration is shown just above its arrow. Note that there is no relationship between the length of an arrow and the duration of the activity. The arrows identify dependency relationships. The numbers above the arrows show durations. Read through the rest of Figure 16.8 using the descriptions printed below the project network as a guide and make sure you understand each event.

Some of the activities in Figure 16.8 are shown as dashed lines. These **dummy activities** link parallel events and consume neither time nor resources. For example, consider Figure 16.9. It shows two possible project networks for starting an automobile. In the top one, event 5 just "hangs there," with no apparent relationship to the rest of the network. Below it is another version with a dummy activity, 2-5. Clearly, activity 5-6, *Fasten seat belt*, begins after the driver enters the car (activity 1-2).

The Earliest Event Time

The project network defines the dependency relationships between the events. Given a clear sense of the order in which events must occur, the analyst can prepare a schedule.

The project network shows how the activities are related.

FIGURE 16.8

A project network for the inventory system.

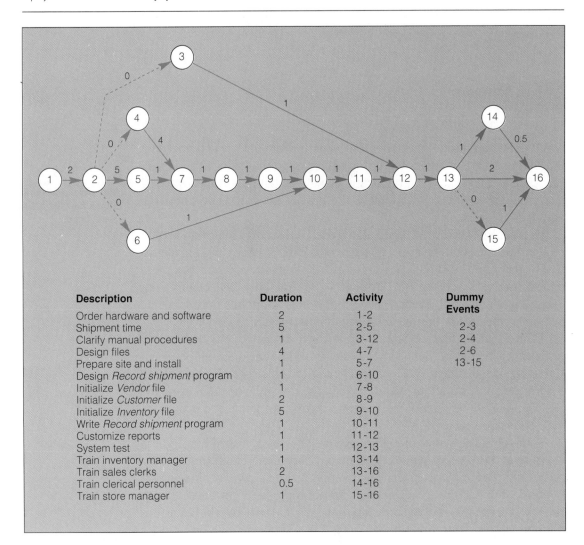

Description	Duration	Activity	Dummy Events
Order hardware and software	2	1-2	
Shipment time	5	2-5	2-3
Clarify manual procedures	1	3-12	2-4
Design files	4	4-7	2-6
Prepare site and install	1	5-7	13-15
Design *Record shipment* program	1	6-10	
Initialize *Vendor* file	1	7-8	
Initialize *Customer* file	2	8-9	
Initialize *Inventory* file	5	9-10	
Write *Record shipment* program	1	10-11	
Customize reports	1	11-12	
System test	1	12-13	
Train inventory manager	1	13-14	
Train sales clerks	2	13-16	
Train clerical personnel	0.5	14-16	
Train store manager	1	15-16	

FIGURE 16.9
Dummy activities link parallel events.

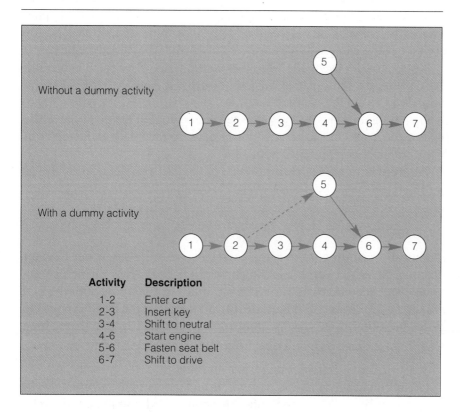

Without a dummy activity

With a dummy activity

Activity	Description
1-2	Enter car
2-3	Insert key
3-4	Shift to neutral
4-6	Start engine
5-6	Fasten seat belt
6-7	Shift to drive

The first step is to compute the **earliest event time (EET)** for each event. The EET is the earliest time the event can possibly begin. By convention it is zero for the first event. To compute the earliest event time for all the other events, work from left to right and follow these three rules:

The EET is the earliest time the event can possibly begin.

1. Select all activities that *enter* the event.
2. For each entering activity, sum the activity's duration and the EET of its *initial* event.
3. Select the *highest* computed EET, and record it in the event circle.

An event occurs when *all* the activities that enter it are completed. That is why the *highest* computed EET is selected.

Figure 16.10 shows a completed project network. The earliest event times are recorded near the upper right of each circle. For example, consider event 2. There is only one entering activity, 1-2. Activity 1-2's initial event is 1. Event 1's EET is 0 and activity 1-2's duration is 2 days, so the earliest event 2 can possibly happen is 2 days after the project begins.

Next, consider event 10. It has two entering activities (6-10 and 9-10), so two computations are needed. Event 6's EET is 2 and activity 6-10's duration is 1 day, so the computed EET is 3 days. Event 9's EET is 10 and activity 9-10's duration is 1 day, so the second computed EET is 11 days. The highest computed EET for event 10 is 11 days, so record 11 at the top right of the bubble that represents event 10.

Before you move on, confirm each of the earliest event times in Figure 16.10.

The Latest Event Time

The LET is the latest time an event can occur.

The **latest event time (LET)** is the latest time an event can occur without affecting the project schedule. By convention, the LET of the last or terminal event is equal to its earliest event time, so 16 days is both the EET and the LET for event 16 (Figure 16.10). To compute the latest event time for all the other events, work from right to left and follow these three rules:

1. Consider all activities that *leave* an event.
2. Subtract each activity's duration from the LET of its *terminal* event.
3. Select the *smallest* computed LET and record it in the event circle.

For example, consider event 13. Three activities (13-14, 13-15, and 13-16) leave event 13. Event 14 has a latest event time of 15.5 days and activity 13-14 has a duration of 1 day, so event 13's first computed LET is 14.5 days. Event 15 has a latest event time of 15 and activity 13-15 has a duration of 0 days (it is a dummy activity), so the second candidate LET is 15 days. Do the computation for activity 13-16 yourself; you should get 14 days. Because the smallest computed LET is 14 days, the latest event time for event 13 is 14 days (Figure 16.10).

Why pick the *smallest* LET? The idea is to allow enough time for the most lengthy activity or series of activities. If event 13 actually occurs at time 15.5, event 14 cannot possibly occur before day 16.5 because activity 13-14 takes 1 full day to complete. That would affect the schedule.

FIGURE 16.10
The completed project network.

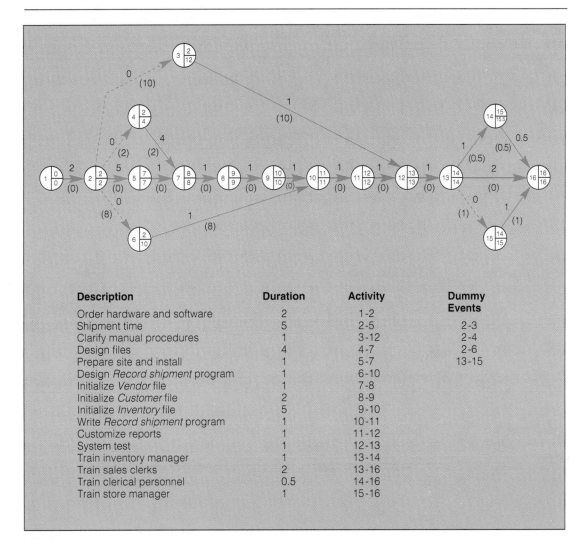

Description	Duration	Activity	Dummy Events
Order hardware and software	2	1-2	
Shipment time	5	2-5	2-3
Clarify manual procedures	1	3-12	2-4
Design files	4	4-7	2-6
Prepare site and install	1	5-7	13-15
Design *Record shipment* program	1	6-10	
Initialize *Vendor* file	1	7-8	
Initialize *Customer* file	2	8-9	
Initialize *Inventory* file	5	9-10	
Write *Record shipment* program	1	10-11	
Customize reports	1	11-12	
System test	1	12-13	
Train inventory manager	1	13-14	
Train sales clerks	2	13-16	
Train clerical personnel	0.5	14-16	
Train store manager	1	15-16	

Next, consider event 12. Only one activity (12-13) leaves it. The LET for event 13 is 14 days (you just computed it) and the duration of activity 12-13 is 1 day, so event 12's LET is 13 days. Before you move on, confirm the remaining latest event times in Figure 16.10.

The Critical Path

Note that the earliest and latest event times are the same for several events (Figure 16.10). Those events define the **critical path;** it is marked by a heavy black line. If the project is to be completed on time, the critical events must begin on time and the critical activities must require no more than their estimated durations.

Slack Time

Activities not on the critical path can (to a point) start late or exceed their estimated durations without affecting the schedule. The extra time associated with an activity, called **slack time** or float time, is computed by subtracting from the latest event time of its *terminal* event both the activity's duration and the earliest event time of its *initial* event:

$$\text{Total slack} = (\text{LET})_t - (\text{EET})_i - \text{duration}$$

Slack time is enclosed in parentheses and recorded below the activity arrow (Figure 16.10). Note that critical path slack times are 0. Slack represents the maximum time the activity can slip without affecting the project schedule. If an activity begins late, of course, its available slack is reduced.

For example, consider activity 6-10. The LET of its terminal event (10) is 11 days, the EET of its initial event (8) is 2 days, and its duration is 1 day. Plug those numbers into the equation and you get a slack time of 8 days. Before you move on, confirm the remaining slack times in Figure 16.10.

PERT and CPM

The project network is the foundation of both **PERT** and **CPM.** PERT (Program Evaluation and Review Technique) gained prominence during the late 1950s when it proved invaluable in scheduling and controlling the Polaris missile program. It is particularly useful in research and development projects where the times required to complete the various activities are uncertain. The critical path is the primary focus of management control, and monitoring the critical events provides an early warning if estimates are inaccurate.

Industry developed CPM (Critical Path Method) to help solve scheduling problems when the activity times are known more precisely. Only by shortening the critical path can the project completion time be improved. Consequently, the critical path defines those activities into which additional resources might be poured to accelerate the schedule.

PROFESSIONAL POINTER   ■

Use Appropriate Tools

Drawing a project network for a simple job is counterproductive because it takes time, and nontechnical people might find the network confusing. Your objective is to communicate the project schedule, not to impress your peers, and a Gantt chart is adequate for most small projects. As a general rule, use the simplest tool that does the job.

Gantt charts break down on large projects, however, because they do not show the relationships between the activities. If you must develop a project network or a similar instrument, use project management software because the charts are difficult to prepare and to maintain manually. Excellent programs are available on a number of platforms, and many CASE products incorporate project management software.

The Project Plan

A complete project plan includes:

1. clear definitions of all design and development activities,
2. a set of deliverables for each activity,
3. clear definitions of how activities are interrelated and how they depend on each other, perhaps in the form of a project network,
4. an activity schedule with milestones and checkpoints, and
5. a budget that identifies resource needs by activity and by time period.

The project plan is the key to project management. Actual progress is compared to the schedule, actual expenditures are compared to the budget, and significant variations suggest that work is not proceeding as planned. Such early warnings can give management an opportunity to intervene in time to make a difference. Many CASE packages include extensive project planning and project management support.

The project plan is the key to project management.

MANAGEMENT'S PERSPECTIVE   ■

Create a Realistic Project Plan

In his classic book, *The Mythical Man Month*, Frederick Brooks suggests that if a project or task is running behind schedule and you add people to the team in an effort to catch up (a normal management reaction), the project will probably fall even further behind. In other words, by the time management determines that the project is in trouble, it might already be too late. The real secret to effective project management is taking the time to create a realistic project plan.

This book started with the words: You can have it fast, you can have it cheap, or you can have it right. Pick any two. Sometimes managers want all three and, being managers, they are in a position to pressure the analyst to prepare a project plan that reflects their wishes (or fantasies). If the objectives are unrealistic, they will not be met. The system will be late, over budget, of low quality, or (most likely) all three. A project plan is essential because it serves as a basis for planning other user activities. However, the key to success is not what you promise, but what you deliver.

Summary

Design is a top-down process. First, systemwide interfaces are defined. Next, application-specific interfaces are designed and a test plan is prepared. The individual components are then designed and developed. Some organizations use a technique called baseline design to determine the priorities of the various design elements. A key factor in managing the design process is preparing a project plan.

The first step in creating a schedule is to list the project's activities and their durations. A Gantt chart is a good choice for showing a small project's schedule. Larger projects might call for a project network with events shown as circles or bubbles and activity lines linking the bubbles. Dummy activities can be used to show precedence. The critical path is defined by a sequence of events with equal earliest event times and latest event times. For events not on the critical path, the computed slack time indicates how long the event can slip without affecting the schedule. PERT and CPM are two project management techniques that use a project network.

The schedule and the cost estimate are key components of the project plan. Actual progress is compared to the schedule, actual expenditures are compared to the budget, and significant variations can give management an opportunity to intervene in time to make a difference.

Suggestions for Additional Reading

Badiru, Adedeji B., and Gary E. Whitehouse. 1989. *Computer Tools, Models and Techniques for Project Management*. Blue Ridge Summit, PA: TAB Books.

Brooks, Frederick P., Jr. 1975. *The Mythical Man Month*. Reading, MA: Addison-Wesley Publishing Company.

Humphrey, Watts S. 1989. *Managing the Software Process*. Reading, MA: Addison-Wesley Publishing Company.

PERT Coordinating Group. 1963. *PERT: Guide for Management Use.* Washington, D.C.: U.S. Government Printing Office, publication number 0-6980452.

Roetzheim, William H. 1988. *Structured Computer Project Management.* Englewood Cliffs, NJ: Prentice-Hall.

Weinberg, Gerald M., and Daniela Weinberg. 1988. *General Principles of Systems Design.* New York: Dorset House Publishing.

Yourdon, Edward. 1982. *Managing the System Life Cycle.* New York: Yourdon Press.

Exercises

1. Why is it a good idea to design interfaces and create a test plan before designing and developing the individual system components?

2. Why is a project development plan necessary?

3. Assume that you are responsible for the project described in the Gantt chart shown in Figure 16.6. Use today's date as a base and explain exactly what your people will do and when they will do it.

4. Briefly explain how a Gantt chart and a project network differ. Under what circumstances would you prefer a Gantt chart? Why? Under what circumstances would you prefer a project network? Why?

5. Using Figure 16.8 as a reference, compute the earliest event time and the latest event time for each event. Then identify the critical path and compute slack time for each activity. Compare your results with Figure 16.10.

6. What are dummy activities? Why are they useful?

7. Assume that you are responsible for the project described in the project network shown in Figure 16.10. Use today's date as a base and explain exactly what your people will do and when they will do it.

8. Explain how a project schedule and a cost estimate can be used to prepare a project budget. Prepare a budget for The Appliance Store's inventory system.

9. Chapter 2 introduced projects for The Print Shop, Jan Tompson's Campus Threads clothing store, and Bill Barnett's automobile dealership. In Chapter 14, Exercise 10, you prepared estimates of costs and benefits for one or more of those projects or for your own project. Identify a set of activities for one or more of those projects and prepare a Gantt chart.

10. Chapter 2 introduced projects for The Print Shop, Jan Tompson's Campus Threads clothing store, and Bill Barnett's automobile dealership. In Chapter 14, Exercise 10, you prepared estimates of costs and benefits for one or more of those projects or for your own project. Define the events, activities, and activity durations for one or more of those projects and prepare a project network. Then compute the earliest and latest event times for each event, identify the critical path, and compute the slack time for each activity.

It is unusual to find a program that does not share data with at least one other program.

17

File and Database Design

When you finish reading this chapter, you should be able to:

—Extract a set of normalized data structures from a requirements specification or a logical system design.

—Select an appropriate file or database organization for a given application.

—Document a data design.

—Discuss the impact of file or database organization on system efficiency.

Data

Consider the partial system flowchart pictured in Figure 17.1 and imagine that the programs, *A* and *B*, are assigned to two different programming teams. Those two programs can be viewed as independent except for a common database file. Because the programs share that file, the format of the data structures and the precise rules for accessing the data must be known to both teams before they can begin designing their programs or writing their code. It is unusual to find a program that does not share data with at least one other program. Consequently, detailed design often begins with file and database design.

FIGURE 17.1
In this partial system flowchart, the database file is common to two programs.

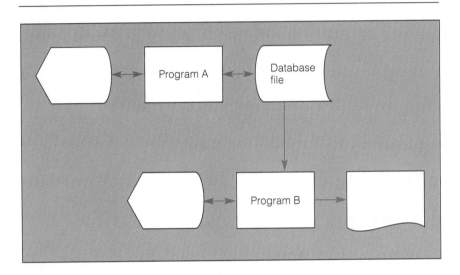

The first step in designing a file or a database is to list its data elements. If a logical model was created during analysis, the set of data elements associated with a given data store represents a preliminary logical data structure. A list of fields from a prototype file, an inverted L diagram from an entity-relationship model, or group items in a data dictionary are alternative starting points. Once you have identified the logical data structures, normalize them.

For example, the inventory system data flow diagram from Chapter 7 (Figure 17.2) shows six data stores, and Figure 17.3 lists the normalized inventory system data you generated in Chapter 6.

PROFESSIONAL POINTER

Prepare Relevant Documentation

The way in which data stores, inverted L diagrams, and similar analysis tools suggest a system's logical data structures is a good example of the step-to-step linkage that is characteristic of a good methodology. People are rarely enthusiastic about preparing models, diagrams, and reports that are promptly filed away, never to be seen again, but they willingly prepare documentation that is relevant to subsequent steps. Good documentation is useful. Documentation for its own sake is a waste of time.

FIGURE 17.2
The data elements associated with a data store suggest a system's preliminary logical data structures.

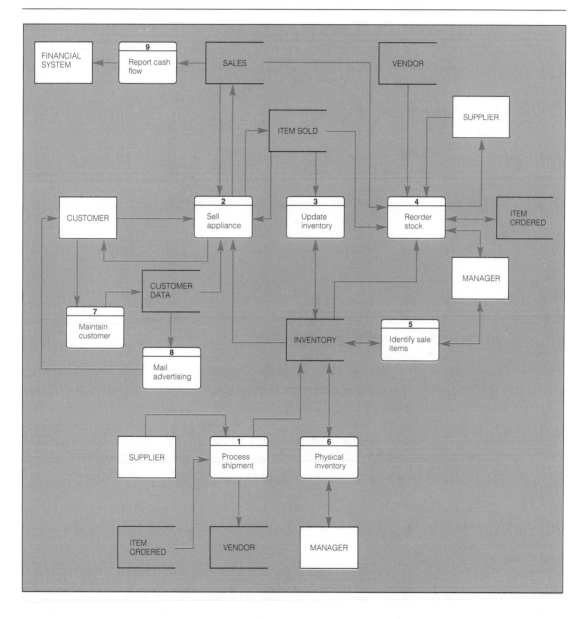

FIGURE 17.3
The normalized inventory system data from Chapter 6.

Sales	Customer	Item sold
Invoice number*	*Customer code**	*Invoice number**
Customer code	Customer name	*Stock number**
Date of sale	Customer address	Quantity
Subtotal		Item total
Sales tax		
Total due		

Inventory	Item ordered	Supplier
Stock number*	*Stock number**	*Supplier code**
Description	*Supplier code**	Supplier name
Stock on hand	Reorder time	Supplier address
Reorder quantity	Supplier price	
Reorder point		
Unit price		

*The key field(s).

File and Database Organizations

Given a set of normalized data structures, the next step is to choose file organizations and/or a database management system for each entity. As you probably recall from your first computer-related course, fields are grouped to form records and a file is a set of related records. A database typically consists of several logically related files linked by pointers, indexes, or relationships. A traditional file, in contrast, usually stands alone and holds all the data needed to support a given application.

Traditional Files

Traditional files often contain difficult-to-maintain, redundant data.

One problem with traditional files is that they often contain difficult-to-maintain, redundant data. For example, imagine two programs that generate, respectively, student grade reports and student bills. Both programs need student names and addresses. Because a traditional file holds all the data needed to support the application, *both* the *Financial* file and the *Academic* file would hold student names and addresses (Figure 17.4). Consequently, if a student moves, his or her address must be changed twice.

FIGURE 17.4
One problem with traditional files is that they often contain redundant data.

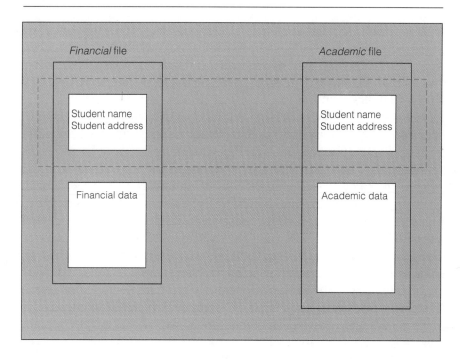

In a traditional file, a record's physical structure and its logical structure are essentially the same, and a clever programmer can take advantage of that fact to make the program more efficient. Unfortunately, if a program's logic is tied too closely to its physical data structures, even minor changes to a data structure can cause significant maintenance problems.

A good database management system helps to minimize data redundancy and data dependency, but many organizations continue to use traditional files in spite of these problems. One reason is compatibility with existing applications. Another is cost; a database management system can be expensive to install, particularly if the firm has numerous existing files and programs that require conversion. On some applications, operating efficiency gives traditional files a decisive advantage over a database. Finally, a traditional file is a reasonable choice when a third-normal-form data structure consists of a single file with no secondary keys.

There are three types of traditional files: sequential, direct access, and indexed sequential.

On a sequential file, records are read and written in physical storage order.

Sequential Files   On a sequential file, records are read and written in physical storage order. For example, transactions might be captured, stored on disk or magnetic tape, and subsequently processed in time order. Often, transactions or master file records are sorted on a key field and then processed in key sequence.

Sequential files can be used to support batch-processing applications. For example, picture a soft drink manufacturer's representative visiting supermarket after supermarket, counting units of his or her firm's products, taking reorders, and recording the counts and reorders on a hand-held terminal (Figure 17.5). Overnight, the transactions are read into a computer, sorted by product code, merged with other representatives' transactions, and used to update a master file. Subsequently, sales reports are prepared and reorders are readied for shipment the next morning.

Note the nature of this application. Transactions are captured in time order, sorted, merged, and processed as a batch. Results are needed the next morning, so response time is measured in hours rather than minutes or seconds. Sequential files are very efficient on such applications.

However, a sequential file should *not* be used if the system requires quick access to specific records. For example, a telemarketing company might have its operators call home telephone numbers in sequence, but you would not even consider looking up a friend's number by starting with A and reading sequentially through the telephone book.

The records on a direct access, or random access, file can be read or written in any order.

Direct Access Files   The records on a direct access, or random access, file can be read or written in any order. Because a program can directly access a specific record, response time is very good. As a general rule, master files that support interactive or real-time applications should be direct access rather than sequential, and real-time tasks that call for extremely tight response times should consider using direct access files instead of a database.

Compared to a sequential file, a direct access file has more overhead and thus needs more space to hold the same amount of data. Additionally, average processing time per transaction is higher because it takes longer to process a given number of direct access records than an equivalent number of sequential records. (Direct access's response time advantage applies to a specific transaction, not the average of all transactions.)

FIGURE 17.5
A typical sequential batch application.

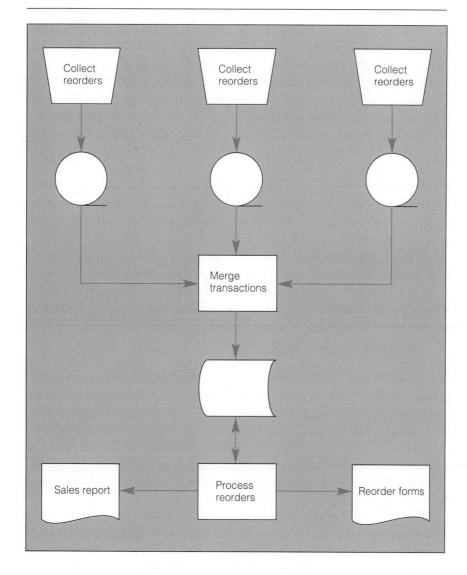

An indexed sequential file is a compromise between sequential and direct access.

Indexed Sequential Files   An indexed sequential file is a compromise between sequential and direct access. Records are stored in key order so they can be accessed sequentially. Additionally, an index relating logical keys and disk addresses is maintained so the data can be accessed directly. Problems occur when the file is maintained. Rather than shifting all the records each time data are added or deleted, new records are stored in an overflow area and the space associated with deleted records is unused. Over time, slack space and overflow data can severely impact the efficiency of both sequential and direct access, so frequent file reorganization is necessary. Do not use indexed sequential files when the data are volatile.

Database Structures

A database consists of a set of related files.

Hierarchical Databases   A database consists of a set of related files. In a hierarchical database, the file links form a hierarchy; for example, Figure 17.6 shows a student *Name and address* file with links or pointers to an *Academic* file, a *Financial* file, and an *Activity* file. In this example, the *Name and address* file is the parent and the other files are its children. Database access starts at the top of the hierarchy and flows downward, so it is possible to access a student's *Academic* file starting from his or her name and address record, but not vice versa. Note that a parent can have many children, but a child can have only one parent.

Network Databases   In a network database (Figure 17.7) the links or pointers can describe relationships between any two files in any direction, so a child can have many parents. For example, if the *Name and address* file contains a link to the *Academic* file and the *Academic* file also contains a link to the *Name and address* file, a given student's grade report might be prepared starting with *either* file. Because links are relatively easy to add to a data structure, the distinction between hierarchical and network databases has practically disappeared.

The relational model has become the de facto microcomputer standard.

Relational Databases   The files that form a relational database are best visualized as two-dimensional tables or spreadsheets (Figure 17.8). In a given file, each column holds a single field and each row holds a single record. Files are linked by pointers or, more generally, relations. The relational model has become the de facto microcomputer standard, and data normalization suggests logical data structures that are compatible with a relational database.

FIGURE 17.6
In a hierarchical database, the various files are linked in a hierarchy and each child can have one and only one parent.

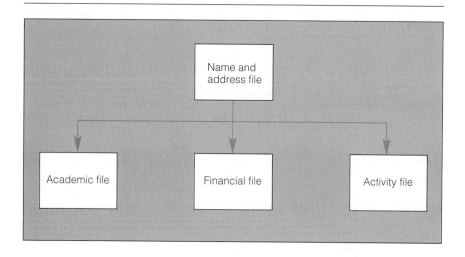

FIGURE 17.7
In a network database a child can have many parents.

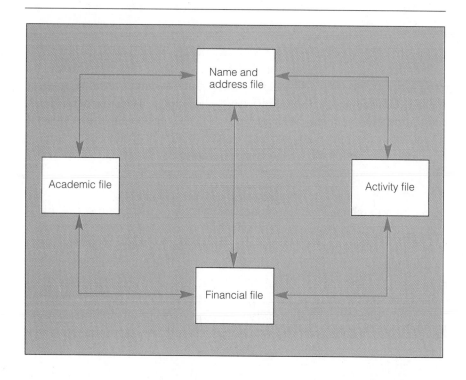

FIGURE 17.8
A relational database consists of a set of related files that are best visualized as two-dimensional tables or spreadsheets.

	Field-1	Field-2	Field-3	Field-4	Field-5
Record-1					
Record-2					
Record-3					
Record-4					
Record-5					
Record-6					
Record-7					
Record-8					
Record-9					

Given today's technology, hierarchical and network databases are physically more efficient than relational databases because they can access data more quickly and they utilize less storage space to hold the same amount of data. Consequently, they continue to be widely used, particularly in mainframe environments. Current research is focused on the relational model, however, and many experts expect relational databases to largely supplant the hierarchical and network models.

Standards

Selecting a database structure is not an everyday task. In most organizations, a standard is developed (or selected) by a team of experts and then used for all subsequent applications, and similar standards (planned or de facto) might be defined for traditional files as well. If your organization has a standard database or file organization, use it unless you have a very good reason not to. If your firm does not yet have a database standard, defining one should become a high-priority task. The selection of a database management system should be based on much more than the requirements of a single application.

The selection of a database management system should be based on much more than the requirements of a single application.

FIGURE 17.9
A dBASE IV file creation screen.

Layout	Organize	Append	Go To	Exit				`1:34:38 PM`

Bytes remaining: 3933

Num	Field Name	Field Type	Width	Dec	Index
1	STOCK_NUM	Character	5		Y
2	DESCRIPT	Character	40		N
3	STOCK	Numeric	5		N
4	R_QUAN	Numeric	5		N
5	R_POINT	Numeric	5		N
6	U_PRICE	Numeric	7	2	N

Database	A:\INVENTOR	Field 6/6	ExclLock	Caps

Documenting a Data Design

The objective of file and database design is to convert the normalized logical data structures from analysis into the physical data structures that will be stored and manipulated by the system. Start by selecting a file organization or database management system for each entity. The data management technique you choose will impose a set of rules for describing the data to the system. For example, under dBASE IV you define a file through the file creation screen (Figure 17.9), while COBOL files are defined through ENVIRONMENT DIVISION and DATA DIVISION entries.

Each field's attributes (data type, field length, precision, and so on) can be extracted from the data dictionary. Given this information, you can prepare a complete set of data descriptions, ideally in source code form. (Some CASE products automatically generate source code in a variety of languages.) Subsequently, instead of recoding picture clauses or data declarations in each program, the programmers can work with standard data descriptions. That saves time and eliminates a common source of error.

Additionally, the analyst or designer should define in source code form the rules for accessing the data. With traditional files, the necessary documentation might consist of job control or command language statements, COBOL DATA DIVISION entries, file declarations and similar code. With a database, standard environments, views, queries, or data access subroutines might be written. The idea is to allow the programmer to focus on application logic instead of physical I/O.

Another useful datum is the physical size of the database or file. Sum the field lengths to get bytes per record. Then multiply by the number of records (from the requirements specification) to get the total number of data bytes in the file. Add overhead for your database or file structure, factor in additional space for growth, and you have a good estimate of the amount of disk space you will need.

Efficiency

Data in third normal form are generally easy to maintain. For most files and databases that is a compelling reason to use third normal form, but sometimes an analyst or designer will choose to sacrifice ease of maintenance to gain speed or to better utilize physical storage space. Be careful, however, because poor design decisions made in the name of efficiency can have negative consequences. As a general rule, it is wise to base your physical file and/or database design on third normal form and to leave the efficiency-driven fine-tuning to specialists.

Poor design decisions made in the name of efficiency can have negative consequences.

■   **PROFESSIONAL POINTER**

Don't Focus on Hardware Efficiency

Back in the 1960s, the need to efficiently utilize expensive hardware drove many computer applications. For example, one technique used by early hackers was to define a set of two or more magnetic tape drives as input devices. The program started by reading a block of records from the first drive. As soon as the first I/O operation was completed, the program issued an I/O request against the second drive and started processing the first block.

If the block size, the computer's processing speed, and the speed of the tape drive were perfectly balanced, a block of data from the second drive entered memory just as the processing of the records from the first block was completed. By toggling back and forth between the tape drives, the programmer kept a continuous stream of data flowing through the computer, and that improved throughput.

The problem was that the application was totally hardware dependent. If you upgraded to a new processor, the program would not work. Changing tape drive models had a similar impact. In some cases, timing was so tight that moving the tapes from drives 1 and 2 to drives 3 and 4 was enough to disable the program.

The point is that focusing on hardware efficiency can be dangerous. Such advantages as reduced access time and reduced space requirements are easy to defend in a cost/benefit analysis. The costs associated with inflexibility, hardware dependency, maintainability, and so on are less tangible and, consequently, easy to ignore, but those costs still exist and they can be substantial. Sometimes hardware efficiency is achieved at the expense of system efficiency.

Conserving Space

Disk is the current secondary storage standard. A disk's surface is divided into concentric circles called tracks that, in turn, are divided into fixed-length sectors. For example, a double-sided, double-density 5.25-inch diskette contains 40 tracks on each side and each track holds nine 512-byte sectors, yielding a total of 360 kilobytes of storage space. It is the contents of a sector that moves between the disk's surface and the computer's memory. Data are physically read and written one sector at a time.

The logical data structures suggested by data normalization rarely match the fixed sector size. For example, if a single 100-byte logical record is stored in each 512-byte sector, 412 bytes of storage capacity are unused (Figure 17.10a). However, if five of those 100-byte logical records are blocked to form a 500-byte physical record and that physical record is stored in a single sector, only 12 bytes are wasted (Figure 17.10b). Consequently, data are normally stored on disk in blocked form.

With one *block* per sector, data move between the disk's surface and the computer's memory a block at a time. Software (the database management system, the operating system, a device driver, or an access method) is used to assemble a program's output logical records to form blocks that are subsequently transferred to disk. That same software disassembles input blocks to get the logical records the program needs.

On a large database, even a few slack bytes per sector can add up to a great deal of wasted space. On some systems, additional space efficiency

FIGURE 17.10
Data are normally stored on disk in blocked form.

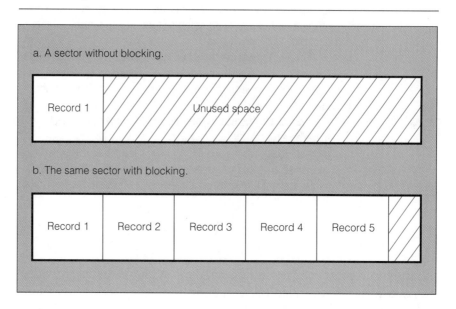

a. A sector without blocking.

| Record 1 | Unused space |

b. The same sector with blocking.

| Record 1 | Record 2 | Record 3 | Record 4 | Record 5 | |

is obtained by using spanned records. For example, imagine that five complete 100-byte records plus the first 12 bytes of the sixth record are stored in the first sector (Figure 17.11). The second sector would contain the last 88 bytes of the sixth record, the next four 100-byte records, and the first 24 bytes of record 11, and so on. Spanned records are also used when the logical record length exceeds the sector size.

The problem with spanned records is that two or more physical I/O operations might be required to access a single logical record. In the previous example, the first 12 bytes of record number 6 are stored in the first sector, and the remaining 88 bytes are stored in the second sector. Consequently, to get logical record number 6, physical sectors 1 and 2 would both have to be read. Because only one sector can be read at a time, two physical I/O operations would be needed, and each I/O operation takes time. Using spanned records sacrifices speed for storage efficiency.

Generally, blocking and spanning are system software functions and thus are not subject to the designer's control. However, by adjusting the logical data structure size to more closely match the sector size, the designer can have a profound impact on space utilization. For example,

FIGURE 17.11
Spanned records.

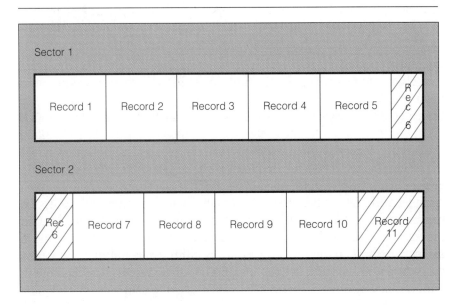

imagine a 260-byte third-normal-form logical record. Without spanning, only one of those records could be stored in each 512-byte sector. However, if four bytes were shifted to another data structure, each sector could hold two of the resulting 256-byte logical records, and the physical space needed to store the file would be cut in half. You might pay a slight speed or maintenance price, but improved space utilization would probably be worth more than that incremental cost.

It is not quite that simple, of course. For one thing, the available space per sector might be less than the full 512 bytes because of access method or database overhead. Also, not all disks use 512-byte sectors and, depending on the hardware used, other variables might have to be considered. Achieving hardware efficiency demands considerable technical expertise and often leads to hardware dependency. However, the point is still valid: Coordinating logical and physical record sizes can save space.

Another possibility is to merge files. For example, imagine a retail store that maintains its customers' home and business addresses. If the store is located on a restricted military base where everyone works for the Army, the government, or one of three subcontractors, adding an employer key to

By adjusting the logical data structure size to more closely match the sector size, the designer can have a profound impact on space utilization.

each customer record to link it to a small employer file makes both logical and physical sense. However, if the local economy is so highly diversified that the number of different employers approaches the number of customers, the designer might be able to save space by eliminating the employer pointer and merging the employer name and address into the customer record.

Before you merge two files, compute the net change in space requirements. Combining an employer file and a customer file eliminates the entire employer file plus a key in each customer record. On the other hand, it adds the employer data structure to each customer record. Unless merging saves space, stay with third normal form.

Be careful, however. By merging two files, you eliminate one of them, and that complicates both data access and file maintenance. For example, merging an employer file into a customer file makes it difficult to access customers by employer, and if the store frequently targets sales by employer, the extra processing costs might cancel the value of the space savings. Also, merging files almost always introduces redundancy (some customers *will* have the same employer) and that complicates file maintenance. Once again, achieving hardware efficiency demands considerable technical expertise.

Achieving hardware efficiency demands considerable technical expertise.

Reducing Access Time

Physically reading or writing a diskette is a three-step operation. First, the diskette drive accelerates from rest to a constant rotational speed and the access mechanism is positioned over the desired track (seek time). Next, the desired sector rotates to the read/write head (rotational delay). Finally, the data flow between the diskette's surface and memory (data transfer time). Because a hard disk rotates constantly there is no need to bring the disk up to speed, but seek time, rotational delay, and data transfer time still remain.

The secret to reducing data access time is to minimize the physical steps.

The secret to reducing data access time is to minimize those physical steps. For example, imagine a program that displays an individual's name, address, and telephone number. If the name and the telephone number are stored on separate files, collecting the data requires two complete physical I/O operations. However, if the files are merged, the same data can be obtained with a single I/O operation in roughly half the time. If a particular set of data elements is frequently accessed together, it sometimes makes sense to merge them into the same physical record even if third normal form suggests otherwise.

Of the three components that make up data access time, seek time is by far the most significant. On a hard disk, it is a function of the number of tracks that separate the access mechanism's current position from its target position. Consequently, to minimize seek time, files that cannot be merged can be stored on adjacent tracks. On some systems, the database designer can specify the physical disk addresses to be allocated to each file. On many systems, the simplest way to ensure that two files are stored on adjacent tracks is to create them one after the other. In either case, the addition or deletion of records will eventually erode the advantages of physical proximity, so regular disk reorganization is essential. Disk optimization software can help.

On a microcomputer, a single interface board normally controls access to all the disk drives, so only one drive can be active at a time. In contrast, a mainframe's disk drives are linked to the computer through a channel (Figure 17.12). Because a channel has its own processor and memory, it can overlap certain physical operations. For example, a seek command might be issued for disk 2 while the channel waits for the completion of a prior seek on disk 3.

A large mainframe might have two or more banks of disk drives linked to the system through separate channels. Because channels can function independently, such systems can access data from two different drives simultaneously. If selected files are placed on separate disks accessed via separate channels, it is possible to gain speed by overlapping complete physical I/O operations. Simultaneous operations save time, but balancing and scheduling hardware operations is tricky. Once again, seek expert help.

MANAGEMENT'S PERSPECTIVE

Information Is a Resource

It is by exchanging data and information that the various parts of the organization communicate with each other and coordinate their efforts. Those organizations that most efficiently store, manipulate, recall, and distribute information enjoy a significant advantage over their competitors. Information may well be the organization's most important asset.

By imposing consistent rules for describing, storing, maintaining, and retrieving data, a database standard makes it possible for all segments of the organization to share their data. An organization that lacks such a standard creates artificial barriers that make it difficult for certain groups to share what they know, and that can lead to competitive "blind spots." If you lack the ability to treat information as a corporate resource, you are going to find it difficult to compete with firms that can. A good database standard is a necessary first step.

FIGURE 17.12
A mainframe's disk drives are linked to the computer through a channel.

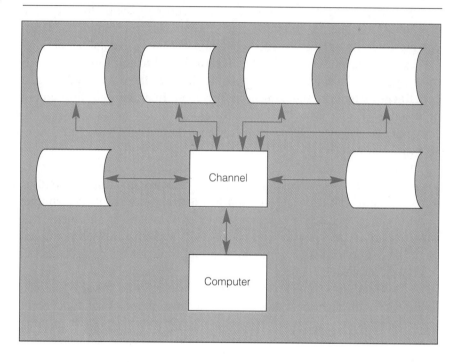

Summary

Because a system's programs are linked by files and databases, detailed design often begins with file and database design. The first step in designing a file or a database is to group its data elements to form logical data structures that can then be normalized.

The next step is to select a file or database organization for each data entity. On a sequential file, records are read and written in physical storage order. The records on a direct access or random access file can be read or written in any order. An indexed sequential file is a compromise between sequential and direct access.

In a hierarchical database, the file links form a hierarchy. In a network database links can describe relationships between any two files in any direction. A relational database consists of a set of related files that are best visualized as two-dimensional tables. Database files are linked by pointers or, more generally, relations.

Physical efficiency can be improved by conserving space and reducing access time.

Suggestions for Additional Reading

Date, C. J. 1986. *An Introduction to Database Systems*. 4th ed. Reading, MA: Addison-Wesley Publishing Company.

Dutka, Alan F., and Howard H. Hanson. 1989. *Fundamentals of Data Normalization*. Reading, MA: Addison-Wesley Publishing Company.

Martin, James, and Carma McClure. 1988. *Structured Techniques: The Basis for CASE*. Englewood Cliffs, NJ: Prentice-Hall.

Exercises

1. Detailed design often begins with file and/or database design. Why?

2. What is a logical data structure? Identify one or more sources of logical data structures.

3. Briefly compare traditional file structures and databases. Cite both advantages and disadvantages for each.

4. Distinguish between sequential, direct, and indexed sequential file structures.

5. Distinguish between hierarchical, network, and relational database structures.

6. Briefly explain how to document a physical data design. Physical data structures are sometimes documented in source code form. Why?

7. Using the programming language or database management system of your choice, define physical data structures for each of the data entities in Figure 17.3.

8. Discuss several techniques that might be used to conserve disk space.

9. Discuss several techniques that might be used to reduce disk access time.

10. Chapter 2 introduced projects for The Print Shop, Jan Tompson's Campus Threads clothing store, and Bill Barnett's automobile dealership. In subsequent chapters you identified the data elements required by one or more of those projects or for your own project and documented them in the form of a data dictionary, a set of data stores, a set of inverted-L diagrams, and/or a set of prototype master files. Using those preliminary logical data structures, normalize the data. Then select a database management system or a file organization and prepare physical data structures for each data entity.

Know the user.
Know the task.

18

The User Interface

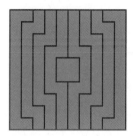

When you finish reading this chapter, you should be able to:

—Define the term *user interface.*

—Identify the information from analysis and high-level design that serves as a base for user interface design.

—Outline the user interface design process.

—Define and document a process or procedure.

—Design simple reports, forms, and screens.

—Design and test a dialogue.

—Explain the purpose of a user manual.

Designing the User Interface

A **user interface** is a point in the system where a human being interacts with a computer. The interface can incorporate hardware, software, procedures, and data. The interaction can be direct; for example, a user might access a computer through a screen and a keyboard. Printed reports and forms designed to capture data for subsequent input are indirect user interfaces. Note that a well-designed user interface serves as both a connector and a separator, linking the user to the computer and protecting the computer from the user.

Before you begin designing user interfaces you must first know the user and understand the task to be performed. Much of the information you will need is collected during analysis and high-level design. Symbols on the system flowchart identify necessary reports, screens, forms, and keyboard operations. On the data flow diagram, flows from sources and to destinations might suggest a need for user interfaces. From the data dictionary you can compile lists of data elements that are input by or output to users. The requirements specification identifies user needs, user characteristics (skill, training, and so on), and task requirements.

In the past, when computers were expensive and people were (relatively) cheap, users were expected to interact with the computer on the machine's terms, but that is no longer true. Given today's technology, a user interface must be designed to allow the user to perform his or her job as effectively as possible. Machine efficiency should, of course, be considered, but only if it does not conflict with the primary objective. That is why user involvement is essential.

A user interface must be designed to allow the user to perform his or her job as effectively as possible.

The first step in user interface design is to define the processes, procedures, and other tasks the users must perform (Figure 18.1). Given a set of tasks, you can design the necessary screens, reports, and forms. Next, the dialogues that control the exchange of information between the computer and the user are designed. Finally, a user manual is written to document the various procedures, screens, reports, forms, and dialogues.

Designing User Processes

Identifying Processes

Much of the information you need to design the user processes is collected during analysis and high-level design and thus can be extracted from the logical model, the system flowchart, the data dictionary, the requirements specification, and other documentation. For example, Figure 18.2 shows a system flowchart for one alternative solution to the inventory problem. The symbols that represent manual procedures, reports, documents, and screens suggest a need for a user interface, while the program symbols and on-line file symbols do not.

FIGURE 18.1
The user interface design process.

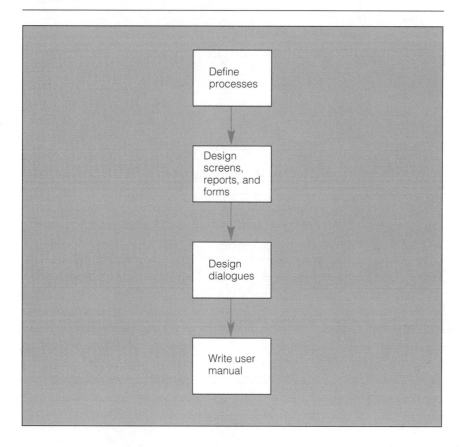

Figure 18.3 lists the inventory system components that suggest a need for user involvement. For example, symbol 1 is a predefined process that includes a manual procedure for handling sales transactions, and symbol 3 identifies a form (the *Sales receipt*) that is completed during the *Sell appliance* process. Symbol 4 represents a data entry screen. Someone must enter the data, so *Enter data* implies a data entry process. The symbols that imply user processes are marked with an asterisk. Note that the unmarked symbols represent forms or documents that are input to or output by a process.

FIGURE 18.2
A system flowchart for an inventory system.

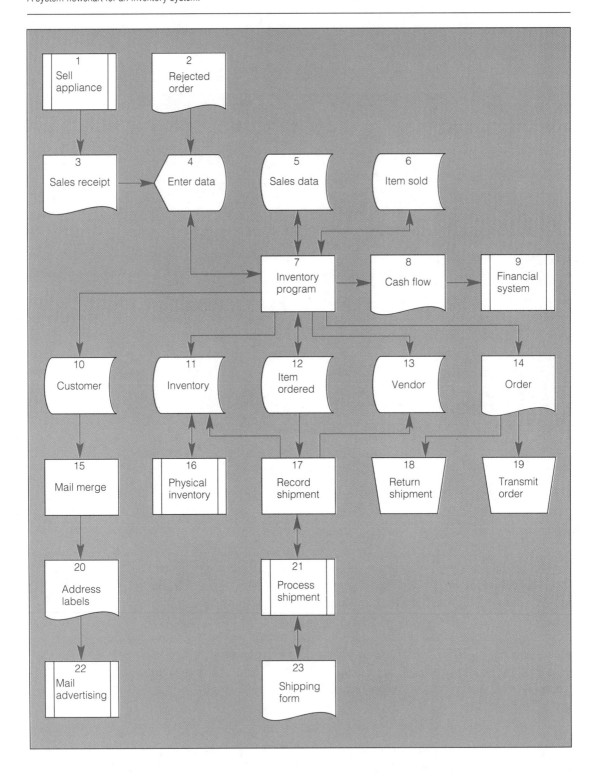

FIGURE 18.3
A list of the inventory system components that suggest a need for a user interface.

Symbol	Title	Represents
1*	*Sell appliance*	Manual procedure
2	*Rejected order*	Paper form
3	*Sales receipt*	Paper form
4*	*Enter data*	Screen
8	*Cash flow*	Printed report
14	*Order*	Printed document
16*	*Physical inventory*	Manual procedure
18*	*Return shipment*	Manual procedure
19*	*Transmit order*	Manual procedure
20	*Address labels*	Printed report
21*	*Process shipment*	Manual procedure
22*	*Mail advertising*	Manual procedure
23	*Shipping documents*	Paper form

*A likely user process or procedure.

Documenting Processes

At the beginning of the system development life cycle you prepared process descriptions to help you understand the present system. Near the end of analysis you studied and documented the processes once again in an effort to define what the new system must do. As you near the end of the life cycle and start detailed design, your focus shifts to how each process *should be* performed. The tools might be the same, but your intent is different.

1. List the Steps   Once you have identified the processes, you can begin to design them by listing the steps that should be performed. For example, Figure 18.4 describes the manual procedure implied by *Sell appliance*. Note that the trigger event (the event that starts the process) is listed first; in this case, handling a sales transaction begins with the arrival of a customer. The other entries describe the primary steps in the process, identify who is responsible for each step, and list each step's inputs and outputs.

Step 3a references a price tag, but that document or form does not appear on the system flowchart. Often, as you study a portion of a system in greater detail, you will discover elements that were overlooked, implied, or assumed earlier.

FIGURE 18.4

The steps in a *Sell appliance* process.

---

1. Trigger event: Customer enters store.
2. Customer selects merchandise.
   a. Sales clerk helps customer.
3. Sales clerk writes *Sales receipt.*
   a. Obtain *Unit price* from price tag.
   b. For each item purchased:
      (1) Record *Stock number.*
      (2) Record product *Description.*
      (3) Record *Quantity.*
      (4) Record *Unit price.*
      (5) Compute and record *Item total.*
   c. Compute and record *Subtotal.*
   d. Compute and record *Sales tax.*
   e. Compute and record *Total due.*
4. Sales clerk accepts payment.
   a. Cash.
   b. Credit card.
   c. Check.
5. Sales clerk marks *Sales receipt* paid.
6. Sales clerk files copy of *Sales receipt* for data entry.
7. Sales clerk gives copy of *Sales receipt* to customer.
8. Sales clerk gives merchandise to customer.
   a. Small items.
   b. Large item pick-up.
   c. Schedule delivery.

2. Identify Input and Output Data Flows   Given a process description, the next step is to identify its input and output data flows. Figure 18.5 lists the data output by the sales transaction process. Each of those data elements and composites must either be input to or computed within the process, so identify the source of each one. (You might find the necessary information in the data dictionary.) Note that the sales receipt data come from the customer, the salesperson, the price tag, and the system (the invoice number is preprinted on the sales receipt). Note also that four values are computed within the process (Figure 18.6).

Consider another example. Symbol 4 in Figure 18.2 identifies a data entry step; a clerk will read the sales receipts and input the data to the *Inventory program*. To document the data entry process, you need a list of the

FIGURE 18.5
A sales receipt is composed of these data elements and composites.

Sales receipt (Invoice)	**Source**
Invoice number	System
Customer code	Customer
Customer name	Customer
Customer address	Customer
Date of sale	Salesperson
Item purchased	
Stock number	Price tag
Description	Price tag
Quantity	Salesperson
Unit price	Price tag
Item total	Computed
Subtotal	Computed
Sales tax	Computed
Total due	Computed

fields that constitute a sales receipt (Figure 18.5), a list of the fields that are displayed on the screen or input through the keyboard, and a flowchart or list of the steps in the data entry process.

3. Identify Other Process Attributes   There is more to understanding a process than just listing its steps, inputs, and outputs, however. A sense of the (often subjective) priorities associated with the various process steps can be important in designing a good system. For example, when handling a customer transaction, responding quickly to the customer, making the sale, and accepting the payment take precedence over collecting the data, so operating procedures might direct the sales clerk to skip nonessential fields during busy periods and complete the sales receipts during slack times.

Note also how the processes are related. For example, a sales receipt is output from *Sell appliance* and input to *Enter data,* so the receipt serves as an interface. When the sales receipt form is designed, its effect on *both* processes must be considered, and design compromises might be necessary. *Cash flow* (symbol 8) is another example. It acts as an interface between *Inventory program* and *Financial system,* so both the program and the needs of the financial system must be considered when that document is designed.

There is more to understanding a process than just listing its steps, inputs, and outputs.

FIGURE 18.6
The *Sell appliance* data come from these sources.

System

Invoice number

Customer

Customer code
Customer name
Customer address

Salesperson

Date of sale
Quantity

Price Tag/Sticker

Stock number
Description
Unit price

Computed

Item total
Subtotal
Sales tax
Total due

The environment represents a potential system constraint. For example, it would probably be a mistake to expect an automobile mechanic whose hands were covered with grease and oil to enter data directly into a computer, and people whose work takes them away from sources of electricity or a system access port require special equipment to capture data electronically.

Other environmental factors have legal, moral, and ethical (as well as financial) implications. For example, over the past several years researchers have identified a variety of problems associated with video terminal use ranging from repetitive stress injuries, to eyestrain, to the possibility that exposure to low-level radiation might represent a hazard for pregnant women. Such factors must be taken into account when procedures are designed. Many organizations have adopted explicit ergonomic standards for user interfaces.

Consider the nature of the end user, too. Such variables as education, training, skill, and handicaps serve to limit what a given person can reasonably be expected to do. The system must fit the user. To achieve that goal, you must understand the user.

Finally, consider legal and auditing requirements. For example, if a company's auditing rules specify that a physical copy of each sales receipt be retained for a period of one full year, the ability to create, store, and retrieve those copies must be built into the system. If state law requires that all documents used to compute an employee's pay be retained until six months after the fiscal year ends, and pay is computed in part as a commission on sales, then there is a legal reason to maintain a file of sales receipts. Such details can make the difference between a successful system and an embarrassing failure.

4. Walk Through the Process   Given a preliminary design, the next step is to physically walk through the process with the people who will actually do the work. If the process asks the user to do something that is impossible or unrealistic, he or she will tell you (either directly or indirectly). Listen to the users, observe their reactions, and change the process as necessary.

> **If the process asks the user to do something that is impossible or unrealistic, he or she will tell you.**

5. Document More Formally   Once the design settles down, document the process more formally using such tools as structured English or a process flowchart (Figure 18.7). Many other tools are available; follow your own organization's internal standards.

Reports, Forms, and Screens

In addition to designing and documenting the processes, you must also design the reports, forms, and screens required by each one. Consider traditional **reports** first. They were common long before computers were invented, but they are still worth studying because they continue to be used and they are the source of some important concepts and definitions.

> **Traditional reports are the source of some important concepts and definitions.**

Designing Reports

Figure 18.8 illustrates the format of a traditional control breaks report. It begins with a **report header** or a report title that identifies the report. Other identifiers, such as the report date and the person or department responsible for compiling the report, are often included in the report header. Sometimes, a separate title page is printed or displayed. On multiple-page reports, the report title is often repeated at the top of each page or screen.

The body of the report is divided into an imaginary grid of columns and rows (or lines). **Column headers** near the top of each page or screen identify the field displayed in each column. Each row holds a single **detail line** that displays the appropriate field values from a single report file record (in this case, from a single sales receipt). Note in Figure 18.8 that the stock number and the description are repeated on each detail line for

FIGURE 18.7
A flowchart for the *Sell appliance* process.

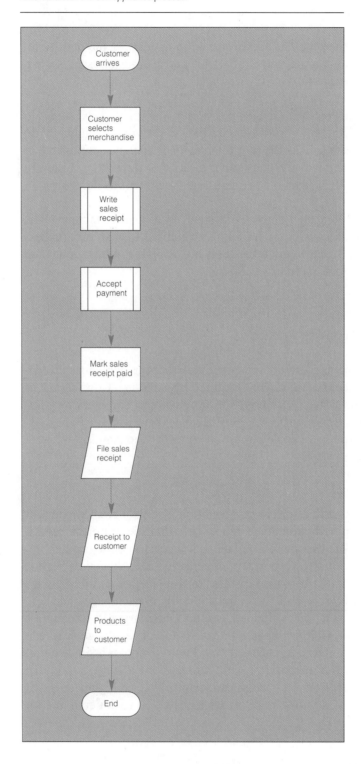

FIGURE 18.8
The format of a control breaks report.

	Sales by Stock Number March 16, 1994			
	STOCK NUMBER	DESCRIPTION	INVOICE NUMBER	QUANTITY
	17593	19" color TV	13352	1
	17593	19" color TV	13367	1
	17593	19" color TV	13375	1
		Subtotal		3
	17594	21" color TV	13351	1
			13358	2
			13362	1
			13370	1
		Subtotal		5
	17596	24" color TV	13366	1
		Subtotal		1
		Report total		9

Labels at left (top to bottom):
- Report header (Page header)
- Column headers
- Detail lines
- Summary line
- Detail lines suppressed
- Summary line
- Detail line
- Summary line
- Report summary

stock number 17593, but the repetitive values are suppressed on the detail lines for the second item, stock number 17594. Suppressing repetitive data tends to make the report easier to read, but either approach is acceptable as long as you are consistent.

The data that are used to generate a report are usually sorted or indexed by one or more key fields; in this case, the stock number serves as the key. Because the source records are accessed in key order, the detail lines for all records with the same key value are grouped together on the report. For example, all the records for stock number 17593 will be read (and thus printed or displayed) before the first stock number 17594 record is read.

A change in the value of the key field is called a **control break.** For example, when the first record for stock number 17594 is read, it is reasonable to assume that all the stock number 17593 records have been

FIGURE 18.9
Page or screen width is the primary constraint on report design.

HEADERS	STOCK NUMBER	DESCRIPTION	INVOICE NUMBER	QUANTITY	TOTAL
Header width	6	11	7	8	
Data value	12345	20 characters	12345	9,999	
Data width	5	20	5	5	
Column width	6	20	7	8	**41**

(Report width) = (sum of column widths) + (white space)

processed. When a control break occurs a **summary line** (Figure 18.8) can be printed. Summary lines typically hold a count of the number of records or the sums of selected fields in the control group, or both. Some reports feature multiple control fields, with primary control breaks, secondary control breaks, and so on. If desired, summary lines can be printed at each level control break. In some reports, the detail lines are suppressed and only summary lines are printed.

Most reports end with a **report summary** line, section, or page. On multiple-page reports, page summaries are common, too. Page numbers and a page header are usually added to lengthy reports.

To lay out a report, start by defining the report title and the page title lines. Be sure to include the report date and page numbers (if necessary). Then turn to the body of the report. You can print or display as many lines as you want, but the number of characters that can be arrayed across a page or a screen is limited, so width is the primary constraint on report design.

To determine the column width for each of the report fields, start with the column headers (Figure 18.9). Lengthy, multiple-word headers can be spread over two or more lines, so for each column, count the number of characters in the widest header line and record the header widths. Then note the biggest possible value (including decimal points, commas, signs, dollar signs, and other punctuation) for each field, count the number of characters in the field, and record the data widths. Finally, compare the header width and the data width and select the larger value. That number is the column width. If you add the widths of each of the columns, you get the number of characters required to display the data.

FIGURE 18.10
Some report design guidelines.

1. Include only the necessary fields.
2. Include *all* the necessary fields.
3. Make important data easy to find.
4. Use clear, meaningful, descriptive column headers.
5. Clearly distinguish data from descriptive information. For example, use uppercase for headers and mixed case for data.
6. Use white space and positioning to group related fields.
7. Use a visual cue (such as asterisks, key words, and/or spacing) to identify summary lines.
8. Left justify character fields and their headers.
9. Right justify numeric fields and their headers.
10. Use rules consistently.

You will also need a few characters of blank space (or white space) to separate the columns. A single space might be enough for closely related columns, but you'll probably want to use two or more spaces to enhance readability. Add white space to the sum of the column widths and you get the report width. If that number is bigger than the paper or screen width, you have a problem and you'll have to modify or delete one or more columns. Otherwise, subtract the report width from the paper or screen width and you get the number of unused spaces that can be distributed across the line to enhance the balance, symmetry, overall appearance, and readability of the report.

Report design is a bit of an art, but Figure 18.10 lists some guidelines that might help you get started. In the past, reports were planned on paper, but modern screen design tools, report generators, and prototyping tools can simplify the process by suggesting reasonable report layouts and doing the necessary calculations for you. Such tools are often found in CASE software. Many of these software tools can generate source code to represent the report layout in a programming language.

Modern screen design tools, report generators, and prototyping tools can simplify the process.

Designing Forms

Many applications call for paper **forms;** for example, Figure 18.11 shows a sales receipt form for the inventory system. Forms are typically used to capture data, although sometimes the forms themselves are retained in long-term storage. A form image can be displayed on a screen and used as

Forms are used to capture data.

FIGURE 18.11

A sales receipt form for the inventory system.

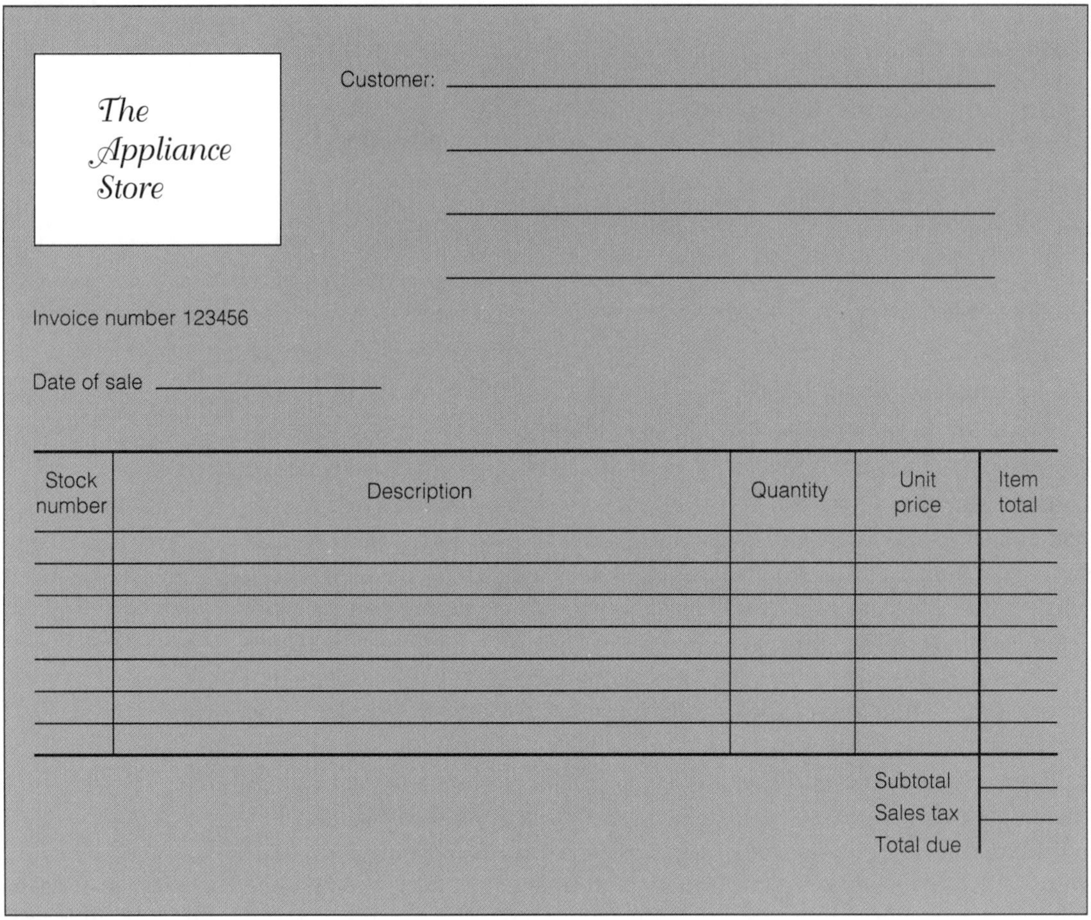

a template for data entry. Completed forms can be scanned or the data can be input to a computer through a keyboard.

Some forms support free-form data recording; for example, note the lines for entering customer data on Figure 18.11. Sometimes, single-character blocks or printed examples show the user exactly where to record the values for specific fields. Checklists are also popular; the available choices

FIGURE 18.12
Some form design guidelines. Note that many of the report design guidelines from Figure 18.10 can also be applied to forms.

---

1. Proximity implies association.
2. Use lines, boxes, color, and white space to group related fields and to visually separate groups of fields.
3. Anticipate the order in which the user is likely to enter the data. Fields that are normally entered together (for example, name, address, and telephone number) are usually related and thus should be grouped.
4. Consider the source of each field and group fields from the same source.
5. If you are familiar with database terminology, group fields (or attributes) that are associated with the same entity.
6. Provide clear, unambiguous directions and captions.
7. Clearly distinguish captions and directions from the data.
8. Provide examples where appropriate.
9. Use boxes, color, lines, and white space to show where the data should be recorded.
10. Allow enough space. Don't try to jam too much on a single page or a single screen.

are listed on the form and the user selects an entry by marking it in some way. It is not unusual for a form to incorporate different data recording techniques for different fields.

Common or "standard" forms can be purchased from most office supply stores, and many form design software packages include libraries of sample forms and form templates. Form design is an art, but you might be able to get help from an office supplies store, a print shop, or a graphics designer. If you must design an original form, consider starting with an existing form and customizing it to fit your needs. Figure 18.12 lists some guidelines.

Designing Screens

A display screen plus a keyboard is the most common human/computer interface. A screen can be used to display a report or to simulate a paper form, but more dynamic images can be displayed, too. Among the features you can use to capture the user's attention or communicate information are color, reverse video, blinking characters, lines, boxes, shapes, graphics, and animation. Because the screen is linked to a computer, you can electronically verify the data as they are entered, and that can have a significant effect on data integrity.

A display screen is the most common human/computer interface.

FIGURE 18.13

On some screens, the user initiates an action by selecting an icon or by making a choice from a horizontal or drop-down menu. This example shows a Microsoft Windows screen.

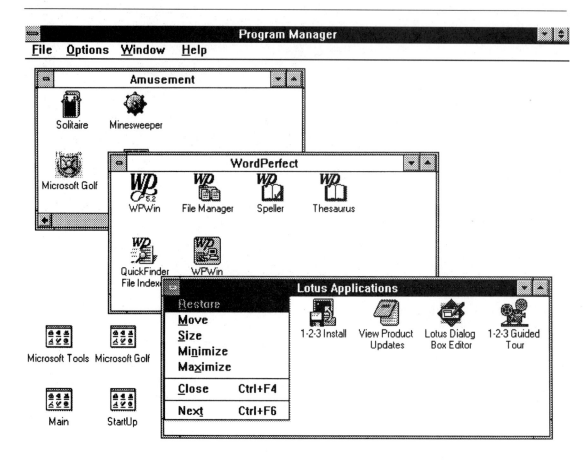

Over the past several years, a number of screen techniques have come into common use. Many applications use a command language, function keys, or icons to let the user initiate actions. Others utilize menus. Often, a horizontal menu across the top of the screen lists primary options, with secondary options selected from a drop-down or pull-down menu.

On some screens, different menus, sets of related icons, or sets of related data are grouped in windows. Systems such as Microsoft Windows (Figure 18.13) and the Apple Macintosh allow the user to directly manipulate

FIGURE 18.14
This screen allows a data entry clerk to enter customer data from an invoice.

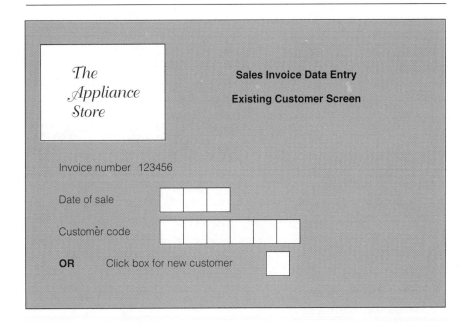

windows, icons, menus, and pointers. Data capture techniques include fill-in forms, question and answer, and WYSIWYG, an acronym for "What You See Is What You Get." WYSIWYG systems often allow the user to directly manipulate the data on the screen; modern word-processing software is a good example.

A given application might call for several screens. For example, Figure 18.14 shows a screen that might be used to enter customer data from an invoice. The *Invoice number* is generated by the system. Note that *Date of sale* and *Customer code* are entered into predefined boxes that effectively prompt the data entry clerk. New customers do not have customer codes, so clicking on the bottom block starts the new customer data entry process. A subsequent screen might display the customer's name and address from the customer file and ask the data entry clerk to confirm or correct the information.

Individual items purchased might be input through another screen (Figure 18.15). Note that the *Invoice number, Date of sale,* and customer

FIGURE 18.15

Once the customer data are entered and verified, this screen allows the data entry clerk to enter the items purchased from an invoice.

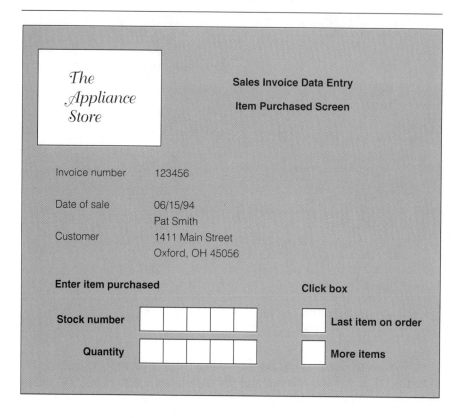

information that were previously entered are displayed in light type. On this screen the data entry clerk enters the stock number and the quantity purchased and then clicks a box to indicate if this is the last item on the receipt or if there are more items to be input. In response, the program uses the stock number to access the inventory file, gets the description and the unit price, computes the item total, and displays for confirmation the data associated with one item ordered on a subsequent screen.

Like form design, screen design is a bit of an art, but Figure 18.16 lists some guidelines that might help you get started. Several excellent screen design programs are commercially available, and prototyping tools can help, too; you might find such tools in your CASE package.

FIGURE 18.16
Some screen design guidelines. Note that many of the report design guidelines from Figure 18.10 and the form design guidelines from Figure 18.12 can also be applied to screens.

1. Design for the user.
   a. Get the user involved in screen design. (Screen design is an excellent application for prototyping.)
   b. Avoid adding features just because they are technically feasible.
   c. Avoid the temptation to "show off."
2. Use familiar structures.
   a. Take advantage of what the user already knows.
   b. Simulate existing forms and reports on the screen.
   c. Follow the conventions of applications the user already knows.
3. Each screen should support a complete operation or a complete set of related operations. For example, use one screen to collect customer data and another screen to collect item purchased data.
4. Provide feedback. Following any transaction or operation, tell the user what happened.
5. Support easy recovery from errors.
6. Facilitate backward migration. For example, allow the user to back up one screen by pressing the escape key.
7. *Never* leave the user hanging. No matter what happens, it should always be possible to recover.
8. Be consistent. Use the same conventions on all parts of the screen and on all screens.
9. When using menus:
   a. Limit menu breadth (the number of choices on a given menu).
   b. Limit menu depth (the number of menus you must navigate to reach a choice).
   c. Excessive breadth is better than excessive depth.
10. If possible, give the user a choice between navigating menus and issuing commands.
11. To avoid confusion, grey out or blank unavailable options.

PROFESSIONAL POINTER   ■

Use Existing Software

Platforms such as Microsoft Windows and the Apple Macintosh have established de facto standards for displaying windows, icons, menus, button bars, and similar logical elements and for performing such tasks as pointing, dragging, and selecting. Subroutines or objects to support those screen elements and functions are available in several programming languages. If you have access to such software, use it. The fact that object-oriented programming encourages the development of such reusable code is one reason why the object-oriented approach looks so promising.

The idea of reusable software has a double impact when it is applied to the user interface. Using existing, tested, debugged software is more efficient than writing custom code for each application, but that's obvious. (Why reinvent the wheel?) The second impact is a bit more subtle, but it could be even more significant. If every programmer uses the same software to implement the user interface, then the interface will look and act pretty much the same in every application. As a result, users will be able to transfer their knowledge of one system to other systems, and that can have a significant impact on training costs and error rates.

Dialogues

A **dialogue** (or **dialog**) is the exchange of information between a computer and a user. Reports, forms, and individual screens are static; think of them as individual slides or still pictures. A dialogue, in contrast, is dynamic. Imagine a series of screens arranged to form a slide show or a motion picture and you have a good mental image of a dialogue.

When you design a dialogue, focus on the complete process. For example, to a clerk entering sales data, a transaction consists of all the steps needed to enter the data from a single sales invoice, including error recovery. Thus, entering that transaction might involve several discrete steps and several screens (Figure 18.17). Entering the next transaction means repeating the same steps and using the same screens. The dialogue defines the set of screens and the order in which they are accessed.

In effect, the dialogue is a merger of the process and the screens that support that process. Although this chapter presents process design, screen design, and dialogue design as discrete steps, they really are tightly interwoven. Like so many analysis and design tasks, user interface design is an iterative process.

The point of dialogue design is to allow the user to complete the task as quickly and as efficiently as possible, but be careful. To many people, the word *efficiency* refers to the hardware, not the user. Given such a definition of efficiency, it is easy to justify designing a clumsy, confusing dialogue in an effort to save computer time or keystrokes.

Efficiency is a function of response time. Traditionally, response time was defined as the interval between the instant a command was issued and the instant the response began to appear on the screen, but that definition ignores the user. A more useful definition of response time includes the following elements:

1. *System response time* is the traditional definition.
2. The *display rate* determines how quickly the complete screen appears.
3. *User scan/read time* is a measure of how long it takes the user to read and understand the screen.
4. *User think time* consists of a cognitive phase during which the user evaluates the screen and a perceptive phase during which the user decides what to do.
5. *User response time* includes a motor phase during which the user performs a physical action (press a key, point and click) and a sensory phase during which the user waits for feedback.

A dialogue is the exchange of information between a computer and a user.

The dialogue is a merger of the process and the screens that support that process.

FIGURE 18.17
The dialogue defines the set of screens and the order in which they are accessed.

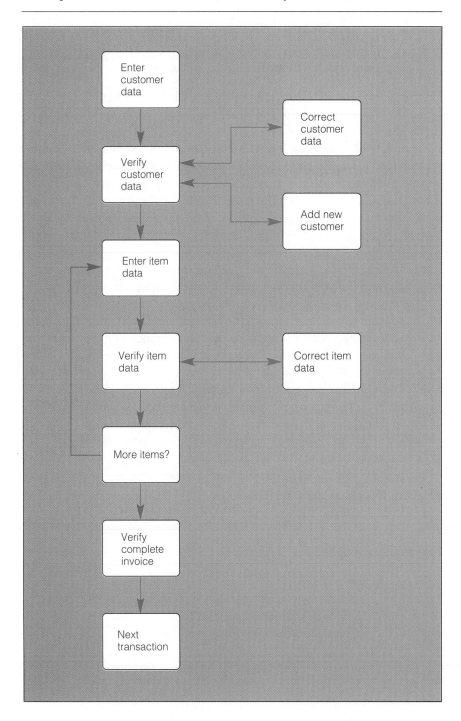

6. *Error time* is the time spent making and recovering from errors. This factor does not occur on all the screens, so think of error time as an expected value (the time multiplied by the probability of occurrence).

Response time can be estimated or measured for each screen. Transaction response time is the sum of the response times for all the screens in the dialogue.

People tend to form their own **mental model** of a system. For example, a video card game lets you visualize cards on a table, a video golf game lets you pretend you're actually playing golf, and a flight simulator gives you a sense of flying an airplane. The mental model helps the user understand how the system works. A good mental model allows the user to predict the system's response to a given stimulus, and the more accurate those predictions, the more intuitive the system appears. When the user understands the system at an intuitive level, the need for training declines, the error rate improves, and the user becomes more efficient.

A good mental model allows the user to predict the system's response.

Try to select a mental model that makes sense to the user; for example, if the user filled out a paper form in the old system, consider simulating that form on the screen. If you cannot base a mental model on the user's experience, take the time to train the user to understand your mental model and be prepared to adjust the model if he or she has trouble understanding it. You might consider using a known metaphor such as the Microsoft Windows desktop. There is no need to create new software, and time spent on Windows training might simplify training for future applications.

Figure 18.18 lists some guidelines for designing dialogues. Students who want more detail should read one or more of the references listed at the end of the chapter. Dialogues are, by definition, interactive, so prototyping is a powerful tool for dialogue design.

Prototyping is a powerful tool for dialogue design.

■   **PROFESSIONAL POINTER**

Reflect the User's Mental Model

Many years ago, I was involved in designing and developing an on-line labor data collection system. There were two sources of input: a plastic badge that identified the worker and a punched card that identified the job. Workers reported their activities through a data entry terminal by inserting their badge in one slot, inserting the card in a second slot, and pressing a button.

Most of the workers quickly learned how to use the new system, but one guy kept inserting his badge in the card slot and jamming the terminal. This problem occurred again and again, as often as

FIGURE 18.18
Some guidelines for designing dialogues.

---

1. Recognize the user's mental model, and use it if possible.
   a. Train the user to understand the mental model.
   b. When faced with a design decision, choose the option that is most consistent with the user's mental model.
2. Never generalize from yourself or your peers.
   a. Work from the user's perspective.
   b. Get the users involved.
   c. Design a dialogue that makes sense to the user, not to the technical experts.
3. Do not assume the user's response. Let the user work with the screens, observe how he or she responds, and change the dialogue as necessary.
4. Be consistent.
   a. Every screen should act and feel the same.
   b. A given action should always produce the same result.
5. Do not force the user to remember transient information from screen to screen.
6. Let the user control the interaction.

once a week, and it was always the same person. People accused him of being stupid. Then they accused him of sabotage. He almost lost his job.

Finally, we discovered the reason for his confusion. His bank had recently installed a cash machine. His plastic credit card resembled a worker badge. The credit card reader was on the right side of the bank terminal, but the badge reader was on the left side of the data collection terminal. In his mental model, he saw the two machines as essentially the same, so he unconsciously followed the pattern he already knew. Had we placed the badge reader on the right side of the terminal, this problem might never have occurred. The point is that users *will* form mental models, and the best user interface reflects the user's model.

The User Manual

The last step in the user interface design process is to write a **user manual** to document the procedures, the reports, the forms, the screens, and the dialogues. The user manual should outline the procedures (perhaps in flowchart form) and explain how to perform necessary tasks. A common approach is to walk the user through each step using realistic screen images, sample forms, and sample reports to illustrate what should happen. To document a dialogue, include a complete set of sample screens, clearly explain what each screen means, and add explicit error recovery procedures.

Given a well-designed user interface, a well-written user manual, and adequate training, the user should be able to access and utilize the system with little or no additional help.

Finally, test the user manual on *real* users. Given a well-designed user interface, a well-written user manual, and adequate training, the user should be able to access and utilize the system with little or no additional help.

■   **MANAGEMENT'S PERSPECTIVE**

Insist on Standards

One of the most important contributions management can make to user interface design is to insist on and enforce standards. You might begin by establishing a committee to define a user interface standard for the organization. Then assign skilled programmers to develop subroutines or objects to implement key elements of that standard and insist that your analysts, designers, and programmers use the standard software in all future systems. As enhancements and improvements emerge, encourage your people to add them to the library and to reuse them in other programs.

If you are considering adopting object-oriented programming in your organization, user interfaces are an excellent place to start. Few programmers enjoy coding menus and laying out screens, so they are usually more than willing to accept tools that simplify those tasks. Objects to implement windows, icons, pointers, menus, and other basic elements are available in several programming languages that support the Microsoft Windows and Macintosh environments, and comparable objects can be found to support other platforms. Given a base that works, you can build on it.

Summary

A user interface is a point in the system where a human being interacts with a computer. The first step in designing a user interface is to define the user processes. One way to document a process is to prepare a process flowchart. The trigger event for a process is the event that starts the process.

Given clearly defined processes, the next step is to define the necessary reports, forms, and screens. A traditional report begins with a report header. Column headers identify the field displayed in each column. Each row holds a single detail line. When a control break occurs a summary line can be printed. Most reports end with a report summary.

Paper forms are typically used to capture data. Screens are defined to support user access to the system through a keyboard/display device. Commonly used screen elements include windows, icons, menus, and pointers, and popular data capture techniques include fill-in forms, question and answer, and WYSIWYG.

A dialogue (or dialog) defines the exchange of information between a computer and a user. Dialogues should be designed to enhance user efficiency. Efficiency is a function of response time, which includes machine time, user time, and error recovery time.

People tend to form their own mental model of a system. The mental model allows the user to predict the system's response to a given stimulus, and the more accurate those predictions, the more intuitive the system appears.

The last step in the user interface design process is to write a user manual to document the procedures, reports, forms, screens, and dialogues.

Suggestions for Additional Reading

Galitz, Wilbert O. 1989. *Handbook of Screen Format Design.* Wellesley, MA: QED Information Systems, Inc.

Mayhew, Deborah J. 1992. *Principles and Guidelines in Software User Interface Design.* Englewood Cliffs, NJ: Prentice-Hall.

Rubin, Tony. 1988. *User Interface Design for Computer Systems.* Chichester, England: Ellis Horwood, Ltd.

Exercises

1. What exactly is a user interface? Why is user interface design so important?

2. Outline the steps in the user interface design process and briefly explain what happens during each step.

3. The first step in designing a user interface is to define the user processes. Why do you suppose the analyst starts with the processes?

4. Briefly explain how to document a process.

5. Describe the components of a traditional report.

6. What is the function of paper forms? What is the function of a screen? Briefly distinguish between using paper forms and using screens to capture data. What are the advantages and disadvantages of each?

7. What is a dialogue?

8. Users tend to form their own mental model of a system. What does that mean? Why is it important?

9. What is the purpose of a user manual?

10. Chapter 2 introduced projects for The Print Shop, Jan Tompson's Campus Threads clothing store, and Bill Barnett's automobile dealership. In Chapter 13 you developed several alternative physical designs for one or more of those projects. Select one of those physical alternatives and identify the necessary user interfaces. Then document the processes and design an appropriate set of reports, forms, and dialogues.

The purpose of the test plan is to ensure that the system does what it was designed to do.

19

Developing a Test Plan

When you finish reading this chapter, you should be able to:

—Explain why a test plan is necessary.

—Outline the contents of a test plan.

—Describe the necessary testing levels.

—Generate test data.

—Explain how to conduct a technical inspection.

The Test Plan

Files, databases, and user interfaces are designed before the other components because they often link two or more entities. Before the hardware experts, the program designers, and the developers begin working on the individual components, you should also develop a **test plan.**

The purpose of the test plan is to ensure that the system does what it was designed to do. To prepare one, start by extracting the system test criteria from the requirements specifications (Figure 19.1). Then derive interface and component tests from the system test plan. Finally, base the

FIGURE 19.1
A test plan involves several levels of testing.

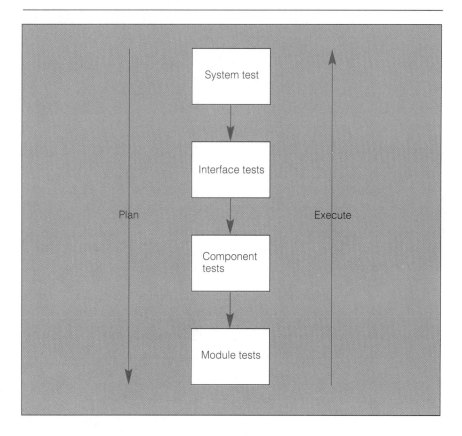

module tests on the component tests. The plan is executed in reverse order, with module tests performed first and the system test performed last.

The heart of any test plan is the **test data.** Each individual test should include not only a set of input data but also a reasonable sample of expected results and a list of expected errors caused by intentionally bad or out-of-control data. The idea is to clearly identify what the output should be. If the actual output matches the expected results, the system or the component passes the test.

In addition to the test data and the expected results, you must also clearly define the test logistics. Identify (by name, by position, or both) the people who will conduct each test and the people who will evaluate the results. (They should be different.) Develop a test schedule and a set of operating procedures, and specify the testing environment and necessary resources. Finally, indicate the criteria for passing the test and assign responsibility for the pass/fail decision. As a general rule, no one should be responsible for evaluating his or her own work.

The test plan represents the system's acceptance criteria. One danger is that the designers and the programmers will work to the test plan and not the requirements, but if the plan is derived from the requirements, this risk is diminished. Formal inspections and walkthroughs (to be discussed in detail later in this chapter) can help ensure that the requirements are actually met.

The test plan represents the system's acceptance criteria.

Testing Levels

The System Test

The **system test** is planned first and, for obvious reasons, performed last. Its purpose is to ensure that the system meets the requirements. A secondary objective is to build user confidence.

The requirements specifications are the ultimate source of the system test criteria, and each logical requirement must be tested. For example, assume that one inventory system requirement is to prepare an emergency reorder within one hour. You might test that requirement by issuing, at a randomly selected time, a request for a reorder. To pass the test, the system would have to produce the appropriate reorder documents within one hour of the request.

The requirements specifications are the ultimate source of the system test criteria.

A preliminary **expert test** should be performed by the people who developed the system (Figure 19.2). Do not rely exclusively on this test, however. It is difficult for anyone to objectively evaluate his or her own work, and a system's developers can often (unconsciously) anticipate and avoid problems before they even happen. Some companies conduct a second expert test by assigning a team of skilled but disinterested technical experts to try to "break" the system. Another option is **worst-case testing** where everything that can possibly go wrong is allowed to happen.

Expert testing should be followed by a **user test** in which user personnel or other user representatives, given only normal training and a copy of the user's manual, exercise the system. Because the system was designed to

The user is the only one who can certify that the needs have been met.

meet the user's needs, the user is the only one who can certify that those needs have been met. Additionally, a successful test builds user confidence.

The **final system test** follows written procedures, uses real input data, and compares the results to a set of expected output values. It involves all the system components including hardware, software, data, manual procedures, auditing procedures, and security procedures. User personnel (rather than technical experts) should enter the data, operate any end-user equipment, and perform any manual procedures. The system test ends with a formal user sign-off that implies user acceptance of the system (Figure 19.2).

The final system test might include a **parallel run** in which both the old system and the new system process the same data (Figure 19.3). The results are then compared and differences are carefully evaluated. Sometimes differences highlight bugs in the new system. Sometimes long-standing errors in the old system are uncovered. The point of a parallel run is not to duplicate the old system's output but to ensure that the new system's output is correct.

■   **PROFESSIONAL POINTER**

Include Outside Perspectives

Several years ago, a banking equipment manufacturer challenged a small group of technical consultants to try to break the security on a new automatic teller terminal. The consultants, who were familiar with the company's computer system, were given minimal documentation and turned loose. Two hours later, they had a reasonably complete set of account numbers and personal identification numbers and were able to make imaginary withdrawals through the automatic teller terminal at their leisure. Needless to say, security procedures were redesigned before the product was released for sale.

The consultants succeeded in breaking the system by exploiting a weakness in the computer's operating system that was only indirectly related to the automatic teller terminal. Because that weakness was (from the developer's perspective) outside the boundaries of the system, it is unlikely that they would have found it. In this case, the decision to challenge a group of outsiders saved the company a potentially embarrassing and expensive loss. There is an old saying: Better the devil you know than the devil you don't know. Expert testing is worth the time and the money.

Interface Tests

Once the system test plan is written, the analyst turns to the networks, files, databases, system software, courier services, and other interfaces that

FIGURE 19.2
The system test includes several stages.

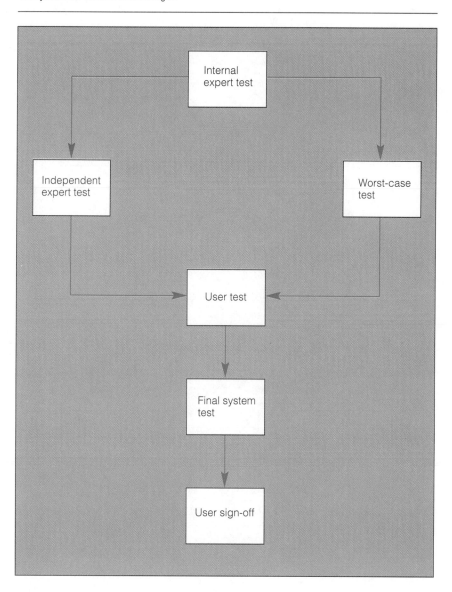

FIGURE 19.3
In a parallel run, both the old system and the new system process the same data and the results are compared.

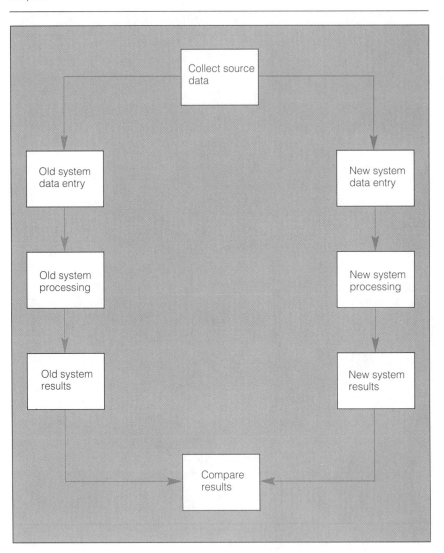

link two or more components. The reason is simple. If the component plans are developed first and the responsible people make different assumptions about a shared interface, at least one of the component plans will have to change. However, if the interface is planned first, component planning can assume a common interface.

Technical experts normally plan the **interface tests.** For example, a database administrator might define the sampling rules for verifying database contents and a network consultant might specify a set of network test signals and expected responses. **Stress tests** of extreme conditions are important; for example, the fact that each of 20 workstations can successfully communicate with a network controller does not necessarily prove that the network can deal with 20 concurrent transmissions. The actual test should be performed by someone other than the person who defined it (a skilled technician, for example).

Key system interfaces often don't exist until just before the system is released. For example, creating a network can be a lengthy task, so other components that depend on it are usually designed and developed in parallel with the network. A common solution is to use mathematical techniques to model or simulate the network. The model then becomes a reference for creating a test plan.

Testing Hardware

Many large organizations employ specialists to test, install, and maintain hardware. A small firm might hire a consultant or rely on the analyst for hardware testing. Some organizations even use the equipment manufacturer's representative.

Basic electronic functions are normally tested first. Many hardware components come with their own **diagnostic routines,** which should be run. Modern electronic equipment is highly reliable; if a component survives the first several hours of operation, it usually continues to work until the end of its useful life. However, start-up failures are common, so many hardware test plans include a **burn-in** period; for example, a computer and a disk drive might be tested by running a program that repetitively reads and writes the disk for several hours. Stress tests are also a good idea. Simultaneously activate all the system's equipment. Then run the system at or near its environmental (temperature and humidity) limits.

> **If the interface is planned first, component planning can assume a common interface.**

> **Start-up failures are common, so many hardware test plans include a burn-in period.**

FIGURE 19.4
Black-box testing ignores what happens inside the module or component.

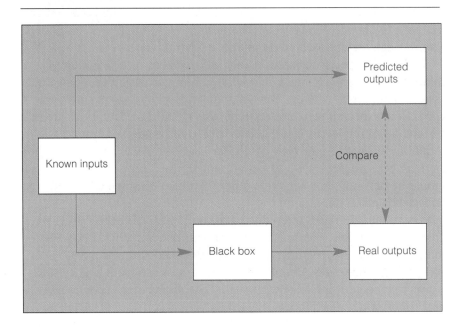

Testing Software

Have you ever searched through your own code for hours trying to find an elusive bug only to have a colleague point it out after a cursory glance at your listing? If you have, you know how difficult it is to objectively test your own work. We tend to see what we *thought* we wrote, not what we really wrote.

We tend to see what we *thought* we wrote, not what we really wrote.

In most organizations, software testing is the programmer's responsibility, and that can be dangerous. Although self testing might be reasonable at the module level, care should be taken to ensure that someone other than the author looks at the code. Often this responsibility falls on the project team leader. Prior to a formal test, walkthroughs and inspections can help.

Programs and program modules are often subjected to **black-box testing** (Figure 19.4). Given a set of input data, the expected outputs are predicted. The data are then input, and the outputs are captured. If the actual results match the expected values, the program passes the test. If not, the responsibility for studying the contents of the black box and correcting the problem rests with the programmer, not the tester.

Each module should be tested independently. Whenever possible, derive the module test data from the program test data. Once the modules have been checked, test the complete program from the top down. Start with a control structure and dummy subroutines and verify that each subroutine is activated. Next add the computational modules one by one and retest the program after each new module. If the results are wrong, the problem often lies in the most recently added routine.

Begin software testing with a limited amount of test data; if something is wrong with a module or a program, you often know it quickly. Next, input a realistic set of test data. Finally, conduct stress tests; for example, enter concurrent transactions from every possible terminal, or fill a database with the maximum expected number of records. It is surprising how often programs fail because extreme conditions were never tested.

Testing the Procedures

Manual procedures, auditing procedures, and security procedures are easily overlooked when the test plan is created, and that can be a mistake. Poorly designed or unclear procedures can cripple a system.

Poorly designed or unclear procedures can cripple a system.

The responsibility for testing the procedures usually rests with the analyst. Initially, a draft procedure might be tested in the lab, with technical personnel reading the instructions and doing *exactly* what they say. (The results can be humorous.) Next come controlled user tests, with selected users walking through the procedures and suggesting improvements. Finally come live tests with real users and real data.

Generating Test Data

The requirements specification and the data dictionary are the primary references for generating system test data. Between them, they identify the necessary data elements and suggest the appropriate data structures. Test data should be devised to test each requirement. Data volumes, acceptable ranges, response times, arrival rates, and many other parameters can be extracted from the requirements.

Test data should be devised to test each requirement.

User Data

Many analysts build their test data around **historical data.** For example, to test the inventory system you might use last month's actual sales and shipment data. Although historical data lack scientific rigor, they are realistic and they are not affected by the analyst's biases. Additionally, the fact that the system can process real data helps to build user confidence.

Assemble test data to simulate a representative or worst-case day, week, or month.

Historical data are often cyclic, so don't just select a single day, week, or month at random. Instead, ask the user to identify patterns, peaks, and valleys. Then assemble test data to simulate a representative or worst-case day, week, or month. For example, if a retail store's inventory system can successfully process test data based on last year's pre-Christmas rush, the system should be able to handle just about anything it encounters.

In addition to realistic historical data, ask the user to suggest extreme or unusual conditions. In particular, look for scenarios that could not be handled by the old system; often they exist only in anecdotal form. Sometimes exceptions really are exceptions, but if the new system can process extreme cases, user confidence is greatly enhanced.

Logical Analysis

Many programmers believe that the objective of software testing is to make sure that every line of code in the program is executed at least once, but exhaustive testing is neither practical nor very effective. A more realistic approach, called **branch** or **path testing,** is to trace through the program, identify key branch points, and include test data for each condition (Figure 19.5). Special software that traces through the source code, finds branch points, and generates test data is available for several compiler languages.

Branch tests are an effective way to catch many common logic errors.

Branch testing makes intuitive sense to most programmers, but it is far from infallible. For one thing, the sheer number of tests required to evaluate every possible path in a complex program can be imposing. Additionally, a program can pass even a well-constructed branch test and still contain hidden bugs that emerge only when specific sets of conditions occur. Still, branch tests are an effective way to catch many common logic errors.

Data Analysis

Because data entry is outside the programmer's control, bad input data are a common cause of program failure. Data type and range checks help by

FIGURE 19.5
Trace through the program, identify key branch points, and include test data for each condition.

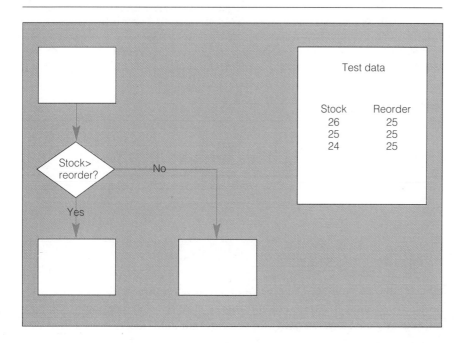

screening the data, but it is impossible to anticipate everything a tired, overworked, undertrained, or devious human being might do.

The idea of **boundary testing** (Figure 19.6) is to try to break a program by testing its limits or boundaries. Start by setting each input data element to its maximum legal value. Define a second record with every element at its minimum legal value. Then generate records for every possible combination of maximum and minimum values. To test for out-of-range conditions, repeat this procedure using values that are just over the maximum and just under the minimum. Test data generation software is one way to create these records.

An analysis of key algorithms might suggest additional test data. Try combinations of out-of-range data values that generate apparently valid answers. For example, if someone works 200 hours per week (which is impossible) at 50 cents per hour (which is illegal), the computed gross pay,

FIGURE 19.6
Use boundary testing to test boundaries or limits.

Requirement: The purchase quantity for any given sales item must be greater than 0 and less than 10.
Requirement: The selling price for any given sales item must not exceed $5,000.
Assumption: A selling price less than $0.01 is illegal.
Test data:

Quantity	Selling Price
9	5000.00
1	0.01
9	0.01
1	5000.00
10	5000.01
0	0.00
10	0.00
0	5000.01

A well-designed program catches bad data before it uses them.

$100, seems reasonable. Finally, include a few records with non-numeric characters in their numeric fields to make sure the data screening logic is working. A well-designed program catches bad data before it uses them.

Volume Analysis

It makes sense to run preliminary tests with limited data. Eventually, however, it is necessary to flood the system.

Because many problems appear after only a few input records are processed, it makes sense to run preliminary tests with limited data. Eventually, however, it is necessary to flood the system. Data volume can be achieved by duplicating test data or by using additional historical data. Maximum data arrival rates can be tested by submitting concurrent transactions from numerous terminals; maintaining an acceptable response time is a common test criterion.

Information on data volumes, response times, and transaction arrival rates can usually be found in the requirements specification. For example, look at these three inventory system requirements from Chapter 11:

- All *Reorders* identified during a business week must be ready to send to the SUPPLIER no later than 3:00 P.M. on Friday afternoon or no later than 3:00 P.M. on the last business day of that week.
- The system must be able to generate at least 50 *Reorders* per week.
- The system must hold data for at least 1,000 unique inventory items.

Because the necessary hardware is often not available until shortly before the final system test is conducted, it is sometimes necessary to simulate arrival rates. For example, you might start the data analysis program, interrupt it, fill the input buffers with subsequent transactions, and then resume processing.

Inspections and Walkthroughs

The purpose of a test plan is to ensure that the system actually does what it was designed to do. Test data help, but not every aspect of a system can be evaluated by processing test data. Using the techniques outlined in this chapter, the test data that might identify an overlooked function might never be generated. Software and other system components can be designed to the test data rather than to the requirements. Documentation and coding standards are sometimes ignored in an effort to meet a schedule or stay within a budget, and test data does not check the documentation. Often, the best way to evaluate such qualitative factors is to conduct an inspection.

An inspection is a formal review of a set of exit criteria conducted by technical personnel. The intent is to ensure that the documentation is technically sound and consistent with the system's objectives and the organization's standards. A successful inspection certifies technical quality and helps to ensure that the component actually performs (rather than merely simulates) the necessary function.

A successful inspection certifies technical quality.

A walkthrough can be viewed as an informal inspection. In many organizations, programmers regularly walk through each others' code as a means of finding logical errors. Before presenting documentation to an inspection team or to management, many analysts, designers, and programmers conduct a walkthrough to fine-tune their presentation.

The Inspection Team

The inspection team is headed by a moderator who distributes the documentation, schedules and conducts meetings, and ensures that the inspection is both thorough and fair. The moderator should be technically competent and unbiased, with no direct involvement in the project. (Some firms use external consultants.) Serving as a moderator is a difficult job with a significant amount of responsibility.

It is difficult for anyone to objectively evaluate his or her own work.

The author is usually the person or the project leader who developed the documentation or the code being inspected. It is very difficult for anyone to objectively evaluate his or her own work, so the outside perspectives of the moderator and the inspectors are crucial to the inspection process. The author is available to answer technical questions, but should refrain from defending the work.

The inspectors should be technical professionals who, while not directly involved in preparing the documentation, have a stake in the outcome. The individual who was responsible for the previous step and a member of the group that will work on subsequent steps are common choices, although some organizations prefer inspectors who have no direct involvement with the system. During the early life-cycle phases, user representation is important. Normally, two inspectors are assigned, although the size of the team can vary.

Managers should not serve on an inspection team.

Managers should not serve on an inspection team. A manager's comments take on added significance simply because they come from a manager. That can intimidate the other participants, and the inspection can easily degenerate into a discussion of nontechnical management issues. Management's involvement in the inspection process should be limited to reviewing the results.

■   **PROFESSIONAL POINTER**

Focus on Technical Issues

In many organizations, serving as a moderator is a first step up the management ladder. Running an inspection requires managementlike skills, so that makes sense, but if the moderator is perceived as more of a manager than a technical expert, the inspection process might break down. The inspection should focus on technical issues. Management issues should be discussed in the subsequent management review.

The Inspection Process

An inspection is a six-step process (Figure 19.7). The first step is planning. When the documentation is ready to be inspected, the author contacts the moderator and asks that a team be assembled. In some organizations the moderator chooses the members; in others, management assumes this

FIGURE 19.7
An inspection is a six-step process.

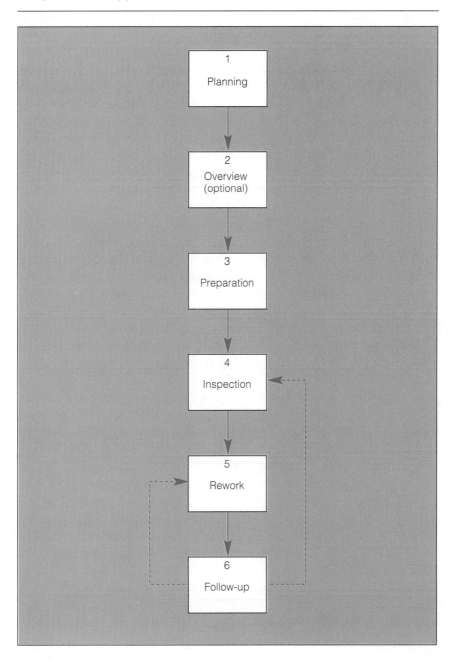

responsibility. Once the team has been named, the moderator distributes the material to be inspected and schedules the inspection meeting or meetings.

If the inspection is late, the project will almost certainly fall behind schedule. Ideally, the inspection should not begin until the author has completed all the documentation, but, realistically, management will pressure both the author and the moderator to begin on time.

If a project is particularly extensive or involves several unique concepts or techniques, it might be valuable for the author to present an overview of the documentation. (Note that the overview is optional.) The overview session should not be allowed to degenerate into a sales pitch or a preliminary inspection. The objective is to help the inspectors understand the documentation. The danger is that the author may bias the other members, making it easy for them to overlook errors, so the author's presentation should stick to the facts.

During the preparation step, the moderator and the inspectors independently read the documentation and note questions or potential problems. If the participants do not do their homework, the inspection is a waste of time. Contact between the inspectors and the author is a source of possible bias, and many firms prohibit it, although such rules are difficult to enforce. At the very least the participants should be aware of the potential for bias and should avoid discussing the documentation.

The inspection session is conducted by the moderator. One of the inspectors (not the author) serves as the reader and paraphrases the documentation. Paraphrasing involves at least an element of interpretation. If the reader paraphrases incorrectly, the documentation is probably unclear, and unclear documentation often points to errors. During the inspection session, the author's primary responsibility is to answer questions.

The objective of the inspection session is to find errors, *not* to correct them.

The objective of the inspection session is to find errors, *not* to correct them. All participants, including the moderator, the author, and the reader, inspect the documentation; anyone, including the author, is allowed to identify errors. The moderator maintains an error log (Figure 19.8), noting each error and estimating its severity. If excessive numbers of errors are encountered, the moderator has the authority to terminate and reschedule the session, because inspecting incomplete or sloppy documentation is a waste of time.

The moderator must control the inspection session. One danger is that the author will defend the work and attempt to deny the existence of any errors. At the other extreme, one or more inspectors might decide to

FIGURE 19.8
The error log lists each error and its estimated severity.

Inspection Error Log

Project: _____   Session date: _____

Module: _____
_____   Moderator: _____
Author: _____
Level: _____   Inspectors: _____
_____
_____

	Error description	Class	Time		Date	Check by
			Est	Act		

Approved by: _____ (Moderator)   Date: _____

conduct a witch hunt. The moderator's job is to see that the inspection is conducted fairly and impartially, and that everyone has an opportunity to participate.

A common point of disagreement involves assigning a measure of severity to each error. The author might see an error as trivial, while an inspector might consider it severe; the result could well be a protracted argument. After a reasonable discussion, the moderator must break in, arbitrarily assign a severity level, and move on. The important thing is that the error be detected; its classification is secondary.

The length of the inspection session should be limited and all participants should be aware of the time limit. A person's ability to critically analyze technical detail fades with time, and plowing through documentation after you have lost the ability to concentrate accomplishes little. Large systems might require more than one inspection session.

Following the inspection, the moderator and the author meet to review the list of errors and estimate rework time for each one. The responsibility for actually doing the rework rests with the author. As each error is corrected, the author notes the actual rework time. This history of estimated and actual rework times can be used to help improve the cost-estimating process.

When the rework is completed, the author and the moderator meet once again to review the results. If the moderator is satisfied with the rework, the inspection process ends. If not, the moderator might request additional rework and another follow-up session, or perhaps schedule a reinspection. If necessary, the inspection team is reconvened and the inspection session, rework, and follow-up steps are repeated.

The Management Review

Following the inspection, the moderator and (sometimes) the inspectors sign a form (perhaps the completed error log) that tells management the project has been reviewed and found technically acceptable. In the subsequent management review, the system's technical validity can be assumed, so management can focus on costs, benefits, schedules, and resources.

Potential Problems

The error reports generated during the inspection session represent a point of concern. People naturally fear that an error report will in some way be used against them and that error rates will eventually creep into personnel evaluations. This puts unnecessary pressure on the inspection team. Management must avoid misusing these data.

Another danger is that an analyst or programmer, fearing criticism or the misuse of an error report, will postpone the inspection until everything is perfect. The moderator must have the authority to insist that the project schedule be followed (within reason) or officially changed. A change in the schedule is, of course, a legitimate reason for management to become involved.

The inspection process puts considerable pressure on the moderator. Without management's authority, this individual must schedule and conduct meetings and order and evaluate rework. The moderator is in a particularly uncomfortable position when a reinspection is required, because reinspection implies that the author did not do a very good job the first time. Sometimes the reinspection is made a formal part of the process and the moderator is given the authority to cancel it. Choosing between "good job" and "no comment" is easier than choosing between "bad job" and "no comment."

The inspection process puts considerable pressure on the moderator.

MANAGEMENT'S PERSPECTIVE   ■

Support Active User Involvement
The final system test ends with user sign-off. By signing off on the system the user formally accepts the system and (by implication) agrees that it solves the problem. The assumption is that the user is making an informed decision. All too often, that assumption is wrong.

In many organizations, the analysts consult with the users during the problem definition stage and then go away and build the system. Some time later, the technical experts deliver the system documentation, conduct a brief training session, conduct a system test, declare the system successful, and ask the user to sign off. That won't work. The only way the user can possibly make an informed decision to accept a system is if the user was involved throughout the life cycle. One of the most important things management can do to ensure a successful system is to insist on and support active user involvement at all phases.

Summary

The purpose of a test plan is to ensure that the system does what it was designed to do. The heart of any test plan is the test data.

The system test criteria are derived primarily from the requirements specifications. A preliminary expert test should be performed by the people who developed the system. A second expert test might be performed by a team of skilled but disinterested technical experts. Another option is worst-case testing. Expert testing is followed by a user test and a final system test.

The system test ends with user sign-off. A system test might call for a parallel run.

Once the system test is defined, the interface tests are planned. Stress tests of extreme conditions are common. Hardware components can be tested by running diagnostic routines. Many hardware test plans include a burn-in period. Programs and program modules are often subjected to black-box testing. Procedures must be tested, too.

The most common source of user test data is historical data. Branch or path testing is based on an analysis of the program logic. Data analysis suggests test data values that can be used for boundary testing. Volume analysis suggests the number of sets of test data needed to fully test the system.

An inspection is a formal review of a set of exit criteria conducted by technical personnel. A walkthrough is an informal inspection.

Suggestions for Additional Reading

Beizer, Boris. 1984. *Software System Testing and Quality Assurance*. New York: Van Nostrand Reinhold Company.

Freedman, Daniel P., and Gerald M. Weinberg. 1982. *Handbook of Walkthroughs, Inspections, and Technical Reviews*. Boston: Little, Brown and Company, Inc.

Howden, William E. 1987. *Functional Program Testing and Analysis*. New York: McGraw-Hill Book Company.

IBM Corporation. 1977. *Inspections in Application Development—Introduction and Implementation Guidelines*. White Plains, NY: IBM Corporation. (IBM publication number GC20-2000.)

Exercises

1. What is the purpose of a test plan?
2. This chapter suggested that developing a test plan should be one of the first tasks performed during the design stage. Why?
3. What happens during the system test phase? Why is all that testing necessary?
4. Distinguish between expert testing and user testing. Why are both types of tests necessary?
5. Why are the system interfaces tested before the hardware, software, and procedural components?
6. Why is it important that user data be included in the test data?
7. Briefly explain how logical analysis can be used to generate test data. Briefly explain how data analysis can be used to generate test data.

8. What is the purpose of a technical inspection?

9. Briefly outline the technical inspection process. Identify the participants and explain what each person does.

10. Chapter 2 introduced projects for The Print Shop, Jan Tompson's Campus Threads clothing store, and Bill Barnett's automobile dealership. Develop a test plan for one or more of those projects. Include appropriate test data.

A good module is cohesive and loosely coupled.

20

Software Design

When you finish reading this chapter, you should be able to:

—Explain functional decomposition.

—Define cohesion, coupling, depth, and breadth.

—Plan a high-level control structure for a program.

—Explain the HIPO technique.

—Create a hierarchy chart and a set of input/process/output charts for a program.

—Evaluate a program design.

Functional Decomposition

Given a project plan, clearly defined file structures and interfaces, and a test plan, you can begin to design the individual components. Functional decomposition is a popular design methodology. The basic idea is to break down (or decompose) a program into modules based on the processes or tasks they perform. Remember, however, that the inputs and outputs are defined before you begin, so the design process is constrained by the data.

A well-designed program consists of a set of independent single-function modules linked by a control structure.

A well-designed program consists of a set of independent single-function modules linked by a **control structure** that resembles a military chain of command or an organization chart (Figure 20.1). At the top is a main control module that calls secondary control structures. At the bottom are the computational routines, each of which implements a single algorithm.

As you may recall from Chapter 8, a prototype is created from the bottom up. You start with a set of detailed, low-level, single-function routines, test them, modify them, and eventually combine them to form a prototype system. The emphasis is on quick response, not precision, and such details as error processing, efficiency, control, security, and documentation are given limited attention. That is why most prototypes are thrown away. Bottom-up design is fine for prototyping, but top-down design is usually a better choice for a production system.

Cohesion and Coupling

Consider the individual modules first. **Cohesion** is a measure of a module's completeness. Every statement in the module should relate to the same function, and all of that function's logic should be in the same module. When a module becomes large enough to decompose, each submodule should perform a cohesive subfunction.

A good module is cohesive and loosely coupled.

Coupling is a measure of a module's independence. Perfect independence is impossible because each module must accept data from and return data to its calling routine. Because global data errors can have difficult-to-trace ripple effects, a module should never change the value of any global data element that is not explicitly passed to it. If that rule is enforced, the parameters list becomes a measure of how tightly the module is linked to the rest of the program. Fewer parameters imply looser coupling. A good module is cohesive and loosely coupled.

Depth and Breadth

A well-designed control structure balances depth and breadth.

Consider the control structures next. A well-designed control structure balances two conflicting objectives: depth and breadth. **Depth** is the number of levels in the control structure. Because each call to a lower level is a potential source of error, shallow structures tend to be better than deep structures. **Breadth,** or **span-of-control,** is a measure of the number of modules

FIGURE 20.1
A program's control structure resembles an organization chart.

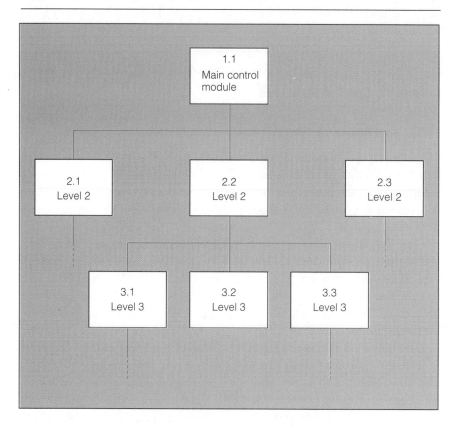

directly controlled by a higher-level routine. Too many subordinates adds to complexity, so narrow structures tend to be better than broad structures.

Narrow structures are usually deep, so reducing breadth tends to increase depth, and vice versa. One rule of thumb for balancing these two parameters suggests that no module should directly control more than seven subordinates. If a given routine has too many subordinate modules, adding a secondary control structure drops some of them to a lower level.

Module size is another useful screen; one page of source code is a common limit. If a module's logic exceeds roughly 50 lines of code, decompose it. If, on the other hand, the logic in a subordinate routine can be merged into its parent without violating the single page rule, merge it. Remember, however, that rules of thumb are not absolute. If breaking one means a better design, break it.

Defining a Control Structure

Afferent, Transform, and Efferent Processes

The first step in decomposing a program is to define its high-level control structure. During analysis, you prepared a logical model that included a data flow diagram that you exploded down to the configuration item level. A program is a physical component that lies just below the configuration item level.

You should be able to obtain a list of the functions performed by a given program from the appropriate configuration item's process description. If two or more configuration items were merged during high-level design, the program will incorporate functions from all the combined processes. That list of functions is one key to defining a control structure for the program.

Identifying the afferent, transform, and efferent processes suggests a basic input/process/output control structure.

The idea is to divide the functions (or subprocesses) into three groups (Figure 20.2). The **afferent** processes gather and prepare input data. The **efferent** processes structure and transmit output data. In the middle, the transform processes convert the input data to output form. Identifying the afferent, transform, and efferent processes suggests a basic input/process/output control structure.

Trigger Events

A program's high-level control structure should reference those tasks that are performed in direct response to its trigger event.

An alternative is to start with the program's trigger event, the event that activates the program or causes it to change from a wait to a run state. Some programs are triggered by an asynchronous event such as the arrival of a transaction or an interrupt. Other applications are driven by the clock; for example, a batch program might be run at the same time every week, and a scientific data collection routine might take a sample every few seconds. A program's high-level control structure should reference those tasks that are performed in direct response to its trigger event.

FIGURE 20.2
Identifying a program's afferent (input), transform, and efferent (output) processes suggests a high-level control structure.

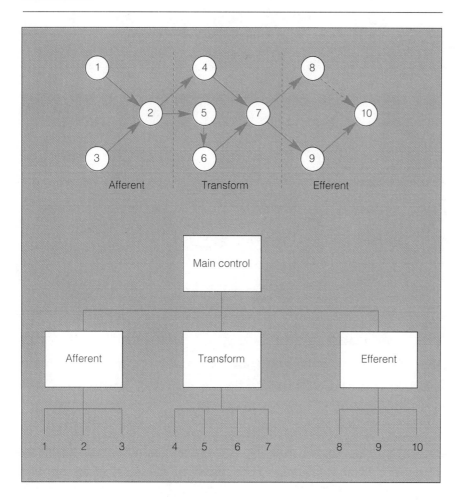

For example, Figure 20.3 shows a control structure for a transaction-processing application. When a transaction occurs, the main control module determines the transaction type and activates the appropriate level-2 routine. That routine, in turn, calls the lower-level routines that get the

FIGURE 20.3
A high-level control structure for a transaction-processing application. Note that each case has a similar level-3 substructure.

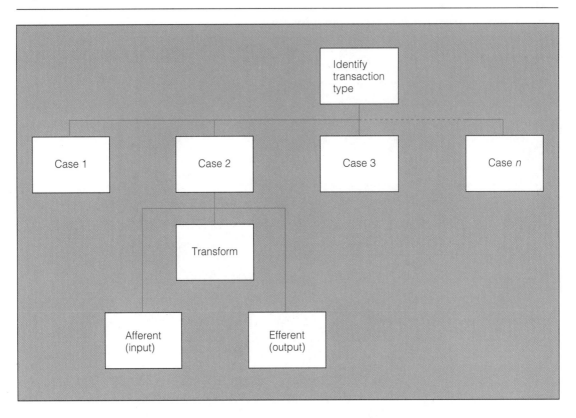

necessary input data, process the transaction, and output the results. In contrast, a batch application is triggered by the clock or by operator action, so it needs separate routines to deal with setup, record processing, and end-of-job tasks (Figure 20.4). Because the input data are collected to form a batch, record processing is a repetitive substructure.

Data Structures

Another technique for selecting a control structure is to analyze the data structures. The point of any program is to accept the input data and convert

FIGURE 20.4
A control structure for a batch application.

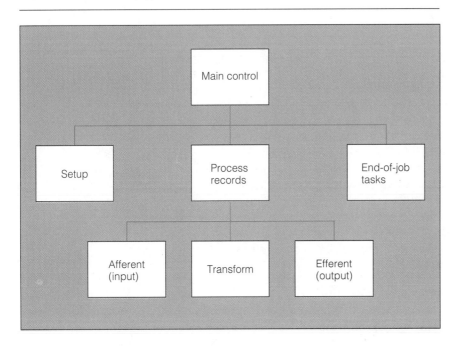

them to the form required for output, so the data actually drive the program design process.

Analyze the output data and determine the order in which the various output substructures will be assembled. Then define the input substructures and the algorithms associated with the data elements in a given output substructure. The data structures will, essentially, dictate both the order in which the logical tasks must be performed and the logical structures needed to support those tasks. Generally, sequential data structures call for sequential logic, conditional structures call for conditional logic, and repetitive structures call for repetitive logic.

The data structures dictate both the order in which the logical tasks must be performed and the logical structures needed to support those tasks.

■

PROFESSIONAL POINTER

Design from the Top Down

Note the parallels between system design and program design. You started designing the system by focusing on its overall structure. Then you turned to the interfaces and designed them. Finally, you began working on the components in the context of the system design. Similarly, you start designing a program by defining its primary control structure. Then you turn to the intermediate control modules before you define the detailed computational routines.

The obvious reason for taking such a top-down approach is to avoid rework. If the control structures and the interfaces are designed first, the lower-level components can assume a common base. If, on the other hand, the low-level components are designed first and the designers do not share the same assumptions, then one or both of those components might have to be redesigned when they are combined.

There are several other reasons for designing from the top down. Given a control structure and/or a set of standard interfaces, the lower-level components can be designed and developed independently, and that simplifies subdividing the work. Top-down design and top-down development are consistent with top-down testing. The structure imposed by top-down design, development, and testing provides a framework for traditional management control techniques. The bottom line is that the top-down approach makes sense.

The HIPO Technique

The **HIPO (Hierarchy plus Input/Process/Output) technique** is a planning and documentation tool that supports functional decomposition. A HIPO model consists of a **hierarchy chart** that graphically represents the program's control structure and a set of **IPO** (Input/Process/Output) **charts** that describe the inputs to, the outputs from, and the functions performed by each module on the hierarchy chart.

A HIPO model consists of a hierarchy chart and a set of IPO charts.

Imagine an inventory management program that performs the functions listed in Figure 20.5, and assume that the requirements call for interactively processing all transactions. This example will be used to illustrate both functional decomposition and the HIPO technique.

The Hierarchy Chart

The first step in creating a hierarchy chart is to plan the high-level control structure.

The first step in creating a hierarchy chart is to plan the high-level control structure. Because the requirements call for interactive processing, Figure 20.3 is a good starting point.

FIGURE 20.5
An inventory program that performs these functions will be used to illustrate functional decomposition and the HIPO technique.

1. Subtract sale quantity from stock on hand.
2. Add sales return quantity to stock on hand.
3. Add incoming shipment quantity to stock on hand.
4. Display the current inventory status for a given product.
5. Print an inventory status report for all products or for a selected class of products.
6. With the inventory manager's approval, modify the value of any data element associated with a given product.
7. With the inventory manager's approval, add a new product to inventory.
8. With the inventory manager's approval, delete an old product from inventory.

Figure 20.5 lists eight transaction types. As a general rule, seven subordinates is a good target, so it might make sense to combine some of them. For example, functions 6, 7, and 8 all require management approval, and grouping them might simplify obtaining that approval. The first three functions are concerned with updating stock on hand, while 4 and 5 are report generation routines that do not modify data; the nature of those tasks suggests two more logical groupings.

Figure 20.6 is one possible high-level control structure for the inventory management program. At the top (1.1) is the main control module, *Process transaction*. It accepts a transaction, determines the transaction type, and calls one of its three subordinates. Note that the level-2 modules represent the three logical groupings just identified. The module names consist of an active verb followed by a subject; such names aid documentation because they suggest the module's function. The level numbers indicate a relative position in the control structure; the lower the number, the higher the level. Some programmers use roman numerals (level I, level II) to designate levels, while others prefer letters (level A, level B).

The IPO Charts

To document the tasks performed by the modules you prepare an IPO chart for each one (Figure 20.7). The top few lines identify the system, the module described by the IPO chart, the chart's author, and the date it was prepared. The *Calls* and *Called by* boxes show the module's parents and

Prepare an IPO chart for each module.

FIGURE 20.6
The primary control structure for the inventory management program.

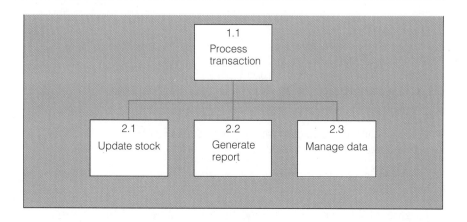

subordinates. The *Inputs* box lists the data elements or data structures that flow into the module; the *Outputs* box lists its outputs. The module's logic is defined in the *Process* box. Finally, there is space near the bottom for local data elements and notes.

The IPO chart in Figure 20.7 describes the main control module, *Process transaction*. The *Called by* box is empty. (Technically, the main control module is called by the operating system.) The three subordinate routines are listed in the *Calls* box. The module's *Inputs* and *Outputs* come next; assume that the output *Transaction class menu* was defined as part of the user interface design process. Drop down to the *Process* box and note that the module accepts a transaction signal, displays a menu, gets a transaction class (the value of the user's menu selection), calls the appropriate level-2 routine, and, as its final act, displays a logo screen. *Transaction class* is the only local data element. The notes provide additional documentation.

Figure 20.7 uses a form of **pseudocode** (Figure 20.8) to define the process. Pseudocode statements resemble compiler source statements, but the syntax is simplified. Structured English (Figure 20.9) and process flowcharts are alternative documentation techniques. Not all processes can be conveniently modeled by a given tool, so for any given process a decision

FIGURE 20.7
An IPO chart for the level-1 main control module, *Process transaction.*

```
IPO CHART


SYSTEM:       Inventory management
MODULE:       1.1, Process transaction
PREPARED BY:  W. S. Davis
DATE:         May 17, 1994
```

Called by:

Calls:
2.1, Update stock
2.2, Generate report
2.3, Manage data

Inputs:
Transaction signal
Transaction class

Outputs:
Transaction class menu
Logo

Process:
```
READ transaction signal FROM keyboard
WRITE transaction class menu TO screen
READ transaction class FROM screen
SELECT transaction class
  CASE (0) EXIT
  CASE (1) PERFORM update stock
  CASE (2) PERFORM generate report
  CASE (3) PERFORM maintain database
  DEFAULT CASE REPEAT SELECT
ENDSELECT
WRITE logo TO screen
```

Local data:
Transaction class

Notes: This is the inventory management program's main control routine. It accepts a transaction, calls the appropriate processing routine, displays the system logo, and then waits for the next transaction.

FIGURE 20.8
Pseudocode is a convenient tool for defining a process.

```
Sequence:
READ data FROM source
stock = stock - sales
WRITE data TO destination
PERFORM process

Decision:
IF condition
  THEN
    PERFORM block-1
  ELSE
    PERFORM block-2
ENDIF

SELECT key
  CASE (1) PERFORM block-1
   .
   .
  CASE (n) PERFORM block-n
  DEFAULT CASE PERFORM block-z
ENDSELECT

Repetition:
WHILE condition DO
  PERFORM block
ENDWHILE

REPEAT
  PERFORM block
UNTIL condition

DO index = initial TO limit
  PERFORM block
ENDDO
```

table, a decision tree, a list of rules, an algebraic formula, or even "sloppy source code" might be a better choice. (Don't try to force the logic to fit the tool.) However, there is a great deal to be said for consistency, so you should follow your organization's standard unless you have a good reason not to.

FIGURE 20.9
Structured English is an alternative to pseudocode.

Sequence:
```
COMPUTE variable
SUBTRACT sales FROM stock
GET record
WRITE record
DO process
```

Decision:
```
IF condition
  THEN block-1
  ELSE (not condition)
  SO block-2.
```

Repetition:
```
REPEAT UNTIL condition-1
  block-1

FOR EACH event
  block-1
```

Decomposing the Control Structure

Figure 20.10 documents the level-2 process, *Update stock*. Recall that this process incorporates the first three inventory system functions listed in Figure 20.5. Each of those three functions calls for a separate module, so the three subordinate routines are listed in the *Calls* block and the process description features a case structure. Assume once again that the output structure named *Update stock menu* is already defined.

The IPO charts for *Generate report* and *Manage data* are similar to Figure 2.10, so they will not be shown. You can see their level-3 modules in Figure 20.11. Because the tasks associated with *Manage data* require management permission, a security check should be one of its sub-processes. In this example, a simple password check is assumed. If more complex security were called for, *Manage data* might have a fourth level-3 module.

Should any of those level-3 modules be further decomposed? The answer depends on their complexity. For example, Figure 20.12 shows an IPO

FIGURE 20.10

An IPO chart for module 2.1, *Update stock.*

IPO CHART

```
SYSTEM:      Inventory management
MODULE:      2.1, Update stock
PREPARED BY: W. S. Davis
DATE:        May 17, 1994
```

Called by:
1.1, Process transaction

Calls:
3.1, Process sale
3.2, Process return
3.3, Process shipment

Inputs:
Process type

Outputs:
Update stock menu

Process:
```
WRITE update stock menu TO screen
READ process type FROM screen
SELECT process type
        CASE (0) EXIT
        CASE (1) PERFORM process sale
        CASE (2) PERFORM process return
        CASE (3) PERFORM process shipment
        DEFAULT CASE REPEAT SELECT
ENDSELECT
```

Local data:
Process type

Notes: This module selects a processing routine for a transaction that changes the current stock on hand for an existing inventory record.

FIGURE 20.11
This control structure decomposes the inventory management program down to individual process types.

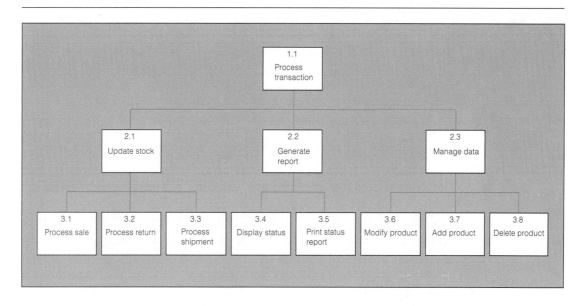

chart for module 3.1, *Process sale*. Because a clear process description can be written on a single IPO chart, there is no need to decompose *Process sale*, so the *Calls* box is empty. Pseudocode is highly compressed, but the roughly one-third page found on an IPO chart rarely expands to much more than a full page of source code.

> **If a clear process description can be written on a single IPO chart, there is no need to decompose the process.**

In contrast, consider *Add product* (Figure 20.13). Its IPO chart refers to four level-4 modules. *Get inventory data* is a relatively complex process that helps the user interactively input several fields, and *Verify inventory data* performs range and type checks on each of those fields. Processes 4.3 and 4.4 are *Compute reorder quantity* and *Compute reorder point*. If the pseudocode for those four modules were added to Figure 20.13, the process would not fit on a single IPO chart, so they drop to level 4 (Figure 20.14). Writing the new record to the database is a simple operation, so there is no need to decompose it.

FIGURE 20.12

An IPO chart for the level-3 module, *Process sale*. Because the process can be adequately described on a single IPO chart, there is no need to decompose it to level 4.

IPO CHART

SYSTEM: Inventory management
MODULE: 3.1, Process sale
PREPARED BY: W. S. Davis
DATE: May 17, 1994

Called by:
2.1, Update stock

Calls:

Inputs:
Sales transaction screen
  Stock number
  Quantity
Inventory file
  Stock on hand

Outputs:
Sales transaction screen
Stock on hand

Process:
WRITE sales transaction screen TO screen
READ stock number, quantity FROM screen
READ stock on hand FROM inventory file KEY stock number
SUBTRACT quantity FROM stock on hand
REWRITE stock on hand TO inventory file KEY stock number

Local data:

Notes: Update inventory stock level to account for sales.

FIGURE 20.13

An IPO chart for level-3 module, *Add product.* Because the logic is relatively complex, the process should be decomposed.

```
IPO CHART


SYSTEM: Inventory management
MODULE: 3.7, Add product
PREPARED BY: W. S. Davis
DATE: March 17, 1994
```

Called by:
2.3, Maintain database

Calls:
4.1, Get inventory data
4.2, Verify inventory data
4.3, Compute reorder quantity
4.4, Compute reorder point

Inputs:
Stock number
Description
Stock on hand
Reorder point
Reorder quantity
Unit price
Estimated sales
Reorder time

Outputs:
Inventory record
  Stock number
  Description
  Stock on hand
  Reorder point
  Reorder quantity
  Unit price

Process:
PERFORM get inventory data
PERFORM verify inventory data
PERFORM compute reorder quantity
PERFORM compute reorder point
WRITE inventory record TO inventory file KEY stock number

Local data:

Notes: This module creates a new inventory file record.

FIGURE 20.14
The inventory management program decomposed to level 4.

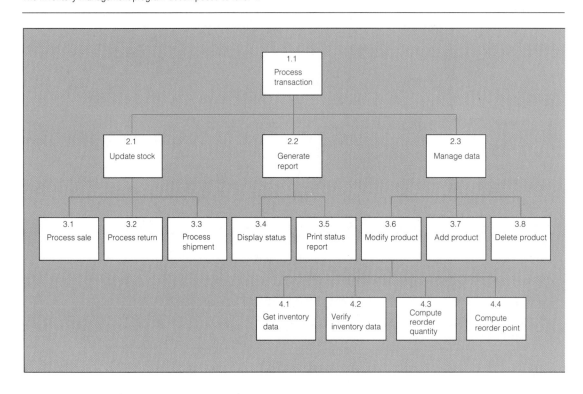

Maintaining the Documentation

A complete HIPO documentation package consists of a hierarchy chart plus one IPO chart for each module at each level. For a large program, the documentation can be quite lengthy.

As the program changes, the documentation must be maintained.

As the program changes (and it will), the documentation must be maintained. A significant change to the hierarchy chart usually implies a change in the program's basic control structure. Such major changes are usually followed by a formal review that should include the documentation. Some CASE products incorporate software that helps you create and maintain the hierarchy chart, and the IPO charts are really process descriptions, so CASE can help.

The IPO charts are the real problem. Technically, even a minor change in the program code should trigger a change to the appropriate IPO chart, but it doesn't always happen. The secret is to make maintenance easy. In some organizations, a technical writer or a clerical assistant is assigned the task of maintaining the documentation. Other organizations have their programmers embed the IPO charts in the source code as comments, perhaps the easiest form of documentation to maintain.

The secret to maintaining documentation is to make maintenance easy.

The IPO charts pictured in this chapter show only the most basic information. Some designers prefer more elaborate IPO charts, with arrows that graphically depict the flow of data from the input block, through the process, and to the output block (Figure 20.15). However, unless an organization has professional documenters or a dependable software-based documentation system, it is unlikely that such charts will be maintained. Sometimes, simplicity is an advantage.

Evaluating the Design

Morphology

One way to evaluate a program design is to examine its **morphology,** or form. Each module decomposes into several lower-level routines, so you would expect to see the number of modules increase as you move from level 2 to level 3, increase again as you move to level 4, and so on. Eventually, however, you reach a level where only some modules require additional decomposition, so the number of routines at each level begins to stabilize and then to decline.

For example, the inventory management program's hierarchy chart (Figure 20.14) shows one module at level 1, three at level 2, eight at level 3, and four at level 4. Figure 20.16 is a simplified version of the hierarchy chart that emphasizes the number of modules at each level. Note the shape; some people describe it as a mosque or a cigar. Most good control structures have a similar shape, with the number of modules at each level increasing, then stabilizing, and then declining.

Morphology is subjective; over the years, people have noticed that good designs tend to have that characteristic shape. You should not consciously

FIGURE 20.15
Some designers prefer more detailed IPO charts. Note that parameters passed to lower-level routines are listed as outputs and parameters returned by those routines are listed as inputs.

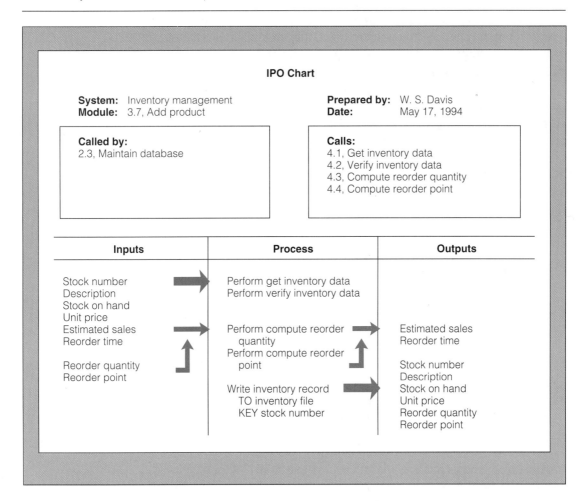

Morphology is subjective; over the years, people have noticed that good designs tend to have a characteristic shape.

try to make your control structure resemble a mosque. Instead, you should complete your design first. Then check its morphology. If the shape seems reasonable, the design is probably a good one. If your design deviates significantly from that shape, restudy it. For example, if you had chosen to implement all eight primary functions from Figure 20.5 as level-2 modules,

FIGURE 20.16
The morphology of a good design tends to resemble a mosque or a cigar.

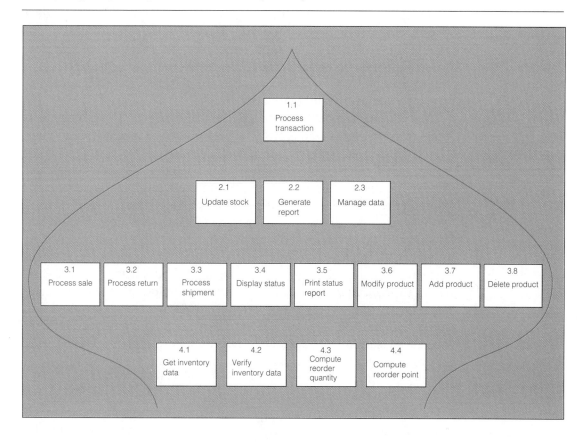

your imaginary mosque would look rather flattened. The decision to group
the primary processes into three categories was probably a good one.

Flow of Control

Tracing the flow of control through the program is a second useful check.
Control should flow from the top down, following the lines that link the
modules. A module may call only its own subordinates. Upon completing
its work, a module should return control to its parent. The analyst should
carefully check each IPO chart to ensure that these rules are not violated.

**Control should flow
from the top down.**

Data Flows

Modules are linked by data flows. For example, picture an input module that reads a record and passes a data structure to its parent. That control routine, in turn, extracts the appropriate elements from the data structure, passes them to other subordinates, accepts new or revised data elements in return, and builds an output data structure. Eventually, the output structure is passed to an output module.

If a module erroneously changes the value of a global data element, that error can ripple throughout the program. Consequently, no module should be allowed to modify any global data element that is not passed to it, and only those elements that are essential to a module's function should flow to the module. Each IPO chart's inputs and outputs should be carefully checked with this "need to know" principle in mind.

Only those elements that are essential to a module's function should flow to the module.

Whenever possible, the data entering and leaving a process should be identified at the *data element* level. A common mistake (really, a shortcut) is passing a complete data structure to a routine that needs only a few data elements. List the fields that compose each referenced data structure. Then check the data elements against the process description. If *every* data element name (or the complete structure) is either referenced or passed to a lower-level module, keep the data structure name. If only some fields are referenced, substitute a list of data elements.

Missing or superfluous data elements can cause problems, too. Read through the process description. Every referenced data element must either come from an input device, be computed within the process, be passed from the module's parent, be passed back from a subordinate routine, or be identified as a local data element. Every input data element must either be used in an algorithm or listed in the output block. Every computed data element must either be output or used by a subsequent algorithm. Every output data element must either be input to the process or computed within the process. If you discover missing data elements, add them; if you discover unreferenced data elements, delete them.

One way to trace the data flows between modules is to create a **structure chart;** Figure 20.17 illustrates a partial structure chart for *Modify product* and its subordinates. Start with the hierarchy chart's lowest level. Pick a module, find its IPO chart, and then copy the name of each data element that flows from the parent or back to the parent alongside the data

FIGURE 20.17
Use a structure chart to trace the data flows between modules.

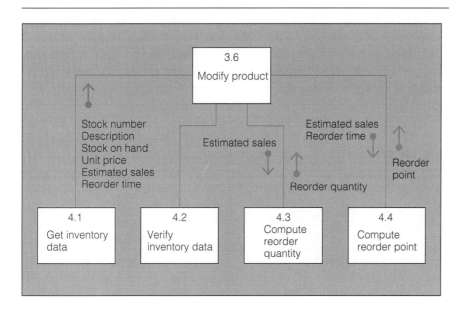

flow line. Add arrows to indicate the direction of flow. Then move on to another module. When you finish a level, move up to the next higher level, and continue until you reach the main control module. As a further check, you might independently prepare a second structure chart from the top down; its data flows should match the first chart's.

If you find yourself writing too many data element names on a flow line, you may have identified a tightly coupled module that should be redesigned. Look for redundancies, too. If the same set of data elements appears on several data flows, you might be able to group those elements to form a data structure. Modules that process the same data structure are often logically related, and grouping them under the same control structure might suggest a better design.

Adding explicit data flows to a hierarchy chart makes it difficult to read and almost impossible to maintain, so structure charts are not documentation tools. The purpose of a structure chart is to verify a design.

If you find yourself writing too many data element names on a flow line, you may have identified a tightly coupled module.

The Inspection

Ask the author to justify each design decision.

The last step in evaluating a program design is to inspect the hierarchy chart, the IPO charts, and (perhaps) the structure chart. In addition to reviewing the documentation, the inspectors should ask the author to justify each design decision. The point is not to criticize the design but to ensure that it is based on clear, logical thinking. The designer should be able to articulate a coherent design strategy. If he or she cannot, perhaps there was no strategy. Good designs are consistent, not random.

■ **PROFESSIONAL POINTER**

Start with What You Know

It is not always possible to design from the top down. Sometimes you know a great deal about the detailed processes but very little about the system's overall structure. If so, you can make a reasonable case for designing from the bottom up. Sometimes a few of the intermediate control structures are clear but both the overall program structure and the detailed computations are murky. Given such a scenario, it might make sense to design from the middle out. As a general rule, you should start with what you know and design around it.

Be careful, however, because detailed computations and intermediate control structures should not drive overall program design. If circumstances force you to start at the bottom or in the middle, your initial routines should include only essential functions and be easy to modify. (Think of them as prototypes.) As you build the control structures, make sure that each new module is compatible with the already designed routines or redesign those lower-level routines to fit the new structure. After you have a preliminary version of the overall control structure, you can begin to add the details from the top down.

■ **MANAGEMENT'S PERSPECTIVE**

Custom Versus Commercial Software

Back in the 1960s, computer time cost perhaps $1,000 per hour and programmers were paid about $10,000 per *year*, so assigning technical experts to optimize custom-designed programs made economic sense. Today, unless your firm is in the business of marketing software, it is difficult to economically justify writing custom code because commercial software is so much less expensive.

Today, many companies see software "development" as a three-step process. First they look for an appropriate commercial software package. If no acceptable package is found, the design and development work might be subcontracted to a specialist. Only if the job cannot be done by a subcontractor is serious consideration given to writing the code in-house.

The problem with commercial software is that it is written for the broadest possible audience. You can probably find software to do just about everything you need, but it is difficult to find a commercial program that does everything exactly the way you want it done. That can lead to inefficiency and extensive retraining. Don't ignore those costs when you consider commercial software.

Subcontracting creates its own problems. When work is subcontracted, the requirements specification must be carefully prepared because it forms the basis of a legal agreement between your firm and the subcontractor. The fact that you assign the work to another firm does not mean that you can ignore it, either; subcontractors must be managed. Once the project leaves your organization, you can lose control over quality, so careful coordination and clear acceptance criteria are essential.

Perhaps the most significant implication of both purchased software and subcontracting is a loss of competitive advantage. Anything subcontractors can do for you they can do for your competitors. Nondisclosure clauses might buy you a year or two, but software is relatively easy to reverse engineer, and very few software copyright infringement suits have ever been successful. The best way to keep critical software or systems away from your competitors is to create them internally and hide them behind a sophisticated security system.

There is no competitive advantage in a better payroll program, so purchase or subcontract payroll. An algorithm that determines the selling price of new products is a different matter, so develop your pricing system in-house. Draw a line somewhere between those two extremes and use it to guide the subcontracting versus in-house development decision.

Summary

Functional decomposition is a popular design methodology. The basic idea is to break down (or decompose) a program into modules based on the processes or tasks they perform. A well-designed program consists of a set of independent single function modules linked by a control structure. Cohesion is a measure of a module's completeness. Coupling is a measure of a module's independence. A good module is cohesive and loosely coupled. Depth is the number of levels in the control structure. Breadth, or span-of-control, is a measure of the number of modules directly controlled by a higher-level routine. Balancing depth and breadth is a key design issue.

One way to define a high-level control structure is to group subprocesses into three categories. The afferent processes gather and prepare input data. The efferent processes structure and transmit output data. In the middle, the transform processes convert the input data to output form. Those groupings define a traditional input/process/output structure.

Options include analyzing the process's trigger event and studying the data structures.

The HIPO technique is a planning and documentation tool that supports functional decomposition. A HIPO model consists of a hierarchy chart that graphically represents the program's control structure and a set of IPO charts that describe the inputs to, the outputs from, and the functions performed by each module on the hierarchy chart. Processes are commonly defined by writing pseudocode or structured English statements or by drawing process flowcharts.

One way to evaluate a program design is to examine its morphology, or form. You should also trace the data flows and control flows between modules by creating a structure chart.

Suggestions for Additional Reading

Gane, Chris, and Trish Sarson. 1979. *Structured Systems Analysis: Tools and Techniques.* Englewood Cliffs, NJ: Prentice-Hall, Inc.

Katzan, Harry, Jr. 1976. *Systems Design and Documentation: An Introduction to the HIPO Method.* New York: Van Nostrand Reinhold Company.

Warniew, Jean-Dominique. 1976. *The Logical Construction of Programs.* New York: Van Nostrand Reinhold Company.

Yourdon, Edward, and Larry L. Constantine. 1979. *Structured Design.* Englewood Cliffs, NJ: Prentice-Hall, Inc.

Exercises

1. Briefly explain functional decomposition.

2. What is cohesion and why is it important? What is coupling and why is it important?

3. Distinguish between depth and breadth. Why must these two factors be balanced?

4. Explain how identifying a software component's afferent, transform, and efferent processes can help you design a high-level control structure. Explain how analyzing a process's trigger event can help you design its control structure.

5. Briefly explain the HIPO technique for designing and documenting a program.

6. When you use functional decomposition to design a program, how do you know when to stop decomposing?

7. Prepare IPO charts for the inventory management program processes called *Generate report* and *Manage data* (Figure 20.6).

8. What is morphology? How does morphology help you evaluate a program design?

9. Explain how a structure chart can help you evaluate a program design. Prepare a structure chart for the inventory management program by adding the data flows that appear in the various chapter IPO charts to the hierarchy chart pictured in Figure 20.14.

10. Chapter 2 introduced projects for The Print Shop, Jan Tompson's Campus Threads clothing store, and Bill Barnett's automobile dealership. In Chapter 13 you planned several physical alternatives for one or more of those projects. Create a hierarchy chart, a set of IPO charts, and a structure chart for one or more programs selected from those alternatives. Your design should take into account the files, databases, and user interfaces you designed in previous chapters.

Object-oriented software is coming. The question is when, not if.

21

Object-oriented Design

When you finish reading this chapter, you should be able to:

—Define key object-oriented terms.

—Distinguish between an operation and a method.

—Explain the purpose of the object request broker.

—Explain the objectives of object-oriented design.

—Extract object components from object structure and object behavior models.

—Define a class structure.

—Assign data to classes.

—Assign methods and operations to classes.

The Object-oriented Approach

Although the object-oriented approach might seem new, the basic idea has been around for quite some time. As early as 1961, Kristen Nygaard and Ole-Johan Dahl created the first object-oriented programming language, Simula 1, and in the 1970s a team headed by Alan Kay developed an object-oriented language called Smalltalk for Xerox Corporation. If the object-oriented approach is such a good idea, why did it take so long to gain acceptance?

In the 1970s, the dominant computer applications performed traditional business data-processing tasks. Simula 1 was designed to support large-scale simulations running on scientific computers, but such applications represented a very small segment of the market. Traditional techniques were appropriate for writing traditional software, so there was no real need for object-oriented programming.

In addition to limited need, we did not have the technology to support object-oriented systems. Until recently, most computers featured a single main processor that executed instructions in a fixed sequence. Object-oriented software is not very efficient on a serial computer, and there was little pressure to create software to take advantage of hardware features that did not yet exist.

Times are changing. Today's networks, multiple-processor configurations, and parallel processors have made serial computers all but obsolete. Modern integrated applications demand quick response to complex queries from multiple concurrent sources, and traditional software is not very effective on such applications. Information systems have become potential sources of competitive advantage, so lengthy development times and extensive application backlogs can no longer be tolerated. We now have both the technical capability and the need. That is why object-oriented software is here to stay.

Designing Objects

Key Terms

Chapter 9 introduced object-oriented analysis. This chapter covers object-oriented design, so before you begin it might be wise to briefly review a few key concepts.

An object is a thing about which you score and manipulate data.

An object is a thing about which you store and manipulate data. To avoid being swamped by the sheer number of objects, you group similar objects to form classes or object types. Both data (attributes) and methods (processes) are associated with an object. In an object-oriented program, each object's data and methods are bundled so that the only way to access the data is through the object's own methods. Hiding implementation details in this way is called encapsulation.

Objects interact with other objects by transmitting and responding to signals. Signals are generated by events. An event occurs when an object's state changes, and a change in state usually implies a change in the value of one of the object's attributes. The only way to change an attribute is through one of the object's own methods, so events imply methods.

A key goal of object-oriented software is creating reusable code. One concept that helps support reusable code is called inheritance; each subclass borrows (or inherits) attributes and methods from its superclass. Polymorphism is another concept that leads to reusable code. A given method is considered polymorphic if it produces similar results in different objects or at different levels.

Operations

In addition to the components just listed, objects also contain **operations.** An operation is an external view of the object that can be accessed by other objects. When you request an operation, you view the target object as a black box. You provide inputs and the object returns the appropriate outputs, but exactly how those outputs are generated is hidden. An operation is implemented by one or more methods. The methods are private; the operation is public.

An operation is an external view of the object that can be accessed by other objects.

For example, if you want to update stock on hand to reflect the arrival of a shipment, you might request an operation named *Update stock* (Figure 21.1). The act of requesting the operation generates a signal. In response, *Update stock* might activate methods to get the necessary data, verify the data, and change the value of the inventory object's *Stock on hand* attribute before sending you a confirming signal. The operation, its inputs, and its outputs are known. The methods that carry out the process and the data those methods act upon are hidden.

Within a system, a given object can request certain operations that belong to other objects. Allowing one object to transmit a signal directly to another would jeopardize object independence, however, so such requests are generally routed through an object management routine called the **object request broker** (Figure 21.2). Its function is to accept requests and pass them to the appropriate operation in the target object. Note that the requesting object has no need to know which object filled its request.

FIGURE 21.1
Methods are private and hidden. Operations are public.

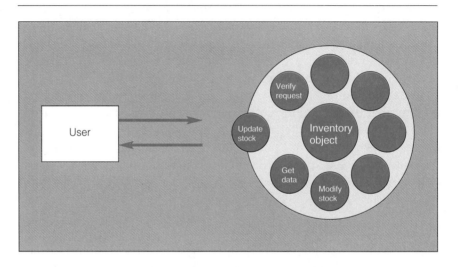

The operation that initiates the request can also be external to the system. For example, a customer's decision to purchase or return a product is an event that generates a signal (the customer's arrival at the checkout station). In response, an operation (*Handle customer transaction*) associated with a system object (*Sale*) is activated. Operations allow external entities to communicate with the system's objects and those objects to communicate with each other.

Operations allow external entities to communicate with the system's objects and those objects to communicate with each other.

Design Objectives

During analysis, you modeled object structures and object behavior by preparing object-relationship diagrams, state-transition diagrams, network diagrams, and object flow diagrams. Those models imply data, methods, events, signals, and operations. During design, your objective is to more fully define and organize those components.

An object contains a data structure, methods, and operations. Start by compiling a list of the necessary data elements and tasks and then allocate the data, methods, and operations to the appropriate objects.

Objects transmit and respond to signals, and signals are generated by events. For any given object you must identify the signals to which it responds, the signals it transmits, the events that generate the signals, the

FIGURE 21.2
Requests for operations are routed through the object request broker.

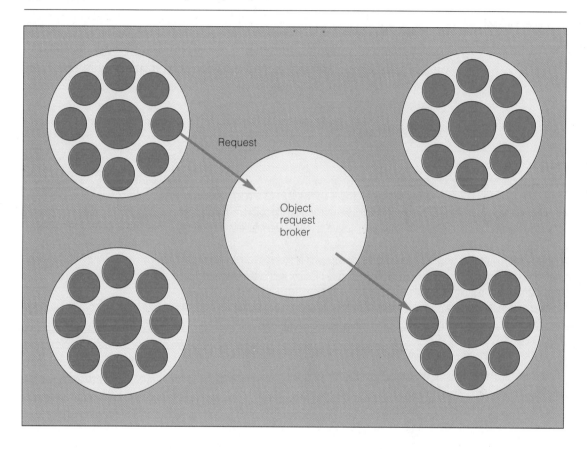

operations that transmit or react to the signals, and the methods that carry out those operations.

Signals can take many forms. Some are transmitted electronically across a network. Others are broadcast using wireless media. In some cases, the transfer of paperwork from office to office via FAX or courier can represent a signal. In batch applications, the signal might be generated by a clock or a calendar. If a signal is to be transmitted and received, both the transmitter and the receiver must agree on the precise nature of that signal. It is the designer's responsibility to select or design an object request broker or some other mechanism for exchanging signals.

Once you have identified the data, methods, operations, events, and signals that are associated with each object, the next step is to organize the objects.

Once you have identified the data, methods, operations, events, and signals that are associated with each object, the next step is to organize the objects. Start by defining a set of appropriate object classes. Then specify the data structures and methods that are associated with each class and be sure to take advantage of inheritance as you move down the class structure. Finally, review the design and look for polymorphism and other opportunities to implement reusable code.

■   **PROFESSIONAL POINTER**

Adjust to Change

Great engineering is simple engineering. History is replete with examples to support that contention. Today, that argument is used to promote object-oriented software. To its proponents, the object-oriented approach is the answer to many of the problems affecting the software industry because object-oriented programs are so much simpler to design, develop, and maintain than are traditional programs.

Perhaps you wonder why, if the object-oriented approach is so simple, it seems so difficult. The problem is that object-oriented programming demands a different way of thinking. Most programmers learned how to program the old way, and before they can begin to write true object-oriented software they must first unlearn the very skills that have made them successful. That is difficult, both intellectually and psychologically. When faced with a need to unlearn old skills and learn new ones, most people balk.

As hardware and software continue to evolve, object-oriented software will become more and more common. A decade from now it will be difficult for people who reject the object-oriented approach to earn a living designing or writing software. Don't hide behind your old skills. The only constant in the computer field is change, and if you cannot adjust to change you cannot be a computer professional.

Identifying Components

Object Structure

Before you can begin to organize the system's objects, you must first identify the components that constitute each one.

Before you can begin to organize the system's objects, you must first identify the components that constitute each one. Every object has a data structure at its core and contains methods and operations. Many of the components are suggested by the diagrams you prepared during analysis. This chapter will focus on the object called INVENTORY.

FIGURE 21.3

The object-relationship diagram identifies the system's objects.

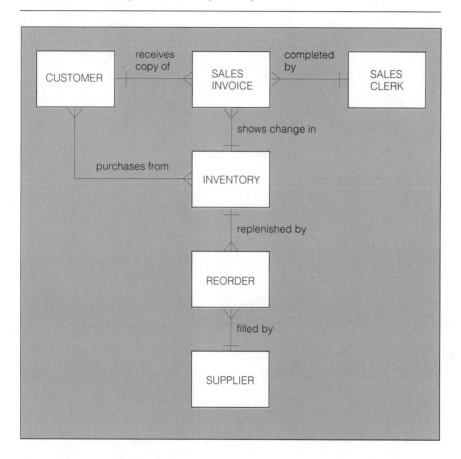

Consider the object-relationship diagram first (Figure 21.3). Note that INVENTORY is related to two other objects, SALES INVOICE and REORDER. (You can ignore its many-to-many relationship with CUSTOMER because it can be converted to two one-to-many relationships with SALES INVOICE.) Relationships imply communication. One object communicates with another object by requesting an operation, so INVENTORY will contain operations related to SALES INVOICE and to REORDER. The object-relationship

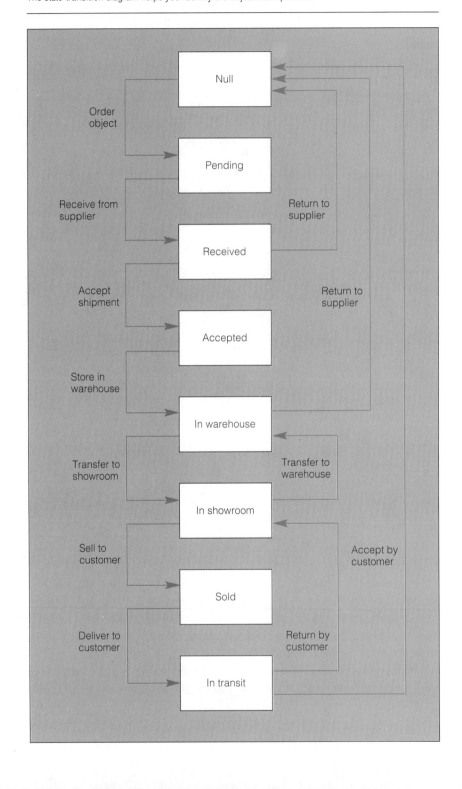

FIGURE 21.5
Changes in state imply events, signals, operations, methods, and attributes (data).

Operations	Methods	Attributes	Signals
Order object		*Stock number*	from Management
		Promise date	
		Order status	
Receive from supplier			from Shipment
Accept shipment			from Management
Reject shipment			from Management
Store in warehouse	*Update stock*	*Stock on hand*	from Management
		Location	
	Create entry	*Description*	
		Unit price	
		Reorder quantity	
		Reorder point	
Transfer to showroom			from Management
Sell to customer		*Serial number*	from Sale
Deliver to customer			from Sale
Accept by customer			from Customer
Return by customer			from Customer
Transfer to warehouse			from Management
Return to supplier			from Management

diagram does not reveal the exact nature of those operations or the methods that support them, but it does suggest that the operations must exist.

The state-transition diagram (Figure 21.4) reveals more information about the object. Each change in state implies an event that generates a signal. Those events and signals, in turn, imply operations, methods, and data.

Events and signals imply operations, methods, and data.

For example, the act of ordering stock begins with a management decision. That decision impacts stock levels, so the object called INVENTORY needs an operation (call it *Order object*) to respond to management's signal (Figure 21.5). The (as yet unnamed) method activated by that operation changes the values of such attributes (data) as *Promise date* and *Order status*.

The act of storing a shipment in the warehouse is another good example. The operation called *Store in warehouse* responds to a management decision (the signal) to accept the shipment. If the product already exists in

FIGURE 21.6
The network diagram suggests links between objects.

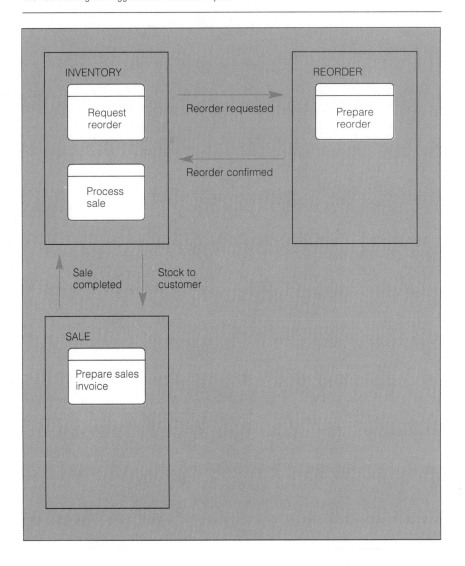

FIGURE 21.7
Links imply signals, which imply events, operations, methods, and attributes.

Operations	Methods	Attributes	Signals
Request reorder	*Check stock*	*Stock number* *Stock on hand* *Reorder point*	to REORDER
Confirm reorder	*Change status*	*Order status*	from REORDER
Support sale	*Check stock*	*Stock number* *Stock on hand*	from SALE
	Hold item	*Serial number* *Location* *Item status*	to SALE

inventory, only two attributes (*Stock on hand* and *Location*) are affected. However, if the product is a new one, those two data elements plus four more must be changed. Thus *Store in warehouse* activates one of two possible methods: *Update stock* or *Create entry*.

Work through each change in state and compile a list of each object's operations, methods, and attributes and the sources and/or destinations of each signal (Figure 21.5). Initially, your list might include missing pieces, but as you continue to study the analysis documentation, you will almost certainly discover more components.

Object Behavior

After you finish studying the object structure models, turn to the object behavior models. The network diagram suggests links between objects (Figure 21.6). For example, INVENTORY requests a reorder from the REORDER object. That reorder request implies an operation that generates a signal. The signal might be transmitted over a network. The request might be part of a list of products that is printed at the end of the day. Before design is finished, you must define the precise nature of that signal because it influences operations in both INVENTORY and REORDER. The operation also implies a method and data; in this case, *Stock on hand* might be compared to the *Reorder point* (Figure 21.7).

Operations imply signals, methods, and data; signals imply events, methods, and attributes.

In a second communication, the REORDER object confirms the order. That signal implies a second operation which, in turn, implies one or more methods and one or more attributes. Note that INVENTORY also communicates with SALE, and those signals imply events, methods, and attributes, too (Figure 21.7).

The object flow diagram (Figure 21.8) is another source of operations and methods. For example, consider the methods (the round-cornered rectangles) that communicate with INVENTORY. *Customer selects item* is an operation that clearly belongs to SALE, *Issue reorder* is part of REORDER, and *Update inventory* is part of INVENTORY. However, because those operations communicate with at least one other object, companion operations are needed to transmit, receive, and act on the signals.

Defining Classes

Selecting a Class Structure

Given a list of operations, methods, attributes, and signals, the next step is to define a set of object classes.

Given a reasonably complete list of the operations, methods, and attributes that make up an object and the signals transmitted and received by the object, the next step is to define a set of object classes. There are several possible INVENTORY class structures. For example, Figure 21.9 shows a superclass called *Inventory*. Below it is a subclass called *Product* that represents groups of virtually identical products (for example, 21-inch Sony color television sets). At the bottom of the class structure are the individual objects or items in inventory (for example, a particular 21-inch Sony color television set).

Figure 21.10 shows another possible class structure. It resembles the first option, but it adds two new classes called *Warehouse* and *Showroom* that identify the physical location of each item in inventory. As the designer, it is your responsibility to choose between alternative structures. If adding two more classes improves data access or makes it easier to implement inheritance, the second option might be a better choice. In this case, however, an item's location can probably be tracked by maintaining an attribute at the object level, so there is little to be gained by adding the two classes.

FIGURE 21.8
The object flow diagram suggests operations and methods.

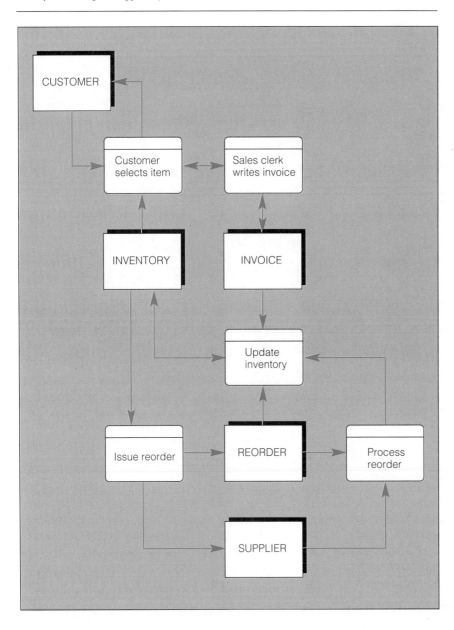

FIGURE 21.9
This INVENTORY class structure includes three levels.

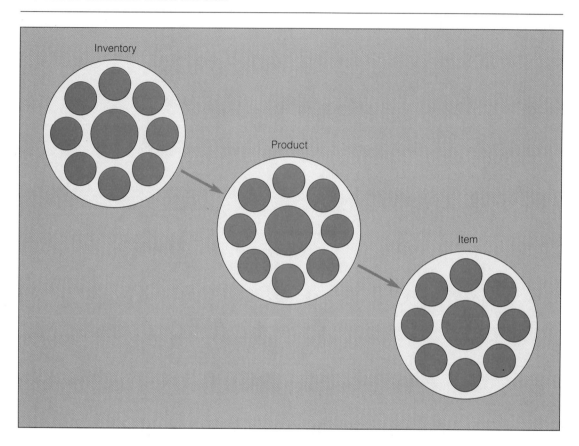

Assigning Data to Classes

Assume that the three-level class structure pictured in Figure 21.9 has been selected for INVENTORY. What attributes should you associate with each class?

The superclass should hold those attributes that are common to every subclass.

Start with the superclass. It should hold those attributes that are common to every product and to every item in inventory. You might include data elements that describe such attributes as total inventory value, the firm's line of credit for financing inventory, the physical inventory schedule, and so on.

FIGURE 21.10
This INVENTORY class structure adds additional classes that identify individual items by location.

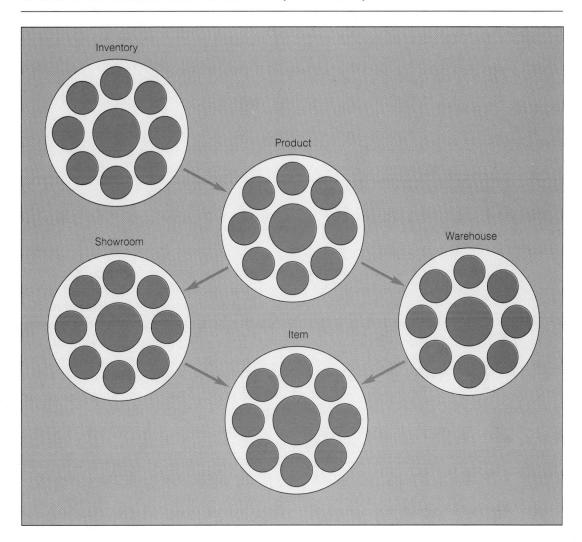

At the subclass level, include attributes that describe a product. Examples include stock number, description, stock on hand, reorder point, reorder quantity, and so on. Most of the attributes that would have been stored in a traditional inventory file or database are found at this level.

At the object level, include attributes that are unique to a specific item in inventory, such as its location (showroom or warehouse) and its serial number. Note that a product inherits a set of attributes from the superclass and that each item inherits attributes from both the superclass and the intermediate class.

Once you have defined the logical data structure associated with each class, normalize the data. Then use the normalized data to design a physical data structure for each class using techniques similar to the ones you studied in Chapter 17.

Assigning Methods and Operations to Classes

The next step is to assign the methods and operations associated with an object to the appropriate classes. Start by preparing something like an IPO chart (Chapter 20) for each method and each operation. In addition to documenting inputs, outputs, and procedures, clearly distinguish between data that belong to the object and data that come from or go to external objects and entities via signals. Operations represent interfaces with components external to the object, so you might have to design a user interface using techniques similar to the ones you studied in Chapter 18.

Normally you assign a method to the class that holds the attribute or attributes it manipulates.

In many cases, the data structures will tell you the appropriate class for each method or operation. Normally you assign a method to the class that holds the attribute or attributes it manipulates. If a given method affects data at two or more levels, assign it to the higher class because the lower class can inherit the logic. An operation should be assigned to the class that holds the method or methods it activates. If an operation deals with methods at more than one level, assign it to the highest class. Figure 21.11 shows the INVENTORY class structure with some of its operations and methods in place.

After you assign the methods and operations to classes, study the logic and try to identify opportunities for reusing portions of the code. For example, operations that respond to the arrival of a shipment, a customer sale, and a customer return all activate methods that change the value of

FIGURE 21.11
The INVENTORY class structure with some of its methods and operations in place.

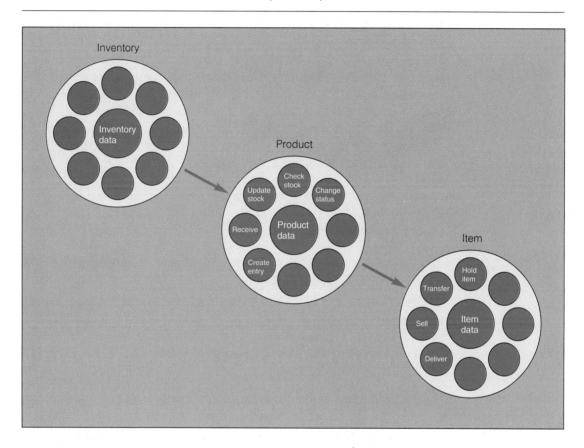

Stock on hand for the affected product or products. Those methods are not really unique (they are more like variations on a theme), so it might make sense to create a *Modify stock on hand* method and reuse it.

Once you have finished preparing preliminary designs for all the object classes, review the logic associated with each method to see if you can find routines that produce similar results in different objects. Such polymorphic logic can often be reused.

Object-oriented CASE

Conceptually, there is little difference between storing processes, data entities, or objects on a CASE repository. Object-oriented modeling techniques are comparable to traditional modeling techniques, and data and processes can be associated with objects just as easily as they can be linked to database files or program modules. Once the various components are recorded in the repository, they can be assigned to classes without reentering them, and the analyst can take advantage of this facility to try several alternative class structures. The CASE repository provides a structure for implementing reusable code, too. Don't be surprised if your first postgraduation job has you using a CASE product to design object-oriented software.

Object-oriented Languages

Object-oriented languages, such as Simula and C++, are designed to work with classes, operations, methods, signals, encapsulation, and other object-oriented concepts, so the design techniques discussed in this chapter lead to design elements that are readily implemented in such languages. Unfortunately, those languages have not yet gained wide acceptance, and the number of programmers trained to use them is limited.

Until we have a standard object-oriented language and a critical mass of programmers trained to use it, traditional languages and traditional software will continue to dominate.

Traditional languages, such as COBOL, Pascal, and BASIC, were not designed with objects in mind. New object-oriented versions of many of these languages are being developed and some are already available, but no generally accepted standard has emerged. Until we have a standard object-oriented language and a critical mass of programmers trained to use it, traditional languages and traditional software will probably continue to dominate. The switch to the object-oriented approach is coming, however. The question is when, not if.

■   **MANAGEMENT'S PERSPECTIVE**

Moving to Object-oriented Development

It is not unusual for an organization's software development group to have a lengthy backlog of work. In some cases, if a project is approved today, work might not begin for a year or more because previously approved projects are still waiting for resources. In today's economy, firms that do not react quickly find it difficult to compete. Timely information is the key to quick reaction, and information systems are the source of timely information, so those backlogs simply cannot be tolerated. Object-oriented programming is a possible solution.

There are problems associated with switching from traditional software development to the object-oriented approach, however. Few current programmers were trained to write object-oriented code, so retraining costs can be extensive. Even after your people are retrained, their productivity might actually decline for a time as they learn the new approach and establish a base of reusable code. In other words, if you switch to object-oriented software, things will probably get worse before they get better.

Replacing the old technical experts with new ones isn't the answer, either. It is expensive because qualified object-oriented programmers are in short supply. Also, replacing people rather than retraining them raises ethical and legal questions. You might subcontract the work, but this means sacrificing control. The idea of subcontracting work (hence, ceding control) to gain competitive advantage is almost an oxymoron.

Sooner or later, your organization will have to decide if the object-oriented approach should become your new standard. It is a difficult decision, but it's the kind of decision managers are paid to make. Good luck.

Summary

An object is a thing about which you store and manipulate data. Similar objects can be grouped to form classes or object types. In an object-oriented program, data and methods are bundled so that the only way to access the data is through the object's own methods. Hiding implementation details in this way is called encapsulation.

Objects interact with other objects by responding to signals that are generated by events. Events occur when an object's state changes. Each subclass inherits attributes and methods from its superclass. A given operation or method is considered polymorphic if it produces similar results in different objects or at different levels.

An operation is an external view of a process that is implemented by one or more methods. Methods are private; operations are public. The object request broker defines the rules for requesting operations and for exchanging signals.

The first design step is to identify each object's data, methods, operations, and signals by studying object structure and object behavior. You then define a class structure for each object and assign data, methods, and operations to the appropriate classes. The data that form the core of a class are converted to a physical data structure using traditional data design techniques. Methods and operations are defined in much the same way as traditional modules and procedures.

Object-oriented programming languages are designed to work with methods, operations, signals, and data structures. Traditional programming languages are not. Until a standard object-oriented language emerges and a critical mass of programmers is trained to use it, traditional languages and traditional software will probably continue to dominate.

Suggestions for Additional Reading

Budd, Timothy. 1991. *An Introduction to Object-Oriented Programming.* Reading, MA: Addison-Wesley Publishing Company.

Martin, James, and James J. Odell. 1992. *Object-Oriented Analysis and Design.* Englewood Cliffs, NJ: Prentice-Hall, Inc.

Winblad, Ann L., et al. 1990. *Object Oriented Software.* Reading, MA: Addison-Wesley Publishing Company.

Exercises

1. Define the following terms: *object, class, method, signal, encapsulation, inheritance,* and *polymorphism.*

2. What is an operation? Clearly distinguish between an operation and a method.

3. What is an object request broker? Why is something like an object request broker necessary?

4. What are the objectives of object-oriented design? Briefly explain how object-oriented design differs from object-oriented analysis. What do these two phases have in common?

5. What can you learn about a system's objects by studying object structure? What can you learn about a system's objects by studying object behavior?

6. Briefly explain how to design a class structure. Why is it necessary to design a class structure?

7. Why is it necessary to assign an object's data elements to classes? How do you convert the preliminary logical data structures created by those assignments to physical data structures?

8. Explain how methods and operations are assigned to classes. How are those methods and operations documented?

9. Until we have a standard object-oriented language and a critical mass of programmers trained to use it, traditional languages and traditional software will probably continue to dominate. Do you agree? Why or why not?

10. Chapter 2 introduced projects for The Print Shop, Jan Tompson's Campus Threads clothing store, and Bill Barnett's automobile dealership. Design a set of objects to support one or more of those applications.

The GARS Project:

22

Design

The Project Plan

The system's requirements were defined during analysis. Based on those requirements, alternative solutions were identified and a high-level system design was selected and documented (Figure 22.1). Your group is charged with developing a prototype GARS system, so the next step was to identify the prototype's components (Figure 22.2); note that the two functions added to the essential list by marketing (Chapter 15) are included. Given that list of components, you can begin to plan the details.

The first step is to prepare a project plan. You have already spent 3 months on analysis, so the work must be done in 15 months if you are to meet your original 18-month deadline. Start by listing the primary activities to be performed and the estimated personnel months to complete each one (Figure 22.3); note that 40 analyst months and 56 programmer months are available to do the job. Figure 22.3 shows one possible plan for allocating analysts and programmers to the various tasks. Dividing personnel months by the number of people assigned to each task gives you an estimate of the task's duration.

Figure 22.4 shows a completed project network for this plan. Activities 1-2 and 2-3 are planning tasks that must be completed before programming can begin. Once the system control routines and service functions have been designed the programmers can begin to write the code (activity 3-4) while the analysts design the system management logic (activity 3-5). As subsequent planning phases are completed, additional programming can begin, so the number of parallel tracks increases as you move across the project network.

There are several critical paths through the network and only two of the activities have any slack time. This is a very optimistic plan that allows little room for error; if anything goes wrong you will almost certainly miss the targeted completion date. Note also that the final event (number 14) occurs 16 months after the project begins. The extra month allows time to complete a system test. Except for 10-13, every activity along the critical path that runs horizontally from event 1 to event 14 represents analyst time, so the only way to accelerate the completion date is to assign more analysts, and it is unlikely that management will allocate those resources.

FIGURE 22.1
A system flowchart for the GARS system.

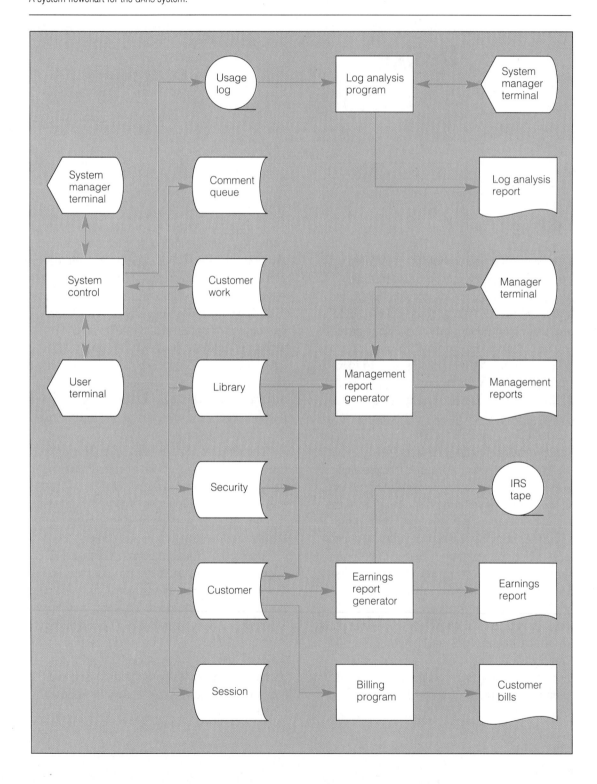

FIGURE 22.2
A list of functions that will be included in the prototype.

Function	Plan	Program	Total	Cumulative
Overhead	12	0	12	12
System control				
Check user number	1	1	2	14
Check password	1	1	2	16
Identify service requested	3	3	6	22
Charge for service	2	4	6	28
Log usage	1	1	2	30
Access games library	1	3	4	34
Access sports/ski information	1	1	2	36
Access system information	1	1	2	38
Develop new game	1	1	2	40
Access work space	1	1	2	42
Store user comments	2	4	6	48
Access customer information	1	1	2	50
*Accumulate (fixed) royalty**	2	4	6	56
Analyze log contents (basic)	2	6	8	64
Report generator (partial)				
Library usage	1	3	4	68
Analyze customer information	1	3	4	72
*Earnings report (basic)**	2	2	4	76
Billing	2	6	8	84
Maintenance and backup	2	10	12	96
Totals	40	56	96	

*Added by marketing

FIGURE 22.3
The estimated personnel requirements and durations for each activity.

Activity	Design			Programming		
	AM	Count	Duration	PM	Count	Duration
Plan system	12	3	4	0	0	0
System control						
Service routines	9	3	3	11	5	2.2
Management routines	9	3	3	15	5	3
Analyze log	2	1	2	6	6	1
Generate reports	4	2	2	8	3	2.67
Billing	2	2	1	6	3	2
Maintain and backup	2	1	2	10	5	2
	40			56		

FIGURE 22.4

A project network for the GARS prototype.

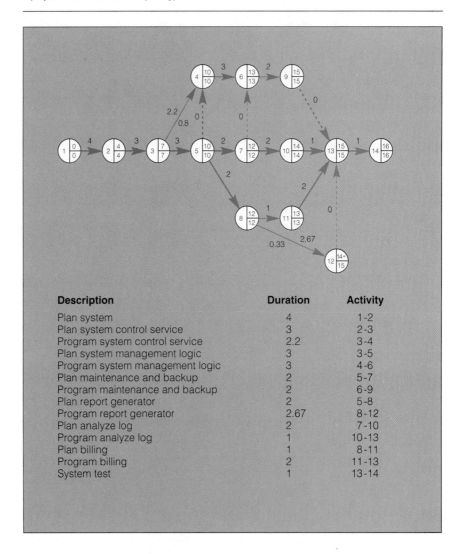

Description	Duration	Activity
Plan system	4	1-2
Plan system control service	3	2-3
Program system control service	2.2	3-4
Plan system management logic	3	3-5
Program system management logic	3	4-6
Plan maintenance and backup	2	5-7
Program maintenance and backup	2	6-9
Plan report generator	2	5-8
Program report generator	2.67	8-12
Plan analyze log	2	7-10
Program analyze log	1	10-13
Plan billing	1	8-11
Program billing	2	11-13
System test	1	13-14

FIGURE 22.5
Estimated personnel requirements by month.

Month	Analysts	Programmers
1	3	0
2	3	0
3	3	0
4	3	0
5	3	0
6	3	0
7	3	0
8	3	4
9	3	5
10	3	5
11	3	5
12	3	5
13	3	7
14	3	6
15	3	14
16	3	0
Total	48	51

Figure 22.5 summarizes personnel requirements by month. Note that the number of analysts assigned to the project remains constant, the programmers begin working in month 8, and the number of programmers increases dramatically as additional parallel work begins. During months 14 and 15, the bulk of the planning is done so the analysts can help with the programming on activities 10-13 and 11-13.

The completed project plan is inspected and then reviewed by management. You were authorized to allocate 40 analyst months and 56 programmer months (96 personnel months) to the GARS prototype, but the plan calls for 48 analyst months and 51 programmer months for a total of 99 personnel months. Additionally, the system will be finished in 16 instead of the targeted 15 months. As part of your presentation you indicate that assigning an extra analyst will allow you to complete the job within 15 months but because of the extra cost that would entail you think delaying the prototype by one month is a better option.

Should management choose to do so, they could terminate the project at this point. To date, three analysts have been working on the GARS prototype. If design and development are authorized, those analysts will keep working and several programmers will be assigned, so the firm's financial commitment will increase dramatically. If a mistake has been made, now is the time to correct it.

Assume, however, that management agrees with your recommendation and approves the plan just outlined. You have a 1-month extension for testing, and your analysis team will remain intact throughout the testing period. It's time to begin detailed design.

Data Design

The system's files and databases link the programs, so start with the data. One of your objectives is to make GARS compatible with the existing SSCIS system. The *Library*, *Customer*, and *Security* databases (Figure 22.1) are similar to their SSCIS equivalents, so you can adopt the SSCIS organizations and copy the associated data structures from the data dictionary into the CASE repository. Analysis revealed several attributes that must be added to *Customer* and to *Security* to account for royalty payments and game playing charges, but the data structures are easy to modify.

The *Customer work* and *Session* databases are needed for system control. They are not databases in the traditional sense because they hold work in progress and the various addresses, pointers, constants, and counters needed by the system control routine. The SSCIS system has a file similar to *Session* to track customer transactions so you can build on it, but given the duration of a typical SSCIS session, there was no need for a customer work file. There is a model you can use for *Customer work*, however. Writing a game is just like writing a program, and playing a game is similar to testing a program, so you can treat *Customer work* as a software library and apply the rules associated with the available compilers and interpreters for accessing it.

Once the file specifications are recorded in the CASE repository, the CASE software is used to generate the source code and the commands or job control language statements that describe each database file. That will save the programmers time and ensure that data references are consistent from program to program.

Designing the Interfaces

Given a set of clear data definitions, the next task is to design the remaining interfaces. GARS will run on a network. Such options as the telephone system, cable TV, various broadcast media, and several others are possible long-term GARS platforms, but the prototype will run on the existing SSCIS network so those decisions can be postponed for now. Because you plan to piggyback on SSCIS, several key system control routines can, with minor modifications, be reused.

The GARS prototype will essentially be treated as a SSCIS option, so several SSCIS screens and dialogues can also be reused, but new screens and dialogues are needed to interface with the game playing and new game creation functions. Following analysis, the data that must be displayed on those screens are recorded in the CASE repository, and the SSCIS screens define a set of interface standards, so the new screens and dialogues are relatively easy to design. Once design is finished, the CASE software generates a set of source code to define each screen. During the programming phase, that source code will be incorporated into the appropriate routines, thus saving the programmers time and ensuring consistency across programs.

The CASE software is also used to create preliminary prototype reports based on the attribute descriptions stored in the repository. Those preliminary reports are then reviewed with the users, improved, and modified, and that cycle continues until the report formats are acceptable. Once again the CASE software is used to generate source code to support the finished reports that can be incorporated into the GARS prototype's report generation routines.

Defining the Test Plan

The purpose of the GARS prototype is to provide marketing with the information they need to estimate revenue potential. When the prototype is finished, the code (at this prerelease stage it is often called beta code) will be released to a selected group of SSCIS customers who will be asked to perform a beta test. That beta test is a key part of the system test plan, but considerable testing is required before the beta code is released.

The individual modules, routines, and programs will, of course, be tested as they are completed. During the system test period your analysis team will exercise the system by converting a few popular electronic games to GARS format, storing the games on the system, and playing the games several times. Given an initial games library, you then plan to invite selected THINK, Inc. employees to play the games. Several interested programmers have already volunteered to create original games during their spare time, and you have accepted their offers. A final internal test will be conducted by a small group of highly skilled programmers who call themselves "The Terminators." They are well known within THINK for their ability to exploit logical weak points and "break" systems. Given such extensive testing, most of the serious bugs should be found before the prototype is released to the outside beta testers.

Designing the Software

Like the data and the interfaces, many of the GARS prototype's programs can be based on the equivalent SSCIS routines. For example, the high-level control structure for the SSCIS *System control* routine is designed to separate system functions from end user routines (Figure 22.6). That control structure makes sense for GARS, too.

Certain tasks are restricted to the system manager; they appear on Figure 22.6. Figure 22.7 shows the major routines controlled by *Service session*. Security functions and the logic that computes and stores billing information are found on this path. The routines controlled by *Manage session* are shown in Figure 22.8. This is where you find the modules that access the various libraries and respond to user requests. Note that royalty payments are accumulated by a level-4 module on this path. Most of the logic that deals with financial matters is found under *Service session,* but royalties are unique to game playing so accumulating royalties fits well here.

Given a high-level control structure, the next step is to prepare a hierarchy chart and a set of IPO charts for the *System control* program. Because much of the logic is derived from SSCIS, you might be able to reuse a great deal of existing code, and that can save considerable time. The schedule is tight, so your design policy is to adopt the SSCIS standard unless it clearly does not fit.

FIGURE 22.6
A high-level control structure for the *System control* routine.

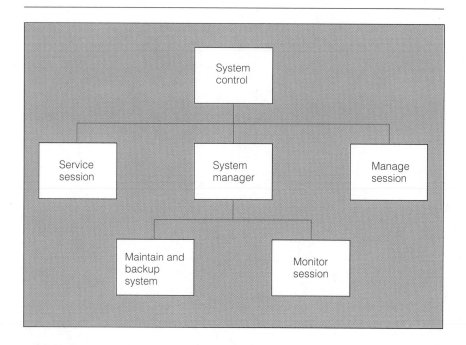

FIGURE 22.7
Service session controls lower-level routines that are not directly accessed by the user.

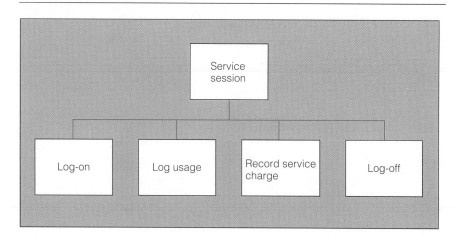

FFIGURE 22.8
Manage session controls routines that perform end-user tasks.

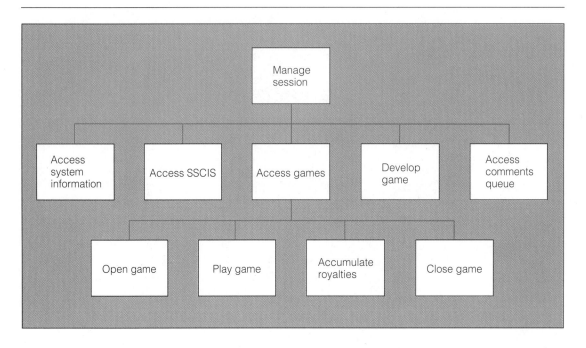

The GARS programs that analyze the usage log and generate management reports and bills are pretty straightforward, but you still must prepare detailed documentation before programming can begin. Maintenance and backup procedures are the system manager's responsibility, so they are accessed through the *System control* program (Figure 22.6).

Inspections and Management Reviews

As each program's design is completed, it is inspected to ensure that valid code can be written to the specifications. Although project managers and lead programmers will certainly review the code, higher-level management does not normally get involved with the technical details associated with individual programs because THINK, Inc., frowns on micromanagement. You will be expected to generate regular status reports, of course, and management will intervene if the project begins missing key target dates, but as long as work continues to progress on schedule you are authorized to design and develop the GARS prototype.

Exercises

1. Briefly explain how to prepare a project plan. Why is a project plan necessary?

2. Management has the authority to terminate a project before design begins. Why might management choose to do so?

3. The design stage often begins with data design. Why?

4. Much of the GARS design was borrowed from or based on SSCIS. Why? What advantages are realized by taking that approach?

5. Briefly explain the process used to design the GARS software. Although the programs are not object oriented, several object-oriented principles were used. Cite some examples and explain why those principles make sense.

When the cost of maintaining a system begins to exceed the cost of replacing it, the system life cycle ends.

23

After Design

When you finish reading this chapter, you should be able to:

—Explain why care must be taken when adding new people to a project team.

—Discuss the system development phase, including hardware installation, data installation, and software development.

—Explain the importance of user training.

—Discuss the system release phase.

—Discuss system maintenance.

System Development

The system has been designed, but a great deal of work remains to be done. The time has come to install the hardware, initialize the databases and files, select or write the software, train the users, and test the system. This book is about systems analysis and design, so the **system development** stage will not be covered in depth, but this chapter will highlight several key issues.

Project Management

The project network identifies a set of checkpoints or target dates for designing and developing the system, but it is impossible to foresee every contingency. Plans change. A module will prove more difficult than anticipated. A programmer will discover a better way to implement an algorithm. Another programmer will prove less skilled or less dedicated than expected. Analysis errors will be uncovered after programming begins. Equipment will fail or arrive late. Accidents will happen, and people get sick, resign, and accept reassignment.

Developing an information system and digging a ditch are very different tasks, and management techniques that work for one cannot necessarily be applied to the other. For example, if one of the programmers suffers an injury, a replacement will need time to learn the system. The replacement's training will almost certainly involve the other programmers, so they will lose time, too. In fact, replacing the injured person can actually affect the schedule more than waiting until he or she is able to return to work.

Fred Brooks discusses a similar problem in *The Mythical Man Month*. Based on his experience developing the operating system for the IBM System/360, he argues that assigning additional personnel to an already late activity is likely to cause that activity to fall even further behind schedule, largely because of the need to train the new people. Whenever a target date is missed, management will be tempted to add people in an attempt to get back on schedule, but new people should be added to the project team with extreme care.

Assigning additional personnel to an already late activity is likely to cause that activity to fall even further behind schedule.

■   **PROFESSIONAL POINTER**

The Turnpike Effect

The Pennsylvania turnpike was the nation's first superhighway. Before it was built, the planners conducted extensive surveys in an attempt to estimate the likely traffic load. The engineers then multiplied the maximum load estimates by a safety factor and designed the road for that worst-case volume.

A few days after the turnpike opened, traffic volume exceeded the worst-case estimates and just kept growing. Apparently, people who had never seen a turnpike before could not imagine using one until they actually experienced the convenience of a modern superhighway. Once they did, the old roads became obsolete and the turnpike became the route of choice, literally overnight.

This phenomenon, an unexpected surge in demand after new technology is released, has come to be called the turnpike effect. It is not limited to highway construction. For example, in the computing field it seems that each time service is improved, new, unexpected users emerge. An exasperated computer center manager once told me that the demand for computing power, by definition, exceeds the existing supply no matter what that supply might be.

The collective wisdom of technical experts is usually wrong when it comes to predicting the future. The turnpike effect is one reason for our tendency to underestimate the impact of change. When it comes to technological change, the future is almost always surprising.

Installing the Hardware

Early in the design phase, the analysts prepared a set of procedures for installing and testing the hardware. Simply installing the hardware is not enough, however; you must also ensure that the site is adequate. There must be enough space to hold the computer and its peripherals and to store such supplies as paper, ribbons, diskettes, backup media, forms, cleaning supplies, documentation, and procedure manuals. Depending on the system, you might need a desk, storage cabinets, a printer stand, and other pieces of furniture. Additionally, you must consider such ergonomic factors as lighting, air flow, and work space.

Ensure that the site is adequate.

Utilities represent another potential problem. Although most small computer systems are designed to run on standard household current, the equipment can easily tax the limits of existing wiring, particularly in older buildings. Obtain a copy of the technical specifications for the hardware you plan to install and determine how much current each component requires. Then have a qualified electrician check the installed wiring and determine if it is adequate. Also, check the computer's power supply to ensure that it can support all the internal components. A better power supply is one of the things you pay for when you purchase a more expensive machine.

Inconsistent power can cause transient errors and even disk failures. Power surges are particularly bad because they can destroy sensitive internal components. Never run a computer without a surge protector between the machine and its power source. Other electrical equipment can cause power to fluctuate, so you might consider installing a dedicated line for the computer. Lost power can be disastrous, so you might also consider

Never run a computer without a surge protector between the machine and its power source.

installing an uninterruptable power source (UPS), particularly if you plan to use the computer to support interactive applications.

Air conditioning is another factor. Computers are heat sensitive, and heat-related problems are difficult to trace. The computer itself generates heat, and that can add to the air conditioning load. If there is any question about the capacity of existing air conditioning equipment, get the advice of a qualified heating and air conditioning expert. The cost of inadequate air conditioning is often measured in excessive downtime and high mainte-nance costs.

If your system includes a network, it might be necessary to install com-munication lines. Some local area networks use existing telephone lines; if that is your plan, check with the telephone company to ensure that the ex-isting lines and switching equipment can handle the new load.

Nothing is more annoying than having expensive equipment sit idle be-cause someone forgot to check the electrical outlet or the telephone jack. The time to identify physical site problems is before, not after, installation. **Planned expenditures are always better than surprises.** Preparing the site can be expensive, but planned expenditures are always better than surprises. Remember to order supplies, too. It would be a shame to be unable to test the system because there was no ribbon for the printer.

Installing the Data

Because the data serve as an interface between numerous system compo-nents, the system's files and databases are defined early in the design stage. Given the nature of the data documentation, much of the work of actually creating the file and database structures is already done, but someone must write the appropriate source code or describe the data structures to the database management system. Once the files and databases are defined they must be initialized. This is a one-time task, so consider hiring tempo-rary data entry clerks to do it.

Writing the Software

During the development stage, the programmers write, debug, and docu-ment the software. This book assumes that you have completed a program-ming course or have prior programming experience, so the task of writing software will not be covered. Given the quality and availability of today's commercial software, it often makes more sense to purchase a program than to write it. Another option is subcontracting software development.

It is difficult for programmers to debug their own code. (Have you ever searched for hours in a vain attempt to find a bug, only to have a friend spot it in seconds?) When you read your code, you tend to see what you *meant* to write, not what you really wrote. Much as an author relies on a copy editor to spot errors in spelling, punctuation, and sentence structure, a programmer should have other technical experts review his or her code. That is the essential idea behind a walkthrough.

Assuming that the modules were designed to be independent, changes that are limited to a single module, such as a better way to implement an algorithm or a redefinition of a local variable, can probably be left to the programmer. However, modifications that involve global variables are much more dangerous because they can affect other modules. Evaluating the impact of such changes is the analyst's responsibility. The programmers must understand the difference between local and global changes and must clear all global changes with the project leader.

The programmers must understand the difference between local and global changes and must clear all global changes with the project leader.

PROFESSIONAL POINTER   ■

Precision Versus Creativity

"We need creative programmers like we need creative bricklayers." When Ker Orr, a well-known systems consultant, opened a presentation with those words, he caught everyone's attention. He then went on to argue that programming, like bricklaying, is a craft that demands precision rather than creativity, and that both the programmer and the bricklayer should work strictly in the context of a plan.

Numerous examples can be cited to counter Mr. Orr's opinion. The original version of Lotus 1-2-3 was written primarily by a single individual, Jonathan Sachs. Wayne Ratliff was largely responsible for creating the dBASE program that established a standard for microcomputer data management. In fact, a surprising number of our most innovative software products were created by individual programmers or by small teams. Maybe we really do need creative programmers.

On the other hand, Lotus Development Corporation currently employs hundreds of programmers to maintain and enhance Lotus 1-2-3. Constrained by the "look and feel" of the existing product, their work does indeed demand precision, and opportunities for truly creative programming are rare. Mr. Orr was at least partially right. For most programmers, precision is more important than creativity.

Training the Users

As part of user interface design, a user manual was written to document the system's procedures, reports, forms, screens, and dialogues. In addition to procedures for performing system tasks, preparing paperwork, entering data, and distributing output, you must also prepare backup, recovery, auditing, and security procedures. Clear backup and recovery procedures will not keep the system from failing, but they can help to cushion the impact when the system does fail.

Before the system is released, the users must be trained to use it.

Before the system is released, the users must be trained to use it. The user manual and the written procedures form the core of the training plan. Initially, the analysts and other technical experts should show the users how to perform the various tasks. Gradually, the experts should do less and the users more until the users clearly understand the system. Following the initial intensive training period, the users should begin to work on their own but the experts should be available to provide quick, accurate technical support. Over time the level of technical support should decline, but facilities for answering user questions should be maintained for the life of the system.

In addition to the primary users, you must also train backup personnel. If possible, have the primary person train his or her backup. Finally, remember that people retire, resign, suffer injuries and illnesses, and earn promotions, so there will be turnover. Training does not end when the system is released; it is an ongoing activity. Design your training plans so they can be used to train new personnel in the future.

System Release

You planned a system test in Chapter 19; now is the time to carry out that plan. A preliminary expert test should be performed by the people who designed and/or developed the system. Some organizations conduct a second expert test by assigning a team of skilled but disinterested technical experts to try to "break" the system. Another option is worst-case testing where everything that can possibly go wrong is allowed to happen. Expert testing should be followed by a user test in which user personnel or other user representatives, given only normal training and a copy of the user manual, exercise the system.

The final system test follows written procedures, uses real input data, and compares the results to a set of expected output values. It involves all the system components including hardware, software, data, manual procedures, auditing procedures, and security procedures. User personnel (rather than technical experts) should enter the data, operate any end-user equipment, and perform any manual procedures.

The system test often reveals problems that must be fixed before the user can assume responsibility. Once those problems are resolved, the system is released to the user. In most cases, the **system release** process includes a formal user sign-off that implies user acceptance of the system. Following release, the analyst's work is essentially done.

Some time after the system is released, a **postrelease review** should be scheduled. During the review process you should investigate any remaining problems and compare the project's objectives, cost estimates, and schedules to the actual outcomes. The idea is not simply to find discrepancies but to explain them. Knowing why mistakes were made is the key to improving your organization's analysis, design, scheduling, and cost-estimating procedures.

The final system test involves all the system components.

Knowing why mistakes were made is the key to improving your organization's procedures.

Maintaining the System

Maintenance begins as soon as the system is released. The purpose of maintenance is to keep the system running at an acceptable level. Backup procedures are part of maintenance. Preventive maintenance is perhaps the best way to avoid excessive equipment downtime. Some bugs will slip through the system test and show up weeks, months, or even years later, and removing those bugs is a maintenance task. Algorithms will change and management or the user will request new or improved features. New systems will interface with old ones, so new input and output procedures will be developed. Hardware will be upgraded. The only systems that do not require maintenance are systems that no one uses.

Maintenance is expensive; it is not unusual for the cost of maintaining a system to, over a period of time, exceed the cost of developing that system. The best way to minimize maintenance costs is to design systems with ease of maintenance in mind. Eventually, the expected cost of maintaining a system will begin to exceed the estimated cost of replacing it. When that happens, the system life cycle ends and the life cycle of a new system begins.

The best way to minimize maintenance costs is to design systems with maintenance in mind.

Incidentally, software maintenance costs are a primary consideration when choosing between purchased, subcontracted, or internally developed software. The cost of maintaining your own programs is variable and difficult to predict, but with purchased and subcontracted software, maintenance becomes an easy-to-budget, fixed-cost item. Given the nature of the budgeting process, managers hate surprises. That is one reason why so many firms choose to subcontract software development.

Some Final Notes

The methodology presented in this book was generalized from numerous sources. You will probably use a different methodology when you begin working as an information systems professional. Although details will differ, the underlying principles and objectives of the new approach will almost certainly be consistent with the methodology you now know. If you understand why you performed each task and created each model, you will have little trouble learning how to use a different methodology.

If you understand why, you will have little trouble learning how.

The analyst's methodology is a general purpose problem-solving tool that can be applied to a variety of problems. Remember, however, that a methodology is just a tool. By itself it does not guarantee success anymore than a quality typewriter guarantees a good term paper. Systems analysis demands skill, creativity, and hard work. It is an exciting profession.

■   MANAGEMENT'S PERSPECTIVE

Be Sure Sign-off Means Acceptance

The fact that a system is released does not guarantee its success. If the system is unwieldy or it fails to solve the user's problem, it simply won't be used, and someone's name on the bottom of a formal document will not change that outcome. Management must take steps to ensure that user sign-off really implies user acceptance.

One key is to insist on user involvement throughout the life cycle. To help achieve that objective, some organizations have their application analysts report to user management rather than to technical management. Another suggestion is to involve user representatives whenever user-related documentation is inspected.

Management should also avoid pressuring the user to accept the system. That advice is difficult to follow when a user group rejects an expensive system just before it is scheduled to be released, but last-minute user reluctance can be a sign of more basic problems. Perhaps the analyst failed to involve the user. Perhaps the user needs more training. Take the time to understand why the user is hesitating. The result might be a better system.

Summary

System development is a busy time. The project network identifies a set of checkpoints or target dates for designing and developing the system, but no plan can foresee every contingency. Within the context of the plan the site must be prepared and the hardware installed and tested. The database and file structures must be defined and initialized. Software must be written, purchased, or subcontracted. Users must be trained.

The development period ends with a system test and system release. The release process normally includes formal user sign-off. A postrelease review should be scheduled after the user accepts the system. Once a system is released, maintenance begins. The key to minimizing maintenance costs is to design the system with maintenance in mind. When the cost of maintaining a system begins to exceed the cost of replacing it, the system life cycle ends and the life cycle of a new system begins.

Suggestion for Additional Reading

Brooks, Frederick P., Jr. 1975. *The Mythical Man Month*. Reading, MA: Addison-Wesley Publishing Company.

Exercises

1. New people should be added to the project team with extreme care. Why?
2. Briefly explain why site preparation is so important.
3. The task of initializing a system's files and databases can often be performed by temporary personnel. Why?
4. Why is it so difficult for programmers to debug their own code?
5. Why is training so important?
6. Briefly explain what happens when a system is released. The release process normally includes formal user sign-off. Why?
7. What is a postrelease review and why is it important?
8. Why is maintenance necessary? Cite some examples of activities or occurrences that require maintenance.
9. When the cost of maintaining a system begins to exceed the cost of replacing it, the system life cycle ends and the life cycle of a new system begins. Explain that statement.
10. Prepare a report on maintenance programming. In addition to general concepts from the literature, cite specific examples from your school's computer center, your employer's computer center, or both.

Glossary

Activity   A task to be completed.

Afferent   A process that gathers and prepares input data.

Alias   An alternate field name.

Alternative   A choice, or option.

Analysis   The act of rigorously and completely defining and verifying the system's logical requirements. To attack a problem by breaking it into subproblems.

Analyst's workbench   A set of CASE tools that cut across life cycle phases.

Attribute   A property of an entity.

Automation boundary   A line drawn around one or more processes, grouping them so they form a single program or procedure. A set of automation boundaries defines a family of alternative solutions.

Balance   A characteristic of an exploded flow diagram in which each input from and output to the parent level is accounted for.

Baseline design   A design technique that attempts to ensure that a functional system is delivered on time and within budget by completing the key 20 percent of the system first.

Behavioral requirement   A requirement that defines something the system must do.

Benefit   An outcome that improves conditions. Often, an outcome that results in increased profits.

Black box   A routine, module, or component whose inputs and outputs are known but whose contents are hidden.

Black-box test   A test that focuses on the input and output data rather than the contents of the component.

Bottom up   To build a system or to estimate a system's cost by starting with its lowest-level, detailed modules.

Boundary   A limit. In a system, an external entity that is independent of the system but that communicates with the system.

Boundary testing   Testing that tries to break a program by testing its limits or boundaries.

Branch testing   Testing in which key branch points are identified and test data are included for each condition. See *path testing*.

Breadth   A measure of the number of modules directly controlled by a higher-level routine. See *span-of-control*.

Burn-in   Running hardware for several hours in an attempt to catch start-up failures.

Cardinality   A measure of the relative number of occurrences of two entities.

CASE   An acronym for Computer-Aided Software Engineering or Computer-Aided Systems Engineering.

CASE framework   A frame of reference for developing applications.

CASE tool   A tool that automates a single task in the system development life cycle.

CASE toolkit   An integrated set of tools that supports one life cycle phase.

Cause-and-effect diagram   A diagram used to suggest or to document a problem's possible causes and secondary symptoms.

Checklist   A list of alternatives or factors to be considered. Used primarily as a memory aid to ensure that key points are not overlooked.

Class   A group of similar objects. See *object type*.

Cohesion   A measure of a module's completeness.

Column header   Information at the top of a report column that identifies the contents of that column.

Competitive procurement   A set of procedures for subcontracting work through a bidding process.

Composite   A set of related data elements. See also *data structure*.

Computer-aided software (or systems) engineering   A set of software tools designed to automate key parts of the system development life cycle.

Computer software configuration item   A high-level, discrete software component.

Configuration item level   An imaginary line on a data flow diagram that links all the configuration items.

Configuration items   The functional primitives and the data stores that appear at the lowest level of decomposition.

Consistent   A requirement that does not conflict with other requirements.

Constraint requirement   A requirement that limits or constrains the design. For example, a computer system might be restricted by available space.

Context diagram   A data flow diagram that documents the system's boundaries. See *level-0 data flow diagram*.

Contingency factor   An amount added to a cost estimate to allow for unanticipated costs and risk.

Control break   A change in the value of a key (or control) field.

Control structure   A logical structure that controls the execution of two or more lower-level modules.

Correct   Every listed requirement must actually be a requirement.

Coupling   A measure of a module's independence.

CPM   Acronym for Critical Path Method. A project management technique that uses a project network when the activity times are known more precisely.

Critical path   A path through a project network defined by a sequence of events with equal earliest event times and latest event times.

Customer   The person (or group) who pays for and consequently makes the final decision about an information system.

Data   Facts. Attributes of an object.

Database   A set of related files.

Data dictionary   A collection of data about a system's data.

Data element   An attribute that cannot be logically decomposed.

Data flow   An arrow symbol in a data flow diagram that represents data in motion.

Data flow diagram   A logical model of the flow of data through a system.

Data normalization   A technique for designing easy-to-maintain, efficient logical data structures.

Data store   An open-ended, rectangular symbol in a data flow diagram that represents data at rest.

Data structure   A set of related data elements. See also *composite*.

Decision support system   A computer-based information system that adds remote intelligence to a management information system.

Depth   The number of levels in a control structure.

Design   The stage during which a specific physical solution is planned.

Design requirement   See *constraint requirement*.

Destination   An independent entity that receives data from a system.

Detail line   A line on a report that holds data from a single input record.

Development   The stage during which the system is created.

Development costs   One-time costs that occur before the system is released to the user.

Diagnostic routine   A hardware test that is often supplied or recommended by the supplier.

Dialogue (or dialog)   The exchange of information between a computer and a user.

Dummy activity   An imaginary activity with duration zero used to show precedence in a project network.

Duration   The time required to complete an activity.

Earliest event time (EET)   The earliest time an event can possibly begin.

Economic requirement   A requirement that defines a financial limit.

Efferent   A process that structures and transmits output data.

Electronic data-processing system   An early computer-based information system. Usually a stand-alone, serial-batch application.

Encapsulation   Hiding implementation details by bundling data and methods in an object so that the only way to access the data is through the object's own methods.

End user   A person who actually utilizes all or part of a system.

Entity   An object (a person, group, place, thing, or activity) about which data are stored.

Entity-relationship diagram   A model of a system's data that stresses the data and shows how the system's primary data entities are related.

Event   An occurrence that generates a signal. The completion of an activity.

Executive information system   A computer-based information system that adds such technical innovations as enterprise modeling, parallel processing, virtual reality, and multimedia to a decision support system base.

Expert test   A test performed by the people who developed the system or by other technical experts.

Explode   To decompose a process in a data flow diagram to a lower level.

Feasibility study   A study conducted early in the system development life cycle aimed at determining if the project is technically, economically, and operationally feasible.

Field   A physically stored data element.

File   A set of related records.

Final system test   A system test performed by user personnel.

First normal form   A data structure with no repeating sets of data elements.

Flowdown principle   Each low-level requirement must have a single high-level parent.

Foreign key   A key to some other entity.

Form   A paper document (or a simulated document on a screen) usually used to capture data.

Functional decomposition   A popular design methodology in which a program is decomposed into independent, single-function modules. Also, the act of exploding a data flow diagram.

Functional primitive   A process (or transform) that requires no further decomposition.

Functional requirement   A requirement that identifies a task that the system or component must perform.

Gantt chart   A chart that shows a project schedule as a series of horizontal lines.

Global data   Data that are shared by two or more higher-level processes.

Hardware configuration item   A high-level, discrete hardware component.

Hierarchy chart   A graphical representation of a program's control structure.

Hierarchy plus Input, Process, Output (HIPO) technique   A planning and documentation tool that supports functional decomposition.

HIPO   Acronym for Hierarchy plus Input, Process, Output technique.

Historical data   Data that were previously processed.

Information system   A set of hardware, software, data, procedural, and human components that work together to generate, collect, store, retrieve, process, analyze, and/or distribute information.

Inheritance   The principle that allows an object to get attributes and methods from its superclass.

Inspection   A formal review of a set of exit criteria conducted by technical personnel.

Intangible benefit   A benefit that cannot be measured in financial terms.

Interface requirement   A requirement that identifies a link to another system component.

Interface test   A test of a component that links two or more other components.

Inverted L chart   A tool for documenting the attributes associated with an entity.

IPO chart   A chart that describes the inputs to, the outputs from, and the functions performed by a single module.

Joint application development (JAD)   An alternative to traditional interviewing in which systems requirements are defined in an intensive three- or four-day meeting.

Key   The attribute or group of attributes that uniquely distinguishes one occurrence of an entity from all other occurrences.

Latest event time (LET)   The latest time an event can possibly occur without affecting the schedule.

Level-0 data flow diagram   A data flow diagram that documents the system's boundaries. See *context diagram*.

Level-1 data flow diagram   A data flow diagram that shows the relationships that link the primary sources, destinations, processes, and stores.

Level-2 data flow diagram   An explosion of a level-1 data flow diagram.

Level-3 data flow diagram   An explosion of a level-2 data flow diagram.

Local data   Data that are known only within one part of the system.

Logical data flow diagram   A data flow diagram that does not suggest physical references.

Maintenance   Postrelease activities that keep the system running at an acceptable level.

Management information system   A computer-based information system with multiple users sharing a central database and integrated applications over data communication lines.

Many-to-many relationship   Each occurrence of entity A is associated with one or more occurrences of entity B, and each occurrence of entity B is associated with one or more occurrences of entity A.

Mental model   A model of a system that allows the user to predict the system's response to a given stimulus.

Method   A process or activity that manipulates data.

Mini-spec   The process description for a functional primitive.

Modifiable   Able to be modified at a reasonable cost.

Morphology   The shape or form of a program.

Network diagram   A model of object interaction.

Nonbehavioral requirement   A requirement that defines an attribute of the system.

Object   A person, place, thing, or activity about which data are stored and manipulated.

Object flow diagram   A model of object interaction that resembles a data flow diagram.

Objective   A desired outcome.

Object-relationship diagram   A model of object structure that resembles an entity-relationship diagram.

Object request broker   A routine or other component that defines the rules for requesting operations and for exchanging signals.

Object type   A group of similar objects. See *class*.

Occurrence   A single instance of an entity.

One-to-many relationship   Each occurrence of entity A is associated with one or more occurrences of entity B, but each occurrence of entity B is associated with only one occurrence of entity A.

One-to-one relationship   Each occurrence of entity A is associated with one occurrence of entity B, and each occurrence of entity B is associated with one occurrence of entity A.

Operating costs   Continuing costs that begin after the system is released and last for the life of the system.

Operation   An external view of the object that can be accessed by other objects.

Parallel run   Concurrently running both the old system and the new system on the same data.

Partition   To break a problem into subproblems.

Path testing   Testing in which key branch points are identified and test data are included for each condition. See *branch testing*.

Performance requirement   A requirement that specifies such characteristics as speed, frequency, response time, accuracy, and precision.

PERT   Acronym for Program Evaluation and Review Technique. A project management technique that uses a project network when the activity times are uncertain.

Physical data flow diagram   A data flow diagram that identifies the system's physical processes and physical data stores.

Platform   A specific operating system running on a specific computer.

Polymorphism   An operation or method that produces similar results in different objects or at different levels.

Postrelease review   A review of the system development process conducted after the system is released.

Prime item development specification   A set of design requirements for a hardware configuration item.

Problem   A difference between things as desired and things as perceived.

Problem definition   The act of identifying a problem's cause.

Problem recognition   The act of identifying a problem.

Problem statement   A written document that defines a problem by listing its symptoms, identifying a set of objectives for solving the problem, and indicating the problem's scope.

Process   An activity that changes, moves, or manipulates data.

Process description   A formal documentation of a process.

Process flowchart   A technique for graphically documenting a process.

Project network   A project management tool that shows events as circles or bubbles linked by activity lines.

Project plan   A management plan for completing a project. Usually, a set of milestones, a schedule, and a budget.

Prototype   A reasonably complete, working model of a system.

Prototyping   To define a system's requirements by building and testing a prototype.

Pseudocode   A technique for documenting a process or a module that resembles program code.

Quality requirement   A requirement that defines a quality standard. Often stated as an acceptable error rate, the mean time between failures, or the mean time to repair.

Record   The set of fields associated with an occurrence of an entity.

Relationship   A link between two data structures or entities.

Release   The act of turning a system over to the user.

Report   An organized presentation of data.

Report header   Information at the beginning of a report (or at the top of each page) that identifies the report.

Report summary   Information at the end of a report that summarizes the entire report.

Repository   Storage that holds information on all the system's objects or components and serves to integrate the various models and phases.

Requirements specification   A document that clearly defines the customer's logical requirements (or needs).

Response time   The maximum allowable time to complete a process once the trigger event has occurred.

Schedule   A series of events with estimated completion times.

Scope   A sense of a problem's magnitude.

Second normal form   A data structure in which no data element depends on only part of a concatenated key.

Signal   A message that allows objects to interact with other objects.

Slack time   For events not on the critical path, the time an event can slip without affecting the schedule.

Software requirements specification   A set of design requirements for a computer software configuration item.

Source   An independent entity that provides data to a system.

Span-of-control   A measure of the number of modules directly controlled by a higher-level routine. See *breadth*.

State   A set of attribute values for an object.

State-transition diagram   A model of an object's state changes.

Steering committee   A committee consisting of representatives from various user groups that accepts, rejects, and prioritizes information system proposals.

Stress test   A test in which the system is exposed to extreme conditions.

Structure chart   A hierarchy chart on which the data flows and control flows between modules are traced.

Structured analysis   A logical modeling technique that utilizes data flow diagrams, a data dictionary, and process descriptions.

Structured English   A technique for documenting a process that resembles a cross between simplified English language sentences and program code.

Summary line   A line on a report that summarizes one or more detail lines.

System   A group of components that function together in a meaningful way.

System development   The phase during which the system is created.

System development life cycle   The basis for most system development methodologies.

System flowchart   A tool for documenting a physical system in which each component is represented by a symbol that visually suggests its function.

System release   The act of turning a system over to the user.

System/segment design documents (B-specs)   A set of specifications that define the logical requirements for each configuration item.

System/segment specifications (A-specs)   A set of specifications that define the system requirements down to the configuration item level.

System test   A test of all the system's components designed to ensure that the system meets the requirements.

Systems analyst   A person who plans and designs an information system.

Tangible benefit   A benefit that can be measured in financial terms. Usually implies reduced costs, enhanced revenues, or both.

Testable   Able to be tested at a reasonable cost.

Test data   The data that make up a test plan.

Test plan   A set of tests intended to ensure that the system does what it was designed to do.

Testing   The act of exercising a component, a program, or a system to ensure that it works.

Third normal form   A data structure in which each data element is a function of the key, the whole key, and nothing but the key.

Top-down   To build a system or estimate a system's cost by starting with the top, high-level components.

Traceability   The ability to trace any given requirement back to a higher-level requirement and to identify the lower-level requirements that satisfy it.

Transform   A process that converts the input data to output form. See also *process*.

Trigger event   The event that starts or activates a process.

Unambiguous   Subject to only a single interpretation.

Understandable   A requirement that is clear to the user and to other nontechnical people.

User   A person who uses the output generated by a system.

User interface   A point in the system where a human being interacts with a computer.

User manual   Formal documentation of a system's procedures, reports, forms, screens, and dialogues.

User sign-off   Formal acceptance of a system by the user.
User test   A test conducted by user personnel.

Verifiable   Able to be verified at a reasonable cost.
Verify   To prove the truth of by the presentation of evidence.

Walkthrough   An informal technical inspection.
Warnier-Orr diagram   A diagramming technique for showing how data are structured.
Worst-case test   A test in which all test data are set at their worst possible values.

Index